Danzón

Currents in Latin American and Iberian Music

Currents in
Latin American
& Iberian Music

Walter Clark, Series Editor

Nor-tec Rifa!
Electronic Dance Music from Tijuana to the World
Alejandro L. Madrid

From Serra to Sancho:
Music and Pageantry in the California Missions
Craig H. Russell

Colonial Counterpoint:
Music in Early Modern Manila
D. R. M. Irving

Embodying Mexico:
Tourism, Nationalism, & Performance
Ruth Hellier-Tinoco

Silent Music:
Medieval Song and the Construction of History in Eighteenth-Century Spain
Susan Boynton

Whose Spain?
Negotiating "Spanish Music" in Paris, 1908–1929
Samuel Llano

Federico Moreno Torroba:
A Musical Life in Three Acts
Walter Aaron Clark and William Craig Krause

Agustín Lara
A Cultural Biography
Andrew G. Wood

Danzón
Circum-Caribbean Dialogues in Music and Dance
Alejandro L. Madrid and Robin D. Moore

DANZÓN

*Circum-Caribbean Dialogues in
Music and Dance*

Alejandro L. Madrid and Robin D. Moore

OXFORD
UNIVERSITY PRESS

OXFORD
UNIVERSITY PRESS

Oxford University Press is a department of the University of Oxford.
It furthers the University's objective of excellence in research,
scholarship, and education by publishing worldwide.

Oxford   New York
Auckland   Cape Town   Dar es Salaam   Hong Kong   Karachi
Kuala Lumpur   Madrid   Melbourne   Mexico City   Nairobi
New Delhi   Shanghai   Taipei   Toronto

With offices in
Argentina   Austria   Brazil   Chile   Czech Republic   France   Greece
Guatemala   Hungary   Italy   Japan   Poland   Portugal   Singapore
South Korea   Switzerland   Thailand   Turkey   Ukraine   Vietnam

Oxford is a registered trade mark of Oxford University Press
in the UK and certain other countries.

Published in the United States of America by
Oxford University Press
198 Madison Avenue, New York, NY 10016

Library of Congress Cataloging-in-Publication Data
Madrid, Alejandro L.
Danzón: circum-Caribbean dialogues in music and dance / Alejandro L. Madrid and Robin D. Moore.
pages ; cm
Includes bibliographical references and index.
ISBN 978-0-19-996580-9 (hardback : alk. paper)—ISBN 978-0-19-996582-3 (pbk. : alk. paper)
1. Danzones (Music)—History and criticism. I. Moore, Robin D. II. Title.
ML3400.M33   2013
781.64—dc23   2013006423

To Ginnie Moore, words can't describe my sense of loss, no one ever had a better mother. And to Lorraine Leu, my constant companion, my *media naranja*, my love, who inspires and supports me in so many ways. Thank you for coming all the way from Bristol to make my life complete. And thank you for our daughter Eva; what a joy to share that experience together.
—Robin

To my parents, Alejandro and Ana Bertha for their unconditional love and support. This one is especially dedicated to my dad for inadvertently instilling in me a deep love for Cuban music and culture. And to Ekaterina, my wonderful and encouraging partner, for bearing with my crazy writing habits with a beautiful smile on her face, timely words of advice, and unflagging love.
—Alejandro

La memoria no hace nada por sí sola.
Sólo es fértil cuando el olvido la reverdece.
El olvido que recuerda a la memoria es la nostalgia.
La nostalgia no hace nada por sí sola.
Sólo el olvido.

Memory does not do anything by itself.
It is only fertile when forgetting revives it.
Nostalgia is the forgetting that triggers memory.
Nostalgia does not do anything by itself.
Only forgetting.

Jaime Moreno Villarreal, *Fracciones*

CONTENTS

LIST OF FIGURES

LIST OF MUSIC EXAMPLES

ACKNOWLEDGMENTS

This project developed out of interests shared by the authors that we discovered while we were both affiliated with the University of Texas at Austin (2005–2006). Each of us had spent time in Cuba and Mexico and were attracted to the danzón, in part due to its striking revival over the past twenty years. The fact that the danzón's history spanned a century and a half and that its influence transcended national boundaries drew our attention, as did the surprising lack of academic interest it had generated of late. Our discussions would have never resulted in a book, however, if we had not received generous funding from multiple sources. The eventual fashioning of a joint research plan took inspiration from the Collaborative Research initiative of the American Council of Learned Societies (ACLS).[1] This program supports groups of two or three scholars who undertake research that none could complete effectively on their own. The intent of the grant is to expose scholars to literatures, regions, or even disciplines that they have little familiarity with and to encourage them to incorporate new material from those sources into their work. Our danzón proposal received funding from the ACLS during the 2011–2012 academic year, and thus we approached the project together. Alejandro brought to it a background in musicology with specialization in Mexico and familiarity with literature on cultural studies, transnationalism, performance theory, and other topics. Robin contributed his training in ethnomusicology, cultural anthropology, and expertise on literature related to Cuban music and history. The writing of the manuscript progressed quickly, as Alejandro had received previous funding from the J. William Fulbright Foreign Scholarship Board, the Institute for Research on Race and Public Policy, and the Office of Social Science Research at the University of Illinois at Chicago, and made multiple research trips to Cuba and Mexico between 2006 and 2011. Robin received similar support from the Lozano Long Institute of Latin American Studies at the University of Texas, and from the university's central administration during the 2009–2010 academic year.

1. www.acls.org/programs/collaborative/. The National Endowment for the Humanities has established a similar program: www.neh.gov/grants/research/collaborative-research-grants.

Prior to undertaking this work, scholarship for both of us had been a relatively individualistic affair; collaborative research thus represented a significant change. The ACLS does not define the nature of collaboration for its awardees or provide guidelines to follow, so we first had to define the logistics of the partnership. Initially we considered writing separate chapters for the volume, but eventually rejected that idea in favor of a model involving close collaboration on virtually all essays. The need to collectively organize the content of each chapter led to more discussion, occasional delays, and sometimes last-minute changes. In the end, however, collective writing generated text in a fairly consistent style and helped reconcile our distinct academic voices and perspectives on the page more effectively than working individually.

The many advantages to collaborative research soon became obvious. Multiple authors bring a greatly expanded knowledge base to any project, of course, both theoretical and region-specific. The large number of professional contacts each of us had greatly facilitated access to material in various countries. Collective writing resulted in a constant process of external evaluation, much like having a built-in peer reviewer looking over the other's shoulder at every step. Reading each other's work thus helped us avoid minor pitfalls such as problems with wording or terminology. We also helped each other draw connections between music making in Cuba, Mexico, and the region that might have otherwise gone unnoticed.

Of course, the success of collaborative projects depends greatly on the rapport of the individual participants, their respect for each other's opinions, and their willingness to compromise as appropriate. If collaborators don't have a strong personal relationship they may prove unable to complete their work. In our case, happily, the process proved enjoyable. Support from the ACLS and from our respective institutions allowed us not only the opportunity to collaborate on writing but also to conduct fieldwork together in Havana, Matanzas, and Santiago, Cuba, which we found especially rewarding.

A number of museums, libraries, and institutes facilitated our study and deserve special thanks here. In Cuba they include the Biblioteca Nacional José Martí, the Casa de las Américas, the Centro de Investigación y Desarrollo de la Música Cubana (CIDMUC), the Instituto de Lingüística, and the Museo Nacional de la Música in Havana; the Archivo Provincial Vivac and Biblioteca Gener y del Monte in Matanzas; and the Biblioteca Elvira Cape, Casa del Caribe, and the Unión de Escritores y Artistas Cubanos (UNEAC) in Santiago. In Mexico we offer thanks to the Biblioteca del Centro Nacional de las Artes, the Centro Nacional de Investigación, Difusión e Información Musical "Carlos Chávez," and the Hemeroteca Nacional in Mexico City; the Centro de Apoyo a Investigaciones Históricas and the Centro Regional de Investigación, Documentación y Difusión Musical "Gerónimo Baqueiro Foster" in Mérida, Yucatán; and the Fototeca Nacional in Pachuca, Hidalgo. In New Orleans we accessed important information in the Williams Research Center, part of the Historical New Orleans Collection, and in the Hogan Jazz Archive and Howard-Tilton Memorial Library at Tulane University. In Miami, staff at the Cristóbal Díaz Ayala Collection of Latin American Music (part of Florida International University's Green Library) provided special assistance, as did those at the Agrasánchez Film Archive in Harlingen, Texas.

Likewise, countless individual friends and colleagues contributed to our research. They conducted independent archival work at our behest, transcribed interviews, generated musical graphics, digitized old recordings, provided access to scores and photographs from personal collections, offered dance lessons, discussed their own compositions and performances, invited us to festivals, suggested books for consultation, read and critiqued multiple draft copies of essays of the manuscript, and served as key interviewees. To all of them we owe a great debt. They include Juan Camilo Agudelo, Lizette Alegre González, Arsenio Alemán, Eduardo Alvelo, Andrés Amado, Jacky Avila, Maru Ayala, Xóchitl Bada, Miguel Bada del Moral, Egberto Bermúdez, Kjetil Klette Bøhler, Chris Boyer, Enrique Martín Briceño, Will Buckingham, Tania Camacho Azofeifa, Guadalupe Caro Cocotle, María de los Ángeles Chapa Bezanilla, Ireri Chávez, Andrew Davis, Rodolfo de la Fuente, Sergio de la Mora, Cristóbal Díaz Ayala, Paul Eiss, Ben Fallaw, Carole Fernández, Tomás Fernández Robaina, Orlando Enrique Fiol, David Garcia, Radamés Giro, Jesús Gómez Cairo, Verónica González, Neris González Bello, Daniel Guzmán Loyzaga, Olivia Hernández Nolasco, Heidi Igualada, Simón Jara Gámez, Benjamin Lapidus, Tania León, Lorraine Leu, Shane Lief, Hettie Malcomson, Peter Manuel, Vivian Martínez Tavares, Sue Miller, José Luis Navarro, Luis Pérez Sabido, Ekaterina Pirozhenko, Bruce Raeburn, Jesús Ramos-Kittrell, José Antonio Robles Cahero, Marcela Rodríguez, Brenda Romero, Ruth Rosenberg, Terry Rugeley, Julian Serrao, Alex Stewart, Ned Sublette, Yosvany Terry, Susan Thomas, Lester Tomé, María de los Ángeles Torres, Claudio Ugalde, Alicia Valdés, Alvaro Vega, Miguel Velasco, Daniel Vernhettes, Elio Villafranca, María Elena Vinueza, Chris Washburne, and Miguel Ángel Zamudio Abdalá. Thanks to colleagues at the Tepoztlán Institute for the Transnational History of the Americas for their insights, specifically Marisa Belausteguigoitia, Frank Guridy, Jill Lane, Laura Gutiérrez, David Sartorius, Micol Seigel, Rodrigo Torres, and Freddy Vilches. And special thanks to Frances Aparicio, Peter Manuel, Lester Monts, and Manuel Rubio for supporting our applications for funding with letters of recommendation at various stages.

We owe a special debt of gratitude to musicologists Liliana González Moreno and Ada Oviedo Taylor for their help in facilitating our final research trip to Cuba. Both proved invaluable: they organized our daily activities, contacted interviewees and performance groups, provided access to official documents, introduced us to center directors and other key contacts, helped steer us through countless bureaucratic snags, and worked side by side with us as we read through books and journals. Thank you, Lili and Adita.

Finally, we extend our thanks to Walter Clark, Adam Cohen, Suzanne Ryan, Erica Woods Tucker, Patterson Lamb, and others at Oxford University Press for their interest in our project and their work in seeing it through to publication. Thanks to our anonymous reviewers for all their suggestions at various stages. And thanks to Norm Hirschy for help in designing and supporting the OUP website accompanying the publication of our book. We hope that the sound files, images, videos, scores, links, and other materials posted there will prove a useful complement to the text that follows.

Alejandro L. Madrid, Cornell University
Robin D. Moore, University of Texas at Austin

ABOUT THE COMPANION WEBSITE

www.oup.com/us/danzon

Oxford has created a password-protected website to accompany *Danzón. Circum-Caribbean Dialogues in Music and Dance*, and readers are encouraged to take full advantage of it. The website includes sound files, scores, and videos of the music examined in the book, images from the authors' fieldwork and archival research, and a list of external music and video links that further illustrate the authors' discussions. The authors hope these materials will prove a useful complement to the text that follows.

Recorded examples available on the website that relate directly to the authors' argument are signaled throughout the text with Oxford's symbol ☻.

You may access the companion website by typing in username Music5 and password Book1745.

Danzón

CHAPTER 1
Danzón Matters

Mapping Out the Issues

For those raised in the United States, attending the many danzón gala events held throughout Mexico today feels like a journey into the past. Stepping into the expansive, glittering halls used for such occasions one is reminded of descriptions of the big band jazz era. On stage, large ensembles are arranged, often with fifteen or more members, that boast extended saxophone and trumpet lines in addition to trombones, percussion, and rhythm instruments. Musicians dress in colorful, coordinated outfits such as off-white double-breasted suits with contrasting shirts and ties. They adorn the stage and their music stands with banners, ribbons, or other items featuring the name and logo of the orchestra. The *salones* (halls) themselves provide ample dance floors of polished stone tile illuminated by glittering chandeliers. The dancers, primarily middle-aged couples or singles and a few younger enthusiasts, arrive in similarly immaculate attire. Women display their finest party dresses, styled hair, and shoes; men wear suits or linen *guayaberas*. They sit together around the edges of the hall, often eating multi-course meals or ordering bottles of rum or tequila with mixers for their table and consuming the contents over the course of the evening. For extended periods during live sets the tables empty as everyone rushes to the dance floor, waiting with their partners in front of the orchestra for the next song to begin or finding new partners among their friends. Danzón performances often last five or six hours or more; free dancing alternates with formally staged presentations by expert instructors or open dance competitions in front of a panel of judges. Similar to the case of tango and swing, the danzón revival of recent years has generated a large and devoted following. Mexican fans travel around the country to attend the many high-profile festivals held annually, in addition to taking part in local events or those abroad in Havana or Matanzas, Cuba. Danzón has become a central part of their lives, a passionate obsession.

Derived from European court dances of the eighteenth century such as the contradance and popularized in the New World thereafter through various French and Spanish colonies (including Louisiana), the danzón is a fascinating form that ties together the entire Atlantic region. The earliest references to the term "danzón" date from the 1840s among the black community in Havana and Matanzas; by the 1870s, white social clubs began to embrace it as well, transforming it into a form of mass entertainment. The following decade, touring Cuban musicians and exiles of the Wars of Independence brought the music and dance to Merida, Veracruz, Mexico City, New Orleans, and other cities in the circum-Caribbean region. Between the 1880s and the 1920s, danzones represented one of the most influential forms of Latin American dance music, with enthusiasts in Costa Rica, Colombia, the Dominican Republic, Guatemala, New Orleans, Puerto Rico, and elsewhere.[1]

Early danzón repertoire was played by ensembles known as *orquestas típicas* consisting primarily of European-derived instruments such as the violin, acoustic bass, clarinet, trombone, and cornet. In addition, they included the *timbales*, a Cuban percussion instrument with Middle Eastern and Spanish antecedents first used in black and mulatto military battalions about 1800, and the *güiro*, a gourd scraper. Both instruments played rhythmic patterns featuring a prominent *cinquillo* (five-note syncopated pattern; see Ex. 2.1) as well as related rhythms derived from Afro-Caribbean heritage.[2] Cuban performers increasingly rejected the orquesta típica format as of the 1910s in favor of the smaller *charanga francesa* featuring flute, violins, and piano as principal melodic instruments. Mexicans, however, continued to play in larger bands featuring brass and woodwinds known as *danzoneras*. Danzones reached an early peak of popularity in Cuba in the 1910s and 1920s, and in Mexico in the 1930s and 1940s. Subsequently, they fell out of fashion in both countries for a time, but (especially in Mexico) have experienced a strong revival since the 1990s.

Danzón structure is highly sectional with multiple contrasting segments, reflecting the influence of nineteenth-century military marches, dance suites, and other

1. Information about the widespread sale of recorded danzones in Colombia around 1910 and the 1920s has been compiled in Edgar J. Gutierrez S., *Fiestas: once de noviembre en Cartagena de Indias. Manifestaciones artísticas, cultura popular, 1910–1930* (Medellín: Editorial Lealón, 2000), 146–49; and in Egberto Bermúdez, "From Colombian 'National' Song to 'Colombian Song,' 1860–1960," *Lied und populäre Kultur / Song and Popular Culture*, No. 53 (2008), 167–259. Discussion of danzón compositions within Guatemalan repertoire is found in *Música guatemalteca para piano: antología histórica, siglos XIX–XXI* (Guatemala City: Universidad de San Carlos de Guatemala, Dirección General de Investigación, Centro de Estudios Folklóricos, 2008), 24, 32; and throughout Julio César Sánchez Castillo, *Producción marimbística de Guatemala* (Guatemala City: Impresos Industriales, 2001). The danzón appears to have been introduced to Costa Rica and other nearby countries by Cuban refugees who resettled there, fleeing the Wars of Independence against Spain. In the case of Costa Rica, Antonio Maceo himself led a settlement of 100 families that established themselves in Guanacaste beginning in 1892. See Amparo María Ballester López, "Antonio Maceo y la mansión de Nicoya," http://verbiclara.wordpress.com/2011/12/06/antonio-maceo-y-la-mansion-de-nicoya/ (accessed on June 28, 2012). Peter Manuel discusses the influence of danzones on Dominican dance music in "The Dominican Republic. Danza and the Contradanced Merengue," *Creolizing the Contradance in the Caribbean* (Philadelphia, PA: Temple University Press, 180); Edgardo Díaz Díaz (electronic communication, February 20, 2012) notes that it became popular in Puerto Rico following the US occupation of 1902.

2. Partial examples of early danzón recordings can be heard on Itunes, for instance, samples of the CD *The Cuban Danzón: Its Ancestors and Descendants* (Smithsonian Folkways FE 4066, 2004), as well as on the website accompanying this book.

repertoire of the day. Danzones have almost always been composed and notated by trained musicians, but often allow performers to interpret the score with a certain degree of melodic and rhythmic improvisation more characteristic of traditional/folkloric repertoire. The pieces feature European harmonies, yet both melodic lines and percussion patterns incorporate rhythms characteristic of West African traditions, as mentioned. Rhythms performed on the timbales involve tapping on the shell of the drums and playing on both dampened and open heads, techniques derived from Afro-Caribbean hand percussion. Finally, danzones incorporate a sense of *clave* or timeline: the constant repetition of a single two-measure rhythmic cell that serves as a structural basis for each composition. This practice is characteristic of West African music as well and is found widely in Afro-Latin dance repertoire, including salsa. Danzones thus demonstrate a fundamental hybridity, reflecting musical influences from Western and non-Western sources.

The danzón today is considered emblematic of Cuba's national music, yet for decades the elite of society rejected it as "African" and "barbaric." Commentaries in Cuban newspapers of the 1880s and 1890s attacked it because of its associations with prostitution and "improper" racial mixing. Mainstream attitudes shifted substantially in the early twentieth century, however, owing in large part to new racial discourses that emerged during the final years of the war against Spain. In the context of a heightened sense of nationalism after 1898 and a desire on the part of Cuba's white leadership to avoid discussions of ongoing racial inequality, references to the danzón's origins among the black population all but disappeared. The music enjoyed a period of broad acceptance as a result. Shortly thereafter, the influence of other local and regional musics such as Cuban *son*, jazz, and the bolero first transformed the sound and structure of the danzón and eventually eclipsed its popularity.

Danzón has been one of the most prominent forms of music and dance in Mexico since the late nineteenth century as well, and has been continuously appropriated by distinct groups and social classes. The bourgeoisie first embraced the music at the turn of the twentieth century as one of many imported cultural forms; later, it resounded in the working-class dancehalls of Mexico City, Veracruz, and elsewhere, reflecting the rise of a vibrant urban popular culture and social liberalization in the years after the Mexican Revolution (1920–1950). The music provided a means of experiencing/embodying Afro-diasporic heritage, but also displacing it at a time when state cultural discourse largely excluded blackness from constructs of *mexicanidad*. As a result of its gradual resignification as a marker of local heritage, the danzón has retained a core base of support; today, many Mexicans consider it their music, disregarding its Cuban origins.[3] In recent years, imbued with influences from salsa and big-band jazz, it has served as a powerful referent of Mexican urban culture for composers of symphonic music, film music, mariachis, vocal artists, and others.

3. Such views have led the Centro Nacional de Investigación y Difusión del Danzón, A.C. (CNIDDAC), on a campaign to have the danzón officially declared cultural patrimony of Veracruz. See Rosario Manzanos, "Proponen al danzón como Patrimonio Cultural de Veracruz," *Proceso*, no. 1751 (May 23, 2010). The initiative has not prospered.

At the turn of the twentieth century, the dynamic musical style that would eventually come to be called jazz was emerging in New Orleans, shortly to become North America's signature music. In its earliest manifestations, it featured brass and wind instruments such as the trumpet, trombone, and clarinet; often the trumpet would play variations on a primary melody while the clarinet and trombone invented countermelodies above and below the original, all supported by the rhythm section and percussion. Though clearly unique, this style of performance had parallels in the danzón and related forms. In the early recordings of artists such as such as Pablo Valenzuela, Felipe Valdés, and Enrique Peña one can hear the same sorts of instruments, performance styles, and improvisational approaches adopted by early jazz pioneers. Yet this fact is largely unrecognized by jazz scholars, and the specifics of the process by which popular Caribbean dance music overlaps with performance traditions in New Orleans remain to be explored.

Throughout the twentieth century, danzón repertoire influenced (and frequently was influenced by) many other forms such as Cuban *son*, bolero, cha cha chá, and mambo. Its early recordings are among the first styles of African American music to be recorded as played by African Americans themselves, nearly a decade before jazz discs appeared. The music has developed countless variants for audiences of distinct classes and races, often straddling boundaries between traditional, popular, and classical music and confounding simplistic categorization. Its many creolized elements speak to processes of exchange and dialogue between countries more than to particular forms of national expression. Finally, its social meanings and associations have changed radically through time, the result of incorporation into distinct ideological projects. For all of these reasons it merits further attention. A dialectical approach is fundamental to understanding the danzón as well as arguably early jazz and many other fin-de-siècle forms of music and dance (Argentine tango, Brazilian *maxixe*,[4] Cuban *habanera*,[5] etc.) that are stylistically similar to the danzón and have circulated widely throughout the Atlantic region.

Despite its historical significance, its popularity in Mexico, its links to early jazz and to current Latin dance repertoire, the danzón remains poorly researched. Academic studies of it are virtually nonexistent; most current literature on the topic is far from rigorous, long out of print, and concerned with only a single dimension of its history or practice. Literature from Cuba typically focuses on the music's early development there; writings from Mexico describe only specific scenes in that country. The current study addresses some of these shortcomings by combining multi-site research, historical/archival work, and ethnography; by linking danzón history to recent literature related to race, transnationalism, performance, revivalism, and other topics; and by framing present-day danzón performance as a dynamic component of African

---

4. The maxixe is a Brazilian urban popular dance music that appeared in Rio de Janeiro around 1870. Like the danzón, it was extremely sectional and employed many of the same melodic figures as popular Caribbean musics of the period.

5. A slow duple-meter song and dance form employing the famous "habanera bass" rhythm found in Bizet's *Carmen* and many other European works, as well as in some US ragtime. See Chapter 2.

diasporic culture. We investigate the initial dissemination of the danzón, how different groups have embraced it, and how it has come to reflect new social realities. Our study uses music and dance as a lens through which to examine the transnational construction of culture in the Americas, both historically and in the present. In order to keep the project manageable, detailed case studies focus only on the Gulf of Mexico region, primarily Cuba, Mexico, and New Orleans.

Danzones and related forms demonstrate the common influences found in North American and Latin American culture and suggest that both are part of the same broad process of colonization and adaptation. They underscore that traditions throughout the region developed as local reinterpretations of European repertoire, often by musicians of African descent, and that such artistry has circulated widely for centuries. The history of the danzón is intimately linked to the Atlantic slave trade through particular melodic/rhythmic figures, instruments, and/or styles of performance. Likewise, it is tied to the growth of international commerce since it largely spread along trade routes to Cartagena, Veracruz, New Orleans, San Juan de Puerto Rico, and elsewhere. It provides important insights into various historical periods in the countries where it became popular. Its constant movement helps to expand frames of musical and cultural analysis beyond national boundaries and to concentrate on broader movements and interactions. From questions of colonialism to changing local imaginaries, from struggles over individual emancipation and pleasure to questions of social control, the danzón is a unique manifestation that provides important insights into lived practice. It allows us to observe how local experiences result from sustained interactions within regions often not understood as interrelated areas.

QUESTIONS OF GENRE, STYLE, AND MEANING

The focus of our study on what is usually described as a music genre has necessitated reflection on what exactly a genre is, whether the danzón is best described by such a term, and whether it might potentially contribute new insights into theories of genre. In various disciplines such as literary studies, linguistic anthropology, film criticism, and folklore, genre studies have a long history dating back at least to Mikhail Bakhtin's influential essays of the 1920s. Musicologists came later to the discussion but since the 1980s have published substantially on genre theory as well.[6]

6. Examples of publications on musical genres since the 1980s include Franco Fabbri, "A Theory of Popular Music Genres: Two Applications," in *Popular Music Perspectives*, ed. David Horn and Philip Tagg (Exeter: A. Wheaton, 1982), 52–81; and Johan Fornäs, "The Future of Rock: Discourses that Struggle to Define a Genre," *Popular Music* 14, no. 1 (1995), 111–25. Simon Frith's *Performing Rites: On the Value of Popular Music* (Cambridge, MA: Harvard University Press, 1998) includes a chapter on the topic; Keith Negus wrote the first book-length work devoted to it, *Music Genres and Corporate Cultures* (London: Routledge, 1999); Steven Pond also challenges traditional notions of genre in his discussion of musical fusions at the core of *Herbie Hancock's* Head Hunters: *The Making of Jazz's First Platinum Album* (Ann Arbor: University of Michigan Press, 2005). Latin American music

Notions of genre serve as organizing principles for academics and the mainstream public alike, as well as for industry groups, performers, and others. They establish shared conventions, helping define appropriate behaviors, contexts for, and readings of cultural expression. Genres are established through acts of repetition and made meaningful through performance and related discourse. They are simultaneously enhanced and/or challenged through experimentation, the playful transgression of style boundaries through time. We view genres as dynamic, socially defined categories in constant dialogue with broader social processes and transformed structurally and/or conceptually according to the needs of the moment. The danzón offers potential insights into such processes, given the striking degree of its transformations in meaning and form over time.

Genre-related publications have been prominent among musicologists in many countries, though they have not always entered into dialogue with broader literatures. Eduardo Sánchez de Fuentes, an early scholar of Cuban music, wrote extensively on genres including the danzón beginning in the 1920s, as did Emilio Grenet in the 1930s, both within a larger discussion of African- and Spanish-derived cultural influences on the island.[7] Their approach was largely descriptive, generating categories of national repertoire and noting prominent stylistic features. In Mexico, Rubén M. Campos took a similar approach in the 1920s, followed by Gabriel Saldívar and Vicente T. Mendoza in the 1930s and 1940s; they focused their taxonomic efforts on the *canción mexicana* (Mexican song), the *romance* (epic ballad), local *son* and *jarabe* traditions, and the *corrido*.[8]

From the 1940s through the 1960s, Cuban Odilio Urfé introduced the notion of "genre complexes" in presentations during public lectures, as well as in program notes accompanying stage productions designed to educate the public about historical forms of popular music (see Chapter 5).[9] His notion, linking broader styles of performance perceived as related, proved influential on later generations of Cuban scholars. Argeliers León, a preeminent musicologist of the mid-twentieth century and a student of Fernando Ortiz, adopted Urfé's term in the 1960s. He also introduced "multigenre

---

scholars who have published on the topic include Martha Ulhoa, "Pertinência e musica popular-Em busca de categorías para análise da musica brasileira popular," www.hist.puc.cl/iaspm/pdf/Ulloa.pdf; and Rubén López Cano, "Favor de no tocar el género: géneros, estilo y competencia en la semiótica musical congitiva actual," in *Voces e imágenes en la etnomusicología actual*, ed. Josep Martí and Silvia Martínez (Madrid: Ministerio de Cultura, 2004), 325–37 and available online at http://lopezcano.org/Articulos/2004.Favor_tocar_genero.pdf. See also the other authors mentioned in the introduction.

7. See, for instance, Eduardo Sánchez de Fuentes, *El folk-lore en la música cubana* (Havana: Imprenta El Siglo XX, 1923); and Emilio Grenet, *Popular Cuban Music. 80 Revised and Corrected Compositions Together with an Essay on the Evolution of Music in Cuba*, trans. R. Phillips (Havana: Secretary of Agriculture, 1939).

8. E.g., Rubén M. Campos, *El folklore y la música mexicana* (Mexico City: Secretaría de Educación Pública, 1928); Gabriel Saldívar, *Historia de la música en México* (Mexico City: Secretaría de Educación Pública, 1934); and Vicente T. Mendoza, *El romancero español y el corrido mexicano. Estudio comparativo* (Mexico City: Universidad Nacional Autónoma de México, 1997 [1939]).

9. Danilo Orozco, electronic communication, February 13, 2012.

complex" a few years later in an apparent attempt to further emphasize interrelations between at least partially distinct musical genres or subgenres. León's written work is heavily influenced by Marxist thought and provides a nuanced discussion of Cuban genres in the context of Caribbean history and socioeconomic development. He emphasizes the emergent nature of forms such as the danzón and their many permutations through time, yet neither he nor Urfé theorize the concept of genre.[10]

Through the mid-1980s, discussions of genre still tended to be descriptive rather than providing a dynamic model for musical study, thus reflecting the state of musicological research internationally. Victoria Eli Rodríguez and Zoila Gómez García in Cuba extended past studies of genre complexes to the entire Latin American region, inspired by earlier work along similar lines by Argentine Carlos Vega.[11] Others such as Olavo Alén wrote about Cuban music in the 1990s using notions of genre complexes as an organizing principle.[12] Alén's work adopts problematic categories, for instance, contrasting the racially unmarked phrase "Cuban music" (implicitly white/Hispanic) with "Afro-Cuban music" and thus implying distance between Afro-Cuban and national heritage. No "Hispano-Cuban" category is used to complement "Afro-Cuban," for instance, which would make a special category for black genres more appropriate. Additionally, many of the "Cuban" musical categories Alén mentions such as *son*, rumba, and danzón could as easily be considered "Afro-Cuban," given the prominence of black and mixed-race performers and audiences to their development.

Recent scholarship in Cuba and elsewhere recognizes the need for more dynamic constructs of genre as a basis for future study. Mercedes de León Granda called in 1996 for greater attention to the various elements of genre (musical, social/contextual, ideational) and how they are produced and circulate among given groups.[13] Leonardo Acosta criticized mainstream Cuban musicology for acceptance of an overly static concept of genre complexes and a fixation on discrete categories that often obscure as many musical relationships between forms as they illuminate.[14] Danilo Orozco's work notes that past discussion of genre tends to downplay both the complex amalgam of elements taken from a diversity of sources, local and global, and the creative ways individual artists compose or perform that transcend genre categories. Orozco uses a diversity of terms to describe the ways musicians combine

10. Jesús Gómez Cairo, "Dos enfoques sobre géneros de la música cubana: Odilio Urfé y Argeliers León," *Clave* 13, no. 1 (2010), 34–38.

11. Victoria Eli and Zoila Gómez García, *Música latinoamericana y caribeña* (Havana: Editorial Pueblo y Educación, 1995).

12. Olavo Alén, *Géneros musicales de Cuba. De lo afrocubano a la salsa* (San Juan, Puerto Rico: Editorial Cubanacán, 1992).

13. Mercedes de León Granda, "Lo cubano, en música. Un problema de estilo o de género," *Cúpulas* 1, no. 1 (1996), reprinted in *Clave* 12, no. 1–3 (2010), 55–59. Her particular interest was on the relationships between national musical style and genre.

14. Leonardo Acosta, *Otra visión de la música popular cubana* (Havana: Letras Cubanas, 2004), 38–72. The chapter in question is entitled "De los complejos genéricos y otras cuestiones." It was published in English translation as Leonardo Acosta, "On Generic Complexes and Other Topics in Cuban Popular Music," *Journal of Popular Music Studies*, 17 (2005), 227–54. Translated by Raúl Fernández and Daniel S. Whitesell with an introduction by Raúl Fernández.

stylistic elements that often contrast or conflict with one another: paragenre, intergenre, interstyle, dance intergenre, musics of transition, and others.[15] In 2010, the
preeminent Cuban musicology journal *Clave* devoted an extended special issue—the
only publication that year— to the notion of genre and its place within musicology,
contributing to critical reflection on past practices.

Any focus on the categories or stylistic features associated with a given music
inevitably risks oversimplification, as well as the downplaying of linkages beyond
a given category and the constant innovation that characterizes musical performance, composition, and dance. A focus on the normative features of genre tends
to shift analysis from music making itself—from processes, performance, and individual agency—to fixed products and general tendencies, thus confounding a
comprehensive understanding of style and form. In many countries, normative
typologies of national music genres continue to dominate musicological discussion. The resulting constructs and discourses prove resistant to change, owing in
part to support from elite institutions and/or governmental agencies invested in
particular forms of heritage.[16] By contrast, our study emphasizes the many unique
manifestations of the danzón as conceived by individual performers and dancers,
and the conscious aesthetic choices that gave rise to them.

With some exceptions, recent studies take more care to define the concept of
genre and consider how particular musical categories emerge, how they change over
time, how the experience of genre functions socially, how the same genre may be
perceived differently by different communities, and so on. Literature from the United
States and Europe emphasizes the role of the corporate music industry in defining
and disseminating notions of genre and suggests that such categories may conflict
with the views of grassroots communities.[17] Growing consensus exists on the need to
make social life and firsthand observation of musical practice the basis of any study
of genre whenever possible. Likewise, more consideration has been given to the
many groups potentially contributing to genre formation above and beyond the
music industry including the mass media, educational institutions, or state officials,
as well as individuals.[18]

Drawing on recent scholarship, we define the danzón as a "performance complex"
rather than a genre or genre complex, emphasizing through this shift in terminology
our primary concern with music making and human action as opposed to categories

15. Danilo Orozco, *Nexos globales desde la música cubana con rejuegos de son y no son*
(Havana: Ediciones Ojalá, 2001), 10–11, 16, 42, 49. Orozco (1944–2013) was one of the
Cuban scholars most closely in dialogue with interdisciplinary scholarship on genre from
Europe and the United States.

16. Fabian Holt, *Genre in Popular Music* (Chicago: University of Chicago Press), 15.

17. E.g., Negus, *Music Genres and Corporate Cultures.*

18. On the importance of centering genre study on social practice, see Danilo Orozco,
"Qué e(s)tá pasando, ¡Asere! . . . Detrás del borroso 'qué sé yo y no sé qué' en la génesis y
dinámica de los géneros musicales," *Clave* 12, no. 1–3 (2010), 64. For a discussion of
the various actors influencing genre formation and discourse, see Liliana González
Moreno, comp., "Género, forma, lenguaje, estilo y demás complejidades." *Clave* 12, no. 1–3
(2010), 111.

or taxonomies.[19] The danzón is best conceived as a particular kind of music and dance that exists within unique cultural webs of production, circulation, and signification. It can be viewed not only as a form of music making but as a space of affect[20] experienced in the minds and bodies of groups of people who share certain conventions.[21] The danzón manifests itself in participatory events and performance. Individual and collective understandings of it derive from the same activities, mediated by conflicting ideologies, perspectives, and initiatives on the part of various groups. Performance complexes such as the danzón help organize cultural creation and reception, yet derive their meanings from broader realities. As suggested in the writings of Richard Bauman, William Hanks, and others, they are historically defined frameworks of orientation, interpretive procedures, and sets of expectations that structure music making and dance.[22] They constitute a habitus in Bourdieu's sense of the term, a way of perceiving and cognitively organizing the world.[23] Rather than fixed structures, forms such as the danzón function as schemata, rough guidelines that dialogue constantly with other cultural and social practices. Performativity is a central notion in defining these complexes.[24] It emphasizes the power cultural of practices to do something as they are enacted by collectivities or individuals. Focusing on the danzón as a performance complex allows us to inquire into what happens when the danzón happens. Thus, we interrogate how the affective relations people establish

19. See Ramón H. Rivera-Servera, "Musical Trans(actions): Intersections in Reggaetón," *Trans. Revista Transcultural de Música*, No. 13 (2009), www.sibetrans.com/trans/a62/musical-transactions-intersections-in-reggaeton (accessed on July 20, 2012).

20. María de los Ángeles Córdoba and Natalí Méndez Díaz discuss genre similarly as a "mundo de sentido" or "world of feeling," drawing on the work of Spaniard Héctor Fouce, in "El género en la música: una aproximación a su estudio," *Clave* 12, no. 1–3 (2010), 91. The idea bears some similarity to Raymond Williams's earlier discussion of "structures of feeling" in *Marxism and Literature* (New York: Oxford University Press, 1977), 128–35.

21. Holt, *Genre in Popular Music*, 2, 7.

22. William Hanks, "Discourse Genres in a Theory of Practice," *American Ethnologist* 14, no. 4 (1987), 676–77, 687–88. Hanks is a linguistic anthropologist who draws on Richard Bauman's work as well as that of other folklorists and anthropologists in defining genre. See, for instance, Richard Bauman, *Verbal Art as Performance* (Prospect Heights, IL: Waveland Press, 1977); and Joel Scherzer, *Kuna Ways of Speaking: An Ethnographic Perspective* (Austin: University of Texas Press, 1983).

23. Pierre Bourdieu, *Outline of a Theory of Practice* (New York: Cambridge University Press, 1977).

24. Throughout the book we use the terms "performative" and "performatic" following the convention proposed by Diana Taylor for the field of performance studies, in which "the performative becomes less a quality (or adjective) of 'performance' than of discourse [and the performatic] denote[s] the adjectival form of the nondiscursive realm of performance." In other words, performatic refers to the theatrical qualities of performance while performative refers to discursive performativity or the realm of "what happens when music happens." See Diana Taylor, *The Archive and the Repertoire. Performing Cultural Memory in the Americas* (Durham, NC: Duke University Press, 2005), 6; see also Alejandro L. Madrid, "Why Music and Performance Studies? Why Now? An Introduction to the Special Issue," *Trans. Revista Transcultural de Música*, No. 13, 2009, www.sibetrans.com/trans/a1/why-music-and-performance-studies-why-now-an-introduction-to-the-special-issue (accessed July 20, 2012).

with the music and dance as they experience them (while playing, listening, dancing, selling, or buying it) allow them to continuously reconstitute themselves.

THE MUSICAL PERFORMANCE OF RACIAL DIFFERENCE

Discussion of race-related themes have surfaced for years in music literature, though most studies fail to clearly define the notion of race; to provide a frame for thinking of various racialized historical periods and their related practices; or to discuss existing literature on music and race and the analytical approaches other authors have taken. We define race as an emergent complex of meanings that reference broader social conflicts, ideologies, and interests through the categorizing of human bodies. Although racial terminology derives from biological difference, the selection of particular features as significant is inevitably a social process and subject to frequent change.[25] Hierarchical notions of race associated with the late nineteenth and early twentieth centuries resulted largely from the conquest of Africa and the Americas and related ideologies that justified mass human subjugation. One could argue that the field of ethnomusicology itself developed slowly out of similar processes of conquest and conflict.[26]

Racial debate thus derives from broad socioeconomic realities and can be understood only in that context. The study of music and race involves an examination of the "racial formation" of a given period: the overarching processes by which racial categories are generated, experienced, and transformed through time. Ideologies associated with a given racial formation justify or sustain its particular forms of social organization. Additionally, the interpretation of racialized practice requires the study of "racial projects," conscious efforts to alter existing racial dynamics or dogma by means of new interpretations or representations of race.[27] Racial formations associated with early danzón performance include the highly stratified colonial/postcolonial societies in Cuba and Mexico in which non-white individuals tended to occupy marginal positions, and in which dominant society perceived Afro-descendant cultural forms as primitive at best. Racial projects influencing the circulation or reception of the danzón include the "racially blind" propaganda espoused by José Martí and other Cuban revolutionaries in the 1890s as well as the rhetoric of *mestizaje* based on a European-indigenous dichotomy proposed by José Vasconcelos and embraced by the Mexican government in the 1920s, as discussed in Chapter 3.

25. Michael Omi and Howard Winant, *Racial Formation in the United States: From the 1960s to the 1990s*, 2nd edition (New York: Routledge, 1994), 54–56.
26. Many prominent scholars of non-Western music first gained exposure to such repertoire as the result of colonialist initiatives. Jaap Kunst, for example, worked as a civil servant in Dutch Indonesia before becoming an authority on the gamelan. Helen Roberts began studying Native American music under the auspices of the US government in the wake of the forced relocation of native populations and the seizure of their lands. Gilbert Chase, an early US scholar of Latin American music, was the son of a military officer stationed in Cuba during the first US occupation of that country.
27. Omi and Winant, *Racial Formation in the United States*.

The term "black music" defies essentialist definition. It refers to constructs emerging from dialectic processes, typically between Afro-diasporic groups in the Americas and a dominant social order that defines itself in opposition to blackness. Black music may contain particular rhythms, structures, or performatic features associated with Afro-diasporic groups, yet these elements do not constitute defining characteristics of the repertoire. Rather, black music at any given time (indeed, virtually any inherited cultural form) incorporates influences from various sources that are creatively combined and re-encoded with local meanings. In the Caribbean and Latin American context such reconfigurations are especially complex, frequently encompassing a diversity of elements from indigenous, Afro-descendant, Western European, North American, and other sources. Black musical forms are best conceived as a constantly shifting sonic/semiotic ground of at least potentially divergent claims and ascriptions.[28] Indeed, the Caribbean is recognized as a quintessentially creolized space, a site known for its fluid, multivalent cultures.[29] One useful focus of analysis in such a context is how commonsense notions of "white" and "black" expression shift through time, who contests them, and whose interests or projects they support.[30]

From the perspective of those studying the arts, an important quality of racial experience is that it bridges the realms of the cultural and the social. As in the case of whiteness, notions of blackness frequently derive from socioeconomic hierarchy, practices of spatial exclusion, and so on, but also from the perpetuation of cultural practices such as religious worship and other forms of embodied experience, including music and dance. To interpret racialized meaning, then, is to study the ways that culture and social structure interact. As Howard Winant notes, the connection between culture and structure, at the core of the racial formation process, "gives racial projects their coherence and unity. . . . This is the way racial formation occurs . . . racial formation is the articulation of culture and structure, signification and social organization."[31] Thus, musical performance does not simply symbolize particular attitudes but, as a locus of human action, plays a central role in their formulation. Music making is often implicated in attempts to shift prevailing sentiment and further particular racial initiatives. Music gives voice to racial difference, a fundamental element of human experience, and provides one of the most powerful lenses through which to examine racialized processes on a global scale.[32]

To date, music literature has taken a wide variety of approaches to the study of race. Some studies document the power of music to serve as (at least symbolically)

28. Peter Wade, *Blackness and Race Mixture. The Dynamics of Racial Identity in Colombia* (Baltimore, MD: Johns Hopkins University Press, 1993), 22.

29. E.g., Stephan Palmié, "Ackee and Saltfish vs. Amalá Con Quimbombó," *Journal de la Société des Américanist* 91–92 (2005), 94.

30. Guthrie P. Ramsey, *Race Music. Black Cultures from Bebop to Hip-Hop* (Berkeley: University of California Press, 2003), 37–38.

31. Howard Winant, "White Racial Projects," in *The Making and Unmaking of Whiteness*, ed. Brander Rasmussen et al. (Durham, NC: Duke University Press, 2001), 101.

32. Ronald Radano and Philip V. Bohlman, "Introduction," in *Music and the Racial Imagination*, ed. Ronald Radano and Philip V. Bohlman (Chicago: University of Chicago Press, 2000), 37.

oppositional forms of expression among oppressed groups, as a chronicle of their daily lives, a means by which black diasporic groups can parody or ridicule aspects of dominant society, organize politically, or express solidarity in the face of oppression.[33] Other publications study the music industry to explore issues of financial exploitation, segregation, and related themes.[34] Still others emphasize the ideologically repressive potential of music making, for instance, how early black characters on the US minstrelsy stage furthered political interests in the antebellum south or how discourse surrounding early jazz reinforced notions of black primitivism.[35] Existing studies most closely resembling the approach taken in this volume emphasize the contested nature of black musical meaning, the multiple ways such expression can be interpreted or understood in relation to broader discourses, or the ways in which black musical expression simultaneously reconciles dominant and subaltern values or ideologies through performance, often in uneasy tension.[36]

We assume that racialized music, as part of larger formations and projects, derives its meaning (whether originating in particular black communities themselves or in segments of dominant society) within distinct historical moments. In the same way that analyses of global racial discourses distinguish between the pre- and post-World War II periods and related shifts in notions of race, or that discussions of African American music in the United States have been periodized into phases of Afro-modernism, black consciousness, and post-industrialism, any study of music and race must be attentive to conjunctures of historical specificity.[37] This is especially important in the case of the danzón because it has enjoyed popularity for extended periods in distinct contexts. Its history spans the mid-nineteenth century, rife with overtly evolutionist ideologies, through the post-WWII period and the emergence of more modern notions of race. And its popularization in both Cuba and Mexico corresponds to periods of fundamental reformulations of nationalist discourse, resulting in a valorization of black and working-class expression as collective heritage.

33. LeRoy Jones discusses the development of the US cakewalk from this perspective, for instance, in *Blues People* (New York: Apollo Editions, 1963), 86. Other studies referencing the oppositional potential of black music include Leonardo Acosta's writings on the rumba or Rogelio Martínez Furé's essay on Cuban drums (both printed in English in the Peter Manuel-edited *Essays on Cuban Music. North American and Cuban Perspectives* (New York: University Press of America, 1991), 25–74.

34. E.g., Steve Chapple and Reebee Garofalo, "Black Roots, White Fruits: Racism in the Music Industry," in *Rock 'n' Roll Is Here to Pay: The History and Politics of the Music Industry*, ed. Steve Chapple and Reebee Garofalo (Chicago: Nelson-Hall, 1977), 231–67.

35. Alexander Saxton, "Blackface Minstrelsy and Jacksonian Ideology," *American Quarterly* 29 (1975), 3–28; Ronald Radano, "Hot Fantasies: American Modernism and the Idea of Black Rhythm," in *Music and the Racial Imagination*, 459–82.

36. On polysemy and multiple interpretations of black music, see, for instance, Louise Meintjes, "Paul Simon's *Graceland*, South Africa, and the Mediation of Musical Meaning," *Ethnomusicology* 34, no. 1 (1990), 37–73. George Lipsitz's work on North American musics also resonates with this perspective; see *Time Passages. Collective Memory and American Popular Culture* (Minneapolis: University of Minnesota Press, 1990).

37. Stuart Hall, "What Is the 'Black' in Black Popular Culture?" in *Black Popular Culture*, ed. Michelle Wallace and Gina Dent (Seattle: Bay Press, 1992), 21. On the periodization of African American music in the twentieth century, see Ramsey, *Race Music*, 28–29.

The expansion of studies of whiteness in recent years also has implications for the danzón, given that dominant groups have attempted to distance the music from its associations with the black community at particular moments. Whiteness is difficult to analyze, as it is rarely defined overtly and usually emerges as a category only in opposition to others. But frequent claims as to the importance of preserving white racial "purity" in the face of the danzón's appeal to multi-racial audiences suggest its importance in this case. Notions of whiteness are linked closely to dominant racial anxieties and perceived threats to racial hierarchy.[38] Prior to the early twentieth century, of course, notions of whiteness and white supremacy served as justification for the subjugation of non-white populations. More recently, parallels can be found between discourses surrounding the danzón and ostensibly "colorblind" neoconservative discourses in the United States and elsewhere that conceal deeply race-conscious beliefs.[39] The acceptance of whiteness involves the embrace of unmarked/orthodox cultural and social practices associated with dominant groups. In the context of the populist nationalism associated with Cuba of the 1910s–1920s or Mexico after 1930s–1940s, mainstream critics asserted the predominantly white/European character of the danzón in order to deny the significance of racial difference, avoid uncomfortable discussions of ongoing racial inequality and discrimination, and/or downplay the contributions of Afro-diasporic groups to the nation. Such historical processes have been described in recent literature as whitewashing: discursive strategies of cultural bleaching that defend and maintain white privilege.[40]

TRANSNATIONALISM, CIRCULATION, CIRCULARITY AND THE CIRCUM-CARIBBEAN

Time never dies
The circle is not perfect
                    —Milčo Mančevski, *Before the Rain*

There are moments in academic life when new theoretical concepts overturn earlier frameworks that have prevented the advancement of knowledge. The transnational turn in the humanities and social sciences at the beginning of the twenty-first century was one such moment; it questioned the relevance of the nation-state as a unit of analysis in a globalizing context. It proposed that transnational cultural flows were not new but rather old phenomena, even if past scholars largely failed to perceive them. By documenting the relationship between comparison and subject formation, the transnational turn questioned the comparative paradigm supporting narratives about national character that dominated the humanities in the nineteenth century

38. Howard Winant, "White Racial Projects," 97.
39. Winant, "White Racial Projects," 103.
40. John Gabriel, *Whitewash. Racialized Politics and the Media* (London: Routledge, 1998), 5; see also Arlene Dávila, *Latino Spin. Public Image and the Whitewashing of Race* (New York: New York University Press, 2008).

and much of the twentieth. A transnational perspective makes evident that the categories, subjects, and experiences at the core of discourses of national difference are themselves products of the methods that support and validate such narratives and frequently develop in tandem with other regional fictions.[41]

As helpful as it has been in re-orienting scholarly inquiry, the notion of transnationalism is used indiscriminately at times to refer to processes, relations, and conditions that bear little relation to transborder dynamics. Of particular concern is the frequent use of "transnational" in lieu of "international." While both terms refer to relations beyond the nation-state, the word international most appropriately refers to relations or exchanges between nations; transnational, on the other hand, refer to flows that cut across the national boundaries and render them at least partially irrelevant. Nowadays, for instance, some scholars refer to rock or jazz as transnational music genres regardless of the fact that they are manufactured and consumed largely within national imaginaries. Fans and marketers alike talk about U.S., Argentine, British, or Cuban rock, making it clear that national affiliation still plays a fundamental role in the identification of such music. One could argue that rock in all its manifestations references a cosmopolitan experience but not necessarily a transnational one. In other cases, music literature describes collaborations between musicians living in different countries as transnational. Yet such partnerships have existed for centuries and do not necessarily speak to a transnational experience. Other studies refer to specific bands as transnational because their members are from different countries; nevertheless, a band in itself cannot be transnational although the experience of its individual members or the circulation of its music may be. In sum, "transnational" has too often been used to label cultural artifacts rather than to describe dynamic processes.

Understanding that the indiscriminate use of a term weakens its analytical potential, we propose to reevaluate transnationalism in relation to flows that, to paraphrase Jonathan Xavier Inda and Renato Rosaldo, are simultaneously defined by "more than one place and no one place in particular."[42] Such a model requires an understanding of space that privileges mobility, circulation, transition, and impermanence instead of fixity. Thus, space is no longer the place where one is but rather where one becomes; local spaces are created and defined through their networks of identification. The approach acknowledges the frequent reconfiguration and resignification of culture as individuals establish new relationships and/or perform beyond the limits of conventional national imaginaries.[43]

This book deals with historical as well as contemporary danzón and danzón-related expressive forms that have traversed the Caribbean basin for over a century. In doing

41. Micol Seigel, "Beyond Compare: Comparative Method after the Transnational Turn," *Radical History Review*, no. 91 (2005), 62–63.

42. Jonathan Xavier Inda and Renato Rosaldo, "Tracking Global Flows," in *The Anthropology of Globalization. A Reader*, ed. Jonathan Xavier Inda and Renato Rosaldo (Malden, MA: Blackwell, 2008 [2002]), 23.

43. See Alejandro L. Madrid, "Transnational Musical Encounters at the U.S.-Mexico Border: An Introduction," in *Transnational Encounters. Music and Performance at the U.S.-Mexico Border*, ed. Alejandro L. Madrid (New York: Oxford University Press, 2011), 8–9.

so, it engages notions of space and circulation implied in the term "circum-Caribbean." Linked together by a shared history of colonization, diasporic movement, and immigration, the circum-Caribbean is a geo-cultural region that encompasses the West Indies, the northern coast of South America, the Florida and Yucatan peninsulas, as well as New Orleans and Veracruz. It is precisely the revolving path of the Gulf Stream that best symbolizes the perpetual (yet always renewed) cultural flows explored in this volume and suggests a possible model for thinking about them, the notion of circularity.

"Time never dies, the circle is not perfect," is a recurrent motto in Milčo Mančevski's award-winning film *Before the Rain* (1994). A few years ago, while reflecting on processes of cultural exchange between Europe and the Americas, one of us engaged Mančevski's aphorism and proposed a spiral as a metaphor for how ideas, concepts, or cultural manifestations reappear over time but are transformed in ever-changing circumstances.[44] This perspective emphasizes how culture continues to exist in the remixes that its circulation engenders. Recent scholarship in cultural studies and rhetoric has advanced similar models as ways to appreciate not only the dissemination or regulation of cultural manifestations but also the performativity of narrative in relation to time and identity. Time and self become real when they are organized according to specific narratives, which themselves are meaningful only as long as they engage people's lives; such a model emphasizes the circularity of performativity.[45] This book explores the movement of expressive culture as observed in the ways the danzón has shaped gender, ethnic, class, and racial representations. Its narratives become meaningful as uttered, played, and danced in localized articulations that establish dialogues throughout the region.

NOSTALGIA AND *CACHONDERÍA*: AFFECT AND TRANSHISTORICAL MEANING IN DANZÓN EXPERIENCES

Throughout its history, music scholarship (both musicology and ethnomusicology) has largely failed to achieve broad relevance for the humanities and social sciences. Despite the paramount contributions of a few individuals, the field has yet to produce an intellectual whose work is referenced across disciplines—someone who, by studying music, allows others to see their own work in a different way. We argue

44. Alejandro L. Madrid, "El continuo proceso de intercambio cultural. Leo Brouwer y *La espiral eterna* (1971)," *Pauta. Cuadernos de teoría y crítica musical* 16, no. 66 (1998), 67.

45. Paul Ricoeur, *Time and Narrative Vol. 1*, trans. Kathleen McLaughlin and David Pellauer (Chicago: University of Chicago Press, 1982); Paul Ricoeur, " Narrative Identity," *Philosophy Today* 35, no. 1 (1991), 73–81; Katrina McNeely Farren, "Narrative Identity in Paul Ricoeur and Luce Irigaray: The Circularity between Self and Other," PhD Dissertation, Michigan Technological University (2010), 135–39. The circularity of performativity is also exemplified in the repeated acts necessary for cultural beliefs and signification to exist; it is only through repetition within specific ideological contexts that those contexts are reconstituted, allowing for the formation of subjects whose actions in turn reproduce them. However, as Judith Butler suggests, certain cultural reiterations also allow for challenges to the established conventions that validate such structures. See Judith Butler, *Excitable Speech. A Politics of the Performative* (London: Routledge, 1997), 24–27.

that the reasons for this may have less to do with the sophistication of music scholarship than with the questions asked about music. We make no claim to have resolved the problem, yet we engage with music and dance in an attempt to further interdisciplinary discussions about race, gender, class, and historical/transhistorical meaning rather than borrowing from cultural theory in order to better understand musical practices.

Scholars in many disciplines, from history and sociology to literary and film scholars, find music a fascinating object of research. One reason for their attraction is that they, like most people, have no problem identifying with it and making it their own. Almost everybody has a close, emotional connection with music, yet musicology and ethnomusicology have largely been unable to theorize such affect. Our book strives to place emotion centrally within its intellectual project. Not only does the affect of danzón enthusiasts constitute a central topic of study, a similar feeling motivates our own scholarly interest in the music.[46] Likewise, nostalgic desire represents a central theme; by focusing on the need many dancers and musicians feel to revive the danzón, this book investigates transhistorical meaning: how the meanings of culture change in relation to its reception in the present in multiple ways, thus transcending historical specificity. The project pays close attention to how the danzón acquires meaning under specific circumstances but also refuses to concede that such meaning (even at specific moments) is irreparably fixed by historical contingencies. Instead, we examine how mythologies about the danzón are enacted on the basis of memories, how entire communities have reimagined the past in order to engage with the music they love, and how resultant meanings develop through a complex web of multi-lineal routes and associations.[47] This suggests how reiterations at the core of performative dynamics subvert the presumed linearity and teleology of historical meaning.

Recent Latin music trends have been informed by nostalgia, as evident in the content of Wim Wenders's *Buena Vista Social Club* (1999) film and much of the scholarly criticism it generated.[48] Nostalgia plays a central role in current danzón revivals in Cuba and Mexico; however, rather than invoking a colonialist nostalgia as in the case of Wenders's film or "structural nostalgia," defined by Michael Herzfeld as "the longing of an age before the state,"[49] current revivals of the danzón speak to how insiders imagine themselves in relation to past dance and musical practices. In a manner more evocative of Raymond Williams's residual tradition,[50] or what Svetlana Boym labels

46. E.g., the danzones, mambos, or cha cha chás we grew up listening to at family gatherings, or those that appear ubiquitously in our everyday lives, on new CD releases, or in TV reruns of old movies.

47. For more discussion of the notion of "transhistorical," see Alejandro L. Madrid, "Retos multilineales y método prolépsico en el estudio posnacional del nacionalismo musical," in *Discursos y prácticas musicales nacionalistas (1900–1970): España, Argentina, Cuba, México*, ed. Pilar Ramos López (Logroño: Universidad de La Rioja, 2012). On the relation of these ideas to Svetlana Boym's notion of restorative nostalgia, see note 51 following.

48. E.g., Vicenzo Perna, "Marketing Nostalgia: The Rise of *Buena Vista Social Club*," chapter 9 of his *Timba. The Sound of Cuban Crisis* (London: Ashgate, 2005), 240–63.

49. Michael Herzfeld, *Cultural Intimacy. Social Poetics in the Nation-State* (New York: Routledge, 2005), 22.

50. Williams, *Marxism and Literature*, 121–27.

restorative nostalgia,[51] many danzón enthusiasts attempt to recreate a time in which the danzón and associated practices enjoyed an exalted position within the national imaginary. Our work not only examines nostalgia for past cultural moments but also pays close attention to reflective nostalgia, reinventions that create the past anew, often overriding historical meaning and adjusting it according to contemporary values.[52] Svetlana Boym proposes that, due to its fragmentary nature, reflective nostalgia operates in a manner similar to transhistoricity, creating "a multitude of potentialities, nonteleological possibilities of historical development."[53] Finally, this book engages with nostalgia, music, and dance in relation to the construction of national memory as evident in racial discourses and the related disciplining of dancing bodies.

In order to understand the subjective-affective associations surrounding music and dance that nostalgic experiences reflect, we approach modern evocations of the danzón as "sonic spaces of effective utopian longing" that validate people's "own sentient experience . . . against the grain of models put upon [them] by forces beyond [their] control."[54] Such forces include the gendered and racialized regulation of the body and its pleasure, restrictions on performance, and changes made to normative danzón choreographies.

Danzón dancing has always been identified with an enjoyment of the body that, depending on the historical circumstances, may be interpreted as immoral or as individually liberating. Mexican danzoneros refer to their enjoyment of the dance as cachondería: an experience of subdued lust, subtle sensuality. We believe this term suggests the possible intersection of two types of bodily pleasure; the Adornian notion of Genuß (pleasure) and the Lacanian concept of jouissance (enjoyment). The terms "pleasure" and "enjoyment" have been used interchangeably in critical theory, often referring to sensual pleasure. In his Ästhetische Theorie (1970), Theodor Adorno critiques aesthetic pleasure as class alienation, an "uncritical pleasure" that contributes to the reproduction of dominant ideologies.[55] In the original German text Adorno uses the word Genuß; English versions of the work translate it as either pleasure or enjoyment. Jacques Lacan employs the same word (Genuß as well as its French translation, jouissance) to reference a different kind of enjoyment that implies usufruct and ownership, clearly different from Adorno's concept. Lacan's notion, further theorized by Néstor Braunstein, involves an experience of pleasure that allows for the subject's momentary repossession of his or her body beyond the constraints of disciplining discourses.[56]

51. Svetlana Boym describes restorative nostalgia as a desire to recreate an idealized past. See Svetlana Boym, The Future of Nostalgia (New York: Basic Books, 2001), 49.
52. Boym, The Future, 49.
53. Boym, The Future, 50.
54. Josh Kun, Audiotopia. Music, Race, and America (Berkeley: University of California Press, 2005), 18 and 23.
55. Theodor W. Adorno, Ästhetische Theorie (Frankfurt: Suhrkam, 1970), 26–27.
56. The meaning of the notion of jouissance is often obscure in Lacan's own writings. However, Néstor Braunstein, who has theorized extensively about this Lacanian idea, defines it as "usufruct, the ownership of the object . . . the appropriation and expropriation of enjoyment in relation to the Other." See Néstor A. Braunstein, El goce. Un concepto lacaniano (Buenos Aires: Siglo XXI, 2006 [1990]), 29.

We suggest that cachondería implies a dancing experience that transcends Adorno's rational hegemonic model. Lacan's work helps explain the wide variety of additional ways individuals act and perceive with their bodies beyond alienation or constraint. Of course, in analyzing dance it is often difficult to determine how movements challenge conventions and/or reproduce dominant norms. We propose cachondería as an intersection of Adornian and Lacanian models that encompasses the contradictory feelings dancers have in relation to mainstream notions of how to enjoy their bodies. Cachondería as experienced by danzoneros is a type of pleasure that simultaneously challenges certain conventions about the gendered body and reproduces others.

DANZÓN MATTERS: THE STORIES

The chapters of this volume were written with various audiences in mind, both music specialists and others concerned primarily with cultural history and related topics. Chapter 2 defines danzón music and choreography as a complex of related practices, past and present, noting core characteristics that coalesced in the late nineteenth century. It examines the danzón's early history, including its emergence out of eighteenth- and nineteenth-century figure dance traditions, as well as its relation to variants such as the habanera and Puerto Rican *danza*. Later sections include numerous musical transcriptions and detail about the many styles of danzón in Cuba and Mexico from the 1880s through the 1950s.

Chapter 3 focuses on issues of race, class, and gender associated with the danzón, also from the late nineteenth through the mid-twentieth century. It considers the varied associations of the music over time and the ways in which discourse about music and dance corresponded to broader political projects and pronouncements on national identity. In Cuba, critics tended increasingly to overlook the Afro-Caribbean origins of the danzón in an attempt to align it with Eurocentric notions of an implicitly Hispanic national culture. In 1920s Mexico, the growing popularity of the danzón (at the time a symbol of black Cuban culture) among the working classes allowed for the transfer of anxieties about blackness onto it; simultaneously, it facilitated the discursive whitening of other Cuban forms such as the habanera and their transformation into symbols of mestizo nationalism as conceived by José Vasconcelos and others. Later, in the 1940s, similar discourses distanced the danzón from associations with blackness and prostitution as well, aligning it with working-class Mexican identity.

Chapter 4 engages with literature on early jazz, focusing on the danzón's presence in the city of New Orleans and highlighting stylistic linkages between orquesta típica-style danzón and turn-of-the-century US repertoire. Of special interest is the practice of collective simultaneous improvisation/variation, a practice found both in segments of the danzón and in the jazz idiom marketed commercially as "dixieland." The chapter begins by discussing demographic and other ties between Mexico, the Caribbean, and Louisiana, and the circulation of danzón repertoire performed in the New Orleans area. It proceeds to analyze early recordings of danzón performance in order to document the pervasiveness of improvisational practices in the repertoire.

Chapter 5 examines the decline of the danzón in Cuba and Mexico in the mid-twentieth century as it was overshadowed by newer musical forms such as the mambo, cha cha chá, rock, and protest song. Later, the chapter documents the danzón's slow revival in both countries as advocates established "historical" performance ensembles, regional and national dance associations, and festivals; disseminated films; and made other self-conscious presentations of heritage. In Cuba, resurgent interest in danzones resulted from factors including grassroots initiatives on the part of older enthusiasts and support from government agencies interested in promoting tourism. In Mexico, dancers from Veracruz and Mexico City contributed to the national revival, fundamentally transforming the danzón's choreography and performance practice in the process.

Chapter 6 examines danzón dancing in Cuba and Mexico in detail, analyzing one set of practices in relation to the other. It notes distinct ways of experiencing the music and moving to it in the two countries, varied contexts for performance, and an increasing tendency in Mexico toward presentations of large group choreographies in events known as *muestras*. In addition, the chapter focuses on how the Cuban and Mexican dance scenes have developed in continuous dialogue with each other. Central to this discussion is an interrogation of the experience of pleasure many fans describe in relation to the notion of cachondería as explained earlier. The chapter also focuses on the distinct views Cuban and Mexican dancers have of one another, frequently informed by essentialized notions of race and national character.

Chapter 7 concludes the volume by considering the ways that elements of the danzón and related forms have been reconceived over the past century and a half within compositions intended for the concert hall or commercial recordings rather than for dancing. It begins by discussing repertoire by Louis Moreau Gottschalk, Manuel M. Ponce, Alejandro García Caturla, Aaron Copland, and other classical artists through the mid-twentieth century. It continues with an overview of works by composers of the late twentieth century such as Arturo Márquez, then discusses adaptations of the danzón in Latin jazz compositions (by Chucho Valdés, Emiliano Salvador, Gonzalo Rubalcaba, Arturo Sandoval, and others), protest song repertoire, and rap music. The chapter concludes with a discussion of how the transnational circulation of the danzón has led to its resignification according to changing ideas about heritage. We argue that apparently local traditions are continuously informed by larger artistic and intellectual flows, and that they acquire meaning only in relation to one another.

CHAPTER 2
Danzón as a Performance Complex

Walking into a Cuban bookstore in Havana is always an adventure; one never knows how it will end. With luck, hidden gems may be found alongside the obligatory Marxist-Leninist literature or biographies of Ché Guevara. One evening, a visit to the Ateneo Cervantes bookstore in Old Havana proves especially rewarding. A couple of boxes filled with music scores sit on the floor near the cashier, including piano reductions of danzones from the 1920s. Some appear to belong to the same private collection, as they contain several hand-copied scores by Joaquín Marcoleta. It is particularly surprising to find the danzón "¡Oh Margot! o La borrachita" ("Oh Margot! Or the Little Drunk Woman").[1] Early danzón composers used melodies from many different musics as sources of melodic material, from opera arias to contemporary jazz hits. Nevertheless, "La borrachita," a languid *canción mexicana* by Ignacio Fernández Esperón, "Tata Nacho" (1892–1968), seems like an odd choice to quote, given that the original piece bears little stylistic relation to the danzón nor evokes its festive or bodily associations. However, upon closer examination of the score one finds certain musical commonalities. "La borrachita" works as a danzón adaptation because the canción mexicana's basic rhythmic pattern (Ex. 2.1, measure 1) derives from the Cuban *habanera* as cultivated by late nineteenth-century Mexican salon composers. The fact that forms as different stylistically as the canción mexicana and the danzón, which evoke completely different racial and national imaginaries, both developed in dialogue with the habanera raises questions about the utility of notions of genre and the elements privileged in the labeling of music.

This chapter analyzes the danzón as a performance complex.[2] Thus, we suggest conceiving of the danzón as a loose cognitive category and a space of cultural affect

---

1. This danzón was recorded in 1927 by Antonio María Romeu's orchestra for the Victor label. See Richard K. Spotswood, *Ethnic Music on Record, Vol. 4. Spanish, Portuguese, Philippine, Basque* (Champaign: University of Illinois Press, 1990), 2271.
2. For more information on this topic, see Ramón H. Rivera-Servera's article, "Musical Trans(actions): Intersections in Reggaetón," *Trans. Revista Transcultural de Música*, no. 13 (2009), www.sibetrans.com/trans/a62/musical-transactions-intersections-in-reggaeton (accessed on July 20, 2012).

Example 2.1: Common Afro-Caribbean rhythmic cells found in the Cuban contradanza and related musical forms.

in which musical style is continuously transformed and resignified. More than a genre defined by standard features, the danzón allows for the performance of networks of identification—frequently across genres—by means of shared listening and dance practices. Our analysis considers the many danzón variants that have developed through time, noting the constant processes of change and experimentation that have characterized them. Elements discussed include overall form/structure, the use of particular Afro-Caribbean rhythms and instruments, dance choreographies, the emergence of diverse instrumental ensembles, and widespread practices of intertextual musical quotation or borrowing.

Conventional descriptions of the danzón's musical style privilege its rondo form, often with a concluding montuno (improvisational vamp) section, and the use of the Cuban cinquillo as its fundamental rhythm. While these elements characterize many pieces, the adoption of such a model has favored a teleological conception of the danzón's development, with certain styles considered classic or orthodox and others peripheral; the latter are often described either as proto-danzones, not yet having achieved the genre's "true" essence, or as corruptions or deviations. Contrary to this view, Chapter 2 assumes no definitive danzón style; instead, it underscores the diversity of danzones that have developed in dialogue with a variety of musics. Thus, the chapter examines the contradanza, danza habanera, two-part, three-part, and multi-section danzones of the fin de siècle, and the *danzón cantado, danzonete, danzón de nuevo ritmo, danzón de nuevo tipo*, and variations of *danzones chá* from mid-twentieth century and beyond as part of the same performance complex.

CONTRADANZAS AND DANZAS: THE EARLY PERMUTATIONS OF DANZÓN

Musically and choreographically, the danzón developed out of the contradanza and danza, which in turn represent local variants of the European contradance. Originally a rural pastime of the common people in England, the contradance first appeared in published form in 1659; by the end of the century it had become fashionable among the emerging middle classes of France and the Netherlands (Francophones used the term *contradanse*), with the Spanish adopting it soon thereafter (as the *contradanza*).[3] Its origins among the poor represented a stylistic revolution of sorts, as dances fashionable among elites prior to that time had come from the Parisian court. The rise of the contradance thus reflected the slow decline of the European

---

3. Hilario González, "Manuel Saumell y la contradanza," in Manuel Saumell, *Contradanzas* (Havana: Letras Cubanas, 1981), 6.

aristocracy and a broader acceptance of working-class art forms. The same trend is evident in the popularity of the waltz, derived from the rural German *Ländler*, and the prominence of the Polish polka in the 1830s. The spread of these dance musics suggests a growing distaste for complex, stylized movements associated with the minuet of earlier generations. Interest in the contradance developed in tandem with early nationalist movements in Europe, the first studies of traditional song genres, and an idealization of "the folk" as the embodiment of regional heritage.[4]

The instrumental contradance as exported to the Americas was characterized by repeated binary form (AABB); it featured two contrasting melodies played in variation, both in major keys, accompanied by simple harmonies. The music was played at lively tempos; musicians repeated the overall form multiple times as necessary to accommodate dancers. One of the most common contradance choreographies began with separate lines of men and women facing each other. Participants executed various figures such as approaching and then moving back from their partner or dancing around them and returning to their own line, each over eight-measure phrases of music. In many cases, dancers performed four distinct moves over each repetition of both A and B. At the conclusion of all four phrases, dancers would usually execute the same figures with the next partner down the line, continuing until they had danced with everyone. Choreographies in France more typically involved groupings of two or more couples standing in a square or circle formation whose members executed moves as a unit. That format developed into the quadrille, conceived as a dance suite of multiple tunes played in a specific sequence with distinct steps assigned to each.

The contradance and its variants began to decline in popularity in Europe as early as 1800 but strongly influenced dance traditions of the Americas for much longer. Peter Manuel views the contradance as a nineteenth-century musical lingua franca that tied together much of the region including Mexico, New Orleans (where the quadrille figured prominently in the repertoire of early jazz players), other parts of the United States (the square dance and Virginia reel derive from contradance traditions), and large parts of South America including Venezuela, Brazil, and Argentina.[5] In the Caribbean, contradancing influenced virtually all islands; the music mediated between European and West African stylistic influences, incorporating elements from both to varying degrees. In some instances the extent of West African influence on such repertoire has been extreme. This includes eastern Cuba, where the *tumba francesa* incorporates contradance choreography and dress but accompanies the dance only with large hand drums and idiophones. Other examples include the island of Montserrat where contradance-derived repertoire accompanies the African-derived *jombee* possession ceremony, and in Trinidad and Tobago or Curaçao where similar repertoire contributes to ancestor veneration.[6] Caribbean contradance traditions, and later derivative forms such as the danzón, are distinguished by stylistic fluidity.

4. Curt Sachs, *World History of the Dance* (New York: W.W. Norton, 1937), 428.

5. Peter Manuel, ed., *Creolizing the Contradance* (Philadelphia, PA: Temple University Press, 2009). See also González, "Manuel Saumell," 5.

6. John F. Szwed and Morton Marks, "The Afro-American Transformation of European Set Dances and Dance Suites," *Dance Research Journal* 20, no. 1 (1988), 29.

Their very openness to external influence has transformed the repertoire into sites of contestation in which representations of class, race, gender, and generation are continually negotiated.[7]

By the nineteenth century, Cubans considered local contradance variants their preeminent music genre. The music existed in many forms: as dance pieces interpreted by early ensembles that included violin, the five-key baroque flute, and harp; in the mid-century as repertoire for the *orquesta típica* (discussed later); and as stylized salon repertoire for the piano, written by early nationalist composers Manuel Saumell, Ignacio Cervantes, and others. Audiences danced to the music in theaters, town squares, carnival events, and private parties including *casas de cuna* (mixed-race venues, a precursor to the public dancehall). The form continued to increase in popularity through 1840, coinciding with rapid economic growth and expanded use of slave labor. Black and mixed-race Cubans dominated music making by 1800, owing to the relatively low social status of such work and the fact that these individuals were legally excluded from higher education and many forms of employment.[8]

Cuban contradanzas slowly began to demonstrate creolized elements; most consisted of Afro-Caribbean rhythmic cells such as the habanera rhythm (also known as *ritmo de tango*), the *tresillo*, and the *cinquillo*, and amphibrach (Ex. 2.1). Rhythms of this nature appeared frequently in melodies, and even more often in repeated ostinato bass patterns. Some early contradanzas appear to be "claved" as well, as discussed later, and thus reflect African-derived aesthetic practices.[9] Repertoire as of the 1840s or so also featured a unique manner of playing the *pailas* or timpani influenced by Afro-Cuban drumming traditions, analyzed at the end of this chapter. Danzón orchestras maintained the same practice into the twentieth century.

The most detailed discussion of Caribbean contradanza choreography appears in María Antonia Fernández's publication *Bailes populares cubanos*.[10] Some understanding of contradanza dance movement is relevant to an understanding of the danzón, both because the basic footwork is similar and because certain choreographic figures associated with the early years of danzón performance derive from the contradanza and danza. As in the case of the danzón's musical elements discussed later, its choreographic features draw heavily from other forms, both figure dances and couple dances like the waltz. Fernández describes the basic step of the contradanza, for instance, as involving a right-left-right—left-right-left (RLR–LRL) alternation with the feet gliding close to the ground, much as in the case of the danza, danzón, and even *son*, suggesting that the footwork of popular Cuban dances has changed

---

7. Manuel, *Creolizing the Contradance*, 43.

8. This topic is well represented in existing literature. See, for instance, Alejo Carpentier, *La música en Cuba* (Mexico City: Fondo de Cultura Económica, 2004 [1946]), 136–52; Pedro Deschamps Chapeaux, *El negro en la economía habanera del siglo xix* (Havana: UNEAC, 1971).

9. Manuel (*Creolizing the Contradance*, 67–73) includes an extended discussion of elements that might be considered African-derived in contradanza repertoire. See also pp. 73–77 of Manuel's essay for analysis of claved rhythms found in surviving piano scores.

10. María Antonia Fernández, *Bailes populares cubanos* (Havana: Editorial Pueblo y Educación, 1976), 19–54.

little over the past two centuries. Fernández diagrams a number of figures performed over eight-measure segments of the music including the *alemanda* (allemande), the *molino* (windmill), the *rodeo*, the *ala* (wing), the *puente* (bridge), and so on, largely derived from European sources. Individual moves would be signaled by a lead dance couple and then executed by others, either all at once (in square or circle formation) or one after another (in line formation).

The *paseo* (promenade), another facet of contradanza choreography, involved processing with one's partner, typically from one group formation such as lines into smaller groupings of circles or squares.[11] A version of this move has been perpetuated by present-day Cuban danzón enthusiasts who use it to circle the dance floor with their partner in a leisurely fashion each time the A theme is played, as well as by contemporary Mexican practitioners who refer to it as *descanso*, a moment of rest from dancing. Other figures associated with the contradanza influenced early danzón performance. The *cadena* (chain), for instance, involved four or more couples in a circle formation who processed one after another, women walking clockwise and men counter-clockwise. They wove in and out as they moved past other dancers, briefly grasping hands with those of the opposite sex. Authors such as Eduardo Sánchez de Fuentes describe the cadena as a typical element of the danzón, apparently alluding to the nineteenth century in which many performed it as a figure dance rather than a couple dance. In the same way, early danzón dancers incorporated the *lazo* (lasso), *ocho* (figure eight), *latigazo* (whip), and other collective choreographies; these could be led by a lead couple and performed as an alternative to couple dancing or in alternation with it.[12]

The term *danza* as of the 1820s represented a new name for contradanza-like repertoire. *Danzas* appear to have first been performed publicly in *academias de baile* of the 1840s and later decades,[13] suggesting that their musical and choreographic innovations derive from the popular classes. In general, danzas were performed at a slower tempo than contradanzas and favored duple meter more consistently. The basic footwork dancers performed did not vary, however, and danzas adopted many figures derived from the contradanza, especially the paseo, ocho, cadena, and *cedazo* (sieve).[14]

Choreographically, the only significant innovation found in the danza was its greater emphasis on the cedazo, essentially a "swing your partner" move in which couples held each other loosely at the waist as they turned. The cedazo had been used in contradanzas, often over the final eight-measure repeat of the B section. But by the 1830s, dancers extended the cedazo in many cases to the full length of the music's repeated B section, and frequently extended the B section itself to sixteen or thirty-two measures, or more. Younger enthusiasts, who enjoyed the intimacy and

11. Natalio Galán, *Cuba y sus sones* (Valencia: Pre-Textos, 1983), 163–64. The author suggests on p. 189 that the paseo derives from European sources as well—for instance, Spanish *bolero* dancing that included a rest segment known as a *desplante* or *bien parado*.
12. Galán, *Cuba y sus sones*, 163–64.
13. Galán, *Cuba y sus sones*, 130.
14. Esteban Pichardo, *Diccionario provincial casi razonado de vozes y frases cubanas* (Havana: Editorial de Ciencias Sociales, 1985 [1836]), 222–23. Interestingly, many of these contradanza-derived figures were revived as part of the *rueda de casino* dance craze of the 1980s; see Bárbara Balbuena, *El casino y la salsa en Cuba* (Havana: Letras Cubanas, 2003).

flirtatious nature of the cedazo, are said to have joined the dance only during the B section, avoiding other figures entirely.[15] By the 1860s and 1870s, many danza enthusiasts chose to alternate the cedazo only with the cadena, or remained in a closed embrace throughout, with no recourse to group choreographies.[16] Fernández's study supports this view by describing the danza's basic step as a semi-closed embrace; similarly, she describes the basic footwork of the danza as a box.[17] Thus, present-day characterizations of the danzón as a couple dance and the danza as a figure dance are too simplistic; in reality, both appear to have been danced by couples and in groups during much of the nineteenth century.

THE ORQUESTA TÍPICA ENSEMBLE

Cirilo Villaverde famously described popular dance venues of early nineteenth-century Cuba in his novel *Cecilia Valdés*, and orchestras consisting of violins, cellos, acoustic bass, and clarinet.[18] But by the 1850s, following the invention of piston and rotary valves, cornets and low brass became a feature of such bands as well, and the ensemble later known as the orquesta típica began to emerge. Various authors suggest that orquestas típicas developed out of marching and military bands associated with the *batallones de pardos y morenos* (battalions of mulattos and blacks), segregated fighting units first established by Spanish colonial authorities in 1764.[19] Carpentier describes one such band that included instruments now associated with the standard orquesta típica (such as the bassoon, clarinet, trombone, and bugle/cornet), as well as others (piccolos, French horns) that are not, at least in a consistent fashion.[20] Similar ensembles of varied instrumentation are described as *charangas* in studies of Spanish military music.[21] The process by which military ensembles contributed to the

15. John Chasteen, *National Rhythms, African Roots. The Deep History of Latin American Popular Dance* (Albuquerque: University of New Mexico Press), 158; Hall Estrada, "The Sensuous Habanera," *Cuban Heritage* 1, no. 1 (1987), 26. Note that several authors suggest the meaning of the term cedazo changed at various moments in the nineteenth century, though they do not all agree how. See Eduardo Sánchez de Fuentes, "El danzón," *Social* 13, no. 12 (December 1928), 83; Radamés Giro, *Diccionario Enciclopédico de la música cubana*, Vol. 1, 227–28.

16. Emilio Grenet, *Popular Cuban Music. 80 Revised and Corrected Compositions Together with an Essay on the Evolution of Music in Cuba*, trans. R. Phillips (Havana: Secretary of Agriculture, 1939), 30–31; Galán, *Cuba y sus sones*, 170.

17. A. M. Fernández, *Bailes populares cubanos*, 58.

18. Cirilo Villaverde, *Cecilia Valdés* (Barcelona: Linkgua Ediciones S.L., 2008 [1882]), 44.

19. E.g., Ezequiel Rodríguez Domínguez, *Iconografía del danzón* (Havana: Sub-Dirección Provincial de Música, 14); Galán, *Cuba y sus sones*, 218. See also related discussion of this topic in Chapter 3.

20. Carpentier, *La música en Cuba*, 146–47.

21. Ruth "Sunni" Witmer cites discussion on this topic in the *Diccionario de la música española e hispanoamericana*. See "Cuban *Charanga*: Class, Popular Music, and the Creation of National Identity," PhD Dissertation, University of Florida, Gainesville (2011), 95; and also Ricardo de Latorre, *Historia de la música militar en España* (Madrid: Ministerio de Defensa, 1999), 97.

orquesta típica is not entirely clear, but the military undeniably gave many black and mixed-race performers their first exposure to Western repertoire. Performers presumably left the military and joined theater ensembles or circus bands, formed their own dance orchestras, or in other ways segued to civilian entertainment. Prominent nineteenth-century performers with ties to the military support this view. Tomás Vuelta y Flores (1791–1844), for instance, gained fame as a composer and also directed the banda de Regimiento de Morenos in Havana; bandleader Claudio Brindis de Salas Sr. (1800–1872) was born into a military family, and most members of Matanzas' Orquesta Sin Rival came from the Banda del Segundo Batallón de Voluntarios.[22] The early orquestas típicas are the first groups to play syncopated percussive rhythms on the timbales now associated with the danzón, discussed later.

Surprisingly little is known about the history of the instruments used to play the standard percussion patterns accompanying the danza and danzón in the orquesta típica, or how they first developed. The term *güiro* has Arawak roots, suggesting that it represents an indigenous element of Cuban culture, though some recent scholarship maintains its African origins.[23] Use of the güiro in Cuba has been documented as far back as the late sixteenth century; popular musicians even at that time apparently enjoyed the chance to *rascar el calabazo* (scrape the calabash).[24] Similar instruments are found in Panama, Mexico, and other neighboring countries. The term *timbal* dates back to at least the tenth-century in the Arab world, and to twelfth- or thirteenth-century Spain, where troops used drums of that name to accompany themselves into battle.[25] While some difference of opinion exists in the literature, Curt Sachs believes that Spaniards adopted the timbales after being exposed to them during the Crusades, probably following the attack on Damietta in 1249.[26] The instrument remained a prominent part of Spanish military music through the early nineteenth century[27] and probably arrived in Cuba through Spain well before 1800. Black and mulatto military bands played both the timbales and güiro in the nineteenth century, as did circus bands.[28] Performance techniques derived from West

22. Osvaldo Castillo Faílde, *Miguel Faílde. Creador musical del danzón* (Havana: Editora del Consejo Nacional de Cultura, 1964), 82.

23. Ana Victoria Casanova Olivia, "Güiro o guayo," in *Instrumentos de la música folklórico-popular de Cuba*, Vol. 1, ed. Victoria Eli Rodriguez et al. (Havana: Editorial de Ciencias Sociales, 1997), 156, 164–65. She notes that African instruments similar to the Cuban güiro can be found in Nigeria and among Bantu groups.

24. Fernando Ortiz, *Los instrumentos de la música afrocubana*, Vol. II (Havana: Publicaciones de la Dirección de Cultura del Ministerio de Educación, 1952), 174.

25. Ricardo Fernández de Latorre, *Historia de la música militar de España* (Madrid: Ministerio de Defensa, 1999), 74–75. See also Fernando Ortiz, *Los instrumentos de la música afrocubana* Vol. III, 75, which asserts the importance of the timbales to Spanish soldiers in the twelfth century. Fernández de Latorre includes a painting of such an instrument from 1677, played by a rider on horseback (75).

26. Fernando Ortiz, *Los instrumentos de la música afrocubana*, Vol. III, 69.

27. Fernández de Latorre, *Historia de la música militar de España*, 123.

28. José Luis "Changuito" Quintana and Chuck Silverman, *Changuito. A Master's Approach to Timbales* (New York: Manhattan Music Publishing, 1998),15. Carpentier (*La música en Cuba*, 147) mentions black and mixed-race military bands in Santiago of the early nineteenth century whose percussionists influenced secular dance bands.

African traditions such as playing on the sides of the timbales and dampening the heads to create unique timbral effects appear to have first developed within these groups.

Musicians describe both older and modern timbales (or paila/pailas)[29] as consisting of "male" (*macho*) and "female" (*hembra*) instruments, the latter being the largest and sounding roughly a fifth below the male drum. Many Afro-Cuban percussionists of earlier periods preferred playing the timbales because they lacked the negative, racialized associations of hand drums and thus could be used in public contexts without generating controversy.[30] Nineteenth-century instruments were constructed of brass or copper and resembled small timpani (Fig. 2.1), but by 1900 some groups began to play smaller, cylindrical timbales made of banded wood (Fig. 2.2). Musicians eventually fashioned the same instruments out of tin or steel and played them attached to a stand, perhaps after being exposed to the snare and toms on the US drum set. This refashioned instrument became the modern timbales used in Latin dance bands internationally.

The early 1840s witnessed the rapid expansion of an influential middle class in the black community in Cuba, impacting the realm of music and other spheres.[31] However, arrests, interrogation, imprisonment, and torture surrounding La Escalera in 1844—a reputed conspiracy involving attempts to foment a slave uprising—dealt a serious blow to the orquestas típicas in Havana and Matanzas for decades, and resulted in the death of some musicians.[32] Performance languished for a time in the aftermath. By about 1850, musical life resumed in earnest, however, with danzas

29. For centuries, Cubans have used the term "paila" to refer to any large receptacle of iron or copper, usually in the shape of a half circle or bell. Workers on sugar plantations often employed such vessels to cook down cane juice into crystals, as discussed by Esteban Pichardo (*Diccionario provincial*, 458). By extension, the population used the same word to describe kettle drums because of their cauldron-like shape (see Fig. 2.1). Danzón groups of the nineteenth century used instruments of this sort, but now they appear only infrequently. See Zobeyda Ramos Venereo, "Paila," in *Instrumentos de la musica folklórico-popular de Cuba*, Vol. 2 (Havana: Editorial de Ciencias Sociales, 1997), 409–10. Ramos Venereo notes that the terms "timbales" and "paila" continue to be used interchangeably in Cuba, but that timbales now most often refers to the larger spherical drums used widely prior to 1900, while paila or pailas typically denote the smaller drums played on a stand.

30. Ortiz, *Los instrumentos*, Vol. IV, 415.

31. Prominent musicians of the day included Vuelta y Flores and Brindis de Salas, mentioned earlier, as well as Ulpiano Estrada, José María González, José Miguel Román, and others. Afro-Cubans gained widespread recognition as poets and authors, as well as businessmen, dentists, journalists, visual artists, and others, many based in Matanzas. See Israel Moliner Castañeda, *José Silvestre White y Laffite. Folleto homenaje en el 60o. aniversario de su muerte* (Matanzas: Dirección Sectorial de Cultura OPP, 1978), 2.

32. Miguel Román, for instance, the first violin teacher of José White, was shot in June of 1844, while Vuelta y Flores died the same year as the result of torture; many others suffered imprisonment or exile, effectively ending their careers. Zoila Lapique Becali provides a good overview of the period, and many additional names of the affected. *Cuba colonial. Música, compositores e intérpretes 1570–1902* (Havana: Letras Cubanas, 2008), 141. For discussion of the Escalera's impact on Brindis de Salas, see Ezequiel Rodríguez Domínguez, *Iconografía*, 14.

Figure 2.1: Old-style metal timbales and güiro, used by the Piquete Típico in Havana.

Figure 2.2: Turn-of-the-twentieth-century postcard from Cuba entitled "The Bunga," featuring an early version of the modern timbales/paila made of banded wood. Photo courtesy of the Museo Nacional de la Música, Havana.

favored through at least 1870.[33] Bands formed across the island, many of whose members had previously played in municipal or fireman's bands;[34] they represent the direct antecedents of danzón groups gaining popularity thereafter.

HABANERAS, *BAILES DE FLORES,* AND THE EARLY DANZÓN

The *habanera* deserves mention as a popular variant of mid-nineteenth century dance repertoire, especially in Havana. Estrada defines it as a slower version of the contradanza or danza, sometimes with an expanded formal structure, that is meant to be sung.[35] Note, however, that the term "habanera" is used in multiple ways in music literature: (1) as a rhythm, the habanera or tango-congo rhythm; (2) as a sung variant of the contradanza or danza, intended for dancing, or (3), increasingly in the late nineteenth and twentieth centuries, as a parlor song genre for listening reminiscent of the pan-Latin American *canción* that incorporated the danza's habanera rhythm. Interestingly, the first documented use of the label "contradanza habanera" to refer to vocal music dates from 1836 in Mexico;[36] similar vocal adaptations of Cuban dance music became popular in Spain at roughly the same time.[37] Thus, it is quite possible that the habanera and the practice of singing contradanzas or danzas first became popular internationally and was only later adopted by Cubans themselves.

In Havana, the first reference to a sung contradanza appears in newspaper articles about an event in the Café La Lonja from 1841 in which a chorus sang alongside an orchestra to accompany dancing. The show's novelty generated considerable interest, and the café continued hosting similar events through at least 1843.[38] Composers eventually formalized the habanera as a distinct form, arranging pieces for dance bands, large municipal wind bands, and salon compositions for piano and voice. José White, Eduardo Sánchez de Fuentes, and other Cuban composers wrote memorable habaneras in subsequent decades, but the form generated even more interest abroad,

---

33. Bands active in Matanzas included the orchestras of Los Hermanos Barani, Francisco Valiente, Frijolín, the Unión Matancera, the Marina, El Progreso, el Siglo XX, and of course the Orquesta Faílde, discussed later. See Argeliers León, *Del canto y el tiempo* (Havana: Editorial Letras Cubanas), 264; Raúl Martínez Rodríguez, "La música bailable en el siglo xix en Matanzas," booklet published for the centenary of the danzón (Matanzas: Consejo Nacional de Cultura, 1979).

34. Rodriguez Dominguez (*Iconografía*, 20–22) includes an exhaustive list of orquesta típica–style ensembles active from the 1850s to the 1870s. The most famous directors included Juan de Dios Alfonso Armenteros, clarinetist and founder of La Flor de Cuba in Havana; clarinetist Lino Boza in Santiago; and bassist José Alemán Rodríguez in Havana. (⊕ Picture 2.1) See also Walter Goodman, *The Pearl of the Antilles or An Artist in Cuba* (London: Henry S. King and Co., 1873), 130–31, for a firsthand description of orquesta típica performance about 1870.

35. Hall Estrada, "The Sensuous Habanera," *Cuban Heritage* 1, no. 1 (1987), 26.

36. Galán, *Cuba y sus sones*, 228-29. The piece cited, by an anonymous composer, was entitled "La pimienta" and published in the *Noticioso de Ambos Mundos* in Mexico.

37. Galán, *Cuba y sus sones*, 228–29; Radamés Giro, *Diccionario enciclopédico de la música cubana*, Vol. 2, 229.

38. Lapique Becali, *Cuba colonial*, 132–34.

especially in Spain. As an elite vocal genre, the habanera was embraced in Europe and throughout Latin America by the 1870s. Some of the most famous compositions in the style are by Basque composer Sebastian Iradier, including "La paloma" and "El arreglito," the latter adapted by George Bizet into his opera *Carmen*.

Much less well documented than the habanera song form is its accompanying dance, perhaps owing to the fact that existing habanera studies have used scores as primary documents. Some groups danced the habanera in lines, alternating choreographic figures such as the ocho with closed-couple position. Yet more often it foregrounded an intimate embrace with a partner *en un ladrillito* (on a single little floor tile).[39] Habanera dancing languished, supplanted by the danzón in the 1880s and beyond; Albert Friedenthal provides some of the only detailed descriptions of its choreography as he observed it in elite society events. He suggests that dancers adopted the standard closed ballroom position but held each other more closely. The habanera step apparently involved a simple lateral movement, alternating to the right and left. To begin, the lead dancer's right foot took a small step to the side on the first eighth note of a 2/4 measure. On the second eighth note the dancer slid his left foot along the floor, placing it next to the first. The final two eighth notes of the measure were not danced, then all motion reversed itself beginning with the left foot. Steps for the follower were the exact opposite, beginning with a step to the side with the left foot. Friedenthal specifically contrasts the habanera's basic step with that of the danzón, noting that the latter involved motion forward and back, rather than sideways. He continues: "There are two forms of [habanera] execution: the first, in which everyone dances the entire time as a couple, the other which can only be employed when the [music] alternates between major and minor keys . . . [in the latter, performers] dance as a couple during the minor section and in the major section each grouping of two couples creates figures."[40] Various dances influenced both by the (contra)danza and European ballroom genres thus existed side by side in Cuba with the early danzón.

While beyond the focus of this study, the Puerto Rican danza deserves mention as yet another (contra)danza variant with ties to the danzón. Often referred to a *merengue* in the mid-nineteenth century, the Puerto Rican danza gained widespread popularity beginning in the 1820s.[41] It has the same roots in the contradanza's binary structure but featured a more extended form, typically ABC or ABCD.[42] Peter Manuel and Edgardo Díaz Díaz note that performers referred to the Puerto Rican danza's A section as the paseo and later sections as "merengue" variants. Some B, C, and D sections tended to be longer than in the Cuban danza or danzón and often featured

39. Galán, *Cuba y sus sones*, 164, 240. This terminology is still frequently used today by Mexican danzón dancers, as discussed in Chapter 6.

40. Albert Friedenthal, *Musik, Tanz und Dichtung bei den Kreolen Amerikas* (Berlin: Hausbücher-Verlag Hans Schnippel, 1913), 107.

41. Peter Manuel and Edgardo Díaz Díaz, "Puerto Rico: The Rise and Fall of the Danza as National Music," in *Creolizing Contradance in the Caribbean*, ed. Peter Manuel (Philadelphia: Temple University Press, 2009), 113–154.

42. Although musicians do not refer to the danzón sections as A, B, C, etc., for analytical purposes we use this standard musicological terminology.

semi-improvised *bombardino* (low brass) melodies that functioned as a counterpart to the principal theme. Little information exists on exactly how Puerto Ricans danced to the music, but the choreography included collective figures through about 1840 and then developed into a couple-style format. The heyday of the danza in the late nineteenth century coincided with that of the danzón, and it shared general stylistic similarities such as common rhythmic elements and overall sectional form.[43]

A number of questions central to danzón history remain unanswered at present, including where a dance of that name first developed. The earliest known written reference to a danzón comes from Havana in 1844. Court documents that year related to investigations surrounding the Escalera asked a lawyer named Ambrosio de Aragón whether he had taken part in "a dance that took place in San Antonio with the title of 'danzón or *moros*,'" presumably a black dance. The (white) lawyer denied taking part.[44] The second known reference also comes from Havana. On April 4, 1850, an article in the *Diario de la Marina* commented on a group of street dancers (a *comparsa*) belonging to a troupe called "Tropical" that had performed the evening before in the café Escauriza. The article noted that the group "danced a danzón, executing very pretty figures. Each of the women carried bunches of flowers in their hands and their partners little Spanish flags."[45]

A more detailed description of a dance that appears to involve early danzón dates from the following year in Matanzas, though the term "danzón" is not used to describe it. In March of 1851, the Swedish author Fredrika Bremer wrote a letter about an event she witnessed involving wreaths of flowers and intricate choreographies.

> One night I attended a big dance as a spectator, organized by free blacks in Matanzas as a fundraiser for the House of Charity in that city. Anyone was invited as long as they paid. The dance took place in a theater and spectators filled the seats . . . A banquet table adorned with flowers and lamps stretched across the end of the dancehall. Dancers in all numbered between two and three hundred people. Their dress was in the French style, and many outfits were flashy. Some couples executed, with dignity and precision, a few very boring minuets . . . But the main dance of the occasion was a type of circle dance in which all took part, coming together and separating again, performing innumerable artistic variations, with wreaths of artificial roses. The result was truly beautiful and picturesque, realized with extraordinary precision.[46]

43. Manuel and Díaz Díaz, "Puerto Rico," 146. Refer to the CD accompanying *Creolizing Contradance* for an early recorded orchestral version of Puerto Rican danza, "Laura y Georgina," in which one can hear the bombardino lines mentioned above.

44. Lapique Becali, *Cuba colonial*, 189.

45. Lapique Becali, *Cuba colonial*, 189.

46. Fredrika Bremer, *Cartas desde Cuba* (Havana: Editorial Arte y Literatura, 1995), 70–71. "Un noche asistí como espectadora a un gran baile organizado por los negros libres de Matanzas en favor de la Casa de Beneficencia de la ciudad. El público estaba invitado, si pagaba. El baile se daba en el teatro, y los espectadores llenaban los palcos . . . Una mesa de banquete, adornada con flores y lámparas, ocupaba el fondo del salón de baile. Los danzantes podían ser de doscientas a trescientas personas. Las vestidas, según la moda francesa, y muchas eran muy llamativas. Algunas parejas ejecutaron con dignidad y precisión

A few years later, in December of 1856, the first documented reference to the danzón in Matanzas appeared in the form of a petition to the governor's office. Two free blacks named Antonio Erice and Pablo Gálvez requested permission to rehearse a carnival routine, along with other members of the San Francisco neighborhood. The two stated the rehearsal would involve "a danzón with varied figures" to be presented publicly in February.[47]

Early use of "danzón" thus referenced dancing rather than music, specifically a variant of the same figure dances that had been in vogue for decades but one that emerged in the black community involving large spectacles intended for theaters or carnival. Most seem to have incorporated moves such as the cadena and cedazo derived from the contradanza. Dancers freely varied or elaborated these figures, executing the same turns simultaneously while holding large arches or wreaths of flowers as props.[48] Commentators referred to such choreographies either as danzones or *bailes de flores* (flower dances). At least twenty couples typically took part, often singing as they moved. One influential troupe organized presentations in Matanzas in 1856, as discussed in the newspaper *El Triunfo*.[49] White elites only observed such dancing initially, but by the 1870s they began to imitate the choreographies themselves, generating controversy in the process.[50] Miguel Faílde (1852–1921) first wrote his early danzones in order to accompany events of this nature. He suggested in an interview that the decision to write a new style of danzón music in three or more parts took inspiration from choreographies with multiple sections.[51]

The bailes de flores–style danzón remained popular through the 1880s and beyond, especially among elites, even after most Cubans danced danzones exclusively in couples. A performance involving bailes de flores took place in the elite Club de Matanzas in May of 1879, suggesting that the famous event accompanying New Years' celebrations there in January (and accompanied by a performance of "Las alturas de Simpson," discussed later) consisted of figure dancing rather than couple dancing.[52]

---

algunos minués enormemente aburridos. . . . Pero el gran baile de la fiesta, una especie de corro, en el cual tomaron parte todos los bailadores, agrupándose y separándose, ejecutando innumerables evoluciones artísticas muy variadas, con guirnaldas de rosas artificiales, resultó verdaderamente bonito y pintoresco, y fue realizado con extraordinaria precisión."

47. Israel Moliner Castañeda, *El Teatro Principal de Matanzas* (Matanzas: Ediciones Matanzas, 2007), 170–71. See also Lapique Becali, *Cuba colonial*, 187–88.

48. Israel Moliner Castañeda, personal interview, December 2, 2011, Matanzas, Cuba. See Ezequiel Rodríguez Domínguez, *Iconografía*, 32, for a photo of such an ensemble, apparently recreated on the stage in the twentieth century.

49. Castillo Faílde, *Miguel Faílde*, 87.

50. "Gacetillas. El danzón," *Diario de Matanzas* (November 7, 1878), 3.

51. Félix Soloni, 1929. "El danzón y su inventor, Miguel Faílde. Notas históricas," in *Cuba musical. Album-resúmen ilustrado de la historia y de la actual situación del arte musical en Cuba*, ed. José Calero Martín y Leopoldo Valdés Quesada (Havana: Molina y Compañía, 1929), 1039.

52. *Diario de Matanzas* 2, no. 126, (Friday, May 30, 1879), 3. Odilio Urfé believed that all dancing associated with the formal debut of the danzon in January of 1879 consisted of bailes de flores. See Odilio Urfé, "Danzon, mambo y cha-cha-chá," *Revolución y Cultura* no. 77 (January 1979), 54.

Newspapers mention bailes de flores events in Havana and surrounding towns through at least 1892.[53]

It is possible that the first danzones danced exclusively by individual couples date from 1878 in Matanzas, as asserted by Miguel Faílde's niece,[54] but the record is unclear. Osvaldo Castillo Faílde reproduces commentary suggesting that couple-style danzones may have been popular among working-class residents of Matanzas as early as the 1850s.[55] Odilio Urfé states unequivocally that dancers in Havana rather than Matanzas were the first to reject group figures and adopt a couple-style danzón format, though he does not specify when.[56] Natalio Galán emphasizes that danzones combined figure dancing and couple dancing for many years, as had been the case with the danza and habanera.[57] It appears that the popular classes accepted closed-couple format before the middle classes and elites, black or white. Whole-hearted acceptance of the couple dancing style likely took place in the 1890s during the final years of war against Spain. Cartoons of danzón dancers published during the US occupation depict individual couples, suggesting that that style had become the most typical by 1898; at least one US administrator believed Cuban couples stood too closely together and tried to impose a more "appropriate" distance through proclamation, much to the amusement of the public.[58]

Having discussed the danzón's antecedent dance and music forms, analysis now shifts to early danzón compositions, their typical structural and stylistic qualities, the ways composers frequently deviated from standard practice or adopted elements from other genres of music, and thus the difficulty in defining the "essence" of danzón style. A few representative pieces by the Orquesta Valenzuela are examined in detail as an introduction to early repertoire.

FROM TWO-PART TO MULTI-SECTION DANZONES

One common element used to define the danzón in existing literature is prominent incorporation of the cinquillo, alone or in alternation with other rhythms. The cinquillo may be found in lead melodies, in rhythmic or melodic accompaniment patterns, or

53. For discussion of bailes de flores in Santiago de Las Vegas, see the online biography of José Alemán, www.scribd.com/doc/80518875/Jose-Aleman-Primera-Orquesta-de-Santiago-de-Las-Vegas-Por-Arsenio-Aleman-Agusti-D. Specific references to bailes de flores in El Fígaro include two articles by Raoul Cay entitled "Crónicas" 8, no. 15 (May 1, 1892), 7; and 8, no. 19 (June 5, 1892), 7.

54. Aurora Gómez Faílde, quoted in Castillo Faílde, Miguel Faílde, 89. She suggests this took place in the home of the Condes de Luna, the site where Miguel Faílde apparently first played his three-part version of "Las alturas de Simpson."

55. Castillo Faílde, Miguel Faílde, 87.

56. Nusia López, "Contrapunto, polemica y danzón: habla Odilio Urfé," Bohemia 68, no. 44 [43] (October 29, 1976), 12.

57. Galán, Cuba y sus sones, 163–64.

58. Marial Iglesias Utset, A Cultural History of Cuba during the U.S. Occupation, 1898–1902, trans. Russ Davidson (Chapel Hill: University of North Carolina Press, 2011), photo 9 following page 86 (originally from El Fígaro April 10, 1900, 149). The caricaturist, Ricardo de la Torriente, depicts the dancers as black and as speaking bozal (distorted) Spanish, probably in an attempt to make the image more humorous.

in multiple locations simultaneously. Musicologists refer to the constant alternation between a measure of the syncopated cinquillo and a measure of straighter quarter notes or eighth notes as *danzón clave*, a pattern that serves as the structural basis for other rhythms and melodies played in the piece (see Ex. 2.23). The practice of organizing music around claves or timelines derives from West African traditions, as mentioned; similar rhythmic patterns can be found in the danza and contradanza, as well as in later dance forms such as Cuban *son* and salsa.[59] Note that some early danzón recordings demonstrate inconsistent clave patterns, as do early *son* recordings, yet the use of such timelines in both forms of music is pervasive.[60]

Many danzón scores as of about 1880 are organized into a three-part rondo structure with a recurring A section (ABACA). Various theories exist about how this multipart structure emerged out of binary contradanzas and danzas; Natalio Galán suggests at least three. First, he notes the close similarity between danzones and the structure of the Spanish bolero, a popular style of dance music in Cuba for many years that may have influenced composers. The Spanish bolero consisted of a repeated refrain (serving as a moment of rest between dance segments, similar to the paseo) interspersed with verses (*coplas*) performed to contrasting musical segments.[61] The similarities between such a form and the multi-part danzones discussed later are striking. Second, Galán notes that musicians often performed figure dances in sets, and that taken as a whole they often implied a more elaborate, multi-section form. Thus, the practice of chaining distinct pieces separated by pauses (paseos), may have contributed to the emergence of danzones in three or more sections.[62] Third, he discusses the characteristic elaboration of the B section in danzas of the 1860s (especially in its final repetition) and the incorporation of new, improvised material each time the section was played. Thus, he asserts, improvisational variety began to create an implicitly more complex form (i.e., A-B-A-B1-A-B2, etc.) containing the essence of the multi-section danzón.[63]

Conventional narratives in popular literature suggest that Miguel Faílde's performance of "Las alturas de Simpson" at the Club de Matanzas on January 1, 1879, represented the birth of the danzón as a distinct musical form.[64] Jesús Flores y Escalante,

59. For additional discussion of the concept of clave accompanied by musical examples, see Robin Moore, *Music in the Hispanic Caribbean. Experiencing Music, Expressing Culture* (New York: Oxford University Press, 2010), 66–67.

60. Thanks to Peter Manuel for bringing this issue to our attention. One example of irregular danzón clave appears in "Jamón con yuca" (Ham and Cassava Root) by the Orquesta Valdés, recorded in Havana in 1907 and available on *Hot Music from Cuba 1907–36* (Harlequin CD 23, 1993). Most of the piece has an implicit or explicit 2–3 clave, but it abruptly switches to 3–2 at 2:43.

61. Galán, *Cuba y sus sones*, 190.

62. Galán, *Cuba y sus sones*, 191, 194. See also Manuel, *Creolizing the Contradance*, 78.

63. Galán, *Cuba y sus sones*, 169.

64. Many Cuban musicologists disagree with such an assertion. See discussion in Carpentier, *La música en Cuba*, 237; Radamés Giro, "Danzón," *Diccionario enciclopédico de la música en Cuba*, Vol. 2 (Havana: Letras Cubanas, 2007), 8; Zoila Lapique Becali, *Cuba colonial. Música, compositores e intérpretes, 1570–1902* (Havana: Letras Cubanas, 2008), 187–89.

for instance, acknowledges the existence of pre-Faíldean danzones but describes "Las alturas" as having a new musical structure.[65] The truth of the assertion is difficult to establish, as Faílde wrote at least two different danzones titled "Las alturas de Simpson." The first, composed in the summer of 1877, is a two-part danzón that bears no musical resemblance, formally or melodically, to the piece known today by that title.[66] The two-part version follows the conventions of contradanzas and danzas of the time: it consists of a repeated eight-measure A section followed by a repeated eight-measure B section.[67] Although the habanera rhythm is used prominently in the A section, the cinquillo is not used at all, as can be seen in Example 2.2.[68]

Faílde's second extant version of "Las alturas de Simpson" is a three-part danzón, consisting of a repeated eight-measure A section and longer sixteen-measure B and C sections. The last four measures of the A section and the C section feature the cinquillo clave prominently,[69] but the B section only includes the cinquillo during the final cadence (Ex. 2.3).

"Las alturas de Simpson" had been played publicly before its famous debut in the Club de Matanzas for white elites—for instance, in the Condes de Luna's residence for the Saint Aurora celebration in August of 1878.[70] Since two-part danzones remained popular well into the 1890s, it is not entirely clear which version of the piece Faílde performed in 1878–1879, although various sources assert it was the newer three-part version.[71] Scholars also disagree as to whether Faílde's three-part score represented the first composition in that style; some ascribe the creation of three-part danzones to Raimundo Valenzuela rather than Faílde.[72] In any case, the

65. Jesús Flores y Escalante, *Imágenes del danzón. Iconografía del danzón en México* (Mexico City: Asociación Mexicana de Estudios Fonográficos, A.C., 2006 [1994]), 7.

66. A manuscript of this version was published in Osvaldo Castillo Faílde, *Miguel Faílde*, 88. The piece is named after a neighborhood of Matanzas renowned for its social life and beautiful women.

67. As mentioned, the repetition of the AABB contradanza/danza form was standard practice. For example, it is evident in the recording of "San Pascual Bailón" released in 1962 in *Antología del danzón* (Areito LD-3724. Havana: EGREM, 1962); Jorge Vistel Colombié's recording of "San Pascual Bailón" and "El dedo de Landaluce" with the Piquete Típico Cubano in *Piquete Típico Cubano. Danzones* (self-produced, without date); and Francisco Ulloa's recording of "Dulce María" released in *Francisco Ulloa y su Piquete Santiaguero. El camaján* (Indigo LC-03428, 2001).

68. This transcription is taken from the manuscript version of Miguel Faílde's danzón as printed in Castillo Faílde, *Miguel Faílde*, 88.

69. Most danzones as of the 1880s adopted a "claved" rhythmic structure in which the cinquillo pattern alternated in every other measure with less syncopated figures, as discussed later in the segment on performance practice.

70. Sigryd Padrón Díaz, "Galicia en el baile nacional cubano: el danzón," in *Galicia-Cuba: un patrimonio cultural de referencias y confluencias*, ed. C. Fontela and M. Silva (A Coruña: Ediciós do Castro, 2000), 405–16.

71. See, for instance, Ezequiel Rodríguez Domínguez, *Iconografía*, 47. Matanzas historian Israel Moliner Castañeda (personal interview, Matanzas, Cuba, December 2, 2011) also maintains the three-part version dates from 1879 and was played at the Club de Matanzas.

72. Elena Pérez Sanjuro writes the following in *Historia de la música cubana* (Miami, FL: La Moderna Poesía, 1985, 566): "*Raimundo Valenzuela fue el creador del danzón de tres partes, con el objeto de poder lucirse con el trombón, que era el instrumento que prefería y dominaba, lo*

Example 2.2: Miguel Faílde, "Las alturas de Simpson" (1877). Two-part version.

Las alturas de Simpson

Miguel Faílde

Matanzas, 7 de junio de 1877

early version of Faílde's "Las alturas de Simpson" does not feature the cinquillo. If this rhythm alone differentiates the danzón from the contradanza, as argued by Carpentier and Giro,[73] the two-part version of Faílde's "Las alturas de Simpson" does not conform to their criteria, at least in piano reduction. One could argue that the presence of the cinquillo may have been more evident in full orchestral versions of the music, or in the unnotated percussion lines. But the same could also be true of earlier contradanzas, as little documentation exists of the performance practice of percussionists of the day. On the other hand, early two-part danzones such as "El llantico" by Félix Cruz and arranged by Raimundo Valenzuela do emphasize the cinquillo strongly,[74] as do many two-part danzones reproduced in the *J. Jacinto Cuevas* collection

que gustó mucho, porque así de ese modo era más largo el tiempo para danzar" [Raimundo Valenzuela was the creator of the three-part danzón, intended to show off his trombone playing, his preferred instrument. The public enjoyed them because it gave them more time to dance with their partner.] However, she provides no proof to support this assertion, or references to scores. Nevertheless, Cleva Solís's earlier essay seems to support the same position. Attributing her argument to Odilio Urfé, she describes Valenzuela's danzón adaptation of the contradanza "El sungambelo" as a "danza-danzón" and suggests it helped create a model for three-part danzones as well as the rondo-like alternation of musical sections in live performance ("En torno a una poesía del danzón," _Islas. Revista de la Universidad Central de Las Villas_ 2, no. 1 [1959], 35). Solís also provides no references to the Valenzuela score nor a date it was composed, making it difficult to evaluate the assertion.

73. Carpentier, _La música en Cuba_, 238; Giro, _Diccionario enciclopédico de la música cubana_, vol. 2, 8.

74. A piano version of this piece is reproduced in Argeliers León, _Del canto y el tiempo_, 268. A hand-written note on the original score in Havana suggests it dates from approximately 1880.

Example 2.3: Miguel Faílde, "Las alturas de Simpson" (1879). Three-part version; arguably the first three-part danzón.

Las Alturas De Simpson

published in Mérida, Mexico, between 1888 and 1894; indeed, their only unique feature vis-à-vis earlier repertoire is the heightened presence of the cinquillo. (🔊 Score 2.1) It is possible that the inclusion of this rhythm did not become established practice among all composers until the end of the 1880s. Sheet music—including many pieces from 1880s Cuba by Raimundo Valenzuela, Felix Cruz, Lino Martínez, Enrique Guerrero, and Miguel Faílde himself, and the Yucatecan collection *J. Jacinto*

Example 2.3(b): *(continued)*

Cuevas[75]—as well as recent scholarship[76]—demonstrate that two-part, three-part, and multi-section danzones coexisted for many years, with and without cinquillo clave, prior to the mid-1890s.[77]

An important topic lost in debates over danzón structure is its relative flexibility as interpreted in performance. Historically informed recordings such as the version of "Las alturas de Simpson" produced by Odilio Urfé in 1954 suggest that dance bands ascribed only loosely to notions of standard rondo form (ABACA); individual segments could apparently be repeated whenever the director cared to do so. In the

75. Havana's Biblioteca Nacional José Martí houses many two-part danzones published in Cuba during the 1880s and 1890s; for example, "La mulata rosa," "Un recuerdo," "Un lazo verde," "La cubana," and "Esperanza" by Enrique Guerrero; "Perico, cuidado con eso" by Pedro M. Fuentes; "El temblol" by Lino Martínez; "El llantico" by Félix Cruz; "El danzón" by Raimundo Valenzuela; and "El valle de Yumurí" by Miguel Faílde. The *J. Jacinto Cuevas* collection was published in Mérida, Yucatán, between 1888 and 1894; with the exception of one danzón by Miguel Faílde in rondo form, all of the other danzones included there are in the two-part convention of earlier contradanzas.

76. Angélica Ma. Solernou Martínez, "Panorama histórico-musical de Santa Clara, 1689–1898." Paper presented at the VII Coloquio Internacional de Musicología Casa de las Américas. March 21, 2012. In this paper, Solernou Martínez provides evidence of two-part danzones published in Santa Clara, Cuba, as late as 1893.

77. Odilio Urfé notes that multi-section danzones could include as many as ten parts joined together by a repeated A section. See Odilio Urfé, "Danzón, mambo y cha cha chá," 56.

case of the 1954 recording, "Las alturas" is interpreted as ABABACAC; the shorter, repeated eight-measure A segments feature prominent improvised variations led by the cornet, and alternate with more fully pre-composed B and C segments.[78] The tempo of this recording is lively (144 beats per minute [bpm]), more of what one might expect of a contradanza or danza. A slower (116 bpm) Rotterdam Conservatory recording of "Las alturas" produced by Cuban Daniel Guzmán interprets the structure as ABACAC, also deviating from standard rondo form, though to a lesser extent.[79] Acerina y su Danzonera recorded the piece in Mexico sometime in the 1950s; their interpretation follows an ABACC form.[80] Discussions of danzón structure in existing literature should thus be understood as score-based and not necessarily representative of the music as actually played.

Raimundo Valenzuela León (1848–1905) was one of the most successful band-leaders in Cuba from the mid-1880s through the early twentieth century, popular both among blacks of all social strata and white elites;[81] his compositions serve as an excellent introduction to early danzones. Born in San Antonio de los Baños, Havana province, Valenzuela trained as a classical instrumentalist on trombone and viola. His orchestra became known for daring arrangements featuring the trombone playing in its highest register. Valenzuela's rigorous technical training is typical of many popular musicians of the period. Miguel Faílde played infrequently in Havana, but the Valenzuela orchestra dominated performance there through the 1910s, doing much to popularize danzones.[82]

Valenzuela's multi-section danzones feature many of the orchestrational traits that characterize the music as performed by orquestas típicas. Along with Faílde, Valenzuela helped standardize arrangements that emphasized timbral and stylistic shifts between segments. His three-part danzón compositions as of about 1879 usually consisted of a repeated eight-measure introduction or paseo (the A theme), performed at a lively tempo by all instruments; a second theme (B), often sixteen measures long and featuring clarinets; and a third theme (C), featuring the brass and representing a climax of sorts. Toward the end of the decade, danzones with four and five sections became popular. Arrangements from that point forward tended to feature a slower and more sentimental C theme played by the violins as well; this was

78. Urfé's recording appeared originally on the LP *Historia del danzón* (Musart M-114, 1954). In 1962, the same recording appeared as *Antología del danzón* (Areito LD-3724. Havana: EGREM, 1962).

79. Daniel Guzmán, prod. *Cuba. Contradanzas and Danzones*. Rotterdam Conservatory Orquesta Típica. Nimbus Records, CD NI 5502. Charlottesville, VA: Nimbus Communications International, 1996. Improvisation is notable in A segments of the Guzmán version as well.

80. The recording was re-released in the compilation *Centenario del danzón: 30 danzones clásicos*. Discos Orfeón, 099441000625. Mexico City: Orfeón, 1993.

81. John Charles Chasteen cites specific venues frequented in Havana by the Orquesta Valenzuela including the Afro-Cuban society La Divina Caridad to the elite white Sociedad del Vedado. See *National Rhythms, African Roots*, 82.

82. Cristóbal Díaz Ayala, *Cuba canta y baila. Discografía de la música cubana. Primer volumen: 1898–1925* (San Juan, Puerto Rico: Fundación Musicalia, 1994), 61.

followed by up-tempo D or D and E segments featuring the brass, known for syncopated rhythms and catchy melodies.[83]

Borrowing themes from preexisting music and incorporating them into danzones became common practice beginning in the 1880s. Since the danzón achieved wide popularity among all sectors of society by the end of that decade, composers appropriated melodies from diverse sources including operas or symphonic music, traditional Afro-Cuban melodies (rumbas, carnival songs), guarachas and boleros, even foreign melodies from Spain, the United States, or elsewhere. The danzón's sectional form and use of contrasting multiple themes made this sort of appropriation easy. Raimundo Valenzuela (see Fig. 2.3) appears to have been the first arranger to adopt the technique, followed in short order by Enrique Peña, Felipe Valdés, Félix Cruz, and others.[84]

Early examples of such melodic borrowing are found in two distinct Raimundo Valenzuela danzones, both entitled "El negro bueno." The original song he took inspiration from, a guaracha by journalist and blackface stage actor Francisco "Pancho" Valdés Ramírez, has a fascinating history of its own.[85] The Valdés Ramírez piece first gained fame in theater shows of June 1868, part of the actor's characterization of a fictitious

83. Eduardo Sánchez de Fuentes, *El folk-lore en la música cubana* (Havana: Imprenta El Siglo XX, 1923), 28; Odilio Urfé, liner notes to *Antología del danzón*.

84. Lid Juárez makes this assertion, specifically mentioning "El negro bueno," discussed later, as the first citational danzón (Lid Juárez, n.d. Program notes accompanying a performance of the Orquesta Félix Gonzalez at the Biblioteca Nacional José Martí from the early 1960s. Archives, Rafael Lam). Octavio "Tata" Alfonso's charanga francesa became well known after 1900 for incorporating *coro de clave* melodies (Rodríguez Domínguez, *Iconografía*, 103).

85. Ironically, given its title, the piece is what would be described in the United States as a "coon song": a racist piece depicting blacks as violent marauders, ready to pull out a knife on any pretext. Pro-independence Cuban audiences, however, perceived the protagonist's readiness to fight as a "revolutionary proclamation," a veiled allusion to the insurgency against Spain and one intended to confound the government's aggressive censorship of theater shows. "El negro bueno" grew in popularity through January of 1869; Jacinto Valdés sang it at that time, the same actor who yelled "Viva Céspedes" and initiated the famous massacre in the Villanueva theater that resulted in multiple deaths, the exile of blackface theater troupes including the Bufos Salas to Mexico, and a blanket prohibition against all blackface comedy in Cuba for a decade. Raimundo Valenzuela was performing in the Villanueva Theater on the evening of the massacre, along with José Alemán, and witnessed the spectacle firsthand. See Rine Leal, *Breve historia del teatro cubano* (Havana: Letras Cubanas, 1980), 67; Leal, *La selva oscura, Vol. 2, De los bufos a la neocolonial* (Havana: Editorial Arte y Literatura, 1982), 17; and Odilio Urfé, "La orquesta del Teatro Villanueva," *Bohemia* 56, no. 10 (6 March 1964), 19 and 98 for an account of the massacre. Walter Goodman, *The Pearl of the Antilles or An Artist in Cuba* (London: Henry S. King and Co., 1873), 168, discusses the censorship of Cuban theater shows in the 1860s. Various authors note the revolutionary associations of the guaracha "El negro bueno" among the general public including Rine Leal, *La selva oscura*, Vol. 2, 17–18; Emilio Bacardí y Moreau, *Crónicas de Santiago de Cuba*, Vol. 4, 2nd edition (Madrid: Breogán, 1973), 50–51; and Ramiro Guerra y Sánchez, *Historia de la nación cubana*, vol. 7 (Havana: Editorial Historia de la Nación Cubana, S.A, 1952), 435. "El negro bueno" continued to be sung by independence fighters in the countryside for decades. See Lapique Becali, *Cuba colonial*, 320, footnote 45.

Figure 2.3: Raimundo and Pablo Valenzuela (second photo below). Photos courtesy of Museo Nacional de la Música Cubana, Havana.

black ruffian named "Candela."[86] Sheet music copies of the original guaracha "El negro bueno" are unavailable, but Cuban singer Joseíto Fernández recorded a version of it in the 1960s that provides insights into its melodies and how Raimundo Valenzuela incorporated them into his arrangements.[87] Examples 2.4 and 2.5 represent the primary themes of the song.

Valenzuela'a first adaptation of "El negro bueno" is a three-part danzón (ABAC as written) that survives only in piano reduction. It dates from 1882 and was published in Havana's *La Revista Musical*.[88] (🔊 Score 2.2) Sections B and C consist of sixteen measures each, separated by the eight-measure repeated A section. Sections B and C are labeled "parts" (*partes*) in the score, though other composers refer to them as

86. Complete lyrics to the guaracha can be found in O. A. Hallorans, *Guarachas cubanas. Curiosa recopilación desde las más antiguas hasta las más modernas* (Havana: Librería La Principal Editora, 1882), 58. The lyrics of the first verse and refrain are as follows: "*Aquí ha llegado Candela / Negrito de rompe y raja / Que con el cuchillo vuela / y corta con la navaja /* [Refrain]: *¡Ay! ¡Ay! ¡Ay! ¡Ay! Vamos a ver / ¡Ay! Chinitica, ¿Qué vamos a hacer? / Si al negro bueno lo quieren prender / Al negro bueno me lo van a desgraciar / Pero ninguno se quiere atracar / Porque si tira se puede clavar.*" Note that the lyrics as recorded by Joseíto Fernández and discussed in the following pages differ slightly from the original version.

87. Joseíto Fernández, *Música popular cubana*. Areíto LP LD-3575. Havana: EGREM, without date.

88. Pérez Sanjuro, *Historia de la música cubana*, 566–68.

Figure 2.3(b): (*continued*)

Example 2.4: "El negro bueno." Verse melody of the original guaracha.

"trios" or "otras."[89] Valenzuela borrowed the first four measures of the two principal melodies from the guaracha and used them as the antecedent phrases of melodies in both the A and B sections of his danzón. Example 2.6, mm. 1, 3, and 5, show how he rhythmically transformed the beginning of the refrain in order to accommodate the danzón's cinquillo clave. Example 2.7, m. 2 shows how he transformed the triplet in the chorus melody into syncopated variations of the habanera rhythm. In both cases, Valenzuela added a new consequent phrase at the end of the melody. In this first danzón adaptation, the C part contains no melodic material borrowed from the guaracha and appears to be newly composed.

89. The term trio derives from European salon dance versions of the minuet and trio; in that context as well "trio" referred to a segment of reduced instrumentation different from the A and B sections of the minuet.

Example 2.5: "El negro bueno." Chorus melody of the original guaracha.

¡Ay, se - ñor cu - ra! ¿Qué va - mos a ha-cer   si al ne - gro bue - no lo quie - ren pren - der?

Example 2.6: Raimundo Valenzuela, "El negro bueno." Piano version, melody of the A section borrowed from the verse of the guaracha (Ex. 2.4).

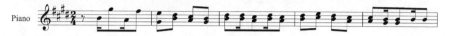

Example 2.7: Valenzuela, "El negro bueno." Piano version, melody from the B section borrowed from the chorus of the guaracha (Ex. 2.5).

Valenzuela's second adaptation of "El negro bueno" is a five-part danzón (ABACA-DAE as written) scored for orquesta típica or *piquete típico* (two clarinets, cornet, trombone, ophicleide,[90] two violins, acoustic bass, and percussion) that survives in the archives of the Museo Nacional de la Música in Havana. (🖉 Score 2.3) The A and D sections consist of repeated eight-bar phrases while the B, C, and E sections are each sixteen measures long. As opposed to Valenzuela's "El negro bueno" piano score, this version includes melodic material from the original guaracha only at the beginning of the final E section. The first quotation borrows from the song's verse and is played in parallel thirds by the violins at the beginning of the E section (Ex. 2.8); Valenzuela employs the melody in a manner similar to that of the danzón discussed previously (Ex. 2.6), but modifies the first cinquillo pattern into a straight descending eighth-note melody, as can be seen in Example 2.8, m.1. This theme in the violins is accompanied by a countermelody (also played in parallel thirds by the clarinets), a bass line consisting largely of a repeated tresillo rhythm (see Ex. 2.1), and brass figures (on the cornet, trombone, and ophicleide) that provides a rhythmic foundation emphasizing the cinquillo.

The second melody borrowed from the guaracha comes from the chorus (Ex. 2.5). This time, violins and clarinets play it, doubling each other (Ex. 2.9) at the very end of the danzón. In this section, Valenzuela transforms the rhythm of the chorus through augmentation so that the sixteenth notes and first triplet from "¡Ay, señor cura! ¿Qué vamos a hacer?" in Example 2.5 become eighth notes and a quarter-note triplet (Ex. 2.9). As was standard practice, the accompaniment of the timbales and güiro is not notated in the score.

90. Rarely used today, the ophicleide (*figle* in Spanish) is a form of low horn made of brass that resembles a bassoon in appearance. It has a trumpet-like mouthpiece but also employs key pads similar to those on a saxophone.

Example 2.8: Raimundo Valenzuela, "El negro bueno." Orchestral version. First melody from the E section, borrowed from the verse of the guaracha.

Example 2.9: Valenzuela, "El negro bueno." Orchestral version. Final melody from the E section, borrowed from the chorus of the guaracha.

Besides offering a glimpse into how composers adapted popular tunes into their danzones, this second version of "El negro bueno" helps us understand the typical scoring for orquesta típica groups. All instruments play throughout the piece, yet Valenzuela creates textural variety by changing the role of the instruments and their combinations from section to section, and within individual sections. The A section is the busiest and loudest. In the first half, the clarinet and first violin present the principal theme in unison, along with the cornet that plays the same material an octave lower, and the second violin that harmonizes in parallel thirds. The second clarinet fills in the texture with a low countermelody. The trombone and the ophicleide provide supporting harmonies and add to the piece's rhythmic drive with syncopated, cinquillo-derived figures, together with the bass.

In the last four measures of the A section the cornet drops the main melody to join the trombone and ophicleide in providing rhythmic and harmonic support. This allows for a smooth transition into the B section featuring the cornet on the main melody against sustained notes played by the violins and the first clarinet and a simple arpeggiated accompaniment provided by the second clarinet. The same style of orchestration continues in section C with the addition of new arpeggiated harmonies on the clarinet and fast repeated notes—reminiscent of the clarinet melodies in section A—over the cornet's melody. The D section reverses the roles of the cornet and clarinets; the latter take over the melody, first in octaves, then in parallel thirds, while the cornet recedes into the background with a simple countermelody. Other instruments continue with lines similar to those in B and C. Finally, the E section features the violins playing a melodic excerpt from the guaracha in parallel thirds against a clarinet countermelody, also scored in parallel thirds. Given the reputation of Pablo Valenzuela, Raimundo's brother, as a master cornetist and improviser, it does not come as a surprise that his instrument features prominently through the first three sections of the danzón. This allowed Pablo to demonstrate his virtuosity as he led the ensemble in performance.[91]

The orchestral version of "El negro bueno" features another important stylistic trait of the danzón: the rhythmic breaks (*remates* or *golpes*) that mark cadences at the end of each section, announcing the return of the refrain or the beginning of a new trio or otra.[92] This is a fundamental characteristic of danzón style and is one of the main features dancers listen to in order to know when the refrain is returning and they should stop dancing, or when a new theme is about to start and they should begin again. The cinquillo is the basic rhythmic unit that characterizes such breaks (Ex. 2.10). In the refrain (A), repeated cinquillos are typically heard at the end of the section over three consecutive bars of music as the harmony typically moves from tonic, often through a secondary dominant (the V/V), to dominant. In trio segments, breaks vary to a greater extent; they may consist of a series of three cinquillos as described, or of only one cinquillo at the very end of the phrase, accompanying the harmonic progression back to the tonic (Ex. 2.11).

Besides taking popular music as a source of melodic inspiration, danzón composers also frequently borrowed from opera and elite music, as mentioned. Raimundo Valenzuela's "Tosca" offers a good example of how such materials were used and transformed. (❸ Score 2.4) Cuban audiences had their first exposure to Giacomo Puccini's *Tosca* at the Teatro Martí in 1902, only two years after its premiere in Rome. Valenzuela composed a danzón of the same name shortly thereafter; his brother Pablo Valenzuela recorded it in 1906, following Raimundo's death.[93] Like "El negro bueno," "Tosca" is a multi-section danzón in five parts for orquesta típica. It is written in G minor, the key used at the beginning of the opera, but shifts to G major in the B and E sections. Valenzuela uses melodies from Puccini's opera prominently in the B, C, and D sections. The themes are taken from Act I, Scene I, the orchestral segment that accompanies Tosca's first appearance on stage (Ex. 2.12), and from the clarinet melody that accompanies Cavaradossi's aria in Act III, Scene I (Ex. 2.14).

Valenzuela first quotes from Tosca's entrance melody, Act I, Scene I (Ex. 2.12), in a very straightforward manner. The entrance theme appears in the first clarinet line, transposed to G major, in the B section of the danzón. Valenzuela makes only minor changes to the original theme. Most noticeable is the addition of an embellishment in measure 6 of the danzón (compare m. 6 of Ex. 2.12 with m. 12 of Ex. 2.13) and another in which he converts the triplets from the original (m. 7, Ex. 2.12) into a simpler dotted rhythm (m. 14, Ex. 2.13). Valenzuela also introduces a cadence using the cinquillo rhythm at the end of the section (Ex. 2.13 m. 15). The composer quotes

---

91. See excerpts of the full score on the website.

92. Mexican musicians refer to these cadences as remates, from the verb *rematar* (to finish). Cubans more typically call them golpes (hits) or *efecto* (effect), especially when emphasizing a transition to the montuno see Dora Ileana Torres, "Del danzón cantado al chachachá," in *Panorama de la música popular cubana*, ed. Radamés Giro (Havana: Letras Cubanas, 1995), 208.

93. The Orquesta Valenzuela recorded "La tosca" on Edison cylinder No. 18910; it has not been reissued. See Cristóbal Díaz Ayala, *Cuba canta y baila*, 157.

Example 2.10: Valenzuela, "El negro bueno." Lower horns emphasize three successive cinquillos at the end of section A. Rhythms leading to the first cadence are further accentuated by the percussionists.

Example 2.11: Valenzuela, "El negro bueno." Clarinet and brass lines emphasize a shorter cadence with a single cinquillo at the end of section D.

Example 2.12: Giacomo Puccini, *Tosca* (1900). Act I, Scene I, "Entra Tosca," main melody.

Example 2.13: Raimundo Valenzuela, "Tosca." Clarinet melody in section B.

Example 2.14: Puccini, *Tosca*. Act III, Scene I, "Cavaradossi's Aria," clarinet melody.

a second melody from Act III, Scene 1 (Ex. 2.14), transposed to G minor, in the cornet line during section C.

Valenzuela's use of this melody represents more than a mere quotation. Here, he transforms the original theme by expanding portions of it through rhythmic elaboration (as in mm. 9 and 10 from Ex. 2.15, corresponding to m. 6 in Ex. 2.14), added material (mm. 6 and 17 from Ex. 2.15), and the addition of sustained or repeated pitches (as in mm. 3–5 and 11–12 in Ex. 2.15, corresponding to mm. 2 and 7 from Ex. 2.14). Of course, changes to the original melody may have been even greater during a live performance than in the written score; the sustained and repeated pitches in measures 3–5 and 11–12, for instance, would have provided the Valenzuelas with plenty of opportunities for improvisation.

Cavaradossi's aria melody appears again at the end of the danzón in the E section. Here Valenzuela includes borrowed material (mm. 7–15 of Ex. 2.14) in the middle and at the end of the clarinet melody with only minor changes. These are largely made in order to fit the melody into the 2/4 time signature of the danzón and to accommodate the added cinquillo of the cadence (see Ex. 2.16).

Both "El negro bueno," and "Tosca" exemplify how composers made musical borrowing and intertextual reference a central aspect of early danzón culture and set a precedent for their use in danzones thereafter. One hears this technique in many other pieces, from multi-sectional "classic" danzones to danzones de nuevo ritmo and danzones chá. Among others, they include "Rigoletito" by Felipe Valdés (borrowing from Verdi), "El cadete constitucional" by Jacobo Rubalcaba (borrowing from Sousa), "La flauta mágica" by Alfredo Brito (borrowing from Mozart), "Oh Margot o La borrachita" by Joaquín Marcoleta (borrowing from Mexican composer Tata Nacho), or "Broadway" by Israel López "Cachao" (borrowing from Rachmaninoff). The same technique is common in danzones from Mexico including "La pajarera" by José M. Prado (borrowing from Mexican folk music), "Rigoletito" by Esteban Alfonzo (borrowing from Verdi), "La giocondita" by Tomás Ponce Reyes (borrowing from Ponchielli),[94] "Lamento borincano" by Carlos Campos (borrowing from Puerto Rican composer Rafael Hernández), or "Concierto de Aranjuez" by Felipe Urbán

94. As discussed in Chapter 3, Tomás Ponce Reyes was a Cuban composer who emigrated to Mexico and made his music career there. Ponce Reyes worked as arranger for Acerina y su Danzonera for many years, composing "La giocondita" for that band.

Example 2.15: Valenzuela, "Tosca." Cornet melody in section C.

Example 2.16: Valenzuela, "Tosca." Cornet melody in section E.

(borrowing from Joaquín Rodrigo). Practices of appropriation provide insights into other styles of music that were meaningful to musicians, audiences, and dancers of the day, and further problematize the notion of the danzón as a distinct genre. Clearly, the music cannot be understood without an appreciation for the gamut of styles in circulation at the time. Intertextual references that first became common in danzón performance continue to appear constantly in Cuban popular music performance, from *son* and modern *timba* dance repertoire to improvised segments within Latin jazz compositions.

FROM ORQUESTA TÍPICA TO CHARANGA FRANCESA AND DANZONERA

The instrumentation of *charanga francesa*–style danzones, increasingly popular throughout Cuba beginning in the 1890s, represented a new permutation of musical elements and formats that had existed in Cuba for some time. Sunni Witmer suggests that French-speaking refugees from St. Domingue at the turn of the nineteenth century may have first formed small ensembles featuring pianos, violins, and flutes; these same immigrants introduced the five-key wooden flute, widely influential across the island in later decades. Witmer has documented the sale of such instruments as early as 1794.[95] Ana Casanova notes that dance bands consisting of three violins, clarinet, flute, violins, bass, timbales, and güiro were common by the early nineteenth century.[96] Villaverde's writings document the presence of similar ensembles in Havana of the 1830s; Galán describes dances of the 1850s (bailes de cuna) as including the five-key wooden flute as well.[97]

95. Witmer, "Cuban *Charanga*," 86; email communication, December 21, 2009.
96. Casanova Olivia, "Güiro o guayo," 165.
97. Villaverde, *Cecilia Valdés*, 39–40; Galán, *Cuba y sus sones*, 218.

The term "charanga" also has a long history, on and off the island. The Spanish used it as early as the sixteenth century to describe informal military bands, as mentioned.[98] Esteban Pichardo defined it in Cuba in the 1830s as "something small, diminutive, or partial, as in a charanga or orchestra of few musicians."[99] For years, "charanga" had pejorative connotations, as in the case of the roughly synonymous "bunga" used to describe ensembles associated with working-class events. Witmer includes graphic reproductions of Cuban charangas from the 1850s that still include trombone, French horn, and clarinet in addition to flute.[100] Over time, performers altered the instrumentation of some charangas to foreground violins and flute as lead instruments; they described the new permutation of the ensemble as a "charanga francesa" (French charanga), apparently in an attempt to make it sound more sophisticated. French culture had positive associations in Cuba, and semantically linking the ensembles featuring flute and violins to France was logical, given their roots in the music of French-speaking refugees who first formed such groups.[101]

Orquesta típica bands, with their mix of strings, reeds, and brass, worked well in outdoor venues, but some audiences preferred the less strident sound of the charanga francesa, especially indoors.[102] The popularization of ensembles featuring only flutes and violins as lead instruments seems to have been a gradual process across the island, beginning in the mid-nineteenth century; some still included clarinets or oboes for a time. The first charanga francesa known to have played danzón appeared in Matanzas. It was called the Unión Harmónica, a quartet that played for dancers at the beach in the Saratoga summerhouse in July of 1890 and featured piano, flute, violin, and acoustic bass.[103] Other early charanga-style danzón ensembles from Matanzas included the orchestras of Ramoncito Prendes and Miguelito Martínez.[104] Antonio Peñes in Havana deserves mention as one of the first musicians who popularized renditions of the danzón for solo piano performance, in 1892, apparently taking inspiration from the use of that instrument in the charanga francesa.[105]

A central factor differentiating twentieth-century danzón performance in Cuba and Mexico is the whole-hearted adoption of the charanga francesa in Cuba after 1900 and the perpetuation of orchestras featuring wind instruments in Mexico. Various authors have speculated as to why the charanga format proved so much more appealing in Cuba. Díaz Ayala believes that larger danzón groups proved difficult to maintain as of the 1910s and 1920s following the popularization of the *son*. *Son* bands included only six or seven members and thus cost less to hire. Most had less

98. Witmer, "Cuban *Charanga*," 72. She notes (p. 77) that the term is still used in Spain and various former colonies such as Colombia to refer to informal brass ensembles, often used in street processions.
99. Pichardo, *Diccionario provincial*, 211.
100. Witmer, "Cuban *Charanga*," 79.
101. Díaz Ayala, *Cuba canta y baila*, 134.
102. Grenet, *Popular Cuban Music*, 33.
103. Rodríguez Domínguez, *Iconografía*, 94.
104. Castillo Faílde, *Miguel Faílde*, 33.
105. "Crónicas," *El Fígaro* 8, no, 32 (September 11, 1892), 7.

Figure 2.4: Antonio "Papaíto" Torroella and his orchestra. David Rendón (violin), Tata (violin), Faustino Valdés (flute), "Papaíto" Torroella (piano), Evaristo Romero (bass). Photo courtesy of Museo Nacional de la Música, Havana.

formal training and presumably charged less for that reason.[106] The associations of the charanga with a sound perceived as more sophisticated may have also played a factor.[107] Charangas from this perspective made the music more appealing to middle-class listeners and distanced the repertoire from the típica tradition, associated for years with racialized controversy as discussed in Chapter 3.

Pianist and composer Antonio "Papaíto" Torroella (1856–1934) played a fundamental role in popularizing the new charanga format in Havana beginning in 1898.[108] Photos of his ensemble from the turn of the century confirm that he was white and directed an integrated ensemble consisting of two violins, flute, piano, and bass (Fig. 2.4).[109] Band members worked on occasion with a percussionist who played

106. Rodríguez Domínguez, *Iconografía*, 96, 108; John Storm Roberts, *The Latin Tinge. The Impact of Latin American Music on the United States* (Tivoli, NY: Original Music, 1985), 8–9; Cristóbal Díaz Ayala, liner notes to *Early Cuban Danzón Orchestras 1916–1920*. Harlequin CD HQCD-131, 1999; Díaz Ayala, "La invencible charanga," *Encuentro*, Vol. 26–27 (2002–3), 296.

107. Cristóbal Díaz Ayala and Richard Spottswood. Liner notes to *The Cuban Danzón. Before There Was Jazz*. Arhoolie Folklyric CD 7032, 1999.

108. Radamés Giro, *Diccionario enciclopédico de la música en Cuba*, Vol. 4 (Havana: Letras Cubanas, 2007), 200.

109. Ned Sublette, *Cuba and Its Music. From the First Drums to the Mambo* (Chicago: Chicago Review Press, 2004), 308.

either güiro or timpani. Their group increased steadily in popularity through 1910, as documented in the press.[110] Torroella's was the first charanga francesa ensemble to record, in 1906, together with típicas such as the Orquesta Valenzuela. Cristóbal Díaz Ayala includes a list of Torroella's pieces transferred to Edison cylinders during that early session, all of which appear to have been lost.[111] By 1909, a number of charangas began to experiment with the instrumentation established by Torroella. Some added instruments from the orquesta típica: the ophicleide or trombone to support the lower registers, or the cornet as an additional lead instrument.[112] Others incorporated the diatonic harp, the saxophone (associated with newly formed jazz bands), excluded the piano, and/or expanded the string section to include a second violin, viola, and cello.[113] More than twenty-five well-known charangas francesas performed in early twentieth-century Cuba, supplanting the orquesta típica tradition by the mid-1920s. They played for parties and public social gatherings, to accompany silent film, and in fundraising events, frequently for the black community.[114] And increasingly into the 1920s, groups emerged that further fused the instrumentation of the charanga and the jazz band, incorporating instruments such as drum set and banjo.[115] By the 1940s, nearly sixty prominent charangas existed in Cuba playing some combination of danzón, jazz, and *son*.[116]

Pianist, composer, and bandleader Antonio María Romeu (1876–1955) (Fig. 2.5), stands out as the most important figure in the popularization of the charanga francesa after 1910. A prolific artist, he released hundreds of recordings on the Victor and Columbia labels prior to 1925 and composed over 1,500 danzones during his career.[117] Romeu had a much higher public profile than most other bandleaders, in part because he performed for so long (over sixty years), and in part because his

110. E.g. *La política cómica* 1, no. 3 (Sunday, January 14, 1906), 2. See also Lapique Becali, *Cuba colonial*, 326.

111. Cristóbal Díaz Ayala, *Cuba canta y baila*, 143–44. Dick Spottswood notes that the first extant recordings of charanga-style danzón were made in 1915 by the orchestras of pianist Antonio Romeu, flautist Octavio "Tata" Alfonso, and Juan Francisco "Tata" Pereira. See Dick Spottswood, "Appendix," *Lost Sounds. Blacks and the Birth of the Recording Industry, 1890–1919* (Urbana: University of Illinois Press, 2004), 526.

112. Castillo Faílde (*Miguel Faílde*, 33) discusses a charanga francesa in Havana's Ateneo society in 1909 that included muted cornet. Cristóbal Díaz Ayala (*Cuba canta y baila*, 135) mentions Tata Pereira as an early experimenter with lower horns in the charanga. In the liner notes to *Early Music of the North Caribbean 1916–1920* (Harlequin CD HQ CD 67, 1995), he also discusses pianist Ricardo Reverón's early charanga that includes ophicleide; some of its recordings from 1918 can be heard on the CD, and on *Early Cuban Danzón Orchestras* (Harlequin HQCD 131).

113. Rodríguez Domínguez, *Iconografía*, 93, 98; Díaz Ayala, *Cuba canta y baila*, 131.

114. Rodríguez Domínguez, *Iconografía*, 143–48.

115. Charanga-jazz fusion groups of this nature included the Pablo O'Farrill orchestra, the Orquesta Calabaza, and those under the direction of Armando Romeu and Moisés Simons. See Rodríguez Domínguez, *Iconografía*, 127–28, and Leonardo Acosta, *Descarga cubana: el jazz en Cuba 1900–1950* (Havana: Ediciones Unión, 2000), 40.

116. Rodríguez Domínguez, *Iconografía*, 93–142, 159–212.

117. Díaz Ayala, *Cuba canta y baila*, 136–43; Ada Iglesias, "Un músico del pueblo," *Actas del folklore* 1, no. 4 (April 1961), 14.

Figure 2.5: Antonio Romeu and his orchestra, including singer Barbarito Diez (third from left, front). Photo courtesy of Museo Nacional de la Música Cubana, Havana.

group was featured live on the radio for decades.[118] He is the first important piano soloist in Cuban dance music, and the well-known danzón "Linda cubana" from the 1920s (discussed later) was the first composition in which such a solo appears.[119] A child prodigy, Romeu played the piano for social events beginning at age ten in his hometown of Jibacoa, Havana province. In 1899 he moved to the capital, interpreting solo piano renditions of the danzón in the Café Diana and Café Manzanares, accompanied only by the güiro. Frank Emilio Flynn subsequently reinterpreted and released many of Romeu's early compositions in that same style.[120]

Romeu occasionally collaborated with Torroella but started working consistently in dance bands as of 1904 when he joined Octavio "Tata" Alfonso's orchestra. In 1911 he formed his own six-piece charanga consisting of flute, violin, bass, güiro, timbales, and piano. Many virtuoso flautists performed with him through the years and helped establish the tradition of extended flute solos in the charanga idiom.[121] A masterful

118. Giro, *Diccionario Enciclopédico*, Vol. 4, 85. He first performed live in 1931 on La Voz de las Antillas, later in Radio Progreso about 1933, and in about 1939 on the Cadena Azul RHC. Giro discusses several classical composers including Amadeo Roldán and Darius Milhaud who composed pieces based on themes by Romeu, attesting to his fame.

119. Giro, *Diccionario Enciclopédico*, Vol. 4, 85; Sublette, *Cuba and Its Music*, 307.

120. Díaz Ayala, *Cuba canta y baila*, 133; the recording mentioned is *Frank Emilio. Cuban Danzas & Danzones*. Yemayá Records YY9437. Andorra: Discforme S.L., 2007.

121. Iglesias Utset, *A Cultural History of Cuba*, 14; Rodríguez Domínguez, *Iconografía*, 23.

orchestrator, Romeu scored music for various groups and was one of the first to write pizzicato phrases and other idiosyncratic lines for charanga string sections. Perhaps even more important, his timbales player was the first to incorporate *cáscara* (shell) or *baqueteo* (stick) ride patterns on the side of the drum, a practice that would strongly influence salsa and other Latin dance music performance of later decades.[122] Throughout his career, Romeu composed more danzones than any other style of music; along with Antonio Arcaño, he continued to play the danzón in a relatively "classic" instrumental format into the mid-twentieth century.[123] Yet he remained open to external influences—for instance, collaborating with *son* singers Miguel Matamoros and Siro Rodríguez in the 1920s. In the 1940s he organized an orquesta típica decades after other groups had rejected the format, and in the 1950s created a so-called *orquesta gigante*,[124] combining instruments derived from both the típica and charanga into a single group that resembled the present-day Mexican *danzonera*.

While Cuban musicians slowly moved from the brassy sound of orquestas típicas to the more intimate sound of charangas, Mexican musicians developed the danzonera, a type of hybrid instrumental ensemble that borrowed elements from both. The format of the Mexican ensemble changed through the twentieth century as it incorporated influences from swing bands in the 1940s and 1950s. Early danzoneras like Orquesta Babuco led by Tiburcio "Babuco" Hernández—arguably the first danzonera recognized as such and active in Veracruz and Mexico City in the 1910s—differed little from the Cuban orquesta típica.[125] Yet as the charanga became more popular among Cuban musicians, Mexican bands incorporated some of its instruments as well. In the 1910s, for instance, the Yucatecan Orquesta Concha featured cornet, trombone, ophicleide, clarinets, strings (usually violins and bass but sometimes a viola or a cello), and often piano and flute, in addition to percussion. The latter consisted of timbales and güiro; Mexican danzoneras never replaced the timbales with pailas,[126] and only more modern formations complement them with the *tumbadoras* (conga drums). By the 1920s, Orquesta Concha replaced the cornet with two trumpets, eliminated the ophicleide, and added saxophones and two extra clarinets.

In the 1940s and 1950s, Acerina y su Danzonera (Fig. 2.6) had become one of the leading danzoneras in Mexico. Formed by Consejo Valiente "Acerina," the former Concha Orchestra's Cuban timbalero, this band featured two trumpets, trombone, two tenor and two baritone saxophones (occasionally replaced by clarinets), two violins, double bass, piano, timbales, güiro, and claves. Acerina's instrumentation set the standard for later Mexican groups, many of which, also influenced by the big-band format, eliminated the violin section. This is evident in ensembles such as the Danzonera Dimas, Alejandro Cardona y su Danzonera, Orquesta de Carlos Campos, and more recent bands like Felipe Urbán y su Danzonera and the Danzonera de José

---

122. Cristóbal Díaz Ayala, "La invencible charanga," 299.
123. Cristóbal Díaz Ayala, "La invencible charanga," 304.
124. Rodríguez Dominguez, *Iconografía*, 25. This was, of course, the era of other "orquestas gigantes" such as that of Beny Moré.
125. Further biographical information about the musicians discussed here can be found in Chapter 3.
126. See discussion of these terms at the beginning of the chapter, especially note 29.

Figure 2.6: Acerina y su Danzonera, still from the film *Este amor sí es amor* (1962). Photo courtesy of Agrasanchez Film Archive, Harlingen, TX.

Casquera. One can hear elements of Dámaso Pérez Prado's jazz-influenced mambo (first popularized in Mexico) and the big-band cumbias of Colombians Lucho Bermúdez and Pacho Galán in Cardona's ensemble, and those of other groups of the period. In Veracruz, a reduced danzonera format known as *guerrilla* consisting of two trumpets, two saxophones (tenor and baritone), electric bass, güiro, claves, and one timbal became popular among the working classes and it is still frequently used in less affluent events. Although Mexicans have enjoyed danzones in a variety of local instrumental formats—from orquesta típica and marimba ensembles to banda and conjunto norteño—the danzonera with extended trumpet and saxophone lines has become the standard format associated with Mexican danzón.

SON-INFLUENCED DANZONES

Various tendencies are evident in the development of the danzón in Cuba in the early twentieth century; the most obvious include the influence of the *son*, especially the addition of a final montuno-like vamp at the end of many pieces beginning about 1910;[127] and the increasing fusion of the danzón with vocal genres such as the bolero, *canción*, or commercial tango, resulting in countless *danzón cantado* and *danzonete* recordings in the late 1920s. José Urfé is the first composer recognized as having incorporated the *son's* montuno section into a danzón, "El bombín de Barreto" (Barreto's Bowler Hat), though recent evidence suggests that musicians in Santiago such as composer Calixto Varona did so more than twenty years earlier.[128] It is surprising in any case that the *son* began to influence danzón performance by 1910 in Havana and Matanzas, well before the *son* itself became widely popular there.[129] According to Antonio Arcaño, Urfé and Raimundo Valenzuela took a trip to the city of Baracoa at the turn of the twentieth century; the sound of the *son* caught their attention and resulted in their experiments with the added montuno segment.[130] Urfé's "El bombín de Barreto," written for orquesta típica, extended the standard three-part danzón structure (ABACA) with a final montuno (D) featuring a trumpet solo and supporting ostinato riffs on other wind instruments.

It is possible that the inclusion of a final montuno in the danzón also took inspiration from earlier "rumbita" compositions of the comic theater, similarly influenced by Afro-Cuban street repertoire, or from other sources. Vamps had existed for some time in Cuban dance music and of course form the basis of much traditional Afro-Cuban drumming and song. Even some danza scores from the 1860s include what appear to be open-ended montuno segments at the end, as discussed in Chapter 4. In *son*-influenced danzón compositions, the speed of the music tends to increase during the montuno, and corresponding dance steps become looser and more picaresque. This aspect of danzón performance—which also has parallels in traditional Afro-Cuban repertoire—continues to be standard practice in both Cuban and Mexican danzones to the present day.

Antonio María Romeu's "Linda cubana" provides a good example of how early charanga bands incorporated elements of the *son* and how composers integrated such influences into charanga arrangements scored for flute, strings, and piano. (🔊 Score 2.5) A well-known composition, "Linda cubana," premiered in 1926 in the Sociedad Unión Fraternal.[131] It may have been inspired by a similar piece recorded by the

127. Odilio Urfé, "Paternidad verdadera del mambo y el chachachá," *Carteles* 39, no. 36 (September 7. 1958), 14.

128. Yianela Pérez Cuza,"El dancismo en Santiago de Cuba en la segunda mitad del siglo XIX." Unpublished manuscript (2012), 62–63. Elena Pérez Sanjuro (*Historia de la música cubana*, 559) states that "El bombín de Barreto" was first played publicly on December 11, 1910, in the Centro Familiar de Güira de Melena. The title took inspiration from a hat frequently worn by Julián Barreto, Urfé's first violinist. A copy of the clarinet part with a final ostinato is reproduced in Rodríguez Domínguez, *Iconografía*,73.

129. The *son's* popularity in the 1920s could be explained among other things by the fact that commercial recordings became more readily available that decade. However, among local practitioners it was nothing new, especially in the province of Oriente where the music had been around for decades.

130. Antonio Arcaño, personal interview, Havana, Cuba, July 16, 1992.

131. Iglesias Utset, *A Cultural History of Cuba*, 14.

Orquesta Tata Pereira in 1924, also *son*-influenced.[132] Romeu's is a five-part danzón. An A theme (consisting of the typical repeated eight-measure phrase) features a lively melody scored for all instruments, with several prominent cinquillo figures. Theme B (16 measures) is softer, lyrical, and in a lower register. Violins carry the melody, supported by double stops filling out chords on the viola and a soft arpeggiated countermelody on cello; the flute is tacet. The loud C theme, with prominent cinquillos, is considerably longer than the others (40 measures). Initially it presents violins, flute, and piano together on the principal melody, and in later sections contrasts permutations of the violin theme in dialogue with fills and arpeggiation on the piano and flute. In section D (16 measures) the piece finally references a *son* melody taken from Guillermo Castillo's "Tres lindas cubanas," featured in the violins and flute and supported by double stops on the viola and cello, as well as faster runs on cello and piano filling in sustained notes (see Exs. 2.17 and 2.18).

The final section of "Linda cubana" (E) consists of a solo for unaccompanied piano. As other instruments drop out, Romeu recreates the sound of the *son*'s montuno in various ways. First, he plays a vamp figure featuring a melody that alternates straight eighth notes with more syncopated figures, thus continuing to reference clave (Ex. 2.19). Extended, improvised solos in clave themselves are more characteristic of *son* than of danzón. The simple tonic-dominant harmonies in section E are also characteristic of *son*. Romeu's piano solos, played over a relatively constant bassline thereafter, continue to feature right-hand melodies in clave, often alternating cinquillos with straighter eighth-note sequences (Ex. 2.20). He may have been the first to create a uniquely "Cuban" style of popular piano performance based on traditional Afro-Cuban sources. After continuing the solo for some time, Romeu segues to an out-of-time cadenza, then cues the entire group to section D for a finale on Guillermo Castillo's *son* theme.

While Romeu's extended danzón compositions with montuno-style solos continued to enjoy wide popularity through the mid-twentieth century, a new model influenced by José Urfé's experiments involving a truncated danzón form ultimately proved even more influential. (⊘ Picture 2.2) As of about 1940, composers tended increasingly to write only two-part danzones (ABA), followed by a final extended montuno segment (C). This style might be described as *"danzón soneado"* (danzón in a *son* style); composers of such music abandoned the rondo structure in favor of one in which the danzón's stylistic features (i.e., the cinquillo clave, contrasting themes in distinct trios) were relegated to a shorter, introductory segment of the piece.[133] Most

132. The Tata Pereira piece (ABACAD form) is interesting for several reasons; it includes the same "Tres lindas cubanas" *son* melody used by Romeu; it represents a hybrid charanga recording featuring flutes and violins but also an ophicleide playing the bass line; and it includes ostinato patterns played by the full ensemble at various moments derived from *son* repertoire. The ostinati appear before the C theme, in the middle of the C theme (dividing its two sections in half), and before D, the section that includes the melody of "Tres lindas cubanas."

133. Mexican danzoneros often refer to these types of truncated danzones as *danzones mutilados* (mutilated danzones). Thanks to Sue Miller and Hettie Malcomson for this information.

Example 2.17: Guillermo Castillo, "Tres lindas cubanas." Chorus theme as performed originally by the Septeto Habanero in B-flat.

Tres, - tres,___ lin - das cu-ba-nas___ Tres,

Example 2.18: Antonio María Romeu, "Linda cubana." D theme excerpt featuring the melody "Tres lindas cubanas" by Guillermo Castillo.

music making actually occurs within an extended montuno vamp thereafter, as in the *son*. This shorter structure was adopted in renditions of danzones with added lead vocals and/or choruses as well as in the so-called *danzones de nuevo ritmo* (danzones in a new rhythm), both of which are discussed later. Antonio Arcaño described the newer danzón format as consisting most typically of an introduction (A) based on cinquillo rhythms, a B theme with a lyrical, bolero-like melody, a repeat of A, and then the montuno, "the African thing."[134] In Arcaño's "soneado" style, compositions tended to be danced from beginning to end, without a pause during the return of A, which may also reflect *son* influence.[135] From this period onward, at least, the danzón can best be described as an "intergenre" as defined by Danilo Orozco:[136] a fundamentally interpenetrated form that constantly incorporated or moved between elements from other styles of music.

134. Arcaño interview.
135. John Santos, liner notes to *The Cuban Danzón: Its Ancestors and Descendants* (Washington, DC: Smithsonian Folkways FE 4066, 1982).
136. As discussed in Neris González Bello and Liliana Casanella, "La timba cubana: un intergénero contemporáneo," *Clave* 4, no. 1 (2002), 2–9.

Example 2.19: Romeu, "Linda cubana." Claved, montuno-like piano vamp, initiating piano solo in section E.

Example 2.20: Romeu, "Linda cubana." Excerpted piano solo line from section E, alternating cinquillos with straighter figures.

DANZÓN CANTADO, DANZONETE, AND OTHER SUNG DANZONES

The danzón was largely an instrumental style at the beginning of the twentieth century. Nevertheless, the increasing incorporation of brief vocal segments eventually generated a number of sung danzón styles, as mentioned. In addition to vocalized dance repertoire such as the canción habanera, brief vocal parts had existed for some time even within the contradanza and danza of the mid-nineteenth century.[137] Danzón composers and bandleaders reintroduced this practice into three-part and multi-section danzones beginning in the 1890s. An early case is that of Puerto Rican–born cornetist and composer Félix Cruz, whose "Trabajar, compañeros!," a four-part (ABACAD) danzón, introduces a four-measure vocal chorus at the end of the final D section that repeats the title of the piece, *"trabajar, compañeros, trabajar!,"* in alternation with instrumental and/or vocal improvisation. Thus, Cruz provides this danzón with a call-and-response flavor that is typical of many other Afro-Caribbean musical styles.[138]

The practice of introducing vocal refrains soon gave way to more extended vocal lines that vocalists sang throughout the final part of multi-section danzones. Commercial sponsors realized the possibilities that the danzón's catchy rhythms and melodies could offer in enhancing product recognition; thus, a type of danzón-jingle

137. Argeliers León, *Del canto y el tiempo*, 257, 264, 271; Goodman, *The Pearl of the Antilles*, 121–22.

138. This piece is reproduced in Argeliers León, *Del canto y el tiempo*, 251–52; León does not include the year of composition. Helio Orovio argues that the height of Cruz's popularity took place between 1888 and 1898, so he likely composed "Trabajar, compañeros!" at that time. See Helio Orovio, *Cuban Music from A to Z* (Durham, NC: Duke University Press, 2004), 61. Miguel Faílde composed a danzón of similar title, "Trabajar, compañeros, trabajar" in May of 1890 (Castillo Faílde, *Miguel Faílde*, 204).

was born. One early example is "El Favorito," a three-part danzón by Antonio Peñas, probably composed in the early 1890s, whose lyrics in the third section praise the "exquisite feel and look" of El Favorito hats.[139] Danzones of this sort appear frequently in Cuba of the early twentieth century. Examples include Elías Buxeda's "Champán Sport" (1910s) (➌ Score 2.6) and Jorge Anckermann's "Yo quiero Coca Cola" (1916) (➌ Score 2.7); though both are extended, multi-section danzones, they similarly introduce lyrics only in the last section of the piece. Buxedas uses a repeated sixteen-measure melody to suggest that Champán Sport *"mitiga la sed y las penas"* ("quenches your thirst and your sorrows"); Anckermann's thirty-two-bar vocal tells dancers that Coca Cola will provide relief from headaches and fatigue, and cheerfully concludes *"¡Ay Lola! ¡Ay Lola! / cómo me gusta la CocaCola"* (Ay Lola! / how much I like CocaCola). Mexican entrepreneurs also employed danzón melodies for commercial purposes in the 1910s.[140]

"Carta Clara" by Everardo Concha, another commercial piece, exemplifies danzón compositional style in Mexico of the 1910s. (➌ Score 2.8) (➌ Track 2.1) It employs practically the same ensemble used in Cuban danzones for orquesta típica with the exception of an added piano that doubles the clarinet and some string parts. Particularly interesting is the high register of the trombone line—as in Raimundo Valenzuela's style—which also often doubles or takes over the melodic lead from the cornet in a virtuosic fashion. Structurally, "Carta Clara" follows the same format as its Cuban counterparts, including an advertisement in the final section; however, it introduces some stylistic variations. While the voice dominates throughout the final section of Cuban danzones, pieces from the Yucatán have a final section divided into two parts: first the vocal jingle, then a purely instrumental segment. In "Carta Clara," the vocal line extends over the first sixteen measures in the danzón's initial key, D minor, followed by a livelier sixteen-measure melody in D major that concludes the piece. The poetic images in "Carta Clara," however cliché, reflect the impact of modernista poetry on Mexican popular music, as seen in Concha's advice *"cuando la vida con su*

---

139. A copy of "El Favorito" is also reprinted in León, *Del canto y el tiempo*, 253–54. León does not offer a date for this work either, but the fact that it is a three-part danzón in a decade when dancers began favoring longer multi-sectional danzones suggests it may have been composed in the early rather than late 1890s.

140. The repertoire of Orquesta Concha, for instance, one of the most popular danzón bands in Mexico at the time, included many such pieces in its repertoire: "Chocolate La Espiga," "Ytzá," "La bombilla del Meco," "Nacionales de Grajales," "Su majestad El Pizá," and "Habanero Pizá," all by José A. Castilla. They advertise everything from beer and sherry to shirts, chocolate, and cigars. These danzones are part of the Concha Brothers Archive at the Centro Regional de Investigación, Difusión e Información "Gerónimo Baqueiro Foster" in Mérida, Yucatán. One could classify the manuscripts in two groups. The first includes danzones copied on older paper and written in elaborate calligraphy; the second is copied on better quality paper and shows a more standard calligraphy, implying the compositions are more recent. Most of the commercial danzones belong to the second batch, which probably means they were part of the band's repertory prior to their relocation to Mexico City in 1924. Enrique Bryon, a Cuban bandleader who lived in Mérida in 1922, recorded many of them in New York for the OKeh label in September 1923. See Ross Laird and Brian Rust, *Discography of OKeh Records, 1918–1934* (Westport, CT: Greenwood, 2004), 249.

inclemencia / hiera de tu alma la rosa rara / cura tus penas con Carta Clara" ("when life with its inclemency / hurts the rare rose of your soul / cure your sorrows with Carta Clara").[141] Bandleaders also composed noncommercial vocal danzones with lyrics in the final section. In 1910, Antonio María Romeu released "El cometa Halley" (❷ Score 2.9), a waggish and clever tune based on the scare the world went through that year due to the passing of Halley's comet. Eliseo Grenet's (1893–1950) "La mora" (The Moorish Woman, 1918) is arguably the most famous sung danzón in this style. (❷ Score 2.10)

In the 1920s, with the bolero an increasingly fashionable form of sentimental song and the danzón at its apogee as a dance style, many composers and arrangers began to combine them. Given the binary form of the bolero (AB), quite different from the danzón's, one of the first ways to reconcile them was to frame both sections of the bolero with a refrain and transform its structure into a rondo. Guty Cárdenas (1905–1932), one of the first superstars of Mexican music, made his bolero "Quisiera" (I Would Like) into a danzón this way and recorded it in New York with the Orquesta Típica Criolla in 1928. His danzón has an ABACAD structure in which the two themes of the bolero become sections B and C. The danzón's A section features the cinquillo clave pattern prominently. Section B features vocals throughout, while C includes an eight-measure instrumental introduction before the singer's entrance. The fact that the melody of "Quisiera" existed first as a bolero makes it harmonically richer than standard danzón tunes, with multiple internal modulations between and within song segments. The last part (D) is a longer, thirty-four-measure instrumental section divided into two parts. The first sixteen bars feature the bolero melody on various instruments including trombone, cornet, and violin. The last eighteen bars consist of a repeated vamp played by the complete orchestra in tutti.

Danzón fans consider Aniceto Díaz's "Rompiendo la rutina" the first danzonete, premiered by Pablo Quevedo at the Casino Español of Matanzas in 1929.[142] However, more than creating a new style, "Rompiendo la rutina" merely formalized and extended the growing interest in vocal danzones, including those influenced by the *son*. In essence, what characterizes the danzonete is not the presence of vocals or a montuno section—these features had already been present in the danzón—but rather its strict formal organization and the use of call-and-response vocal techniques in the montuno, similar to those employed by *son* singers. Sometimes vocals were performed between soloist and orchestra, sometimes between soloist and chorus. Danzonetes abandon the standard rondo form of the danzón; an eight-bar A section is played without the usual repeat and returns only between sections B and C, not

---

141. *Modernismo* is considered the first truly influential Latin American literary movement, flourishing from the end of the nineteenth century until the 1910s. The kinds of images used in "Carta Clara" are typical of the movement, primarily because of its aesthetic of melancholy ("la vida con su inclemencia") and choice of words ("de tu alma la rosa rara"). For a discussion of the influence of modernismo on popular music in 1920s Mexico, see Alejandro L. Madrid, *Music in Mexico. Experiencing Music, Expressing Culture* (New York: Oxford University Press, 2012), 41–46 and 49–50.

142. Rodríguez Domínguez, *Iconografía*, 160–62.

between C and D.[143] Based on the cinquillo clave, the A section is the only portion of the danzonete that features this rhythm; later segments adopt *son* clave.[144] The B section usually consists of a thirty-two-bar instrumental segment created with two distinct sixteen-measure phrases. The C section consists of a repeated sixteen-measure melody, the first time played by the orchestra, the second time sung. Section C transitions to the estribillo (the montuno-like D section) through a brief bridge that increases the tempo of the music; here, the singer repeats a melodic phrase (often with improvised lyrics) in response to a second melody played by the orchestra or sung by a chorus. Repeated ad libitum, the estribillo provides a space for improvisation and musical exchange between singers and musicians, giving the pieces almost a guaracha-like quality as they conclude.[145] The popularity of the danzonete was rather brief even within Cuba, and it also failed to gain widespread support in Mexico. However, many famous artists sang danzonetes for a time including Fernando Collazo, Joseíto Fernández, Frank "Machito" Grillo, Tata Pereira, Pablo Quevedo, and Paulina Álvarez (Fig. 2.7), known as the Empress of Danzonete.[146]

Another type of sung danzón emerged in the late 1930s as the popularity of danzonete waned: the so-called danzón cantado. This style departed from rondo form even further. Composers included an instrumental introduction conforming to the standard A section of a danzón—a repeated eight-bar phrase with prominent cinquillos, ending with a cadential break—but then avoided repeating it as a refrain, even as they maintained the cinquillo accompaniment throughout the rest of the song. This typically resulted in an ABC form with internal repeats in the B and C vocal sections but with no montuno. In most cases these "danzonized" boleros, guarachas, or sones bear only a tangential formal resemblance to earlier danzones, but fans and musicians alike still consider them part of the repertoire. The wildly popular singer Barbarito Diez recorded precisely this sort of music, frequently accompanied by the

143. This formal organization has its variants, but always avoids rondo form. For example, Rodrigo Prats's "Pensamiento," follows an ABCAD structure.

144. *Son* clave consists of the tresillo pattern (notated in ex. 2.1) played in alternation with two quarter notes on beats 2 and 3 of the next measure. Radamés Giro quotes Aniceto Díaz in describing some of the basic stylistic features of the danzonete and mentions the lack of cinquillo in sections other than A. This makes the B section of danzonetes more like the B section of Mexican danzones, since they also replace the cinquillo with the *son* clave pattern. See Radamés Giro, "Danzonete," *Diccionario enciclopédico de la música cubana*, Vol. 2, 9–10.

145. This is evident in the final section of danzonetes like Aniceto Díaz's "Rompiendo la rutina" and "Son igual que el cocodrilo," as well as Rodrigo Prats's "Pensamiento."

146. Releases such as *La emperatriz del danzón* (EGREM CD 0048, 1993) make clear that Alvarez's later repertoire was extremely varied and heavily influenced by jazz, cha cha chá, boleros, guaguancó, and other genres. This may have been due to arrangements created by the Tropicana house band where she performed for extended periods. Díaz Ayala ("La invencible charanga," 301) notes that the popularity of the danzonete represented one of the few moments of danzón history in which women played a fairly prominent role. The all-female Orquesta Edén Habanero featuring singer Rosario Martínez, for instance, specialized in danzones and danzonetes. See also Raimundo Rodríguez, "El danzón en el cincuentenario de la muerte de Miguel Faílde," *Granma* 7, no. 230 (Saturday, September 25, 1971), 2.

Figure 2.7: Paulina Álvarez, "The Empress of Danzonete" and Everardo Ordaz, pianist and director of her orchestra. Photo courtesy of Museo Nacional de la Música Cubana, Havana.

Antonio Romeu orchestra (see Fig. 2.5), and became known as La Voz del Danzón (The Voice of the Danzón).

An analysis of the wide variety of sung danzones between 1890 and 1950 belies the notion that even this variant had a monolithic musical style. Instead, composers, dancers, and listeners continuously resignified it in the early twentieth century, making it meaningful in a number of different emotional, affective, and commercial contexts, and constantly experimented with new formal structures.

DANZONES DE NUEVO RITMO, DANZONES-CHÁ, AND DANZONES DE NUEVO TIPO

Flautist, composer, and bandleader Antonio Arcaño (1911–1994) looms large as an influential performer during the danzón's final decades of widespread popularity in Cuba. Along with Antonio María Romeu, he continued to play instrumental danzones long after vocal versions became the norm. Arcaño and his band members added new rhythmic, harmonic, and orchestrational elements to the *son*-influenced danzones that became known as *danzones de nuevo ritmo* or *danzones-mambo*. The repertoire influenced generations of performers thereafter and has become the standard for danzones performed by Cuban dance bands today.

Figure 2.8: Arcaño y sus Maravillas, ca. 1940. Photo courtesy of Museo Nacional de la Música Cubana, Havana.

Arcaño began playing music as a teenager to support his family.[147] In 1935 he joined danzonete singer Fernando Collazo's "Maravilla del Siglo" orchestra, performing alongside classical violinist Virgilio Diago and established pianist Ricardo Reverón. In 1937, Arcaño formed his own ensemble, Arcaño y sus Maravillas (Fig. 2.8), consisting of influential instrumentalists such as Israel "Cachao" López on bass, his brother Orestes López on piano, and violinists Félix Reina and Enrique Jorrín. The group often performed with an extended string section consisting of three or more violins, cello, and bass, a format later adopted by others.[148] Arcaño's Maravillas enjoyed popularity across racial and class lines; their fame increased as the result of regular shows on the Mil Diez radio station in between 1943 and 1948.

The repertoire of Arcaño's orchestra represents a heterogeneous mix of the old and new. Structurally, some pieces such as "Como pasaron los años" follow the truncated ABAC structure of danzones described earlier. This piece has an eight-measure introduction featuring motives from Beethoven's fifth Symphony. The lyrical B section includes an introductory melody as well as the A and B themes from "As Time Goes By" (44mm. total) before transitioning to an extended montuno. Other danzones interpreted by Arcaño, such as Félix Reyna's "Angoa,"[149] include three principal themes in rondo form before a segue to the montuno, resulting in a more traditional

147. Arcaño interview; Antonio Romero and Mauricio Saez, "Antonio Arcaño . . . El danzonero mayor," *Tropicana Magazine*, no. 5 (1997), 46–48.
148. López-Nusia, "Contrapunto, polémica y danzon: habla Odilio Urfé." *Bohemia* Vol. 68 No. 43 (29 October 1976), 10-12.
149. This piece takes its name from a well-known danzón dancer, Ricardo Benedit Varela "Angoa" (1909–2009).

ABACAD structure. The majority of the band's danzones conform to one of these two formats, including classics like "Arcaño y su nuevo ritmo," "Doña Olga," "Rapsodia en azul," or "Permanganato." Other pieces, such as Orestes López's "Goza mi mambo," consist entirely of an improvisatory jam over a montuno vamp, complete with chorus vocals, and are devoid of any stylistic reference to the danzón.[150] Danzones of this sort are often referred to as danzones-mambo and influenced the rhythmic structure of the danzón-chá that bands like Orquesta Aragón popularized in the 1950s. Practitioners often use the terms danzón de nuevo ritmo, danzón-mambo, and danzón-chá interchangeably although they are not precisely the same. The danzón-mambo is essentially a variant of the danzón de nuevo ritmo born out of musical effervescence within Arcaño's band, foregrounding the use of ostinato. Danzón-chá represents a fusion of the danzón de nuevo ritmo and cha cha chá, as explained later.

In addition to its formal innovations, danzón repertoire as performed by Arcaño's orchestra features a more daring harmonic vocabulary that often incorporates intervals of ninths and elevenths, cuartal harmonies, diminished chords, melodies in parallel motion, and the use of pentatonic and whole-tone scales that resemble contemporary classical and jazz music practice.[151] The ensemble's recordings typically include a final montuno section that is stylistically different from those in previous danzón repertoire. Yet they are similar to many other experiments among mid-twentieth-century Cuban musicians that foregrounded elements derived from West African heritage such as open-ended, cyclical musical form; layered, polyphonic instrumental and/or vocal melodies; and ostinato patterns repeated in variation.[152] Montunos in Arcaño's repertoire feature a strong rhythmic drive created by the timbales, güiro, and congas. When performed within the truncated danzón format, the montunos tend to be played at a slightly slower tempo, which makes them sound like cha cha chás; when performed by themselves, as in the case of danzones-mambo, they are played faster.

Arcaño added the conga to his ensemble about 1940, an instrument previously considered uncouth and associated only with street rumba and carnival music. The conga drum usually remained silent during the initial A theme, played a bolero-like pattern during the B theme to accompany its lyrical melody, dropped out for the repeat of A, and then entered with a *son*-derived *tumbao* pattern to accompany improvisations in the montuno.[153] Arcaño's arrangements emphasized extended solos on flute and other instruments during the montuno, more than had been the case in earlier bands. Other compositional features as manifested in Orestes López's

150. These tracks can be heard in the compilation *Arcaño y sus Maravillas. Grandes Orquestas Cubanas*. Areíto CD 0034. Havana: EGREM, 1992.

151. Dora Ileana Torres, "Del danzón cantado," 200–204.

152. Robin Moore, *Music and Revolution. Cultural Change in Socialist Cuba* (Berkeley: University of California Press, 2006), 46–51. The text includes background on the varied meanings and uses of the term "mambo," as well as discussing mambo compositions in various styles.

153. Fidel Ortiz Chibás, percussionist of the Orquesta Guillermo Rubalcaba, personal interview, Havana, Cuba, December 5, 2011. For transcriptions of typical tumbao patterns on the conga, see Ex. 2.21.

well-known "Mambo" from the 1930s[154] include syncopated piano and violin ostinato patterns (*guajeos*) that repeat throughout much of the montuno, outlining two–three *son*-clave; two-measure claved bass patterns that first rise a fifth, then fall an octave; relatively static harmonies; interlocking, polyphonic chorus phrases, similar to the patterns of instrumental and percussion lines; and modal solo flute melodies emphasizing a raised fourth or flattened third (see Ex. 2.21).[155]

Percussion patterns associated with the montuno of the danzones de nuevo ritmo tend to be relatively straight, providing a foundation upon which the syncopated vocal and instrumental lines notated above generate rhythmic tension. Both the güiro and the bell on the timbales mark straight time with an emphasis on strong beats. The conga plays on almost every eighth note, marking beats two and four of the 4/4 measure with slaps and open tones. The free hand of the paila/timbales player (not being used to play the bell) play barely audible open and closed tones on the head with the finger tips, coinciding on beat 4 with the conga's open tone and helping the two players stay locked rhythmically.

In the early 1950s, Enrique Jorrín left Arcaño to join the Orquesta América. It was within this band that he first popularized the cha cha chá, a style that developed out of experiments with the danzón de nuevo ritmo. The cha cha chá takes its name onomatopoeically from the rhythmic pattern of the güiro and modern timbales in the montuno section of danzones de nuevo ritmo (Ex. 2.22), and from the shuffle-step patterns employed by dancers. Musically, the cha cha chá is similar to the montuno section of the danzón mambo, although it is usually played more slowly and includes an extended vocal that frames or introduces the final instrumental/improvisatory section. Similarly to Orestes López's "Goza mi mambo," the cha cha chá avoids any overt reference to the danzón by omitting the cinquillo. Instead, it foregrounds rhythms associated with the montuno section throughout.

The popularization of the cha cha chá in the 1950s generated yet another hybrid, the danzón-chá. In practice, the latter is very similar to the cha cha chá but includes an introductory A section typical of the danzón, a lyrical, usually vocalized B section, and a montuno (C) in cha cha chá style with brief, repeated vocal phrases. The danzón-like A section is heard only once and not used as a refrain, similar to the danzón cantado. Every so often, danzones in this style segue directly from the A section to the montuno and do not include a lyrical B segment. In the 1950s, the Orquesta Aragón recorded many danzones-chá; their repertoire included re-makes of older danzones like "Almendra," "Angoa," and "Tres lindas cubanas" as well as newly composed danzones-chá like Electo "Chepín" Rosell's "Bodas de oro" and "La reina

154. Odilio Urfé believed the piece was written in 1935, though other sources mention later dates. See Urfé, "Danzón, mambo y cha-cha-chá," 57.

155. Sue Miller, electronic communication. March 8, 2012. Thanks to Miller for her transcription of Orestes López's "Mambo," Exs. 2.21 and 2.22, based on the 1951 recording of the piece. On many contemporary recordings of "Mambo," bands play the first part of the A section and move directly into the montuno (C section in the original score), thus making it into an AB form. The original version of the score suggests an ABAC form, however, the kind of truncated rondo form discussed by Arcaño. For a recording of the complete piece, see Alberto Corrales y su Orquesta Panorama, *Danzoneando*. Cinquillo CD 123. Havana: Colibrí, 2006.

Example 2.21: Orestes López, "Mambo." Ostinato figures associated with the montuno section. Transcription courtesy of Sue Miller.

Isabel." Rosell's danzones-chá feature an introductory A section divided into two eight-measure subsections; the first features the rhythmic accompaniment of the cha cha chá while the second features the danzón's typical cinquillo cadence.

Julio Valdés also recorded danzones-chá, although they vary significantly from those of the Orquesta Aragón. Valdés's danzones-chá are based on the juxtaposition of two previously composed songs (I and II) organized as follows, A-B-bridge-C-B-(D), where song I appears in section B and song II in section C. The A theme is similar to the A section of danzones-chá employed by the Orquesta Aragón; a final D-section montuno may or may not be included. Valdés's danzones-chá are vocal pieces; segment I usually consists of a short melody while II tends to be a longer bolero melody. Valdés

Example 2.22: López, "Mambo." Percussion patterns associated with the montuno section. In the conga line, P = palm, F = fingers, S = slap, O = open tone. Transcription courtesy of Sue Miller.

uses fragments from pieces like "Caimitillo y marañón" ("Caimitillo and Cashew Fruit"), "El gallo solterón" ("The Unmarried Rooster"), or "El tín marín" ("Eeny, Meeny, Miny, Moe") in the B sections, and boleros like "Cobarde" ("Coward"), "Boda gris" ("Gray Wedding") or "Te las sabes todas" ("You Know All of Them") in the C sections.

At the end of the 1950s and during the early 1960s, Israel "Cachao" López continued composing the kinds of truncated danzones without refrain that the Orquesta Aragón had popularized. López's pieces were multi-section danzones, longer than those recorded by the Aragón (with more sections and expanded improvised solos, ABCD), but maintained the through-composed format and the emphasis on the montuno section. "Año del 61" is a noteworthy example in this style that includes a refrain in the montuno section praising the literacy campaign instigated that year by the revolutionary regime. Some musicians refer to such pieces as *danzones de nuevo tipo*;[156] they may represent the last important structural transformation of the danzón.

Danzones-chá became popular in Mexico due to the influence of Cuban musicians like Enrique Jorrín who lived there between 1954 and 1958; Mariano Mercerón (1907–1975), who made multiple trips to Mexico beginning in 1945; and Arturo Núñez "El Caballero Antillano" ("The Gentleman of the Antilles," 1913–1981), who also settled in Mexico in the 1950s. Mexican musicians soon adopted the new style; Carlos Campos's danzones-chá combined the lush, saxophone-dominated, big-band sound of mid-century Mexican danzoneras with percussion that emphasized the cinquillo during the refrain and the cha cha chá rhythm during the rest of the piece. Campos's danzones-chá are purely instrumental and (unlike Cuban pieces) retain an ABACAD rondo form as heard in his rendition of "Ojos tapatíos" ("Eyes of Guadalajara") and "Lamento borincano" ("Puerto Rican Lament")[157] This format and repertory influenced the development of Mexican *música tropical* (consisting primarily of guaracha-like pieces and cumbia) beginning in the late 1950s as represented in the repertoire of bands like Sonora Santanera.[158]

156. Francisco Ulloa, personal interview, Santiago de Cuba, Cuba, December 6, 2011.
157. These tracks can be heard in Carlos Campos, *Danzones melódicos*. Musart 1930, 1998.
158. A popular legend among Mexican danzoneros argues that Sonora Santanera's most popular música tropical hit, "La boa" (1960), is based on a riff from the vocal montuno in Orquesta Aragón's version of Felix Reyna's danzón de nuevo ritmo "Angoa."

PLAYING DIFFERENCE IN THE DANZÓN

Beyond distinct approaches to form and instrumentation, the non-notated aspects of danzón performance—such as attitudes toward improvisation or techniques employed on percussion instruments—create important differences between the sound of Cuban and Mexican danzones. As explained in Chapter 4, Mexican danzoneras for many years appear to have avoided improvisation, with a few exceptions, like the Orquesta Concha; also, they often (although not always) avoid repeating the A section, which has affected the development of Mexican dance choreography, as described in Chapter 6. However, even more central stylistic disparities between Mexican and Cuban performance practice relate to conceptions of rhythm and to specific rhythmic patterns. For instance, while Cuban musicians understand the cinquillo as an embellished version of the Cuban tresillo (see Ex. 2.1) and cinquillo clave a variant of son clave, Mexican musicians generally conceive of the cinquillo and tresillo as independent rhythms.[159] Thus, Cuban musicians rarely play the tresillo pattern during danzones. On the other hand, Mexicans feature it prominently during the B section of their repertoire, with the güiro player usually switching instruments and playing it on the claves. This is one of the many differences in rhythmic conceptualization that inform Cuban and Mexican danzón performance, the most salient being the understanding of overall rhythmic flow: while Cubans are said to play al aire ("in the air," in a syncopated style emphasizing the upbeat), Mexicans play a tierra ("on the ground" on the downbeat).[160] This not only affects the music; it also influences dancing styles, as discussed in Chapter 6.

The marcha—the cinquillo-based percussion continuo associated with all danzones—makes evident the most important differences between Mexican and Cuban styles of interpretation. The marcha is never notated in danzón scores, yet this rhythmic base, created between the güiro and the timbales, constitutes a central element of performance. Cuban percussionists use two basic forms of the cinquillo clave[161]

159. Hipólito González Peña, timbalero with Danzonera Acerina, suggests that only following the salsa craze of the late 1970s did Mexican musicians realize the close relationship between the cinquillo and the son claves. Hipólito González Peña, personal interview, Mexico City, February 22, 2009.

160. Gonzalo Romeu, who has played danzones with Cuban and Mexican musicians alike, describes the different styles using these terms. Gonzalo Romeu, personal interview, Mexico City, Mexico, September 26, 2011.

161. Descriptions of performance style reflect discussions with Juan Pereira and Carlos Manuel Ruiz Verrier, timbal and güiro players of the Piquete Típico Cubano; Hipólito González Peña, timbalero of Danzonera Acerina; and Marcela Pérez Abreu, güiro player for Gonzalo Romeu's ensemble. Juan Pereira and Carlos Manuel Ruiz Verrier, personal interview, Havana, Cuba, April 3, 2009; Hipólito González Peña, personal interview, Mexico City, Mexico, February 22, 2009; and Marcela Pérez Abreu, telephone interview, October 5, 2011. The assertions of all musicians mentioned were corroborated by historical recordings from the 1910s and 1920s, historically informed recordings by Odilio Urfé's Charanga Típica Nacional from the 1960s and 1970s, and more contemporary recordings by Mexican danzoneras and Cuban charangas.

during the initial paseo or A section.[162] During the first four measures they employ a pattern consisting of a cinquillo (simple or embellished) performed on the larger *hembra* (female) timbal head followed by four eighth notes performed in alternation on the hembra head, macho head, hembra rim, and hembra head (Ex. 2.23).[163] The güiro accompaniment over the same measures consists of a straight cinquillo followed by four eighth notes.

During the last four measures of the A section, Cuban musicians use a *redoble* or variation of the basic cinquillo. This pattern features an embellished cinquillo played on the hembra head in the first measure followed in the second by an amphibrach and two eighth notes played over the macho and hembra heads in a prescribed order. In measure three, performers repeat the cinquillo pattern and end with a cadence on two eighth notes played on the timbales' macho head. In most cases, the rhythms of the four-measure sequence coincide with the rhythm of the danzón's melody. As usual, the güiro pattern mirrors the pattern of the timbales (Ex. 2.24).[164]

During trio/otras sections, Cuban percussionists play variations of the two-measure cinquillo clave pattern. The orientation of the sequence (either a cinquillo followed by four eighth notes or vice versa) is determined by the rhythm of the main melody. Percussionists coordinate their marcha with the melody, avoiding *atravesado/cruzado* (crossed) playing in which the cinquillos of the marcha do not align with those in the melody. Most typically, the timbales play the first half of their standard pattern exclusively on the hembra: a sixteenth note on the rim followed by three sixteenth-note strokes on the head, another sixteenth note on the rim of the hembra and one eight note on the head (Ex. 2.25). The second measure features four eighth notes played in standard fashion as notated in m. 2 of Example 2.23. As before, the güiro player imitates the timbales.

During lyrical trios, the güiro player often shifts from scraping the instrument to hitting it softly on the side in order to keep the volume of the percussion down, yet its patterns remain the same. Historical recordings suggest many variations to the marcha as played by the güiro and timbales, including elaborations of the standard cinquillo clave (see Ex. 2.25). The permutations are endless; Example 2.26, provides a few other examples.[165]

Once percussionists choose to play a particular variation, they generally continue it throughout a given section of the piece. Minor rhythmic shifts between sections

162. As noted earlier, many Cuban musicians and dancers refer to the repeated A section as the paseo since dancers do not dance but rather walk around the dance floor while it is played.

163. Performance on the shell of the drum in addition to the head appears to be a directly African-derived trait. See Ortiz, *Los instrumentos*, Vol. III, 304.

164. Contemporary orquesta típicas such as the Piquete Típico Cubano execute the marcha in this manner; however, historical recordings usually include a final sequence that avoids the amphibrach and eighth-note pattern in measure two and instead features three repeated cinquillos before the cadence at the end of the A section.

165. Variants A and B appear frequently in the 1907 and 1911 recordings of Felipe Valdés's orchestra; C and E are used by Enrique Peña in his 1909 and 1918 recordings; Tata Pereira uses D in his 1924 recording of "Linda cubana."

Example 2.23: Basic Cuban marcha pattern in the first part of the A section. The cross over a notehead denotes a rim shot on the timbal. Lower and higher notes on the timbales denote shifts between the macho and hembra heads.

Example 2.24: Basic Cuban redoble pattern as performed during the second part of the A section.

Example 2.25: Basic marcha pattern during trio/otra sections. The cross indicates a rim shot.

Example 2.26: Cuban marcha variations played on the güiro and timbales during trio/otra sections.

are common in orquestas típicas as well as charangas, although the latter usually feature a smaller range of rhythms. Variations of the cinquillo often appear in the first half of sections B and C, for instance, while the second half usually includes only the unembellished cinquillo clave pattern.

In recordings from the 1920s and 1930s by both orquesta típicas and charangas, one often hears variations of the cinquillo clave even in the montuno. However, following the popularization of danzones de nuevo ritmo most bands chose to accompany the montuno with cha cha chá rhythms, even when playing older pieces. In this style, the güiro employs the pattern notated in Example 2.22, establishing the basic groove and allowing the timbalero to improvise as appropriate.

The realization of the marcha in Mexican danzón diverges significantly from Cuban practice, as mentioned. *Son* clave appears prominently in Mexican danzón recordings as early as 1910, for instance; the Orquesta Babuco's "El premio gordo" from that

Example 2.27: Cáscara-based realization of the marcha in the montuno section. The "o" denotes a technique referred to as *sobando el parche* ("fingering the drum head"), a time-keeping technique that creates a barely audible sound. The macho line is played on the head of the drum.

year superimposes tresillo- and cinquillo-style patterns in both its trios. By the mid-1920s and early 1930s, Mexican orchestras begin to abandon güiro altogether in B or C sections (usually in the section featuring the danzón's main melody) and even the timbales, leaving the percussive foundation to the unaccompanied claves. Another typical trait in Mexican danzón performance is the use of a full two-measure cinquillo clave pattern (sometimes in variation) played over the final redoble portion of the A section instead of the continuous measure-long cinquillo figures or the pattern (notated in Ex. 2.24) preferred by Cubans.[166]

As in the Cuban marcha, the montuno section of Mexican danzones is based on the cha cha chá rhythm notated in Example 2.22. However, instead of maintaining it throughout the section, Mexican musicians tend to combine it with variants of the cinquillo (such as in transcription C of Ex. 2.26) or simply alter it by mirroring the rhythmic pattern of the main melody. Example 2.27 notates one of Acerina's favorite realizations of the montuno marcha based on the *cáscara* (shell) pattern, derived from Cuban rumba guaguancó.[167]

If the use of rhythmic patterns distinguishes the sound of Mexican and Cuban danzones, the technique of playing percussion instruments—especially the güiro—also differentiates the two styles. For instance, Mexican *güireros* often play the montuno's cha cha chá pattern in a sharp and defined manner, distinct from the less pronounced attack of Cuban musicians. This results from a difference in technique; while Mexican musicians scrape the güiro with a sharp motion of the right hand down the instrument, Cuban musicians assist the right hand by moving the güiro with the left hand in the opposite direction at the same time.[168] This produces a stroke with a less acute attack, and one that lasts longer instead of dying away quickly. The timbral difference produced by the two methods allows many listeners to distinguish immediately between Cuban or Mexican percussionists.

166. Note that while this pattern is standard, some Mexican orchestras also use the triple cinquillo during the redoble. Recordings by Acerina y su Danzonera occasionally feature this pattern, and the more contemporary Orquesta Monstruo de Angel "Chino" Flores uses it almost exclusively.

167. Thanks to Hipólito González Peña for providing this information as well as a sketch of the music notation. González Peña, personal interview.

168. Pérez Abreu, telephone interview.

GENRE, PERFORMANCE, AND THE DANZÓN

As discussed in Chapter 1, musicologists since at least the 1960s have been concerned with notions of genre as they pertain to the danzón and related Latin American musics. Argeliers León initiated the most influential discussion of genre complexes in Cuba with his publication *Música folklórica cubana* (1964), subsequently reprinted as *Del canto y el tiempo*.[169] The concept remains potentially useful, but often obscures relationships between genres not recognized as part of a given complex. More important, an over-focus on genre leads researchers to deemphasize music as lived social practice and the creative ways musicians and listeners themselves move fluidly between such conceptual divisions. Leonardo Acosta notes that some styles of music associated with the so-called danzón complex (such as the contradanza and cha cha chá) have virtually nothing in common with one another musically, and any notion that they belong to a discrete group must be questioned.[170] Of course, it is not exlusively through the analysis of form and style that such connections can effectively be drawn, but also through an exploration of how music and dance have been used, modified, and discussed by social actors themselves through time.

Distinct styles of performance contribute to a definition of the danzón as social practice and deserve further exploration in multiple contexts; composers, performers, dancers, and listeners alike have developed clearly defined notions of what the danzón is that transcend discourses of form or instrumentation found in musicological writings. Thinking of the danzón as an affective cultural space in continuous negotiation instead of as a fixed genre emphasizes the multiplicity of connections that have reconfigured and made it meaningful throughout its history. From musicians' intimate ties to the danzón's sounds and rhythms, to the memories tied to particular performance spaces, to the romantic networks the dance floor promotes, to the passion of danzón collectors and aficionados, social practice extends the danzón's meanings beyond the typological constraints of musicology. Affect surrounding the danzón informs how fans come to understand and love the music, and how they see themselves in relation to their surroundings. The danzón's stylistic and formal developments from the mid-nineteenth century through the 1950s resulted from constant dialogues between practitioners across class, ethnic, race, and gender divides. Subsequent chapters explore specific aspects of the danzón's history, circulation, and practice, as well as its power to set into motion a variety of performative behaviors.

---

169. See for instance mention of the "expressive *son* complex" in León, *Del canto y el tiempo*, 144, and commentary in Jesús Gómez Cairo, "Acerca de la interacción de géneros en la música popular de Cuba," *Boletín Música* no. 83–84 (1980), 19–30.

170. Leonardo Acosta, "On Generic Complexes and Other Topics in Cuban Popular Music," *Journal of Popular Music Studies* 17 (2005), 227–54. Translated by Raúl Fernández and Daniel S. Whitesell with an introduction by Raúl Fernández.

CHAPTER 3
Race, Morality, and the Circulation of Danzón, 1870–1940

The danzón is a site in which notions of race and gender have intersected with national imaginaries, producing radically different meanings at particular historical moments. Discursive and ideological shifts surrounding the danzón in Cuba involved movement away from initial associations with African influences and toward association with shared national heritage. Following the music's acceptance by diverse audiences in the 1880s and beyond, critics rhetorically refashioned it as either "white" or as a racially unmarked and implicitly hybrid form in which European elements were presumed to predominate. In Mexico the process was similar, at least as of the 1910s after it gained popularity in major urban centers. Danzón history shares certain characteristics in this sense with that of the banjo and rock music in the United States, or with the marimba in Central America, instruments and forms that have lost their associations with their Afro-diasporic origins owing to the active shaping or erasure of local histories.[1]

Similar processes are evident throughout Latin America at the turn of the twentieth century, a period closely associated with the formulation of new nationalist projects and symbols. Discourses surrounding the Puerto Rican *danza*, Argentine tango, and Colombian *bambuco*, for instance, all demonstrate elite concern over the influence of Afro-descendant culture on national expression. In Puerto Rico, Frances Aparicio suggests that aspects of the danza's structure and texture have been ignored or overlooked as part of "systematic efforts to whitewash African-derived elements

---

1. To reference a few sources related to only one of these debates, Guatemalan musicologists who have denied the African origins of the marimba in the past and asserted its origins among Maya groups include David Vela in *La marimba; estudio sobre el instrumento nacional* (Guatemala City: Editorial José de Pineda Ibarra, Ministerio de Educación Pública, 1962); Marcial Armas Lara in *Origen de la marimba, su desenvolvimiento y otros instrumentos músicos* (Guatemala City: National Government Publication, 1970); and the opinions of various authors reprinted in Mariano López Mayorical, ed., *La polémica de "La Marimba": el poema más discutido de todas los tiempos, consagrado antes de llegar al bronce esculpido en monumento* (Guatemala City: Editorial José de Piñeda Ibarra, 1978).

from Puerto Rico's social imaginary."[2] In Argentina, Marilyn Miller discusses the forced displacement of black tango and milonga performers from Buenos Aires in the second half of the twentieth century. She notes that white musicians and dancers eventually began to impersonate black artists in a form of blackface involving "recognition of the racial other and the absorption of that otherness into dominant forms of ontology."[3] In Colombia, Ana María Ochoa explains that the bambuco's appropriation by elites at the end of the nineteenth century also involved an effort to reject its African origins. Critics rhetorically "creolized" and "purified" the genre in order to create a national dance acceptable to the white and educated.[4]

In nineteenth-century Cuba, the danzón had unambiguously black and thus frequently negative associations. Between 1878 and about 1890, newspapers and magazines carried a surprising number of articles about the music and dance, the majority of them critical in the extreme.[5] Such writings reflected an unease on the part of elites with public dances as sites of cultural and racial mixing, as had been the case for decades. But the attacks became especially heated because of the danzón's popularization during the second decade of the Wars of Independence against Spain, a moment in which white fear of black armed rebellion led to heightened concern over the influence of all things Afro-Cuban. Racialized debates surrounding the music did not represent an isolated phenomenon, therefore, but emerged out of a more generalized fear, often fueled by Spanish war propaganda. In the early twentieth century, by contrast, with the conflict over and as elite whites attempted to retain social privilege while avoiding discussions of discrimination, the topic of race largely disappeared from public discourse. At the same time, references to the danzón's associations with the black community also disappeared.

In fin-de-siècle Mexico, after early acceptance by the bourgeoisie as a dance linked to Cuban exile communities, the danzón also came to be associated with stylized and hyper-sensualized black heritage due to the growing presence of Afro-Cuban musicians, dancers, and blackface theater troupes. Following the Mexican Revolution (1910–1921), working-class Mexican migrants who moved to the capital adopted the dance and refashioned it as a symbol of urban cosmopolitanism and modernity. The continuous flow of Cuban music and musicians to Mexico in the mid-twentieth century and their appearances in popular Mexican *rumbera* films generated new associations between blackness and other Afro-Cuban dance genres like the ballroom rumba, mambo, and cha cha chá. These influences made the danzón seem familiar and tame by contrast. They created an opportunity for local critics to "Mexicanize"

2. Frances R. Aparicio, *Listening to Salsa. Gender, Latino Popular Culture and Puerto Rican Cultures* (Middletown, CT: Wesleyan University Press, 1998), 8.

3. Marilyn Grace Miller, *Rise and Fall of the Cosmic Race. The Cult of Mestizaje in Latin America* (Austin: University of Texas Press, 2004), 94.

4. Ana María Ochoa, "Género, tradición y nación en el bambuco," *A Contratiempo*, no. 9 (1997), 35–44.

5. Various authors, including Osvaldo Castillo Faílde, suggest that the controversy was limited to the early 1880s, but a review of publications even from the early 1890s indicates that negative views of the danzón persisted much longer. See Osvaldo Castillo Faílde, *Miguel Faílde, creador musical del danzón* (Havana: Consejo Nacional de Cultura, 1964).

the danzón over time, and it eventually played a role in post-revolutionary state ide-ologies of mestizo heritage that similarly rendered blackness invisible. The racialized meanings of *mexicanidad* that emerged around danzón performance thus developed at least partially in relationship to and against cultural forms from the Caribbean.

This chapter analyzes shifts in the racialized meanings surrounding the danzón, with special attention to the ways in which discourse about its music and dance aligned with broader racial projects and official pronouncements on national identity. Cuban and Mexican society of the nineteenth and early twentieth centuries shared marked divisions that separated a largely European-descendant middle class and elite from the frequently disenfranchised mixed-race, indigenous, or Afro-descendant masses. In both countries, acceptance of non-European heritage proved central to emergent conceptions of nation in the twentieth century. And yet the ongoing am-bivalence toward non-European (as well as working-class) populations and cultures is evident in the decidedly halting and incremental acceptance of the danzón and popular forms that emerged subsequently.

DANZÓN AND EARLY RACIAL CONTROVERSY IN CUBA

The Cuban revolution against Spain has been described as "unique in the history of the Atlantic world"[6] to the extent that insurgent forces consisted of a racially diverse force and included black and mixed-race soldiers at virtually all levels of command. It is noteworthy that this took place during an era of scientific racism, evolutionist thought, and the rhetorical division of the world into superior and inferior races. Academic literature of fin-de-siècle Cuba drew on the writings of major European intellectuals and philosophers (David Hume, Georg Hegel, Emmanuel Kant) as well as on later works specifically on race by Arthur de Gobineau and others, who depicted Africans as savages incapable of sophisticated thought, dominated by passion, closer to beasts than human beings.[7] Pseudo-scientific studies of phrenology and craniom-etry were practiced assiduously in Cuba as a means of proving black inferiority—for instance, in Henry Joseph Dumont and Israel Castellanos's *Antropología y patología comparadas de los negros esclavos* from 1876. Aline Helg cites similar writings by Fran-cisco Figueras from 1907 and beyond,[8] making it clear that extremely racist views of this nature persisted for some time. The inherent inequality of the races remained unquestioned by dominant Cuban society until at least the 1930s; the only debates regarding race that authors engaged in centered around whether blacks and mixed-race peoples could be civilized over time, given sufficient tutelage by whites. Such views make it clear that the Cuban revolutionary conflict of the nineteenth century

6. Ada Ferrer, *Insurgent Cuba. Race, Nation, and Revolution, 1868–1898* (Chapel Hill: University of North Carolina Press, 1999), 3.
7. Ben Carrington's *Race, Sport, and Politics. The Sporting Black Diaspora* (London: Sage, 2010), 67–68, contains an insightful overview of this topic.
8. Francisco Figueras, *Cuba y su evolución colonial* (Havana: Imprenta Avisador Comercial, 1907).

involved at least as much ideological as physical effort, and they underscore the difficulty war leaders faced in attempting to unify the Cuban population across racial lines. Spanish colonial authorities in Cuba, as might be expected, portrayed themselves not only as guaranteeing prosperity and civilization but as maintaining a social hierarchy that, if dismantled, would result in a race war of epic proportions, as had taken place in Haiti. The revolutionary leadership was compelled to combat such ideas before any military goals could be achieved.

Racial fears among the white Cuban population ensured the fidelity of its citizens to Spain for many years and were only tentatively overcome in 1868. At that time, Carlos Manuel de Céspedes and other white planters famously freed their slaves and then asked them to join the fledgling independence movement in what is now known as the Ten Years War (1868–1878). During the earliest years of rebellion, the overwhelmingly Hispanic insurgent force frequently chose not to give weapons to Cubans of color but instead put them to work digging trenches, cooking, and cleaning.[9] Racial tensions did not surface in the rebel force initially because the limited armed participation of black Cubans in the effort did not threaten existing social hierarchies. Later periods, by contrast, saw the increasing participation of black and mixed-race soldiers. Many came from rural areas and humble origins, or directly from the former slave population. Black and mixed-race insurgent troops, especially, began to free slaves by force to increase their own numbers, often against the wishes of white hacendados.

The growing number of armed rebels of color from the working classes and slave population made a majority of white revolutionaries decidedly uneasy. Beginning in the mid-1870s, white troops began to defect from the war in substantial numbers, in large part for that reason. They often cited a "lack of morality" in the ranks, referring to what they claimed was the tendency of many new recruits to dress in less than full military uniform, bring women into camp to live with them, drink, use informal modes of address, and engage in markedly racialized behavior such as dancing or singing to the accompaniment of drums in the evening. Indeed, photographic evidence even from the final years of revolutionary conflict in the 1890s proves that many insurgents danced and played traditional rumba and related music in the countryside.[10] Spanish authorities fueled racial and class tensions by spreading rumors that black military leaders such as Antonio Maceo and Guillermo Moncada had declared themselves "black emperors," kept white women as concubines, and planned all-out war on the white population. These authorities consistently described black forces as savages or wild animals and characterized insurgents as demographically blacker than they actually were. The result of such effective manipulation of racial fear, in combination with other regional divisions among insurgents, was total capitulation of the white leadership by 1878.[11] For their part, black military leaders

9. Ferrer, *Insurgent Cuba*, 32.
10. Zoila Lapique Becali, *Cuba colonial. Música, compositores e intérpretes, 1570–1902* (Havana: Ediciones Boloña, 2008), 307.
11. Aline Helg, *Our Rightful Share. The Afro-Cuban Struggle for Equality, 1886–1912* (Chapel Hill: University of North Carolina Press, 1995), 48.

of the 1870s were furious at the Pact of Zanjón peace accords signed in 1878 and had no desire to stop fighting. Moncada, Flor Crombet, and others publicly protested the truce; their troops almost immediately initiated another conflict (La Guerra Chiquita, 1879–1880), but failed to gain the support of the white population or to extend the confrontation beyond the far eastern provinces.

This is the highly charged context in which Miguel Faílde and other black bandleaders began performing the danzón, transplanted from the black society ballrooms of Matanzas to white recreational societies on the Western side of the island. The west remained firmly in Spanish hands through the 1890s, and its social life continued unabated after 1880.[12] But the revolutionary campaigns in the east among black and mixed-race insurgents and associated racial fears stoked by Spanish propaganda strongly influenced discourse about the new music. An additional exacerbating factor was the enactment of the Moret Law of 1880, beginning a gradual process of abolition in Cuba that many conservatives opposed and feared. Among other things, it allowed for the greater freedom of movement of black Cubans across the island and into urban areas.[13] As might be expected, the most virulent invective against danzones of the day appeared in conservative, Spanish-controlled newspapers such as *El Diario de la Marina*, *La Aurora del Yumurí*, and *La Voz de Cuba*,[14] as well as in books from the period on Cuban culture and society. During the height of the controversy from the late 1870s through the early 1890s, even some elite black clubs considered banning the music entirely, and many newspapers avoided even printing the word "danzón" in their articles.[15]

It is not inconsequential that music and dance served as the focus of attention of such racialized debates. Many authors emphasize the importance of dance to Cuban society in the nineteenth century, with Havana boasting as many as fifty public dances each night at the turn of the nineteenth century; participants often remained at such events all night, dancing to the point of exhaustion.[16] Dance had long functioned as a point of interracial contact and transgressive behavior, in various senses. Black performers dominated music making and played regularly even in the most exclusive venues beginning in the early 1800s. Over time, Afro-creole versions of European-derived dance music developed an enthusiastic following among local white listeners. Masked events, ubiquitous during carnival season, represented moments in which audiences of various classes and races celebrated together with

12. Dolores María de Ximeno y Cruz, *Memorias de Lola María* (Havana: Letras Cubanas, 1983 [1928]), 202.
13. Jill Lane, *Blackface Cuba, 1840–1895* (Philadelphia: University of Pennsylvania Press, 2005), 161.
14. Castillo Faílde, *Miguel Faílde*, 121.
15. Castillo Faílde, *Miguel Faílde*, 133.
16. Alejo Carpentier, *La música en Cuba* (Mexico City: Fondo de Cultura Económica, 1946),138; Argeliers León, *Del canto y el tiempo* (Havana: Letras Cubanas, 1984), 251; "Gacetillas. Baile y pilitas," *Diario de Matanzas* 2, no. 260 (Thursday, November 6, 1879), 2. Similar references to mixed-race dances in Santiago of the eighteenth century appear in Abelardo Estrada, "Estudio de un libro, su autor, y el ámbito de ambos," Prologue to Laureano Fuentes Matons, *Las artes de Santiago de Cuba* (Havana: Letras Cubanas, 1981 [1893]), 29.

relative impunity.[17] Mixed-race dances appealed strongly to young white men, especially, who enjoyed the libertine environment and the possibility of clandestine trysts they afforded. Music and dance thus created points of strain within a colonial society that justified slavery through the dehumanizing of black subjects and that emphasized the importance of strict divisions between the races. As Ben Carrington notes, "For the colonial racial order to be maintained, and for racial degeneration to be avoided, strict codes of conduct and legal sanctions on sexual practices become necessary to safeguard the imperial project."[18] And in fact, one finds substantial Cuban legislation from mid-nineteenth century Cuba designed to regulate dance activity and keep the races apart in such contexts. Authorities used surveillance, fines, revocation of business licenses, jailing, and other means to enforce racial divisions.[19] Notions of the superiority of European-derived culture and its perceived civilizing force were also central to the colonial project, helping to justify the authority of the state. The broad appeal of the danzón, a dance music closely associated with black Cubans and demonstrating perceptible African-derived influences, conflicted fundamentally with this ideology.[20]

Controversies over the danzón took public outcry over Africanisms in dance music to new heights, but similar criticisms had been voiced in previous decades. Alejo Carpentier cites the newspaper *El Aviso de la Habana* from 1809 characterizing the waltz and contredance as "lascivious" and "diametrically opposed to Christianity."[21] Esteban Pichardo's *Diccionario provincial* from 1836 directly attributes African-derived influences to the danza's music and choreography, noting that Cuban youth swayed voluptuously in their *cedazo* figures "with an African ear and coquettishness."[22] Natalio Galán believes similarly that Cuban contradanza figures were not "walked" as in Europe, but rather danced with short, dragging steps and accompanied by considerable hand and arm movement, all of which commentators of the day ascribed to the influence of the black community. Galán quotes Félix M. Tanco in Matanzas of 1857, who asks "Who doesn't see in the movements of our young men and women when they dance an imitation of the blacks in their *cabildos*? Who is unaware that the basses of the dance bands in our country echo the drums of African

17. De Ximeno y Cruz, *Memorias de Lola María*, 205; Adolfo Dollero, *Cultura cubana. La provincia de Matanzas y su evolución* (Havana: Imprenta Seoane y Fernández, 1919), 115. In *El Fígaro*, references to masked dancing are common as well, e.g., 5, no. 9 (March 17, 1889), 7; or 7, no. 7 (February 28, 1892), 7.

18. Carrington, *Race, Sport, and Politics*, 70.

19. Pilar Egüez Guevara, "Colonial Anxieties over Sex and Race: Regulating 'Public' Spaces and the *escuelitas de baile* in 19th Century Havana." Unpublished manuscript, Center for Latin American and Caribbean Studies, University of Illinois Urbana Champaign, 2008. The author documents such legislation and policing of dance activities beginning in the 1820s through the end of the nineteenth century.

20. Guevara, "Colonial Anxieties"; see also Marial Iglesias Utset, *A Cultural History of Cuba during the U.S. Occupation, 1898–1902*, trans. Russ Davidson (Chapel Hill: University of North Carolina Press, 2011), 56.

21. Carpentier, *La música en Cuba*, 135.

22. Esteban Pichardo, *Diccionario provincial casi razonado de vozes y frases cubanas* (Havana: Editorial de Ciencias Sociales, 1985 [1836]), 223.

tangos?"[23] At least some writers of the 1860s and 1870s continued to criticize the licentious character of the danza with its extended cedazo section and the perceived African influences it had incorporated.[24]

By the same token, the contradanza, danza, and later the danzón slowly developed associations with *cubanía*, local expression, and by extension with the nationalist insurgency against Spain. The contradanza's popularization at the turn of the nineteenth century throughout the Americas coincided with a series of independence movements and had political connotations in many Spanish colonies as a result.[25] Beginning in the 1850s, Cuban danzas began to appear with overtly pro-independence titles; Spanish authorities eventually banned the performance of many of them.[26] If anything, the danzón had even stronger associations with revolution since it emerged in the final decades of the nineteenth century during periods of open warfare. Danzón titles made constant references to aspects of local Cuban experience and many also directly referenced the revolutionary effort.[27] Danzones feted José Martí in the 1880s during his campaigns to organize and fund the Cuban insurrection while based in New York City and featured prominently in the repertoire played by armed rebels themselves for entertainment in the Cuban countryside.[28] Miguel Faílde Pérez (1852–1921) (❸ Picture 3.6) (Fig. 3.1) and other danzón performers collaborated directly with Afro-Cuban insurgent leaders such as Juan Gualberto Gómez and Martín Morúa Delgado. Faílde's danzón "Por nuestra parte sin novedad" took inspiration from Spanish war rhetoric in local newspapers; its controversial reception nearly forced him into exile in 1895.[29]

Faílde, one of the central figures in the popularization of the danzón beyond the black community of Matanzas, played music in that city for many years before his performances began to generate attention. Born to a Galician immigrant father and

23. Natalio Galán, *Cuba y sus sones* (Valencia, Spain: Pre-Textos, 1983), 135. See also page 151 with a quote by Antonio de las Barras y Prado from the early 1860s suggesting that the accompaniment of the danza was perceived as African-influenced: "El compás es el mismo que se tocan los negros con sus tambores e instrumentos para sus bailes grotescos y voluptousos."

24. Anselmo Suárez y Romero, "El baile," in *Artículos de costumbres cubanos del siglo XIX*, ed. Iraida Rodríguez (Havana: Editorial Arte y Literatura, 1974 [1854]), 239–49. See also Zoila Lapique Becali, *Cuba colonial*, 198–99, for commentaries by English observer Samuel Hazard from 1870 who emphasizes the licentiousness of the danza and an article from the Santiago newspaper *El Redactor* in 1862 describing the "Africanized danza" as being incompatible with cultured society.

25. Hilario González, "Manuel Saumell y la contradanza," in Manuel Saumell, *Contradanzas* (Havana: Letras Cubanas, 1981), 17.

26. Ezequiel Rodríguez Domínguez, *Iconografía del danzón* (Havana: Sub-Dirección Provincial de Música, 1967), 40; Galán, *Cuba y sus sones*, 178–79.

27. Castillo Faílde, *Miguel Faílde*, 203–7; Rodríguez Domínguez, *Iconografía*, 11.

28. Galán, *Cuba y sus sones*, 199–200; Ramiro Guerra y Sánchez, ed., *Historia de la nación cubana*, Vol. 7 (Havana: Editorial Historia de la Nación Cubana, S.A., 1952), 434.

29. De Ximeno y Cruz, *Memorias de Lola María*, 236–37; Castillo Faílde, *Miguel Faílde*, 48. Flautist Juan Francisco "Tata" Pereira left musical practice and became an armed rebel in 1896, as did others, see Radamés Giro, *Diccionario enciclopédico de la música en Cuba*, Vol. 3 (Havana: Letras Cubanas, 2007), 218.

Figure 3.1: Orquesta Faílde. Miguel Faílde is standing second from the left in the back row. Photo courtesy of Museo Nacional de la Música, Havana.

a free mulatto mother, Faílde grew up in the small town of Caobas.[30] He learned to play music from his father and at age twelve participated as a cornetist in a Municipal Fireman's band. Together with his brothers Eduardo, a clarinetist, and Cándido, a trombonist, Miguel Faílde first organized an orquesta típica in 1871, all of whose members were black or mixed-race. The ensemble soon achieved a devoted following among the youth of Matanzas, black and white, especially for the intensity of its shows that included raucous shouting from band members (anticipating the antics of Dámaso Pérez Prado by seventy years), Miguel Faílde's virtuosic solos on trumpet, and those of his *timbalero* Andrés Segovia.[31] The Orquesta Faílde played primarily for the dances of white elites as of the mid-1870s, but also in more humble establishments associated with the black working class. Most sources describe Faílde in later years as soft-spoken and refined, known for wearing a gold watch and fob, using an amber cigarette holder, playing chamber music on the viola and violin in his spare time, and moving in prominent literary circles.[32] His strong personal identification

30. Sigryd Padrón Díaz, "Galicia en el baile nacional cubano: el danzón." *Galicia–Cuba; un patrimonio cultural de referencias y confluencias* (A Coruna, Spain: Edicios do Castro do Grupo Sargadelos, 2000), 407.

31. De Ximeno y Cruz, *Memorias de Lola María*, 216; Castillo Faílde, *Miguel Faílde*, 35–44, 63.

32. Castillo Faílde, *Miguel Faílde*, 35–44, 62, 95, 210; León, *Del canto y el tiempo*, 281. One reference to his popularity among elites is found in the *Diario de Matanzas*, Friday, July 27, 1883 (6, no. 176), 3.

with European-derived culture makes the criticisms of his music as barbaric and primitive especially ironic.

The sudden cross-racial appeal of the Afro-Cuban danzón generated widespread concern in the 1880s, and thus many commentators took offense at its mere incorporation into white society gatherings rather than at any particular musical or choreographic characteristics.[33] It appears that large numbers of adolescents began for the first time during this decade to attend public *"fiestas de arroz y frijoles"* with white and black couples in attendance together, adding to such concerns.[34] Mixed-race *casas de cuna* and *academias* or *escuelitas de baile* (informal dance venues), similarly associated with interracial romance, exposed many younger white men to the danzón for the first time and were also denounced.[35] Yet the music appealed to a growing segment of the population and not only the young, making clear that conservative critics did not speak for everyone. Jill Lane describes white danzón performance of the period as "a form of erotic choreographic blackface," allowing Hispanic Cubans to present themselves publicly in a new way that may have felt vaguely African, or at least sexy and transgressive.[36] An article in the *Aurora del Yumurí* in 1879 supports this view, tying the danzón to sexual transgression and possible interracial attraction. The author states "we love the danza, it is so tasty, and even more the danzón, *with girls that shall never be our wives.*"[37] At the same time, the music also constituted a form of local expression and served to distinguish Cubans from Spanish colonials at a time when such distinctions were increasingly important.

Some critics focused their attacks on danzón choreography, underscoring its perceived sexual or licentious nature. Figure dances previously in vogue, such as the contradanza and danza, were largely accepted as clean "family fun."[38] By contrast, the closed-couple format increasingly adopted by danzón enthusiasts exacerbated racial

33. "Rectifique," *Diario de Matanzas*, 2, no. 236 (October 8, 1879), 2.

34. Castillo Faílde, *Miguel Faílde*, 75; Lane, *Blackface Cuba*, 167.

35. Francisco Moreno Chicharro, *Cuba y su gente. Apuntes para la historia* (Madrid: Establecimiento Tipográfico de Enrique Teodoro, 1887), 143. See also Rine Leal, *La selva oscura, Vol. 2. De los bufos a la neocolonial* (Havana: Editorial Arte y Literatura, 1982), 269. Cirilo Villaverde famously depicts interracial dances at casas de cuna in his novel *Cecilia Valdés*, set in the 1830s; clearly they have a long history. Lapique Becali documents the first written references to escuelitas de baile—dances in which unaccompanied men could pay to dance with women—in Havana of 1848 (*Cuba colonial*, 2008, 138). According to Israel Moliner (personal interview, Matanzas, December 2, 2011), similar events became popular in Matanzas in the 1850s, and it is in such venues that the danzón began to catch on among the white Cuban population. Castillo Faílde, *Miguel Faílde*, 215–222, devotes a few pages to the phenomenon of escuelitas de baile, discussing the various Afro-Cuban musical forms danced there in addition to the danzón.

36. Lane, *Blackface Cuba*, 177. Pilar Egüez Guevara ("Colonial Anxieties") discusses the discourses of "decency" surrounding escuelitas, a coded term referencing anxieties about blackness.

37. "Gacetilla. Indecencias," *Aurora del Yumurí* 51, no. 127 (February 2, 1879), 2. The italicized section is found in the original, in English, apparently because it referred to controversial subject matter.

38. Peter Manuel, "Introduction: Contradance and Quadrille Culture in the Caribbean," in *Creolizing the Contradance in the Caribbean*, ed. Peter Manuel (Philadelphia: Temple University Press, 2009), 44.

concerns and extended the scope of the debate considerably. One anonymous author in the *Diario de Matanzas* described danzones as involving too close an embrace and too much butt movement;[39] another in the *Aurora del Yumurí* drew attention to the "unbridled passion" ostensibly associated with its turns and spins,[40] and a third referenced the "lewd thoughts" awakened by dancers' flexible waists.[41] Similar attacks on the waltz had appeared a few decades earlier and emerged at approximately the same time as condemnation of the Brazilian *maxixe*, the tango, and other regional dances.[42] Public dancing of the era clearly referenced a range of controversial social issues including the gradual democratization of many nations, the erosion of hard class lines, changing views of appropriate gender roles, and the expression of public sexuality. But in the Cuban context, commentators often linked such perceived indecency to African heritage, suggesting that the music represented an evolutionary step backward because it came from "inferior beings."[43]

Still other detractors focused on the music itself. One suggested that danzón orchestras made sounds reminiscent of the "virile exclamation of the savage,"[44] others singled out percussive patterns on the timbales that to them recalled the African origins of the music,[45] the "tireless drum that generates ever more enthusiasm the longer it plays."[46] Admittedly, danzón timbales patterns are claved and incorporate techniques derived from traditional West African sources, though commentators of the day probably failed to recognize them. Yet Serafín Ramírez as late as the 1890s compared the sound of danzón percussion to that of an African *cabildo de nación*, denounced the "rude banging" of the timbales and *güiro*, and even the "obstreperous clamor" of the wind parts.[47] Bandleader Raimundo Valenzuela came under particular attack because of the decision to include an African-derived *chéquere* in his band for a time,[48] as did others, presumably, who included the *marímbula* or mouth bow.[49] All such criticisms sought to distance the danzón from Cuban heritage and instead to emphasize elements perceived as foreign or barbaric.

39. "Comunicación," *Diario de Matanzas* (December 27, 1878), 2, 3. The exact quote is as follows: "La danza antigua se componía de muchas y diversas figuras, mientras que el matancero danzón es una serie de cedazos iguales, sin otra figura que el culebreo."

40. "Ja, ja, chúpete ese huevo," *Aurora del Yumurí* (June 30, 1881), 2.

41. Moreno Chicharro, *Cuba y su gente*, 142.

42. John Charles Chasteen, *National Rhythms, African Roots. The Deep History of Latin American Popular Dance* (Albuquerque: University of New Mexico Press, 2004), 5.

43. Castillo Faílde, *Miguel Faílde*, 122; see also Benjamín de Céspedes, *La prostitución en La Habana* (Havana: Establecimiento Tipográfico O'Reilly, 1888), 142–43; Galán, *Cuba y sus sones*, 180.

44. "Gacetilla," *Aurora del Yumurí*, Wednesday, July 20, 1881, quoted in Castillo Faílde, *Miguel Faílde*, 141.

45. *Aurora del Yumurí*, July 30, 1881, quoted in Castillo Faílde, *Miguel Faílde*, 148.

46. *Aurora del Yumurí*, Wednesday, July 20, 1881, quoted in Castillo Faílde, *Miguel Faílde*, 141.

47. Serafín Ramírez, *La Habana Artística. Apuntes por la historia* (Havana: Imprenta del E. M. de la Capitanía General, 1891), 29–30, 395.

48. Zoila Lapique Becali, personal interview, Havana, Cuba, October 1, 1993. See also Lapique Becali, *Cuba colonial*, 269, 271–72; this appears to have taken place about 1886.

49. Galán, *Cuba y sus sones*, 221.

Writers for the Havana magazine *El Almendares* took offense at the titles of many danzones, describing them as disgusting.[50] Many referenced black working-class culture or street slang with phrases such as "La bollera" (a female street vendor), "La guabina" (the name of an Afro-Cuban dance), "La mulata Celestina," "El mondonguito" (roughly, chitlins), and "El yambú" (a style of rumba). Cristóbal Díaz Ayala cites others with even more overt ties to African heritage: "El lucumí," "El ñáñigo," "Mallombero," "El carabalí," "Conconcó Mambó."[51] Such titles apparently represent a self-conscious foregrounding of Afro-Cuban heritage on the part of composers. It is unclear how white adolescents and others more accepting of the new dance perceived them. Certainly they would have been read in multiple ways, just as in the case of the danzón itself: as a manifestation of "otherness" and degeneracy within the colonial context, or as a marker of *cubanía* and local experience, distinct from that of Spain. Just as with referents to Afro-Cubans within the blackface theater, danzón performers and audiences could choose to identify with such titles as a means of obliquely expressing pro-independence sentiment.[52] It seems likely at the very least that danzón performers themselves promoted such patriotic readings, as many strongly supported the revolutionaries.

It should be noted that the blackface theater itself helped popularize and disseminate the danzón in the 1880s and beyond, especially outside of elite circles. Danzones served as the focus of many stage plays from the period, such as *En la cocina* (1880) by Ignacio Sarrachaga, and *El proceso del oso* (1882) by Ramón Morales Álvarez. Jill Lane discusses these works at some length,[53] and many are available in reprint.[54] In Matanzas of the late nineteenth century, blackface stage entertainment achieved such broad popularity that the city supported ten local bufo (comic blackface) companies, all of whom presented daily shows. Music of various sorts represented a prominent feature on the bufo stage—the *guaracha*, the stylized rumba, the *pregón*—but typically included at least one danzón, often toward the end of the first scene. Many famous danzón dancers first gained popularity as part of blackface entertainment, and shows in the famous Alhambra Theater in the early twentieth century invariably began with a danzón.[55]

A surprising number of newspaper articles denouncing the danzón in the late nineteenth century make reference to notions of (white) women's honor, purity, and virginity, suggesting that these characteristics were threatened by dance events. Helg has documented the highly sexualized and gendered nature of Cuban racial discourse

50. Lane, *Blackface Cuba*, 164. See also Ramírez, *La Habana Artística*, 395.

51. Cristóbal Díaz Ayala, *Los contrapunteos de la música cubana* (San Juan, Puerto Rico: Ediciones Callejón, 2006), 148.

52. Robin D. Moore, "The *Teatro Bufo*: Cuban Blackface Theater of the Nineteenth Century," in *Performativity, Power, and the Poetics of Being: Soundscapes from the Americas*, ed. Donna Buchanan (London: Ashgate, forthcoming).

53. Lane, *Blackface Cuba*, 167–70.

54. Rine Leal, ed. *Teatro bufo siglo XIX. Antología tomo II* (Havana: Editorial Arte y Cultura, 1975).

55. Israel Moliner, personal interview, Matanzas, Cuba, December, 2, 2011; Raimundo Rodríguez, "El danzón en le cincuentenario de la muerte de Miguel Faílde," *Granma* (7, no. 230), Saturday, February 25, 1971), 2.

of the late nineteenth century, identifying various tropes including that of the black beast who constantly threatens to rape white women; that of lustful black and mixed-race seductresses who threaten white families and values; and that of the chaste white woman.[56] White women appear invariably in literature and press of the period as virtuous; no image even of lustful white men ever enters public discussion, only those that depict whites as victims of a black onslaught. Much of the ever-present discussion of wantonness, vulgarity, and indecency associated with dances seems to have been code for black influence, whether choreographic or musical, or for the physical presence of black performers or dancers. Lane supports this view, suggesting that the distress caused to white men by the thought of "their" white women dancing to music perceived as African was "extraordinarily acute."[57] The obsession of Cuban society with white women's sexual and racial purity supports notions of white superiority and a need to divide society along racial lines.[58]

Middle-class white women lived restricted lives in nineteenth-century Cuba, largely confined to their homes. De Ximeno y Cruz recalls in her memoirs that she and others considered the home the extent of their universe, the space in which they would live and die, and in which resided "everything that was attractive in life."[59] Luis Martínez-Fernández concluded based on an analysis of travel accounts that "elite white women in Havana were more restricted in their movement and behavior "than [their counterparts] in any other Western society," and likened much of their domestic lives to "imprisonment."[60] As children, women enjoyed considerable freedom, but after adolescence the situation changed. From that point onward their families never let them leave home alone, only when accompanied by friends or relatives and black attendants. They might chat with passersby in the street from behind barred windows, but never for too long, or too often with the same person.[61] Prior to the twentieth century, society did not permit middle-class women to work or in many cases to educate themselves, thus keeping them dependent upon men.[62] They could not move too fast, laugh too openly, cross their legs, put down their fan when in the presence of non-family members, and in other ways conformed to strict social guidelines.[63]

56. Helg, *Our Rightful Share*, 18.

57. Lane, *Blackface Cuba*, 156.

58. Verena Martínez-Alier, *Marriage, Class, and Colour in Nineteenth-Century Cuba* (Ann Arbor: University of Michigan Press, 1974), xiv.

59. De Ximeno y Cruz, *Memorias de Lola María*, 39–40.

60. Cited in Susan Thomas, *Cuban Zarzuela. Performing Race and Gender on Havana's Lyric Stage* (Urbana: University of Illinois Press, 2009), 30.

61. Walter Goodman, *The Pearl of the Antilles or An Artist in Cuba* (London: Henry S. King, 1873). Discussion of leaving the house appears on p. 216, and chatting from windows on p. 213.

62. The following articles discuss women's limited access to education, even in elite circles: "Instrucción de la mujer," *El Club de Matanzas. Periódico de Literatura, Ciencias y Bellas Artes* 3, no. 2 (January 15, 1881), 1–3. Joaquín Balmaseda, "Guía de la mujer. Por la mujer," *El Club de Matanzas* 3, no. 17 (September 1, 1881), 140–41. "Al bello sexo principalmente," *El Club de Matanzas* 3, no. 19 (October 1,1881), 154–55. Ángel de la C. Muñoz, "Eduquemos a la mujer," *El Club de Matanzas* 6, no. 2 (February 1, 1882), 9–10.

63. De Ximeno y Cruz, *Memorias de Lola María*, 71.

Thus, women's public appearances at dances and theater events, even when the women were heavily chaperoned, constituted some of the few contexts in which they could socialize with men at all and represented important moments in their lives.

Constant references to black or mixed-race women either as hypersexual beings or as a social danger in dance settings represent a logical counterpart to discourses of white purity and honor. Of course, concern over racial purity has a long history throughout Latin America. Cuban law extended such beliefs into the legal code by criminalizing mixed-race marriages through 1881; well into the twentieth century social convention continued to be a barrier to formal mixed-race unions.[64] It appears that the Emancipation Proclamation in the United States generated additional fears among Spanish colonials that Cubans of color might hear of such changes and fight for greater equality. As a result, the government enforced existing racial codes robustly through the mid-1870s, with virtually no exemptions permitted.[65] Cuban publications through at least 1890 continue to characterize mulatas either as sexy bombshells or as the corrupters of white society. In the collection *Guarachas cubanas* from 1882, the sexy, seductive mulata appears as a virtual leitmotif in countless popular song lyrics.[66] The writings of Dr. Benjamín de Céspedes, by contrast, represent an extreme example of the opposite characterization. In a short story from 1889 he referred a mixed-race woman as a "devil," corrupting the soul of a white man.[67] In a book publication the previous year he went further, describing mulatas as stunted in their intellectual development, physically deformed, superstitious, and disease-ridden.[68] Preoccupied with the moral laxity of dance events, he made clear that much of his concern derived from the presence of black or mixed-race Cubans and their "debased" cultural forms.

In all parts of the city resounds the penetrating shout of the cornet; calling to the male and female for their hypocritically lewd festivities. From the modest drawing room to the wide salon of haughty society, the confused and delirious arrive to take part, without modesty or decorum, in Sapphic scenes of the bedroom, baptized with the names *danza, danzón*, and *Yambú*. Musicians and composers—typically of the race of color—label their motley tunes with names taken from the most expressive slang . . . whose rhythms are the musical expression of pornography. The timbales

64. Martínez-Alier, *Marriage, Class, and Colour*, 14. References to contemporary negative views toward mixed-race unions can also be found in *El Fígaro* 2, no. 10 (March 11, 1886), 2–3 and no. 11 (March 18, 1886), 4–5, in the section "Dimes y diretes," both commentaries written by Francisco Chacón.

65. Martínez-Alier, *Marriage, Class, and Colour*, 31–32.

66. O. Hallorans, ed. *Guarachas cubanas. Curiosa recopilación desde las más antiguas hasta las más modernas* (Havana: Librería La Principal Editora, 1882), 5, 54, 64–65, 79–80, 89, 94–96, 101, 103. Similar views appear in the writings of European travelers to Cuba from the early twentieth century, for instance, Albert Friedenthal's *Musik, Tanz und Dichtung bei den Kreolen Amerikas* (Berlin: Hausbücher-Verlag Hans Schnippel, 1913), 92.

67. Benjamín de Céspedes, "Brujerías," *El Fígaro*, 5, no. 16 (May 5, 1889), 2–3.

68. Benjamín de Céspedes, *La prostitución*, 173–76.

dissemble their drum rolls of desire; the scrapings of the rasp are like titillations that augment lust, and the clarinet and cornet, in their strident and dissonant competition, seem to imitate anxieties, supplications and yearnings that fight arduously for amorous possession.[69]

This quote is similar to countless others of the day in its conflation of music, race, and sexuality, and in its suggestion that acceptance of the danzón was tantamount to miscegenation. Critics depicted danzón dancing as both frivolous and corrupting, a form of moral danger that threatened Cuban society. It excited base passions, they suggested, referencing the atavistic practices of "barbarous peoples."[70] It incited men and women to act inappropriately and was linked to other vices such as drunkenness, smoking, and prostitution. It would sap the energy of the young, rob them of decorum, and consume their health and innocence.[71]

CUBAN CULTURE AND DANZÓN IN FIN-DE-SIÈCLE MEXICO

Close cultural ties between Cuba and Mexico date back to the sixteenth century, with the establishment of commercial trade routes during the Spanish colonial era. Economic, political, and cultural relations between the two countries allowed for continuous crossings of the border between them involving merchandise, people, ideas, and artistic forms, including music. By the mid-nineteenth century Mexican elites had adopted the contradanza and *danza habanera* into their salons, as Domingo Ibarra documents in his *Colección de bailes de sala y método para aprenderlos sin ausilio de maestro* (1858).[72] The immense success of Sebastián Iradier's "La paloma" in the 1850s and 1860s across class lines—it was reported to be the favorite song of empress Carlota I, as well as a melody used by the underclasses to criticize both the French

---

69. De Céspedes, *La prostitución*, 140–41. The original text is as follows. "Por todos los ámbitos de la ciudad resuena el penetrante alarido del cornetín; reclamando al macho y a la hembra para la fiesta hipócritamente lúbrica. Desde el modesto estrado hasta el amplio salón de la más encopetada sociedad pública, acuden todos confundidos y delirantes a remediar sin pudor ni decoro escenas sáficas de alcoba, bautizadas con los nombres de danza, danzón y Yambú. Músicos y compositores,—por lo general de la raza de color,— rotulan con el dicharacho más expresivo, recogido de la calle o del tugurio, sus abigarradas composiciones, cuyos ritmos son la expresión musical imitativa de escenas pornográficas, que los timbales fingen como redobles de deseos, que el respido sonsonete del *guayo* como titilaciones que exacerban la Lujuria y que el clarinete y el cornetín, en su competencia estruendosa y disonante, parecen imitar las ansias, las súplicas y los esfuerzos de que lucha ardorosoamente por la posesión amorosa." See also p. 98 where he describes the dance music in vogue as "*música ñáñiga*," African in origin.
70. Luis Arias, excerpt from "El baile," *La Aurora del Yumurí*, August 9, 1882, no page, as quoted in Castillo Faílde, *Miguel Faílde*, 152.
71. Castillo Faílde (*Miguel Faílde*) devotes over 40 pages in his book to a reproduction of period newspaper articles that discuss the danzón, many of them in this way. See especially pp. 145, 147, 150–53, 157, and 159.
72. Domingo Ibarra, *Colección de bailes de sala y método para aprenderlos sin ausilio de maestro* (Mexico City: Tipografía de Nabor Chávez, 1862 [1858]), 15–18.

invasion (1862–1866) and the conservative politicians who supported it—shows these musical forms as part of the everyday life of all Mexicans.[73]

The Cuban Wars of Independence led to a continuous exodus through the circum-Caribbean between 1868 and 1898. Mexico became one of the most important destinations of Cuban patriots and their families, who established large communities in Veracruz and Mérida, Yucatán.[74] These immigrants brought with them not only a desire for independence but also their everyday culture. In a continuous process, Mexicans appropriated and made meaningful new Cuban musical styles in dialogue with older forms they had already embraced, together with the racial anxieties and the political overtones associated with such musics at specific moments.

The date of the danzón's arrival in Mexico is difficult to determine with precision. Olavarría y Ferrari first mentions the music in print when describing a series of concerts at Mexico City's Arbeu Theater in 1883. He simply states that "Zapata's orchestra was also applauded for their danzones and other Cuban airs."[75] Olavarría y Ferrari's review of the 1884 season of Miguel de Salas's Bufos Habaneros at Mexico City's Teatro Principal provides more insight into the early reception of such repertoire. He emphasizes that although Mexico City audiences found the blackface "sainetes [one-act skits] and parodias to be extremely monotonous" and frequently heckled them, they responded enthusiastically to the music they performed including "danzones, danzas, and guarachas."[76] In all likelihood, Mexican audiences did not find the bufos humorous because they did not understand the Cuba-specific political allusions and other referents in the dialogue. Yet they seem to have enjoyed the music, as it was similar to the contradanzas and danzas already in vogue. Several other Cuban blackface acts toured Mexico during the same period; Paulino Delgado's troupe in 1882, Pablo Pildaín's in 1884, and Leopoldo Burón's in 1884 and 1889.[77] Since the danzón was already a regular musical feature among Cuban companies it must have been included during their performances in Mexico as well. However, sporadic

73. The French Invasion of Mexico (1862–1866) came at the climax of a long-standing political struggle between Liberals and Conservatives in the country. When liberal president Benito Juárez suspended interest payments to foreign countries in 1861, France invaded and took possession of Mexico. This resulted in the Second Mexican Empire, supported by the conservatives. Maximilian Ferdinand, an Austrian Archduke, and Charlotte of Belgium (both from the Hapsburg dynasty) were crowned emperor and empress consort, becoming Maximiliano I and Carlota of Mexico. They ruled through a bloody civil war that ended with the French withdrawal, the victory of Mexican liberals, and the execution of Maximilian in 1867.

74. Bernardo García Díaz, "La migración cubana a Veracruz," in La Habana, Veracruz, Veracruz, La Habana. Las dos orillas, ed. Bernardo García Díaz and Sergio Guerra Vilaboy (Xalapa, Mexico: Universidad Veracruzana, 2002), 302–304.

75. Enrique Olavarría y Ferrari, Reseña histórica del teatro en México, Vol. 3 (Mexico City: La Europea, 1895), 360.

76. Olavarría y Ferrari, Reseña histórica, 403–404.

77. Leal, Teatro bufo siglo XIX, 183–84, 189–90, 220. Leal confirms that the blackface comedy they showcased, with its many political references specific to Cuba, was poorly received by Mexican audiences, but that the music made a strong impression. "José Valenzuela" is said to have directed the Salas orchestra for a time, a possible reference to Raimundo or Pablo Valenzuela.

performances by foreign performers on tour cannot fully explain the exceptional popularity of the danzón among the Mexican bourgeoisie by the end of the decade.

In 1888, only four years after the Bufos de Salas toured the country, the weekly music magazine *J. Jacinto Cuevas* began publication in Mérida. It made available hundreds of piano scores—mostly by local composers—to the Yucatecan bourgeoisie through its final issue in 1894. Enrique Martín Briceño states that the salon pieces disseminated by *J. Jacinto Cuevas* were extremely popular, as were piano renditions of orchestral music played at weekly social events.[78] The sheet music allowed enthusiasts to perform their favorite pieces at home months after they had been first played at public parties. Among the more than 180 pieces published in *J. Jacinto Cuevas* (Fig. 3.2), over sixty are danzones of the pre-Faildean style in rounded binary form (A-B-A).[79] *La Gaceta Musical*, first published in 1895 as the successor of *J. Jacinto Cuevas*, offers similar repertoire, including a large number of danzones in rounded binary form by local composers.[80] The danzón was so ubiquitous in fin-de-siècle Mérida that local writers began to make jokes about the fact, suggesting that even "a few counter clerks have dedicated themselves to writing danzones."[81] Thus, by the late 1880s and early 1890s the elite of Yucatán had unquestionably adopted the danzón as a favorite music.

The presence of music written by Raimundo Valenzuela and José Marín Verona—in addition to Faílde—among the scores in the *J. Jacinto Cuevas* collection indicates that Yucatecans of the 1890s were familiar with the latest works of contemporary Cuban performers.[82] Some Cuban composers and orchestras, as Martín Briceño argues, may even have visited Mérida.[83] An additional explanation for the presence of recently composed Cuban danzones in Mérida can be found in the long-standing commercial shipping networks established between the island and Yucatán, which probably delivered music scores to the region;[84] and in the growth of the previously

78. Enrique Martín Briceño, "Ecos del Yucatán porfiriano: el semanario musical *J. Jacinto Cuevas*," in *Guía y joyas de los archivos de Mérida*, ed. Maureen Ransom Carty (Mérida: Instituto de Cultura de Yucatán, 2005), 42.

79. Only one danzón in rondo form is featured in the collection, Miguel Faílde's "Trabajar compañero, trabajar," from 1890.

80. A copy of the complete collection of *La Gaceta Musical* is kept at the Centro Regional de Investigación, Documentación y Difusión Musical "Gerónimo Baqueiro Foster" in Mérida. Almost half of the pieces published in the periodical were danzones (19). It included music by some of the same Mexican composers featured in *J. Jacinto Cuevas*, among them Bilo-Río (Julio Río Ceballos), Justo Cuevas, and D. Amésquita.

81. P. Escalante Palma, "Intrinculis," *Pimienta y Mostaza* (February 4, 1894), 1.

82. Jesús Flores y Escalante states that Raimundo Valenzuela's danzón "El combate" (1883) was played during a dance at La Lonja Meridana in 1884, just a year after its composition. See Jesús Flores y Escalante, *Salón México. Historia documental y gráfica del danzón en México* (Mexico City: Asociación de Estudios Fonográficos, A.C., 2006 [1996]), 7.

83. Briceño argues that Marín Verona may have spent some time in Mérida since he wrote the mazurka "Meridana" specifically for *J. Jacinto Cuevas*. See Briceño, "Ecos del Yucatán porfiriano," 46.

84. By the end of the nineteenth century, the Ward Line, New York & Cuba Mail Steamship Company, and the Atlantic and Mexican Steamship Company, among others, had weekly steamers that touched at Veracruz, Tampico, Campeche, Progreso (a few miles from Mérida), Tuxpan, Havana, and New York. See Reau Campbell, *Campbell's New Revised Complete Guide and Descriptive Book* (Chicago: Robert O. Law, 1899), 21.

Figure 3.2: Cover of the Mérida music periodical *J. Jacinto Cuevas*. Courtesy of Centro Regional de Investigación, Documentación en Información Musical "Gerónimo Baqueiro Foster," Mérida, Yucatán.

mentioned Cuban exile community whose members came from affluent and educated families.[85] This last point suggests why the largely white/Hispanic Mexican
bourgeoisie uncritically adopted the danzón without paying much attention to the
racial overtones and controversies surrounding the music in Cuba: they associated
it with the white Cuban elite that had relocated to Mérida. Piano scores of early
danzones published in Mexico—in the pre-Faildean style, very similar to habaneras
and contradanzas—may have also led Yucatecans to consider the danzón a variant
of these dances, by the late 1800s already gentrified and accepted as yet another
cosmopolitan dance form.

The danzones in rounded binary form featured in *J. Jacinto Cuevas* and *La Gaceta
Musical* were available throughout the country by the end of the 1890s. Wagner y
Levien published many of them during that decade, but also started selling danzones
in the rondo form that was becoming fashionable, including Juventino Rosas's
"Flores de Romana," in 1893, as well as a series of danzones by composers from Mexico City and Veracruz 1899.[86] It is likely that these were the kinds of danzones played
at elite events such as in Mexico City's Casino Español as chronicled by *El Nacional* on
January 29, 1895;[87] or at the charity dance sponsored by the American and British
colonies in Mexico City on November 29, 1900, where Carlos Curti conducted the
orchestra and President Porfirio Díaz received special honors.[88]

The 1890s and 1900s witnessed an expanded presence of influential Cuban musicians in Mexico. Many came with bufo troupes, which Mexican audiences were beginning to accept and enjoy. Composer Jorge Anckermann (1877–1941) directed music
for the Gonzalo Hernández bufo company in a successful season at the Circo Teatro
Orrin in Mexico City and a tour of the countryside in 1898,[89] and once again in 1903
with the Raúl del Monte troupe.[90] Anckermann lived in Mexico for an extended
period thereafter, making a living as a musician, composer, and music teacher, and

---

85. Bernardo García Díaz, "La migración cubana," 302–4; and Carlos E. Bojórquez
Urzaiz, *La emigración cubana en Yucatán, 1868–1898* (Mérida: Imagen Contemporánea,
2000), 38.

86. Flores y Escalante, *Salón México*, 29 and 55.

87. *El Nacional* (January 29, 1895), quoted in Clementina Díaz y de Ovando, *Invitación
al baile. Arte, espectáculo y rito en la sociedad mexicana (1825–1910), Tomo II* (Mexico City:
UNAM, 2006), 506.

88. *El Popular* (December 1, 1900), quoted in Díaz y de Ovando, *Invitación al baile*, 725.

89. Enrique de Olavarría y Ferrari, *Reseña historica del teatro en México*, Vol. 3 (Mexico
City: Editorial Porrúa, 1961), 1863.

90. Eduardo Robreño, *Como lo pienso lo digo* (Havana: UNEAC, 1985), 15–16; Flores y
Escalante, *Salón México*, 14; and Enrique Río Prado, *La Venus de bronce: una historia de la
zarzuela cubana* (Havana: Ediciones Alarcos, 2010), 62. Robreño argues that Anckermann's
two trips to Mexico were as musical director of Raúl del Monte's company. However Río
Prado states that the troupe traveled to Mexico for the first time in 1903. This confusion
may have arisen because Raúl del Monte may have worked in Mexico in 1898 as a member
of Gonzalo Hernández's troupe. Anckermann probably went to Mexico in 1898 and
returned in 1903, when he decided to stay after the company returned to Cuba. Flores y
Escalante assumes that Anckermann's second trip to Mexico must have taken place around
1908–1909 when the Teatro Circo Orrín was closed; however, Giro places Anckermann
back in Havana by 1909, when he received a composition award (*Diccionario*, Vol. I, 56).

publishing his danzón "La rumba" there in 1907.[91] Robreño affirms that José Urfé (1879–1957) was also a member of the Raúl del Monte orchestra during the company's second visit to Mexico.[92] One assumes that the activities of these Cuban composers and arrangers, as well as those in other bufo troupes, played an important role in the final adoption of the rondo-form danzón in Mexico as opposed to the rounded binary form associated with the contradanza and habanera. By 1905, the Concha Orchestra in Mérida was already playing danzones in rondo form,[93] and the rounded-binary-style form faded away in subsequent years.

It is difficult to determine with precision how the danzón was danced in Mexico at the end of the nineteenth century or whether it was already a couple dance. However, a few sources suggest a style that combined couple dancing with choreographed figure dancing. In *Colección de bailes de sala*, Ibarra explains how the contradanza and (danza) habanera styles featured couple dancing organized into a series of fixed group choreographies. The dances no longer contained figures structured into circles or squares in which dancers moved collectively, largely avoiding a close embrace with their partner; nevertheless, they did not yet adopt the free couple dancing that characterized danzones later in the twentieth century.[94] The fact that the same Mexican elites who adopted the danzón early on practiced semi-choreographed couple dancing in conjunction with other social dances suggests that they may have danced the danzón in a similar fashion. On February 25, 1906, the Cuban magazine *El Fígaro* dedicated an issue to the activities of the Cuban colony in Mérida. Among other events, it chronicled a dance at La Lonja Meridana, stating that "although there were several danzas, or [more precisely] danzones among the twelve dances in the program, they were not danced by couples. In Mérida, it has become an elegant trend, as in Havana, to *walk* the danzones instead of dancing them."[95] The fact that most other dances at this event were *piezas de cuadro* suggests that, at least among elites, the danzón was also a type of semi-choreographed group dance that included elements of both couple dancing and figure dancing. In contrast, an earlier note by *El Nacional* from 1895 mentions a danzón dance style associated with Cuba, distinct from what Mexican elites favored. The author comments on a social event at Mexico City's Salón Español, describing a danzón played for Gabriel Ibargüen so that he could dance it Havana-style.[96] The orchestra performed the piece for a specific guest, implying that he did not dance it in a group but rather as a couple dance and in a style (*habanero*) different

91. Giro's *Diccionario*, Vol. I (55), suggests that Anckermann lived for two years in Mexico. Evidence that he was still in Mexico in 1907 comes from that year's *Boletín de Instrucción Pública*, which lists his danzón "La rumba" as having being submitted for copyright by Wagner y Levien on October 31, 1907. See *Boletín de Instrucción Pública* (Mexico City: Tipografía Económica, 1907), 650.

92. Robreño, *Como lo pienso lo digo*, 16.

93. A set of particellas copied in 1905 for the Concha Orchestra is kept at the Centro Regional de Investigación, Documentación y Difusión Musical "Gerónimo Baqueiro Foster" in Mérida. They are all danzones in rondo form.

94. Ibarra, *Colección de bailes*, 15–18.

95. "Gran baile en la Lonja," *El Fígaro* 22, no. 8 (February 25, 1906), 98.

96. "Ecos sociales," *El Nacional* (January 29, 1895). Quoted in Díaz y de Ovando, *Invitación al baile*, 506.

from the Mexican norm. It is likely that Ibargüen's couple dancing imitated the independent couple style already popular in Cuba but still uncommon in Mexico in the 1890s. As the danzón became more democratized and gained popularity among the Mexican working classes, however, the figure dancing that presumably characterized it in the nineteenth century gradually disappeared.

Acceptance of the danzón by the working classes in the early twentieth century coincided with a shift in the music's reputation and its identification with exoticism, urban experience, prostitution, and blackness. The danzón is a central leitmotif in Federico Gamboa's description of Mexico City's nightlife and brothel culture as depicted in his novel *Santa* (1903).[97] In Gamboa's characterization, the music and dance accompany acts of sinful sensuality and moral degradation; although he makes no direct reference to the black origins of the danzón, he emphasizes that it is accompanied by one of those "Caribbean rhythms danced with lascivious undulations of the torso."[98] Danzones had circulated in Mexico for over twenty years by 1900, yet this is one of the earliest descriptions to relate it with decadent lifestyles or lustful movements associated with Caribbean culture. One finds similar rhetoric among nineteenth-century Mexican authors describing the habanera or dance presentations of the bufos habaneros, but never the danzón prior to the twentieth century. Clearly, important changes in the uses and circulation of the music were occurring at the time that affected its place in the Mexican imagination.

It was also at the turn of the century that several black Cuban musicians who immigrated to Mexico eventually became central to the popularization of the danzón among the working classes. By all accounts, the influential Tiburcio "Babuco" Hernández (Fig. 3.3) arrived in Mexico in the 1890s and may have been the first Cuban danzón performer to have permanently relocated there. A *timbalero* (kettle drum player), he first attracted audiences as part of a traveling circus act before forming his own dance band.[99] In 1905, Babuco founded a danzón orchestra in Veracruz that soon became popular not only in the port but also in Mexico City.[100] He served as a mentor for percussionist Consejo Valiente Robert "Acerina" (🔊 Picture 3.1) (1899–1987), one of the most famous danzón performers of its "golden age" in 1940s Mexico City. In 1913, Acerina left Cuba for Mexico and also stayed there permanently.[101] Tomás Ponce Reyes (1886–1972), later one of the country's most famous danzón composers and arrangers, settled in Mexico City around that time (see Fig. 3.4).[102] Many other

97. See Federico Gamboa, *Santa: A Novel of Mexico City*, trans. John Charles Chasteen (Chapel Hill: University of North Carolina Press, 2010), 75, 78, 103.
98. Gamboa, *Santa*, 78.
99. Charlie Gerard, *Mongo Santamaría, Chocolate Armenteros, and Cuban musicians in the United States* (Westport, CT: Praeger, 2001), 34–35.
100. Flores y Escalante, *Salón México*, 57.
101. Gabriel Pareyón, *Diccionario enciclopédico de música en México*, Vol. 1 (Guadalajara: Universidad Panamericana, 2007), 20.
102. Gabriel Pareyón, *Diccionario enciclopédico de música en México*, Vol. 2 (Guadalajara: Universidad Panamericana, 2007), 846. Pareyón states that Ponce Reyes moved from Cuba to Mexico around 1900 but does not provide a specific date. Díaz Ayala notes that Tomás Ponce recorded several danzones in Cuba for the Victor label in 1916. The

Figure 3.3: Tiburcio "Babuco" Hernández. Photo courtesy of Fototeca Nacional de México.

black Cuban musicians and dancers figured prominently as entertainers in Mexico between 1900 and 1920; their names (or nicknames) are now part of popular Mexican mythology that ascribes black origins to the danzón. Veracruz-based musicians Eulogio Veytia (acoustic bass), Quiroz (figle), and O'Relly (güiro) from Orquesta de los Chinos Ramírez; Albertico (clarinet) from the Orquesta Típica de Severiano y Albertico; Sonsorico (a violinist), "El Negro" Charles (a timbalero), "Ñame" (a güiro player), as well as dancers La Babuca, La Negra Cuca, and La Mulata Rosario appear

author speculates that although it may have been Ponce Reyes's father, it was more likely Ponce Reyes himself. This would place him in Cuba at least until the mid-1910s. See Cristóbal Díaz Ayala, *Cuba canta y baila: discografía de la música cubana*, Vol. 1 (San Juan, PR: Musicalia, 1994), 128. At any rate, evidence places Ponce Reyes in Mexico by 1925 when he became a member of Julián Carrillo's microtonal music ensemble Grupo 13. "Vientos de fronda," *El Sonido 13* 11, nos. 23–24 (1925), 12–13. The commentary in this journal, which congratulates Ponce Reyes for winning a composition contest in Mexico City, contains two brief references that suggest he was perceived as a black musician by his Mexican colleagues. First, it quotes Ponce Reyes as saying "pero que quiere uté" ["but what do you want"], emphasizing his Cuban accent (*uté* instead of *usted*). Second, it reproduces a comment by Ponce Reyes to Carrillo, "no podía ser yo la mancha de nuestra clase" ["I could not be the stain on our cohort"], jokingly implying that regardless of his black skin he would not be the one to shame his classmates by losing the contest (12).

Figure 3.4: Tomás Ponce Reyes. Photo published in *El Sonido 13* (1925).

prominently in chronicles of early danzón scenes in that city and in the capital.[103] The presence of influential black Cuban musicians in 1920s Mexico is reflected in the lineup of Orquesta Concha at the time (see Fig. 3.6). This shift in racial representation coincides with a change in its imaginary relation to place. Mexico City audiences began to associate the music with Veracruz due to the increasing presence of Veracruz-based danzón musicians in the capital and a recognition that the dance had been adopted there by the working classes since the late nineteenth century. Veracruz's residents have adopted multiple racial discourses strategically through the years, embracing or rejecting blackness depending on various factors but often referring to their city's African heritage as a source of uniqueness and distinction.[104] Yet little

103. Francisco Rivera "Paco Píldora" quoted in Flores y Escalante, *Salón México*, 52–53; Ángel Trejo, *¡Hey familia, danzón dedicado a . . .!* (Mexico City: Plaza y Valdés, 1993), 40; Flores y Escalante, *Imágenes del danzón. Iconografía del danzón en México* (Mexico City: Asociación Mexicana de Estudios Fonográficos, A.C., 1994), 116–22.
104. For an ethnographic exploration of racial discourses in relation to the danzón in Veracruz, see Hettie Malcomson, "La configuración racial del danzón: los imaginarios raciales del Puerto de Veracruz" in *Mestizaje, diferencia y nación. Lo 'negro' en América Central y el Caribe*, ed. Elisabeth Cunin (Mexico City: INAH, 2010), 267–98.

documentation exists as to how they played or danced danzón in the nineteenth century and whether their style was truly unique.[105]

The success of the Gonzalo Hernández and Raúl del Monte's bufo companies in Mexico in 1889 and 1903 overcame the initial reticence of Mexican audiences toward blackface performance. However, only following the 1914 and 1919 seasons of the Arquímedes Pous Theater Company did Cuban blackface gain broad popularity there.[106] Pous established a reputation for superb dialogue, spectacular choreographies, magnificent scenery, and an opulent wardrobe, gradually winning over the public.[107] Mexican audiences demanded that they extend their 1919 season to more than forty performances.[108]

The increasing visibility of black Cuban danzón musicians in Mexico, combined with the sudden success of touring blackface companies, reinforced the connections between blackness and the danzón in the minds of Mexican audiences. As one example, "Almendra" (by Abelardo Valdés, 1938), a classic Cuban danzón whose original lyrics in the montuno include the phrase "son de almendra voy a bailar" ("I will dance an almond song") came to be reinterpreted in 1930s–1940s Mexico as "danzón negro voy a bailar" ("I will dance a black danzón").[109] Thus, a musical form whose racial overtones had been overlooked by the bourgeoisie and aristocracy when they first embraced it in the 1880s was resignified as black as it became popular among the working classes in the 1910s, 1920s, and beyond. This cultural transformation proved particularly important in the elaboration of Mexico's post-revolutionary discourse, projecting racial anxieties about Caribbean blackness onto the danzón. At the same time, it allowed Cuban musical styles previously considered black such as the habanera and contradanza to be whitened and naturalized as "Mexican" during the same period.

José Vasconcelos as minister of education from 1921 to 1924 established the notion of mestizaje at the center of racial discourse within the Mexican revolutionary regime. Vasconcelos's cultural crusade involved a "civilizing" project that privileged the Hispanic elements of Mexican heritage in an attempt to counter what intellectuals and politicians alike viewed as the dangerous and growing influence of US culture in Mexico. Vasconcelos's notion of mestizaje, defined by him as a process of racial and cultural mixing that would create a civilization transcending racial and ethnic

105. Flores y Escalante, Salón México, 39–68; Flores y Escalante, Imágenes del danzón, 35–49; and Trejo, ¡Hey familia, 37–44.

106. Río Prado, La Venus de bronce, 70; and Flores y Escalante, Salón México, 85.

107. As opposed to other actors, Arquímedes Pous's blackface performances were not considered a mockery of Afro-Cubans. Instead, he is described as a "champion in the fight against discrimination in Cuba." Robin D. Moore, Nationalizing Blackness. Afrocubanismo and Artistic Revolution in Havana, 1920–1940 (Pittsburgh: University of Pittsburgh Press, 1997), 48. The success of Pous's company in Mexico was also influenced by a completely different historical context. At the end of the nineteenth century, political polemics surrounded bufo acts favored Cuban independence, while in 1910s the performers freely composed material around other themes.

108. Flores y Escalante, Salón México, 85.

109. These lyrics can be heard in the version of "Almendra" played in Emilio "El Indio" Fernández's classic film Salón México (1949). They could also be interpreted as "danzón, negro, voy a bailar" or "black man, I'm going to dance danzón."

differences, was in fact an ideological project designed to privilege European culture, indigenous assimilation, homogenization, and the whitewashing of ethnic difference.[110] Furthermore, since Vasconcelos's model emphasized only European and indigenous cultures, the erasure of blackness became a central component of mestizaje as well. In the case of music, the presence of musical forms like the danzón (increasingly associated with Cuba) allowed blackness to be projected onto Caribbean influences as if all blackness in Mexico were imported from Cuba. This racial distancing made possible a second rhetorical trend: the transformation of older Cuban forms which had been considered black in the past—the contradanza and habanera—into icons of Mexican identity, both individually and through their stylistic influence on the *canción mexicana*.

DISCURSIVE TRANSFORMATION OF THE DANZÓN IN CUBA

Various factors combined to reduce racialized fear among white Cubans toward the end of the 1880s. The relatively peaceful transition from slavery to abolition (1880–1886) made claims about an impending slave uprising on the island ring increasingly hollow. New waves of white immigration to Cuba from Spain and the Canary Islands, supported financially by the colonial government, resulted in Hispanic Cubans representing a solid 68 percent majority of Cuba's population by 1887.[111] Danzones were not warmly embraced by all Cubans by the end of that decade, but their fusion of European- and subdued African-derived elements did not necessarily strike all listeners as implying that an impending race war lay in the island's near future. And of course the most extreme views associated with articles and books of the period represented an extension of Spanish war propaganda in many cases, not necessarily views accepted by the average reader.

Perhaps even more important to the mass acceptance of the danzón in the 1890s was the crafting of a new discourse of raceless nationality by ideologues of the revolution such as José Martí, Rafael Serra, and Juan Gualberto Gómez. They recognized that earlier rebellions had failed in part because the Spanish had been able to capitalize on racial divisions among the troops. In response to ongoing Spanish warnings about black barbarity and the racial hatred ostensibly harbored by black insurgents, Martí and others began to discuss the history of the insurgency in new ways. Their accounts foregrounded black-white cooperation and suggested that all differences between the races had been resolved on the battlefield during the Ten Years War. They argued that strong identification along racial lines was tantamount to treason, even among black Cubans struggling for equal rights, and should be discouraged.[112] Revolutionaries crafted a revised image of the armed black insurgent: valiant but

110. Marco Polo Hernández Cuevas, *African Mexicans and the Discourse on Modern Nation* (Lanham, MD: University Press of America, 2004), 10–11.

111. Ferrer, *Insurgent Cuba*, 96.

112. José Martí, *Biblioteca popular martiana no. 4. La cuestión racial* (Havana: Editorial Lex, 1959), 27.

innocent, selfless, obedient, and loyal, respectful of existing racial hierarchies, without any independent social or political agenda.[113] And in fact rebel leaders actively suppressed such agendas, implying that any lingering prejudice or injustice would be addressed in an independent Cuba of the future. It is noteworthy that even as progressive a thinker as Martí had no interest in African-derived culture, but assumed Cuba's black population would divest itself of African heritage and embrace European models in order to be treated as equals.[114]

Acceptance of the danzón in Cuba as a prominent national dance was far from a monolithic process; rather, various sectors of the public accepted it to differing degrees and at different times over the course of two or three decades. The first known reference to elite social groups performing danzones appear in the Matanzas newspaper La Aurora del Yumurí in November of 1871, describing choreographed figure dances with wreaths of artificial flowers.[115] But as a couple dance, the form first became widely popular among working-class audiences—and perhaps elites with bohemian tastes—who danced it in recreational societies and public theaters of the 1880s and beyond. Various individuals helped popularize and disseminate the new danzón compositions in three or more sections across the island. They included Miguel Faílde, who toured Cienfuegos and other regions beginning about 1890; Antonio "Papaíto" Torroella, who played early Faílde compositions in Havana after visiting Matanzas; and Raimundo Valenzuela, also based in Havana, who contributed to the elaboration of the danzón's structure and orchestrational style.[116]

Little documentation exists on the specifics of events held at working-class sociedades de recreo in Havana, but Zoila Lapique Becali has recorded the many such venues where danzón bands performed. They included La Sociedad El Pilar, La Sociedad de Recreo de Santos Suárez, La Unión de Peñalver, El Liceo de Jesús del Monte, and El Liceo de Guanabacoa.[117] Theaters had long been associated with libertine and racially diverse dancing as well and in the 1880s became another prominent site of danzón performance. Havana's Diario de la Marina includes accounts of public dances beginning in the 1870s, for instance, describing rowdy behavior in which "one finds dances of every genre and color."[118] Havana's Irijoa theater (later renamed after Martí) opened in 1884 and scheduled many public dances that included danzones from the outset, especially over the Christmas and New Year season. Several theaters developed a reputation for bailes populares featuring the danzón by the 1880s and early 1890s including the Alhambra, the Cervantes, the Payret, and the Tacón. Such

113. Ferrer, Insurgent Cuba, 119, 121.

114. Helg, Our Rightful Share, 45.

115. Castillo Faílde, Miguel Faílde, 86.

116. For discussion of Faílde's tours, see Castillo Faílde, Miguel Faílde, 118. For background on Torroella's involvement in the dissemination of the genre, see Félix Soloni, "El danzón y su inventor, Miguel Failde. Notas históricas," in Cuba musical. Album-resúmen ilustrado de la historia y de la actual situación del arte musical en Cuba, ed. José Calero Martín y Leopoldo Valdés Quesada (Havana: Molina y Compañía), 1040–1041.

117. Lapique Becali, Cuba colonial, 311.

118. Diario de la Marina, May 5, 1877, no page, as quoted in Leal, La selva oscura, Vol. 2, Teatro bufo siglo XIX, 81.

entertainment became increasingly common in the wake of abolition (1886). Elite critics denounced the dances, yet they grew in popularity. On some occasions organizers admitted clientele of any color who could pay the admission fee, while on others they rented the theater to exclusively black or white audiences.[119] A separate entrance existed at the back of some theaters for the poor and/or persons of color at events in which they were not permitted to take part directly.

Somewhat surprisingly, baseball games of the late nineteenth century also proved central to the popularization of danzón among the popular classes in the 1880s.[120] First introduced to the island in the 1860s by affluent Cubans who had studied in the United States and by US expatriates working in the sugar industry, baseball soon gained a substantial following. Prior to the occupation of Cuba in 1898, many Cubans viewed the United States as an inspirational model of progress and free enterprise, and as an alternative to that of Spain. Thus, imported games such as baseball had largely positive, even nationalistic associations. Elite society created the first baseball clubs, but by the mid-1880s entire leagues had formed across the island among all classes and social groups, including networks of black teams. All matches as of that decade ended with a dinner and dance in an outdoor venue or at a summer house at which danzones featured prominently.[121]

The unqualified acceptance of the danzón among elites, especially in Havana, involved an exceptionally long process.[122] The earliest mention of danzón orchestras taking part in the events of Havana's high society appear sporadically in conjunction with carnival. In February 1886, for instance, El Fígaro magazine announced that the Orquesta Valenzuela would play for the opening of a skating rink, and that groups nominally under his direction would play at ten different masked carnival dances in the coming weeks.[123] Raimundo Valenzuela's group became phenomenally popular at this time; he eventually organized half a dozen "Orquestas Valenzuelas" so that they could play simultaneously at various locations. One supposes that his performances for elites included at least some danzones, though early commentators do not mention them. The term "danzón" appears in print in March of 1886 as part of an account of a masked dance for adolescents, but the article states that "Although Valenzuela played danzones, the [youth] didn't dance them out of respect for the older people

119. Nancy González Arzola, Teatro Martí. Prodigiosa permanencia (Havana: Ediciones Unión 2010), 31, 41, 62, 68, 83.

120. Alfonso López, "Las narrativas del béisbol en la construcción del nacionalismo cubano: 1880–1920," in Perfiles de la nación, ed. María del Pilar Díaz Castañón (Havana: Editorial de Ciencias Sociales, 2004), 128.

121. Roberto González Hechevarría, Crítica práctica (Mexico City: Fondo de Cultura Económica, 2002), 257.

122. Occasional commentary in the Diario de Matanzas from the 1870s suggests that some elites there defended the danzón against detractors and believed it could be danced "decently." At this time they must have been referring to bailes de flores, and not to couple dancing, however. Examples include the articles "Seamos imparciales" and "Sobre el baile," both of which appear the same day in the Diario de Matanzas 1, no. 71 (Sunday, December 22, 1878).

123. Ramón Catalá, "Peloteras," El Fígaro 2, no. 6 (February 11,1886), 8; and "Mascaradas," El Fígaro 2, no. 10 (March 11, 1886), 6.

present. They contented themselves with figure dances and polkas."[124] Even more negative views of the danzón appear in April of 1886 in conjunction with the review of a novel by Pablo Hernández entitled *Idilios*. The novelist denounces the danzón in his work as "unpatriotic"; reviewer Mariano Ramiro contests that suggestion as exaggerated, but accepts the broader idea that the dance be prohibited for the public good.[125] Reprints of dance programs even for some elite carnival events in 1888 suggest that many did not include the danzón.[126]

Beginning in about 1889, however, one finds more tolerant views of danzones appearing in the press alongside ambivalent commentary. Some authors strongly defended them—along with other local expression such as stylized rumba music and dance of the blackface theater—as inherently Cuban and thus important, and publications of danzón scores began to appear in pro-independence publications such as the weekly newspaper *Gil Blas*.[127] Raimundo Valenzuela's band received prominent mention in *El Fígaro* beginning with the carnival seasons of 1889 through the final War of Independence in 1895. Writers increasingly referred to him as a composer of national renown rather than merely a bandleader, and the magazine even sponsored events where he was to perform.[128] His name as of 1892 appears alongside phrases such as "king of danzones"; many elites apparently danced to his music openly on the beaches of Marianao, and in exclusive societies such as the Círculo Habanero.[129] Despite the persistence of vocal detractors, resistance to the danzón was clearly in decline. By 1895, Miguel Faílde's group headlined a dance at the elite Casino Español; the Orquesta Valenzuela began offering regular events at the Teatro Irijoa the same year in conjunction with comic sketches of the Salas bufo troupe, where they played to packed houses for two and a half years.[130]

For their part, middle-class leaders of color suggested that the growing popularity of the danzón demonstrated the extent of cultural advancement achieved by black and mixed-race Cubans. Operating within the same evolutionist frame of reference as white contemporaries, mulatto politician Juan Gualberto Gómez expressed pride at the transition from "African *tangos*" and other dances previously embraced by the black community to the more "refined" expression of the danzón.

Isn't it true that dances of the *sociedades de color* have contributed much to the progress, the culture, and the morality of our race? . . . Our youths, in great measure, dedicated themselves to *ñáñigo* gatherings, black *tangos*, immoral dances in the

124. Ramón Catalá, "Peloteras," *El Fígaro* 2, no. 11 (March 18, 1886), 7–8.
125. Mariano Ramiro, "Crítica literaria," *El Fígaro* 2, no 15 (April 15, 1886), 2.
126. E.g., González Arzola, *Teatro Martí*, 65. *El Fígaro* 6, no 4 (February 25, 1888), 8.
127. One example of commentary defending the danzón appears in the article by Antonio Escobar. "Cosas que se van," *El Fígaro* 5, no. 1 (January 13, 1889), 6. Zoila Lapique Becali (*Música colonial cubana, tomo 1, 1812–1902* [Havana: Letras Cubanas, 1979], 268–70) discusses the danzones in *Gil Blas*.
128. *El Fígaro* 5, no. 4 (February 3, 1889), 3.
129. Raoul Cay, "Crónica," *El Fígaro* 8, no. 24 (June 10, 1892), 7; and *El Fígaro* 8, no. 7 (February 28, 1892), 7.
130. González Arzola, *Teatro Martí*, 86; Lapique Becali, *Cuba colonial*, 302.

casas de cuna of Guanabacoa and Albizu heights. . . . Then the societies appeared and such dances represented an advance over tangos and ñáñigo contortions. . . . [W]e should never overlook the fact that in Havana the societies managed to distance [our youth] from barbarous practices . . . that contributed to their truly abysmal moral and intellectual level.[131]

Clearly, the danzón had distinct meanings within the black community from the late 1870s onward. Rather than viewing the danzón's creolized elements as traces of atavism, they associated its popularity among black and white audiences as a symbol of anti-racist ideologies and nationalist pride, and of sophistication. This latter is clear in the lavish attire preferred by middle-class black danzón dancers. An author in the newspaper *La Fraternidad* noted with amazement the "unrestrained luxuriousness" of danzón events and wondered "how much sacrifice, how many hardships and difficult moments" participation in the dance must have cost those attending.[132] Danzones accompanied the most important aspects of black public life, from fundraisers for black schoolchildren to celebrations for black politicians.[133]

Naturally, gradual acceptance of the danzón as the music of all Cubans did not imply that racial divisions had been overcome, only that one form of local music associated originally with blacks now seemed less threatening. Through the 1880s and 1890s, published articles make it clear that the thought of blacks and whites mixing through marriage or even interacting socially remained abhorrent to many whites.[134] And despite a growing recognition that any successful revolutionary effort would entail arming black troops, the idea still generated unease. Martí and other revolutionary propagandists reacted to such concerns by emphasizing the loyalty and subservience of black *mambises*, as mentioned, while less progressive commentators tended to perpetuate racist caricatures of them in which they appeared less threatening, but also ridiculous. Cartoons of black soldiers in the press of the 1880s depicted them as physically less than human, fit only for domestic chores, constantly hungering for white women, or as cannibalistic.[135] Fictional stories suggested they

131. *La Igualdad*, March 14, 1893, 1–2. "¿No es verdad que los bailes que las Sociedades de la clase de color han servido mucho para el progreso, la cultura y la moralidad de nuestra raza? . . . Nuestra juventud, en buena parte, se dedicaba a los juegos de ñáñigos, a los tangos, a los bailes inmorales de la cuna de Guanabacoa, y de los altos de Albizu . . . entonces se crearon las sociedades y sus bailes vinieron a representar un positivo progreso sobre los tangos y las contorsiones del ñañiguismo . . . no debemos desconocer que en la Habana las sociedades prestaron el servicio de alejarlos de aquellas otras prácticas bárbaras que . . . hacían que el nivel moral e intelectual de dicha clase fuera verdaderamente desconsolador."

132. Jimeno Herld, "De Cienfuegos," *La Fraternidad*, December 20, 1888, 3–4.

133. Lane, *Blackface Cuba*, 162.

134. "El garbanzo y el café," *El Fígaro* 5, no. 4 (November 17, 1889), 6. Originally published in the *Crónica Liberal de Cárdenas*.

135. *El Fígaro* 5, no. 29 (August 11, 1889), 5. The soldier, with exaggerated black facial features, is holding a fish. His belly sticks out, he is wearing a silly plumed helmet and house slippers, and has a large spoon hanging by his side where a sword should be. The caption on the image reads "Un negro general cocinero desea cocinar a una señora" (a black chef-general wants to cook a lady).

were inherently superstitious and deluded because of their belief in African-derived religions.[136] With the onset of renewed armed conflict in 1895, pro-Spanish periodicals such as *La Política Cómica* suggested once again that blacks were less than human, that the revolutionary effort was racially motivated, and that military figures such as Guillermo Moncada planned to establish a black monarchy.[137]

Within a few years, dance events largely came to a halt in most cities across the island owing to policies of forced relocation and the devastation of local economies.[138] Yet the conclusion of the war made the population more nationalistic and supportive of local heritage. By the time Spanish troops departed, danzones had become emblematic enough of cubanía to accompany the lowering of the Spanish flag over the Morro castle in Havana.[139] Miguel Faílde himself played danzones in Matanzas to celebrate the arrival of military governor Wilson to that city.[140] The occupation is the moment that ushered in the true heyday of the danzón in Cuba, from 1898 through approximately 1915. While more overtly African-influenced drumming and dance continued to be persecuted, Cubans no longer perceived the danzón as threatening.

Frustrated aspirations for full national sovereignty under US occupation contributed greatly to the wholehearted acceptance of the danzón. Friction with the US military, combined with the strong presence of imported North American music, led to a backlash that exalted all things local.[141] The increasing vogue of the two-step and related foreign dances among the young made elite families more receptive to the danzón as an alternative. As early as 1899 prominent citizens seem to have initiated campaigns urging others to prohibit the two-step in their social gatherings.[142] Playing a danzón or reciting patriotic *décima* poetry during the occupation served as an important means of expressing national pride for everyone at a time when flying the Cuban flag had been outlawed.[143] Marial Iglesias Utset has undertaken the most detailed cultural history of Cuba during this period. Her book describes North American military leaders attempting to do away with local cultural forms and replace them with North American practices, even as Cuban elites promoted "whitened" and gentrified national pastimes. But the masses continued to embrace the guaracha, the blackface theater, Afro-Cuban carnival bands, theater acts featuring local talent, and other vernacular forms, often promoting them strategically as a reaction to US domination. Public celebrations of the danzón also figured prominently among their activities.

136. "Cuentos inverosímiles," *El Fígaro* 5, no 7 (February 24, 1889), 6.
137. E.g., "Festín de caníbales," *La política cómica* 1, no. 29 (June 1895), 1. "El emperador Guillermón," *La política cómica* 1, no. 19 (April 1, 1895), 5. "Sandwiches," *La política cómica* 1, no. 20 (April 9, 1895), 3. "Refuerzos para Maceo," *La política cómica* 1, no. 27 (May 27, 1895), 1.
138. De Ximeno y Cruz, *Memorias de Lola María*, 233.
139. Iglesias Utset, *A Cultural History of Cuba*. 136.
140. Lapique Becali, *Cuba colonial* 2008, 309.
141. Rogelio Martínez Furé, interview, Havana, Cuba, January 20, 1994.
142. Lapique Becali, *Cuba colonial*, 314.
143. Iglesias Utset, *A Cultural History of Cuba*, 1, 4.

Far from aping a North American style of fashionable dance, the Cuban lower-class redoubled its affection for its own way of dancing, even inventing a new kind of dance—the "patriotic dance"—in which the danzón became a symbol of protest against the "civilizing" pretensions of a forced acculturation. . . . As a result, every popular celebration held [from 1898 to 1902] had its corresponding orchestra complete with a full repertoire of Cuban danzones. Dancing the danzón . . . was thus seen as a way to reaffirm *cubanía* . . . outside the milieu of official political life, at social gatherings, and in cockfighting pits and gambling dens, in dancehalls and cafés, the "masses" resisted the prompting to remake themselves; they were determined to live by their own lights.[144]

In the years after 1902, the danzón consolidated its preeminent position as a national musical form. The most exclusive (and of course segregated) dance venues such as the Ateneo and Círculo Habanero featured it regularly in social events, where only a few years earlier it had been shunned. Music critic Serafín Ramírez, who in the early 1890s had nothing but scorn for the danzón, began publishing printed scores of such music in the journal *La Gaceta Musical* in the early twentieth century, together with his collaborators.[145] Danzones dominated the earliest recordings of Cuban music in 1904, underscoring its importance to listeners of the day, and constituted roughly 40 percent of all recordings made in Cuba through 1925.[146] Poets published décimas in local newspapers singing their praises, and white women from elite families played piano reductions of formerly controversial hits from the 1880s in their drawing rooms.[147] (❷ Sheet Music Covers) Sheet music publications from the first decades of the twentieth century make clear that the genre dominated music making at the time; composers used it to comment on many sorts of national and international events with titles such as "La toma de Varsovia" ("The Taking of Warsaw"), "Aliados y alemanes" ("Allies and Germans"), "El dengue" ("Dengue Fever"), "El ferrocarril central" ("The Central Railway"), "El teléfono de larga distancia" ("The Long-Distance Telephone"), and so on.[148] Far from a debased or malignant cultural force, the danzón was by then perceived as embodying a largely white creole essence of Cuban character as defined by dominant society. By the 1920s, conservative activists fought to preserve its centrality to younger audiences in the face of the growing popularity of *son* and jazz.[149]

As part of the rhetorical transformation of the danzón, musicologist and composer Eduardo Sánchez de Fuentes published a series of books and essays denying that any African influences had contributed to its development. In his discussions of

144. Iglesias Utset, *A Cultural History of Cuba*, 57.
145. Lapique Becali, *Música colonial cubana*, 290.
146. Díaz Ayala, *Los contrapunteos*, 45, 48.
147. Castillo Faílde, *Miguel Faílde*, 163–64; Lapique Becali, *Cuba colonial*, 326.
148. Ezequiel Rodríguez Domínguez, *Iconografía del danzón* (Havana: Sub-Dirección Provincial de Música, 1967), 25–26.
149. Eduardo Sánchez de Fuentes, *El folk-lore en la música cubana* (Havana: Imprenta El Siglo XX), 27; Ramón Vasconcelos in Alejandro de la Fuente, *A Nation for All. Race, Inequality, and Politics in Twentieth-Century Cuba* (Chapel Hill: University of North Carolina Press, 2000), 180.

danzón history, he emphasized its historical ties to the contradance as performed in England and France, not the ways in which decades of Afro-Caribbean performers had modified such music in Cuba and elsewhere after 1800.[150] Sánchez de Fuentes likewise failed to mention the decades of public racialized controversy surrounding the danzón. He flatly denied African influences in the habanera as well and asserted the predominance of Spanish characteristics in all Cuban music.[151] If non-Europeans contributed to the unique sound of Cuban music in any way, he suggested—based in part on the work of similarly biased musicologists of the late nineteenth century—it was undoubtedly local indigenous cultures that infused national repertoire with its local flavor, transmitted by means of Indian concubines living with early Spanish settlers.[152] Only in the late 1940s did Fernando Ortiz definitively dispute the erasure of blackness in scholarship of this nature; one of his essays on the subject was subsequently reprinted as the first chapter of *La africanía de la música folklórica de Cuba* (1950).[153]

Racial discourses of early twentieth-century Cuba intersected in various ways with those surrounding the danzón. As might be expected, notions of evolutionism and black inferiority remained widespread. Yet politicians also invoked earlier rhetoric disseminated by revolutionary leaders to suggest that racial problems had been solved. They denounced as racist anyone criticizing the existing social order and placed the blame for any lack of black social mobility on the black community itself.[154] In reality, Cubans of color encountered few opportunities for a better education or increased job opportunities after 1902. Even former combatants and prominent military leaders found themselves shut out of positions in government and denied entry to many private businesses, restaurants, parks, and hotels. Such treatment clashed with their expectations as veterans and generated unrest. The liberal uprisings of 1906 derived largely from racial tensions of this nature, and the creation of the Partido Independiente de Color (PIC) followed outrage over the elections of 1908 in which not a single person of color was elected to political office. Attempts within the black community to mobilize politically resulted in new waves of racial fearmongering in the press. A violent government crackdown on the PIC led to the forced disbanding of the party and the slaughter of thousands of Afro-Cubans in 1912.[155]

Racial tensions of this sort manifested themselves culturally in various ways. As mentioned, local authorities criminalized music and dance forms heavily influenced by African heritage; in some cases, the persecution (especially of religious repertoire) lasted well into the 1950s and 1960s.[156] Most dances and social venues remained

150. Sánchez de Fuentes, "El danzón," *Social* 13, no. 12 (December 1928), 32.
151. Sánchez de Fuentes, "El danzón," 13, 49.
152. Sánchez de Fuentes, *La música aborigen de América* (Havana: Imprenta Molina y Cía.), 53.
153. Fernando Ortiz, *La africanía de la música folklórica de Cuba* (Havana: Editora Universitaria, 1950).
154. Helg, *Our Rightful Share*, 3, 6.
155. Moore, *Nationalizing Blackness*, 27–30.
156. Robin D. Moore, *Music and Revolution. Cultural Change in Socialist Cuba* (Berkeley: University of California Press, 2006), 198–201, 204–213.

segregated in the early twentieth century, as well as parades involving revolutionary soldiers.[157] Recreational societies created by the black community often bore names such as La Armonía, La Unión, La Concordia, and La Fraternidad, reflecting both aspirations for harmonious integration into Cuban society and a desire to avoid further racial bloodshed. In this context, black groups chose to think of the danzón as a form of expression that tangibly demonstrated the union of African and European heritage. Of course, Afro-Cuban musical elements in the danzón tended to be heavily constrained, and the overwhelmingly black performers who popularized it trained on European instruments, wrote compositions based on European harmonic conventions, and often played as hired help for white audiences. Rather than challenging the social order, danzón as social practice thus perpetuated many existing conventions. White and middle-class danzón enthusiasts for their part tended increasingly to overlook or downplay the music's Afro-Cuban origins in the same way they chose to disregard black contributions to the war effort or the denial of full citizenship to the black community. The ambiguity of the danzón in cultural terms and its susceptibility to multiple readings along racial lines contributed greatly to its broad acceptance through the early decades of the new Republic.

TRANSFORMATIONS OF CUBAN MUSIC IN POST-REVOLUTIONARY MEXICO

Mexico's long and bloody civil war extended from 1910 to 1921. The conflict began with a desire among progressive elites to create a democratic system of government after thirty years of Porfiriato—Porfirio Díaz's dictatorship (1877–1911)—but quickly expanded to include demands by the masses for social equality and land reform. The end of armed conflict brought significant social and cultural changes to the country. Political leaders attempted to break with the recent past, requiring the development of new symbols of nationality to represent a closer liaison between the state and the people. These symbols developed slowly out of dialogues among government ideologues, private entrepreneurs, and the everyday cultural expressions of the masses. Fundamental to the reconceptualization of the nation were the processes of modernization, urbanization, and centralization of power in Mexico City. An emphasis on modernization necessitated greater recognition of the nascent urban working class within the public imaginary, and new roles for women as workers. Finally, discourses of mestizaje and an at least rhetorical valorization of indigenous heritage became the official doctrine of the post-revolutionary regime as reflected in the writings of José Vasconcelos (mentioned previously) and the visual art of Diego Rivera, José Clemente Orozco, and many others.

The armed struggle had devastating consequences for the Mexican economy and was particularly hard on peasants and farmers in rural areas, forcing a massive exodus from the countryside to the cities. By 1930, the population of Mexico City quadrupled from that of 1900, thus creating a sizable urban working class. In the 1920s and 1930s

157. Iglesias Utset, *A Cultural History of Cuba*, 55–56.

Figure 3.5: Stage and dance floor of Salón Colonia, Mexico City. Photo property of Simón Jara Gámez, Mexico City dance historian. Used by permission.

many new dances and musical genres circulated in the capital as well. The fox-trot, charleston, tango, one-step, shimmy, and blues all attracted audiences, in turn coming to represent aspirations of modernity among many Mexicans, especially elites. For their part, the working classes preferred the danzón and the bolero—Caribbean musics that flourished in brothels, taverns, and cabarets—as the soundtrack of their new, fast-paced urban lives. The danzón's early associations with refined, aristocratic entertainment at the end of the Porfiriato soon changed; it came to be thought of as a working-class form of moral permissiveness, one with Afro-Caribbean roots.

Many modest dancehalls opened in Mexico City in the 1910s, though most lacked proper dance floors, failed to meet basic standards of hygiene, and were largely unsuitable for dancing.[158] The next decade witnessed the opening of more modern venues, including the legendary Salón México in 1920 and the Salón Colonia in 1922. The large black face on the back of the stage of Salón Colonia (Fig. 3.5) became the trademark of this hall and an icon of the danzón-dominated 1930–1940s Mexican nightlife, further reinforcing the associations between the dance and blackness developed in those decades.[159]

158. Simón Jara Gámez, Aurelio Rodríguez "Yeyo," and Antonio Zedillo Castillo, *De Cuba con amor . . . el danzón en México* (Mexico City: CONACULTA, 2001), 61.
159. After Salón Colonia closed its doors in 2003, El Negro (as dance aficionados call the large decorative mask) became part of the collection of Mexico City's Museo del Juguete.

The new, modernized dancehalls represented a reaction to campaigns against working-class entertainment by the conservative Liga de la Decencia [Decency League], which criticized early venues as unhealthy and as sites for the propagation of indecent dances, especially imports from the United States such as the shimmy.[160] In response, venues of the 1920s promoted social dance as part of a healthy lifestyle and offered low-cost entrance fees and clean facilities.[161] The Salón México and Colonia served as models for subsequent ballrooms of the 1920s and 1930s including the Dancing Corona, Mata Hari Dancing Club, La Playa, Smyrna Club, Salón Los Ángeles, and Tívoli. The proliferation of these venues and the vibrancy of Mexico City's nightlife attracted the best orchestras from the countryside that soon relocated to the capital or spent extended periods of time there. The Orquesta Concha from Mérida (Fig. 3.6), as one example, featuring Acerina on kettle drums, Juan Luis Cabrera on violin, and Tomás Ponce Reyes on bass, performed as Salón México's house orchestra from 1926 to 1938.

Massive migration to the cities resulted in the increasing presence of women in the public sphere. The popularization of the danzón provided Mexican women with a space to negotiate their new status, from individuals largely restricted to domestic spaces to increasingly independent and public actors. Robert Buffington suggests that the danzón craze and salon culture were both "part and parcel" of "the emergence of working-class women as 'modern' subjects" and "structured their participation in post-revolutionary society."[162] Nevertheless, such changes in traditional gender roles also raised concerns about the role of women in Mexican society. Guadalupe Caro Cocotle demonstrates that the struggle between mainstream notions of gender derived from earlier periods and constructs of the new Mexican woman frequently took place in performative spaces involving dance, exemplified by her study of Mexican flappers and the fox-trot and shimmy scenes.[163] However, it was the danzón's ubiquity in the Mexican mass media—especially films—that played a fundamental role in representations of modern Mexican femininity and mediated the fears of conservative social sectors.

Prostitution is one of the recurrent themes of early Mexican cinema. Antonio Moreno's *Santa* (1932), the first Mexican sound film, and Arcady Boytler's *La mujer del puerto* (1933), one of the industry's first blockbuster hits, are both moralistic stories about the downward spiral of indiscretion and tragedy that leads the two female characters to perdition in a brothel. These movies set the tone for representations of urban femininity within a contradictory imaginary that, as Sergio de la Mora argues, depicts the prostitute as the "object of erotic desire who is paradoxically both

160. Amparo Sevilla, *Los templos del buen bailar* (Mexico City: CONACULTA, 2003), 61–68.

161. Jara Gámez et al., *De Cuba con amor*, 69.

162. Robert Buffington, "La 'Dancing' Mexicana. Danzón and the Transformation of Intimacy in Post-Revolutionary Mexico City," *Journal of Latin American Cultural Studies* 14, no. 1 (2005), 89.

163. Guadalupe Caro Cocotle, "La música de las pelonas. Nuevas identidades femeninas del México moderno, 1920–1930." PhD Dissertation, Universidad Nacional Autónoma de México (in process).

Figure 3.6: Orquesta Concha, late 1920s. Consejo Valiente Robert "Acerina" (timbal), Juan Luis Cabrera (violin), Juan de Dios Concha (trumpet, standing left), Pedro Concha (drums), Everardo Concha (saxophone, sitting right), Juan Fernández (trombone), and Tomás Ponce Reyes (bass), among others. Photo property of Simón Jara Gámez, Mexico City dance historian. Used by permission.

pure and corrupt."[164] In both films, as in the case of later movie genres they helped develop—the *cabaretera*, rumbera, and *fichera* films of the 1940s and 1950s—danzones and boleros provide the soundtrack to immorality and prostitution.[165] The fact that these styles of music derive from the Caribbean made them the perfect repositories of "otherness," in opposition to local mariachi and ranchera music that came to represent a male chauvinist Mexican identity in the *comedia ranchera* genre.[166] Thus, while local ranchera music stood for a *mexicanidad* that inculcated mainstream values of paternalistic masculinity such as chivalry, courage, virility, dependability, protection, and domineering control over women, the danzón and bolero became symbols of corrupting "otherness." Using the danzón, a foreign, black music, to symbolize the shame that modern women would face by entering the public sphere proved less controversial than stigmatizing a local music with such associations. Following the

164. Sergio de la Mora, *Cinemachismo. Masculinities and Sexuality in Mexican Film* (Austin: University of Texas Press, 2006), 23.
165. Cabaretera, rumbera, and fichera films were standard features in Mexico by the 1950s. They revolved around the lives of female cabaret singers, dancers, and/or prostitutes.
166. These were musical films revolving around stylized depictions of country lifestyles such as *Allá en el rancho grande* (1936).

dichotomy virgin/whore evoked in de la Mora's analysis of prostitution in Mexican films, women in the public sphere could only be depicted as mother or virgins, the embodiment of virtue (under the control of males), or prostitutes (when escaping male control).

Another aspect of performance that reinforced the danzón's connection with Caribbean culture and blackness was the popularization of the montuno section at the end of many pieces toward the end of the 1920s. Although the montuno from the Cuban *son* was incorporated into Cuban compositions in the early 1910s,[167] Mexicans avoided it well into the late 1920s. This is evident in the catalogue of danzones recorded in Mexico between 1916 and 1929.[168] Orchestras in the 1920s typically played the last section of danzones at a livelier tempo, yet the first proper montunos—based on continuous improvisation over repeated ostinato figures—appear only in the Orquesta Concha's renditions of "Tristeza" (1927) and "Desdén" (1929) at the end of the decade. It is likely that the tendency to incorporate the montuno in such recordings reflects the preferences of dancers and that dance bands had been performing montunos for a few years. The presence of more overt Afro-Caribbean elements in the repertory of Mexican danzón compositions made it easier to associate the music with Afro-Cuban genres like the rumba, and thus with anxieties about otherness.

Mexican composers had written contradanzas and habaneras since the nineteenth century, yet many still considered them foreign music after 1900. Writing in 1917, Manuel M. Ponce makes this clear when he states that although "voluptuous danzones, tangos, and languid danzas . . . have been composed in Mexico, achieving great success, we should consider them imitations of Cuban music."[169] Ponce's reference to "voluptuousness" echoes the tone of nineteenth-century Mexican chronicles that emphasize the sensuality of all Cuban dance forms and go as far as calling them "the illegitimate daughter of the licentious dances performed by blacks in Africa."[170] Yet despite this invective, the habanera rhythm strongly influenced Mexican composition, as mentioned. It became a prominent feature of the canción mexicana by the 1940s, with many of the most popular pieces in that style incorporating the pattern.[171] In the 1960s, Vicente T. Mendoza discussed the process by which the habanera had been transformed into a local romantic song form and listed the former's rhythm as a defining feature of the canción mexicana.[172] The fact that the music

167. Danzón historians often refer to José Urfé's "El bombín de Barreto" (1910) as the first danzón to incorporate a montuno in the final section of the rondo form. See discussion of this topic in Chapter 2.

168. Recordings of danzones in Mexico date from as early as 1906, although international labels like Victor only began to produce a limited number of commercial recordings beginning in the 1910s.

169. Manuel M. Ponce, *Escritos y composiciones musicales* (Mexico City: Cultura, 1917), 16.

170. Ignacio Manuel Altamirano, *Crónicas de la semana* (Mexico City: Ediciones de Bellas Artes, 1969 [1869]), 141.

171. For example, "La borrachita," "La barca de Guaymas," "La barca de oro," "Las golondrinas," "Adios Mariquita linda," and even Manuel M. Ponce's "A la orilla de un palmar," which was popularized in a habanera-based arrangement.

172. Vicente T. Mendoza, *La canción mexicana. Ensayo de clasificacion y antología* (Mexico City: Fondo de Cultura Económica, 1982 [1961]), 75.

anthology in *El folklore musical en las ciudades* includes many canciones in habanera style shows that scholars already recognized the importance of such repertoire in 1930.[173] Even in the 1920s, popular music composers like Ignacio Fernández Esperón "Tata Nacho," Mario Talavera, and Alfonso Esparza Oteo responded to Vasconcelos's *criollista* civilizing project by transcribing vernacular songs—or composing new ones—using the basic rhythmic pattern of the habanera, already well known to Mexican audiences.[174] Academic composers and pedagogues rejected this practice, as they considered popular song unsophisticated and unworthy of the concert hall.[175] Nevertheless, the public embraced the pieces and eventually came to think of them as the most typical variant of canción mexicana. Thus, the "Mexicanization" of the habanera rhythm and its transformation into a national symbol in the post-revolutionary period should be understood within the context of modernization, mestizaje, the popularization of new Cuban styles (especially the danzón), and the formation of a post-revolutionary working class.

The whitewashing of the habanera song form in Mexico began in the nineteenth century. Altamirano referred to it in the 1860s as an "illegitimate daughter of licentious black dances," yet nevertheless considered it a "more moderate and civilized daughter" than its antecedents.[176] From Altamirano's perspective, the adoption of the habanera by Mexican elites appears to have afforded it an aura of decency. This suggests in general terms how the discursive whitening of the habanera functioned in the Mexican context. However, for the habanera to make its way fully into the pantheon of national symbols and to be transformed into the canción mexicana, it had to be divested of all traces of blackness. The popularity of the danzón in subsequent decades and its identification with sensuality, otherness, and blackness converted it into a surrogate recipient of the habanera's Caribbean associations. Discursively erasing the habanera's origins and slowing its underlying rhythm to the point that its previously dance-like character became unrecognizable represented the final steps of

173. See Rubén M. Campos, *El folklore musical en las ciudades. Investigación acerca de la música mexicana para cantar y bailar* (Mexico City: Secretaría de Educación Pública, 1930).

174. The musical side of Vasconcelos's project was inspired by Manuel M. Ponce's call to take traditional canciones mexicanas as the source of a new Mexican music. Ponce first suggested the use of the canción mexicana as the source of national inspiration in a 1913 conference for El Ateneo de la Juventud entitled "La música mexicana y la canción mexicana." He repeated his plea in *Escritos y composiciones musicales* (1917), and "El folk-lore musical mexicano. Lo que se ha hecho. Lo que puede hacerse," *Revista Musical de México* 1, no. 5 (1919), 5–9. For a study of the adoption of the habanera rhythm in the *danza mexicana*, see Joel Almazán Orihuela, "La danza habanera en México (1870–1920)," PhD Dissertation, Centro de Investigación y Docencia en Humanidades del Estado de Morelos (2010). Almazán Orihuela discusses the works of Ernesto Elorduy, Felipe Villanueva, Juventino Rosas, and others.

175. Academic composers referred to their popular music counterparts as *arregladores* (arrangers). They organized the first Congreso Nacional de Música in 1926 partly a response to the polemic over the work of these composers and their songs. See Alejandro L. Madrid, "The Sounds of the Nation: Visions of Modernity and Tradition in Mexico's First National Congress of Music," *Hispanic American Historical Review* 86, no. 4 (2006), 681–706.

176. Altamirano, *Crónicas de la semana*, 141.

the transformation. As of the mid-twentieth century, most critics viewed this type of canción mexicana as a cherished symbol of Mexican character.

A process parallel to the "othering" of the habanera in the mid-nineteenth century is the eroticizing of the dancing female body articulated by its music. Altamirano's description of a woman he calls *la diosa de la danza habanera* (the goddess of habanera dance) suggests such a dynamic:

> [W]ithin the body of that bewitching young woman moves, without a doubt, some unknown god, the ardent genius of African dance, a dance of fire that makes blood boil in the veins; the heart pounds, the eyes languish, and an indefinite smile appears in the mouth . . . her body seemed to be moved by the music's cadence and the sound of the *huiro* [güiro] in a kind of measured trembling rather than an academic movement.[177]

The same links between black expressive culture and eroticism are reproduced in the othering of the danzón as it gained popularity among post-revolutionary Mexican working-class women. Federico Gamboa uses a rhetoric of sensuality in *Santa* to describe early twentieth-century danzones as they came to be associated with prostitution ("Caribbean rhythms danced with lascivious undulations of the torso");[178] such attitudes appear in cabaretera and rumbera films of the 1930s and 1940s. Many contain an implicitly moralist message, reinforced by the imaginary surrounding the danzón and other Afro-Cuban musics: they suggest that by abandoning the private sphere where men protect and control them, women enter a realm of unbridled sensuality that can only lead them to ruin. Negative masculine character types that also reinforce heteronormative values accompany this representation of women. The men with whom dancehall women associate fail to embody the values of paternalistic masculinity privileged by the mainstream; they are either pimps who exploit them or lovers who fail to rescue them from their fate.

David Eng proposes the notion of "racial castration" to explain how Anglo men in the United States perceive Asian men as effeminate in order to enhance their own sense of masculinity.[179] A similar process is evident in mid-twentieth-century Mexico involving an Other defined through Afro-Caribbean culture. Neither Mexican pimps nor black musicians and dancers are portrayed as "real" men in contemporary films because they fail to embody the values of paternalistic machismo; rather, they appear as morally weak and unable to protect, control, or gain the favor of their female partners. Instead of viewing them as racially castrated, one might describe these men as

177. ". . . en el cuerpo de esa hechicera joven se agitaba sin duda algún dios desconocido, el genio ardiente de la danza africana, danza de fuego que hace hervir la sangre en las venas, palpitar el corazón, languidecer los ojos y dibujarse en la boca una sonrisa indefinable [. . .] aquel cuerpo parecía conmoverse a las cadencias de la música y al son del huiro, más bien que por una especie de temblor acompasado que por su movimiento académico." Altamirano, *Crónicas de la semana*, 285.

178. Gamboa, *Santa*.

179. David Eng, *Racial Castration. Managing Masculinity in Asian America* (Durham, NC: Duke University Press, 2001), 2.

Figure 3.7: Scene from *En cada puerto un amor* (1949), featuring Cuban rumbera Amalia Aguilar and black musicians. Photo courtesy of Agrasanchez Film Archive, Harlingen, Texas.

personifying a "failed masculinity," one derived from the embrace of a foreign and corrupted expressive culture, a lack of appropriate moral values, or association with an alien ethnic/racial group.

The arrival of Afro-Cuban music forms like the rumba, mambo, and cha cha chá in 1950s Mexico allowed for a discursive whitening of the danzón similar to that of the habanera in the 1920s. Notions of blackness associated with the new dances (especially the rumba and mambo) facilitated the transfer of the danzón's blackness onto them (Fig. 3.7 shows a typical representation of rumba from the 1949 film *En cada puerto un amor*). Thus, while films like José Díaz Morales and Carlos Schlieper's *Pecadora* (1947), Chano Urueta's *Al son del mambo* (1950), or Emilio "Indio" Fernández's *Víctimas del pecado* (1951) portray the rumba and mambo as savage, sinful dances, other filmmakers simultaneously transform the danzón into the music of the Mexican worker, as in Alejandro Galindo's *Campeón sin corona* (1946), Ismael Rodríguez's *Ustedes los ricos* (1948), and Gilberto Martínez Solares's *El rey del barrio* (1950).[180] The

180. For a more detailed account of the perceived differences between the danzón and the mambo in the 1950s, see David F. García, "Going Primitive to the Movements and Sounds of Mambo," *Musical Quarterly*, no. 89 (2007), 505–23. For a discussion of the rumberas in terms of exoticism, see Gabriela Pulido Llanos, "Las mil y una rumbas. Cuatro cubanas en México," *Dimensión Antropológica* 15, no. 44 (2008), 99–132.

Figure 3.8: Danzón dance scene from *Salón México* (1949). Photo courtesy of Agrasanchez Film Archive, Harlingen, Texas.

perceived primitiveness of the mambo and rumba allow for the construction of discourse surrounding the danzón as a restrained, civilized practice. This dichotomy is evident in the early sequences of Emilio "Indio" Fernández's *Salón México* (1949) in which the director juxtaposes two dancing scenes. First he shows a number of white and *mestizo* couples dancing a slow, restrained, and elegant danzón (Fig. 3.8); almost immediately thereafter the action shifts to a furious rumba display by black musicians and dancers. While the contrast signals the discursive whitening of the danzón, the specific danzón played is the version of "Almendra" discussed earlier with the lyrics "*danzón negro voy a bailar.*" Such contradictory representations inform the particular moment the film was made, as the danzón's associations shifted from Afro-Cuban to Mexican mestizo. Contemporary danzoneros have embraced these mid-century discourses of whiteness and now associate danzones with the epitome of refined Mexican heritage, a form of imagined past practice they strive to recreate in the present (see Chapter 5).

The whitewashing of habanera in 1920s and 1930s Mexico and of the danzón in the 1950s must be understood within the discourse of nation building. The social and political dynamics of both periods allowed for the performance of new gender relations within moralist structures that resonated with the predominant Catholic mindset of Mexicans. The habanera and the danzón supported emergent ideologies of mestizaje in turn by relocating blackness beyond the boundaries of the nation-state.

The racialization of the danzón in both Cuba and Mexico has supported larger nationalist projects as well as the development of racial and moral imaginaries to support them. Racial controversies over the danzón in Cuba emerged during one of the tensest periods of the revolution against Spain. Two large-scale insurgencies, the Ten Years War and the Guerra Chiquita, had just ended inconclusively owing in large part to racial divisions among Cuban troops. Spanish propaganda managed to convince a majority of the white, educated population that the arming of free blacks and former slaves would lead to all-out war against them, miscegenation, and the degeneration of the island into barbarism. As a primary site of racial interaction in urban contexts, ballroom dance music became a focal point for the expression of white anxieties about blackness. Spanish-owned newspapers characterized the danzón as a corrupting influence, a form of rampant vice that threatened the entire colonial project much in the same way that armed revolutionaries themselves did.

By the 1890s, revolutionary leaders began an aggressive ideological campaign to counter Spanish propaganda and re-forge alliances between white and mixed-race forces. This involved reformulating Cuban identity as something that transcended African or European ancestry, and downplaying or choosing to ignore existing racial unease. The danzón, as the preeminent dance music of the day, played a central role in this ideological shift. In an era of ostensibly "raceless revolution," dance music that fused elements of African and European heritage and appealed to interracial audiences served as an ideal symbol of the revised revolutionary project. Yet its subdued incorporation of African-influenced elements could be conveniently overlooked by those who preferred to do so (and there were many). In this way, danzones contributed to liberal consensus of the period that suggested blacks should be part of the nation, but in a subservient role, in the background, expressing "appropriate gratitude" for their emancipation.

Within the space of only about ten years (1888–1898), the racialized invective surrounding danzones in newspapers and books was replaced by universal praise for the music as the epitome of Cuban heritage. To the popular classes and to black performers it represented the triumph of the local, the vindication of mixed-race heritage, and promised greater racial inclusion in an independent Cuba of the future. To elites, danzones had the advantage of referencing inclusion in a relatively nonthreatening way. The music was notated and required formal Western training on a range of symphonic instruments to perform, thus conforming to commonsense notions of European cultural superiority and progress. It reigned supreme in the first decades of the twentieth century, a period that perpetuated a myth of racial harmony and yet whose leaders quickly moved to suppress with violence any independent agency within the black community itself. Only the vogue of more overtly African-influenced styles of music in the late 1920s and beyond would initiate new discussion about the cultural contributions of black Cubans to the nation.

In Mexico, early racial representations of the danzón developed in a trajectory virtually opposite to that of Cuba. The elites who embraced the danzón in Mérida and elsewhere downplayed the form's racial polemics among Cubans and initially considered it a "white" music. Only after the danzón's popularization among the Mexican working classes did elites denounce it, particularly on moral grounds. The gradual association of the danzón with prostitution, indecency, and African-derived heritage allowed for the emergence of new discourses that distanced it from Mexico, as had occurred earlier with the habanera. Such a process would later be reversed; the arrival of the mambo and cha cha chá in the 1940s and 1950s shifted Mexican anxiety about blackness onto these newcomers. In the aftermath, the danzón became a symbol of the mestizo working class. The changing racial connotations of the danzón and habanera demonstrate that Mexican constructs of national racial identity—to which mestizaje is central—acquire meaning through transnational dialogues, and that imagining Mexico has also meant imagining Cuba and the circum-Caribbean region. Racialized representations of musical style must be understood within Vasconcelos's cultural project but are not the sole result of state policy. Rather, the meanings of blackness, whiteness, and mestizaje in post-revolutionary Mexico emerged in dialogue between various actors including government ideologues, private entrepreneurs, literary figures, film producers, and audiences. The danzón is a rich field of popular practice that can be used to examine the complex interplay between state initiatives and individual agency informing notions of race, gender, and class.

CHAPTER 4

The Danzón and Musical Dialogues with Early Jazz

Jazz scholars have repeatedly lamented the lack of historical data describing the emergence of early jazz repertoire in New Orleans.[1] Not only do no recordings of jazz exist prior to 1917, but few written sources from the turn of the twentieth century make any mention of the emergent musical style. As a result, historians have had difficulty discussing the development of jazz with any degree of specificity. Many histories—from Gunther Schuller's influential work in the 1960s to the recent documentary series by Ken Burns—fail to explore this issue sufficiently and imply that "jazz somehow came into existence in the 1890s by an act of spontaneous creation."[2]

In framing jazz as an exclusively North American phenomenon rather than part of broader hemispheric artistic trends, the mainstream jazz community may have created fundamental obstacles for itself in terms of such historiography. Substantial documentation exists about musical forms in the Gulf of Mexico, the Caribbean, and Latin America that were contemporary with and preceded early jazz. Music from Cuba, Haiti, and Mexico, especially, represent central components of New Orleans music, of course, and a significant undercurrent of jazz scholarship as early as the 1950s and 1960s has argued that such influences be considered more central to its development.[3] Literature of this sort has taken multiple approaches to establishing

1. See, for example, Christopher Washburne, "The Clave of Jazz: A Caribbean Contribution to the Rhythmic Foundation of an African-American Music," *Black Music Research Journal* 17, no. 1 (1997), 59; and Gilbert Chase, *America's Music. From the Pilgrims to the Present* (New York: McGraw-Hill, 1955), 476.

2. Ernest Borneman, "Creole Echoes," *Jazz Review* 2, no. 8 (1959), 13. The author critiques this notion of jazz's ostensibly spontaneous emergence.

3. One of the first authors to attempt this was Borneman, "Creole Echoes," 13–15; and "Creole Echoes: Part II," *Jazz Review* 2, no. 10 (1959), 26–27; followed by John Storm Roberts, *The Latin Tinge. The Impact of Latin American Music on the United States* (New York: Oxford University Press, 1979); Thomas Fiehrer, "From Quadrille to Stomp: The Creole Origins of Jazz," *Popular Music* 10, no. 1 (1991), 21–38; and most recently Ned Sublette, *The World that Made New Orleans. From Spanish Silver to Congo Square* (Chicago: Lawrence Hill Books, 2009).

ties between the circum-Caribbean region and the emergence of jazz. The most common has been to discuss migration; demographic patterns; the influence of Cuban, Haitian, or Mexican culture within New Orleans in broad strokes;[4] visits by regional performers to the city; and the presence of performers of Hispanic or French creole heritage within the early jazz scene. The quantity of such data is substantial and paints a convincing picture of sustained contact. A recent publication by Bruce Raeburn suggests that as many as 24 percent of first-generation jazz performers born before 1900 were of Hispanic heritage, for instance, an astounding figure that considers only individuals' ties to the Spanish-speaking Americas, not the many Afro-Creole performers with ties to Haiti.[5]

Another approach to exploring ties between the Caribbean and jazz has been to document the strong presence of Latin-influenced or Latin-inspired music published in New Orleans,[6] or to discuss the presence of discrete musical elements that link Afro-Latin music to ragtime and early jazz. Clearly, many rhythmic and formal commonalities exist between the Cuban (contra)danza and ragtime music, for instance, and are also found in other contemporary music such as Brazilian chôro and maxixe.[7] As mentioned in Chapter 2, specific rhythmic motives discussed by various authors include the tresillo, cinquillo, amphibrach, and habanera or tango rhythm.[8] Doheny examines the ways in which percussionists in early jazz bands perform two-measure rhythmic sequences that conform to Cuban notions of clave, including patterns nearly identical to danzón clave.[9] Chris Washburne extends this line of analysis further, noting at least five different ways in which early jazz repertoire incorporates influences from "claved" rhythms associated with Afro-Cuban music specifically.[10] They include clave-like drum breaks that transition between distinct musical segments of many pieces; claved comping that can be heard on the guitar, piano, or other rhythm instruments in early recordings; and horn riffs or song melodies that conform to clave in the music of Louis Armstrong and others.

4. See, for example, Jack Stewart, "The Mexican Band Legend: Myth, Reality, and Musical Impact: A Preliminary Investigation," *Jazz Archivist* 6, no. 2 (1991), 1–14; "The Mexican Band Legend—Part II," *Jazz Archivist* 9, no. 1 (1994), 1–17; "Cuban Influences on New Orleans Music," *Jazz Archivist* 13 (1999), 14–23. See also the pdf variant at www.arhoolie .com/world/the-cuban-danzon-various-artists.html (accessed on December 30, 2012).

5. Bruce Boyd Raeburn, "Beyond the 'Spanish Tinge': Hispanics and Latinos in Early New Orleans Jazz," in *Eurojazzland*, ed. Luca Cerchiari, Laurent Cugny, and Frank Kerschbaumer (Lebanon, NH: Northeastern University Press, 2012).

6. See, for example, Peggy C. Bordreaux, "Music Publishing in New Orleans in the Nineteenth Century," Master's Thesis, Louisiana State University (1977); and Pamela J. Smith, "Caribbean Influences on Early New Orleans Jazz," Master's Thesis, Tulane University (1986).

7. See Tania Mara Lopes Cançado, "An Investigation of West African and Haitian Rhythms on the Development of Syncopation in Cuba Habanera, Brazilian Tango/Choro and American Ragtime (1791–1900)," PhD Dissertation, Shenandoah University (1999).

8. See Peter Manuel, ed., *Creolizing Contradance in the Caribbean* (Philadelphia, PA: Temple University Press, 2009), 20, for additional commentary.

9. John Doheny, "The Spanish Tinge Hypothesis: Afro-Caribbean Characteristics in Early New Orleans Jazz Drumming," *Jazz Archivist* 19 (2006), 15.

10. Washburne, "The Clave of Jazz," 69–75.

It is remarkable, however, that the danzón has not featured more prominently in existing scholarship on the links between jazz and the Caribbean.[11] Perhaps the plentiful published scores of contradanzas and danzas in music libraries (typically in stylized "salon" form for solo piano rather than as scored for dance band) and the relative scarcity of reedited danzón sheet music has contributed to this oversight. Perhaps the difficulty of conducting research on partially improvised repertoire has been a prohibitive factor. Perhaps the relative marginalization of the danzón in present-day Cuba has obscured its earlier popularity; the shift to *charanga*-style flute and violin format in the 1910s and 1920s may have similarly obscured its earlier wind band format, much closer to that of contemporary jazz bands.[12] Whatever the case, the danzón's relationships to jazz deserve additional attention; its glaring omission suggests that regional forms contributing to the development of early jazz may have been consciously overlooked or ignored in existing literature.

After discussing what is known about the involvement of Latin American performers in New Orleans around 1900 and the extent of danza and danzón performance there, this chapter analyzes a few early danzón recordings as a means of exploring stylistic similarities between such music and that of early jazz. The danzón is potentially significant to jazz researchers in many ways. It was one of the first musics created and recorded by African descendants in the Americas, with early Edison cylinders and 78 rpm records of the music pre-dating jazz discs by more than a decade. Wind band–style danzón flourished in the years just prior to the emergence of jazz, from the 1880s through the 1920s and gained wide popularity throughout the Caribbean region. Along with its antecedent form, the danza, the danzón was performed and disseminated through sheet music in the New Orleans area, and thus first-generation jazz artists had at least some exposure to it directly. The many characteristic elements of the danzón can be analyzed on recordings as dance orchestras actually played them, not merely as they were represented on sheet music reductions for piano, providing a more rounded view of the style. Some of the danzón's star performers on early recordings were cornet players, roughly contemporary with Buddy Bolden and other legendary, though unrecorded, jazz pioneers.

Perhaps most important, improvisational sections in early danzón recordings provide the closest stylistic link between Caribbean music and early jazz. The approach to improvisation in danzones corresponds so closely at times to New Orleans

11. Authors have noted parallels between the two forms, but for the most part they have been discussed in the briefest of terms, primarily in liner notes accompanying historical recordings. See, for example, John Santos, liner notes to *The Cuban Danzón: Its Ancestors and Descendants* (Washington, DC: Smithsonian Folkways FE 4066, 1982); Cristóbal Díaz Ayala, liner notes to *Early Music of the North Caribbean 1916–1920* (East Sussex, UK Interstate Music, Harlequin CD HQCD 67, 1995); and liner notes to *Early Cuban Danzón Orchestras 1916–1920* (East Sussex, UK: Interstate Music, Harlequin CD HQCD 131, 1995); and Dick Spottswood, Cristóbal Díaz Ayala, and Chris Strachwitz, liner notes to *The Cuban Danzón. Before There Was Jazz* (El Cerrito, CA: Arhoolie Productions, Arhoolie Folklyric CD 7032, 1999).
12. Compare the instrumentation of the orquesta típica, discussed in Chapter 2, with early jazz orchestras such as that of A. J. Piron that included a similar mix of violins, brass, reeds, and percussion.

repertoire of subsequent decades that one is forced to wonder whether some sort of musical exchange existed between the two repertoires. At the very least, improvisation in the danzón may provide insight into turn-of-the-twentieth-century performance practice in New Orleans, suggesting how jazz itself emerged in the 1880s out of dialogues between score-based band arrangements and improvised traditional music. The danzón's history and style link early jazz more tangibly to broader regional developments than has been thought before, suggesting a continual process of inter-influences. Analysis focuses primarily on cornet melodies, as they are the easiest to hear on early cylinder discs, but also includes some discussion of violin and clarinet lines, and other instruments.

LATIN AMERICAN AND CARIBBEAN MUSICAL INFLUENCES ON NEW ORLEANS

This chapter explores the similarities and interrelations between the danzón and the earliest manifestations of jazz in New Orleans. Despite suggestions that jazz may have developed simultaneously in various parts of the United States, consensus remains that central to its history was New Orleans, as well as cities farther north connected to New Orleans through river boat traffic along the Mississippi river.[13] Interest here is on the practice of "polyphonic weave,"[14] that is, the foregrounding of various planes of improvisation heard simultaneously, the collective variation associated with both repertoires.

Danzones share a number of common musical features with ragtime, one of the principal antecedent forms of jazz. This is not altogether surprising, given that danzón and ragtime entered the commercial music market almost simultaneously in the late 1880s and that the terms "jazz" and "ragtime" were largely interchangeable through about 1917.[15] Indeed, some of the danzón's influence on early jazz may have come indirectly via its influence on ragtime repertoire. Both ragtime and the danzón followed similar paths of development to the extent that they created characteristic sounds by "ragging" or syncopating European-derived melodies or dances associated with a more straightforward duple meter. The same could be said of cakewalks, syncopated marches and two-steps, and other North American music of the late nineteenth century.[16]

13. Wiley H. Hitchcock, *Music in the United States: A Historical Introduction* (Englewood Cliffs, NJ: Prentice Hall, 1974), 192–93.

14. Mark Tucker, "Jazz," in *Grove Music Online*, Section 1, Definitions, and 2, Jazz and the New Orleans Background (2007).

15. Jack Stewart, "The Original Dixieland Jazz Band's Place in the Development of Jazz," *Jazz Archivist* 19 (2006), 19.

16. Edward A. Berlin, "Ragtime," *Grove Music Online*. Section 1, Stylistic Conventions (2007). The cakewalk rhythm, consisting of an amphibrach followed by two quarter notes, is found both in the repertoire of composers such as Scott Joplin and in Cuban dance music of the mid-nineteenth century as documented by Alejo Carpentier in *La música en Cuba* (Mexico City: Fondo de Cultura Económica, 1946), 151. See also the B section of Manuel Saumell's "El pañuelo de Pepa" from the 1860s that incorporates not only the typical cakewalk rhythm but a melodic style that sounds quite similar to those that would develop later in the United States.

The essential feature distinguishing ragtime from early jazz seems to be that ragtime's syncopated rhythms were largely pre-composed, and that it did not necessarily allow for collective improvisation during performance.

Other specific elements link ragtime to the danzón. Both are highly sectional, with multiple contrasting themes presented in succession, and frequent major-minor contrasts between sections.[17] The structures of specific pieces vary but often approximate a rondo with an A theme that repeats after a statement of the B theme, followed by additional themes; this reflects the influence of contemporary brass band repertoire.[18] Thus, the structure of numerous danzón and ragtime pieces might be represented by either ABACD or ABAC. Many of the same Afro-Caribbean rhythmic cells discussed in Chapter 2 appear in both forms.[19] Such parallels represent part of a hemisphere-wide phenomenon of Afro-Latin influence, as the same motives can be found in nineteenth-century sheet music from Brazil, Colombia, Mexico, and elsewhere.[20] In terms of characteristic elements, the danzón might be viewed as occupying an intermediate position between ragtime and early jazz: its formal structure and pre-composed melodies conform more closely to ragtime music of the period, yet its use of polyphonic texture and allowance for simultaneous improvisation in particular sections aligns it with New Orleans jazz.

Emphasis on the possible interrelations between the danzón and early jazz discussed below should by no means be construed as lack of recognition of the strong francophone Caribbean influences in New Orleans. The city maintained close ties with the French colony of St. Domingue prior to the 1790s. Its residents purchased thousands of slaves from Martinique, Guadeloupe, and St. Domingue in the late eighteenth century;[21] roughly 9,000 more black, white, and mixed-race refugees arrived from St. Domingue following the revolution there in the 1790s, including many musicians.[22] All of this directly supported the singing and dancing in Congo Square beginning in 1817, as well as a variety of commercial musical forms in theaters and music halls. Fiehrer notes that by 1815 half the urban population of New Orleans had come from the West Indies and spoke French Creole.[23] The extent of influence Afro-French traditional music was recognized as late as the 1880s by G. W. Cable who identified eight distinct dance traditions still performed in the area derived from the

17. Allan Sutton, *Cakewalks, Rags, and Novelties. The International Ragtime Discography (1894–1930)* (Denver, CO: Mainspring Press, 2003), xi.

18. Rudi Blesh, "Scott Joplin: Black American Classicist," in Scott Joplin, *Scott Joplin. Collected Piano Works* (New York: New York Public Library, 1971), xvii. Thanks to Chris Washburne for his insights on the formal influence of brass band repertoire on both the danzón and early jazz.

19. See, among others, Doheny, "The Spanish Tinge Hypothesis"; Mark Lomanno, "Topics on Afro-Cuban Jazz in the United States," Master's Thesis, Rutgers University (2007), 52; Roberts, *The Latin Tinge*, 42–43.

20. See Carlos Sandroni, "Rediscutindo gêneros no Brasil oitocentista: tangos e habaneras," in *Música popular na América Latina: pontos de escuta*, ed. Ana María Ochoa and Martha Ulhoa (Porto Alegre: UFRGS, 2005), 175–193.

21. Borneman, "Creole Echoes," 15.

22. Michael Largey, "Haiti: Tracing the Steps of the Méringue and Contredanse," in Manuel, *Creolizing Contradance*, 212; and Stewart, "Cuban Influences on New Orleans Music," 14.

23. Fiehrer, "From Quadrille to Stomp," 26.

West Indies including the *calinda, bamboula, babouille,* and *juba.*[24] Not surprisingly, French Creoles figure heavily among first-generation jazz artists as well. It is important to remember that the French *contradanse* tradition of the late eighteenth century strongly influenced Cuban musical practice of the nineteenth century, especially in terms of contradanzas and danzas, direct antecedents of the danzón. And later variants such as the French Caribbean *contradanse quadrille antillais* (a highly improvisational tradition as well) appear to have influenced the repertoire of early jazz artists such as Buddy Bolden and William Henry Peyton.[25] Rather than viewing Francophone traditions as distinct from those of the Hispanic Caribbean, one might consider them fundamentally interrelated, and yet another way in which musical styles in Cuba, Haiti, New Orleans, and other locations have been in dialogue.

Hispanic- and French-Caribbean musical traditions themselves represented only two strong components of musical influences in New Orleans. The city at the turn of the twentieth century can only be described as cosmopolitan in the extreme, with music being made by significant populations of immigrants from Germany, Austria, Italy, and elsewhere in addition to Caribbean and African-American populations.[26] Typical dance band repertoire in the 1890s reflected this. Concerts regularly featured opera overtures, waltzes, polkas, mazurkas, lancers, schottisches, quadrilles, marches, gallops, and countless other styles,[27] in addition to the contradance, danza, and danzón.

The importance of brass band traditions to New Orleans is worth brief mention, given that brass and wind band groups gained popularity throughout the Americas in the mid-nineteenth century and that early jazz bands and the danzón's orquesta típica also seem to have developed out of brass band ensembles.[28] The turn of the twentieth century represented a heyday of sorts for brass bands; a large number of first-generation jazz artists began their careers in them, and it is in these groups that free melodic improvisation or variation seems first to have developed.[29] New Orleans groups often purchased pre-composed arrangements of ragtime music for brass band published in New York City, suggesting that improvisational practice emerged in dialogue with notated practice and through the involvement of literate and non-literate musicians, as in the case of the danzón.[30]

Much work remains to be done on wind band history in Cuba, but the prominence of such ensembles in the nineteenth century is unmistakable. The orquesta típica

24. G. W. Cable, quoted in Marshall and Jean Stearns, *Jazz Dance. The Story of American Vernacular Dance* (New York: Da Capo, 1994 [1964]), 19.
25. Daniel Vernhettes with Bo Lindström, "Buddy Bolden 1877–1931," in *Jazz Puzzles* Vol. 1 (Paris: Jazz'Edit, 2013) 33–4. See also http://www.jazzedit.org/Pz/jazz-puzzles.html.
26. Raeburn, "Beyond the 'Spanish Tinge,'" 3.
27. Lawrence Gushee, "The Nineteenth-Century Origins of Jazz," *Black Music Research Journal* 14, no. 1 (1994), 18.
28. Leonardo Acosta, *Descarga cubana: el jazz en Cuba, 1900–1950* (Havana: Ediciones Unión, 2000), 6.
29. Washburne, "The Clave of Jazz," 66.
30. William J. Schafer, *Brass Bands and New Orleans Jazz* (Baton Rouge: Louisiana State University Press, 1977), 18–19.

format discussed in Chapter 2 emerged out of military bands associated with black and mulatto military battalions, as well as from municipal brass bands and firemen's bands across the island;[31] many such players also went on to play in theater orchestras, in addition to dance orchestras. Roig includes some discussion of the most prominent brass ensembles active in Havana in the latter nineteenth century, as does Guerra y Sánchez.[32] They included the Banda de Isabel la Católica, directed by Antonio de la Rubia; the Banda del Apostadero de Marina, directed by Angel María Gil; the Banda de Ingenieros, directed by Juan Brochi Spiglianteni; the Banda de Isabel Segunda, directed by Francisco Espino; the Banda de Artillería, directed by Napoleón Carozzi; and the Banda del Regimiento Reina María Cristina and the Banda de Bomberos, directed by Rafael Rojas. Cristóbal Díaz Ayala documents the participation of numerous early danzón composers and bandleaders such as flautist Tata Pereira and Jaime Prats in municipal brass bands of various sorts early in their careers.[33] The same is true of Miguel Faílde, who played in the Municipal Fireman's Band in Matanzas prior to establishing his orchestra.[34] Sublette notes that in the late eighteenth century under Spanish rule, New Orleans and Havana shared the same military band tradition, with performers trained in Havana sent to play in New Orleans for extended periods.[35] Some resettled permanently in the city and contributed to musical life in subsequent decades. It appears that the New Orleans tradition of musicians of color parading in military bands began during the late eighteenth century, since free blacks and mulattos were obliged to serve in segregated military units at the time.[36] Interestingly, the racially segregated military ensembles created in Cuba under Spanish rule (divided into *blancos* or whites, *pardos* or mixed-race, and *morenos* or blacks) have a parallel in the white/creole/black divisions that existed among New Orleans brass bands and other ensembles in the late nineteenth century and beyond. It remains to be determined whether such racial divisions in Cuba corresponded to varying degrees of literate versus improvised performance as was the case generally in New Orleans.

Despite representing a small percentage of New Orleans residents at the turn of the twentieth century, Hispanic performers featured prominently in musical circles. They included Spanish-born danzón composer Carlos Maduell (1836–1900); Mexican-Spanish tuba player Martin Abraham (1886–1981), better known as "Chink" Martin; Mexican-American violinist Paul Domínguez; bandleader Perlops

31. Acosta, *Descarga cubana* 18; Lid Juárez, program notes accompanying a performance of the Orquesta Félix Gonzalez at the Biblioteca Nacional José Martí from the early 1960s. Archives, Rafael Lam.

32. Gonzalo Roig, *Apuntes históricos sobre nuestras bandas militares y orquestas* (Havana: Molina y Compañía, 1936), 8–9. Ramiro Guerra y Sánchez, *Historia de la nación cubana*, Vol. 7 (Havana: Editorial Historia de la Nación Cubana, 1952), 436.

33. Díaz Ayala, *Cuba canta y baila*, 126, 130.

34. Sygrid Padrón Díaz, "Galicia en el baile nacional cubano: el danzón," in *Galicia-Cuba: un patrimonio cultural de referencias y confluencias*, ed. C. Fontela and M. Silva (A Coruña: Ediciós do Castro, 2000), 408.

35. Sublette, *The World that Made New Orleans*, 95 and 103.

36. Sublette, *The World that Made New Orleans*, 113.

Nunez;[37] multi-instrumentalist Jimmy "Spriggs" Palao (1879–1925), apparently of Spanish, Portuguese, or Catalan descent; clarinetist Alcide "Yellow" Nunez (1884–1934), whose family came from the Canary Islands; Spanish-American cornetist Ray López (1889–1970), Mexican saxophonists Florencio Ramos (1861–1931) and Leonardo Rojas Vizcarra (1860–1923): and Afro-French/Mexican cornetist Emanuel Perez (1879–1946; Fig. 4.1), discussed later. Specific biographical information on many individuals remains scanty,[38] but they undoubtedly had some exposure to and appreciation for the danzón as one of the preeminent Caribbean/Latin American musics of the day. This is especially true of individuals such as Russell, Ramos, and Vizcarra who immigrated to New Orleans from Latin America as adults.[39] The Creole Tio family emigrated to the Tampico area of Mexico in the mid-nineteenth century and undoubtedly heard Cuban-influenced repertoire there, as discussed later. Lorenzo Tio Sr. (1867–1908) and his brother Louis "Papa" Tio (1862–1922) eventually moved back to New Orleans; along with Lorenzo's son Lorenzo Tio Jr. (1893–1933), they became highly regarded as pedagogues and performers.[40]

The presence of Hispanic cornet players among early jazz players represents one of the most direct ways that improvisatory danzón performance practice may have spread to New Orleans. Cornetist Emanuel Emile Perez deserves mention as an especially influential early figure, though his direct ties to Latin America are diffuse. Perez was born in New Orleans in 1879[41] into a family of mixed French creole and Mexican roots (his paternal grandfather was from Puebla, but both parents were born in New Orleans; the father moved back to Mexico for a time in search of better employment).[42]

37. No information is available on Perlops's ethnicity or dates of birth and death, but John Storm Roberts describes him as running "one of the first black bands in New Orleans, the 1880s" (*The Latin Tinge*, 37).

38. Indeed, the poor state of research on early jazz musicians even in terms of basic biographical information and where they lived at particular times is shocking; it suggests total disinterest in the subject on the part of mainstream jazz historians. Jack Stewart's articles on Mexican bands in New Orleans provide the best data to date on many of the individuals mentioned. See Jack Stewart, "The Mexican Band Legend: Myth, Reality, and Musical Impact: A Preliminary Investigation," and related articles in the references.

39. Raeburn, "Beyond the 'Spanish Tinge,'" 25–26; and Stewart, "The Mexican Band Legend: Myth, Reality, and Musical Impact: A Preliminary Investigation," 7.

40. Charles E. Kinzer, "The Tios of New Orleans and Their Pedagogical Influence on the Early Jazz Clarinet Style," *Black Music Research Journal* 16, no. 2 (1996), 279–302.

41. There is considerable misinformation in current literature on this issue. Helio Orovio (*Diccionario de la música cubana*, 2nd ed., 1992, 350) and Radamés Giro (*Diccionario Enciclopédico de la música cubana*, Vol. 3 [Havana: Letras Cubanas, 2007], 220) suggest that Perez was born in Cuba, for instance, citing 1863 as his date of birth. But a photo in Berger (Monroe Berger, "Letters from New Orleans," *Annual Review of Jazz Studies* 7 [1994–95], 62–67), taken in 1943 depicts a man younger than eighty who could not have been born that early. And a recent birth certificate that has surfaced thanks to the efforts of Ned Sublette and David Chachere settles the matter.

42. Ned Sublette, interview with David Chachere, Monday November 14, 2011, New York City. The information about Emanuel Perez's father living in Mexico comes from Robert Goffin, *La Nouvelle-Orléans, capitale du jazz* (New York: Édicions de la Maison française, 1946), 68–69.

Figure 4.1: Emanuel Emile Perez (on cornet, back right) and his Imperial Band from 1908. Perez was one of many New Orleans artists of Hispanic and Francophone heritage who contributed to the emergence of early jazz. Photo courtesy of the Hogan Jazz Archive, Tulane University.

Perez began studying classical trumpet with Sylvester Coustaut from the age of twelve, joining the John Robichaux orchestra in 1895, and going on to play in several other top-notch ensembles.[43] These included the Onward Brass Band which he joined in 1900 and directed from 1903 through 1930. From 1901 to 1908 he also directed the six-piece Imperial Orchestra dance band, and in 1923 he formed and directed the Manuel Perez Orchestra. Considered by some "the greatest of all pioneer jazz trumpeters,"[44] Perez collaborated frequently with Lorenzo Tio Jr. and Joe "King" Oliver, and is said to have influenced Louis Armstrong's playing.[45] He developed a reputation both for strong improvisational and sight-reading skills and attracted renowned trumpet students such as Alvin Alcorn Sidney Desvigne, "Natty" Dominique, Rena

43. Giro, *Diccionario enciclopédico de la música cubana,*Vol. 3, 220–21; *Grove Music Online*.
44. See Gilbert Chase, *America's Music. From the Pilgrims to the Present* (New York: McGraw-Hill, 1955), 472; Samuel Charters, *Jazz: New Orleans, 1885–1963,* rev. ed. (New York: Oak Publications, 1963), 44; Jelly Roll Morton in Lawrence Gushee, *The Pioneers of Jazz. The Story of the Creole Band* (New York: Oxford University Press, 2005), 307.
45. Charters, *Jazz: New Orleans,* 61.

"Kid" Henry, Manuel Manetta, and Willie Pajeaud.[46] Other prominent early jazzers such as clarinetist Louis "Big Eye" Nelson DeLisle, and trumpeter Peter Bocage developed their improvisational skills while playing in ensembles under Perez's direction.[47] Perez retired from public performance in the late 1920s following a stroke.

Discussion of Hispanic musicians in New Orleans to date has largely centered on Mexican performers. Mexicans certainly contributed much to New Orleans musical life of the late nineteenth century, but for purposes of this analysis that considers the stylistic influence of the danza and danzón within the region, existing literature raises nearly as many questions as it answers. Mexican bands visiting New Orleans are known to have performed both forms of music, especially the danza. But whether Mexican groups interpreted the repertoire in an improvisatory a manner as was common in Cuba remains to be determined. Further complicating analysis, "Mexican music" and "Mexican band" (as well as "Spanish music" or "Spanish band") seem to have been phrases used generically at times in popular literature and in interviews to reference all Latin American musicians and performers, making it difficult to determine exactly what music or ethnic groups are being discussed in particular sources.

Mexican audiences began to adopt the danzón as their own in the late nineteenth century and had substantial firsthand exposure to the improvisatory style of the Cuban danza and danzón owing to the presence of Cuban musicians who toured and/or relocated there. Performers accompanying *bufo* (blackface comic theater) troupes often played such music to accompany stage acts as well; as mentioned in Chapter 3, they were some of the first to play danzas and danzones for Mexicans. Los Habaneros de Pancho Fernández toured in 1869, for instance, during the height of the danza's popularity.[48] Many more groups arrived during the bufo's "revival" period at the conclusion of the Ten Years War (Spanish authorities prohibited such entertainment between 1869 and 1879 because they perceived the themes of many sketches, and the audiences that frequented them, as pro-independence). As explained in Chapter 3, a number of bufo companies toured Mexico between 1880 and 1892, including the Salas, Paulino Delgado, Raul del Monte, and Nacho López's troupes.[49] As a result of such frequent shows, it seems likely that Mexican musicians visiting New Orleans in the late 1880s and 1890s were familiar not only with the danzón but

46. Manetta took trumpet lessons with Pérez in 1904 or 1905 before playing with Buddy Bolden, the Eagle Band, the Crescent City Band, the King Oliver Band, and other groups; see his obituary in the *Times-Picayune*, Sunday, October 12, 1969, p. 22. Information about Dominique's relation to Perez, and that of most other students mentioned, comes from *Grove Music Online*. See also Charters, *Jazz: New Orleans*, p. 95 for a discussion of Rena and p. 121 for Pajeaud.

47. Kinzer, "The Tios of New Orleans," 286.

48. Rine Leal, *La selva oscura. De los bufos a la neocolonia*, Vol. 2 (Havana: Editorial Arte y Literatura, 1982), 69. Gabriel Pareyón, *Diccionario enciclopédico de la música en México*, Vol. 1 (Guadalajara: Universidad Panamericana, 2007), 52–53, describes the group's performance in some detail, as well as the fact that their attempts to raise money to support the insurrection against the Spanish led to conflicts and a boycott of their shows by pro-Spanish factions in Mexico.

49. Eduardo Robreño, *Como lo pienso lo digo* (Havana: UNEAC, 1985), 15–16; Giro, *Diccionario enciclopédico de la música de Cuba*, Vol. 1, 55.

with improvisatory performance practice associated with the danza and danzón in Cuba. As early as 1884, composers in Mexico began to interpret early Cuban danzones such as those by Raimundo Valenzuela in their own concerts.[50]

Shortly after the arrival of musicians accompanying theater and circus acts, individual Cuban composers and orchestras began arriving in Mexico as well. Cayetano de las Cuevas Galán (1864–1929) was one of the first, establishing himself in Mérida in 1893 and remaining there for the rest of his life. A classically trained violinist, he composed original danzones and directed dance bands.[51] The orchestra of Enrique Peña made multiple trips to Mexico beginning in about 1896 and is said to have played in the United States as part of the same tour.[52] As mentioned in Chapter 3, Tiburcio "Babuco" Hernández also arrived in Mexico in the 1890s.

Multiple performances in New Orleans by the Mexican Eighth Cavalry Band under the direction of Captain Encarnación Payén in the 1880s and 1890s generated considerable enthusiasm for "Mexican music" in New Orleans, including danzas and danzones. Payén's group raised awareness of Latin American repertoire, and several of the band's members (such as Ramos and Vizcarra) settled permanently in the city, establishing themselves as performers of early jazz. Jack Stewart and Gaye Theresa Johnson have discussed Payén's ensemble performing as part of the World's Industrial and Cotton Centennial Exposition from December of 1884 and the tremendous sensation they created, drawing crowds of thousands to nightly concert events.[53] Perusal of the Daily Picayune confirms that the band returned on multiple occasions thereafter. In July of 1888 they performed nightly for a week in the West End Garden amusement park, featuring cornet soloist "Mr. E. López"; the event included several danzas, and may have included the published danzón "Encarnación" by Carlos Maduell that is dedicated to the group's director (see Fig. 4.2).[54] (⊜ Scores 4.1, 4.2) In 1891 Payén's ensemble played in the same venue for three weeks.[55] They returned again in May of 1897 and in July of 1898.[56] Other Mexican orchestras played in the city as well, such as the Orquesta Típica Moderna that toured the US South following the World's Fair in Chicago of 1893.[57]

50. Flores y Escalante, Salón México, 7.
51. Pareyón, Diccionario, Vol. 1, 304.
52. Giro, Diccionario, Vol. 4, 225.
53. See note 4 for references to articles by Jack Stewart. See also Gaye Theresa Johnson, "'Sobre Las Olas': A Mexican Genesis in Borderlands Jazz and the Legacy for Ethnic Studies," Comparative American Studies 6, no. 3 (2008), 225–240.
54. The following Daily Picayune stories document relevant performances: "West End Amusements" (July 22, 1888), 4; "The Mexican Band" (July 23, 1888), 8; "Great Success of the Mexican Band Festival" (July 24, 1888), 4; "West End Concerts" (July 28, 1888), 4; "Mexican Band Farewell Concert" (July 29, 1888), 8. Maduell's danzón dedicated to Payén dates from the 1880s, as well as a second danzón entitled "Melio." (⊜ Score 4.2)
55. "Mexican Band," Daily City Item (June 21, 1891), 4.
56. Relevant articles include "Amusements. Mexican Band and 'Shoot the Chutes,'" Daily Picayune (May 23, 1897), 12; and "Flag Raisings. The Claireborn Market," Daily Picayune (July 27, 1898), 8.
57. Stewart, "The Mexican Band Legend," 4.

Figure 4.2: Representative danzones composed in New Orleans of the 1880s and apparently performed by the Mexican Eighth Cavalry Band.

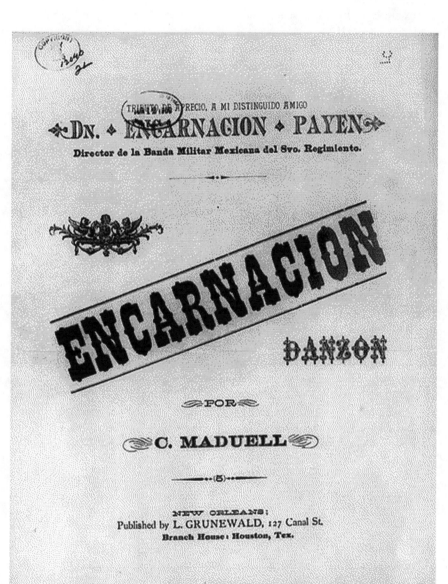

Figure 4.2: (*continued*)

Not only did the Eighth Cavalry Band play danzas for New Orleanians[58] but their concerts inspired a local "mania for Mexican danza and Cuban danzón"[59] and resulted in substantial amounts of sheet music printed in the city thereafter. Local sheet music sales of "Mexican music," which apparently reached upward of 200,000 units,[60] reflected the exploding interest in such repertoire. Newspaper advertisements notified readers of new titles available for purchase.[61] These included arrangements by local composer-arrangers such as W. T. Francis,[62] and others inspired directly by Payén's band and sold by Junius Hart, L. Grunewald, and Narciso Martínez publishers. Examination of the Junius Hart catalogue from 1894 reveals roughly fourteen danza titles, and a danzón, "Las campanillitas." Grunewald published many more such pieces, including two danzones. Of course, the circulation of published scores as piano reductions doesn't necessarily establish the use of improvisation by Mexicans themselves or by local performers, but it does confirm a familiarity with the style.

The cultural ties between Cuba and New Orleans are less well documented than those between Mexico and New Orleans, yet they are significant. As mentioned, the two cities shared the same colonial authority for decades in the late eighteenth century. They were both major ports during the heyday of the danzón, connected to each other and to the entire Caribbean region through common trade routes.[63] Louis Moreau Gottschalk famously traveled to Cuba on multiple occasions in the 1850s and 1860s, publishing Cuban-inspired pieces in New Orleans thereafter such as "Ojos criollos" and "Danses cubaines." Travel between Havana and New Orleans was enhanced by their reputations as exotic "good-time" capitals, and by their common cigar and sugar industries. New Orleans boasted a substantial Cuban expatriate community with social organizations that raised money for the revolutionary effort against Spain in the mid-1890s and undoubtedly listened to the latest musical hits from the island.[64] At least some of the members of the famous Onward Brass Band enrolled in the Ninth Volunteer Infantry, an all-African American unit, in order to fight in the Spanish-American War. They spent about six months in Cuba near the

58. The following *Daily Picayune* articles contain references to particular danza titles in concert programs: "Exposition. Songs Performed," *Daily Picayune* (April 4, 1885), 2; "Pickwick Club Day," *Daily Picayune* (April 22, 1885), 2; "Mexican Band Festival," *Daily Picayune* (July 24, 1888), 4; "Mexican Band," *Daily Picayune* (July 28, 1888), 8. Pieces mentioned in these articles include "Déjame," "A media noche," "Chloe," and "Me gusta bailar."

59. Raeburn, "Beyond the 'Spanish Tinge'"13.

60. Smith, "Caribbean Influences," 95.

61. For instance, one "Mexican Band Music" advertisement appears in the *Daily Picayune* (July 28, 1888), 8.

62. The *Daily Picayune* (February 13, 1887), 6, discusses "La naranja," a danza by W. T. Francis in the Junius Hart Catalogue. William Taylor Francis worked as an arranger and composer for Julius Hart and generated many Latin American pieces for the catalogue. He dedicated some pieces to Payén's daughter, and thus seems to have known the band well.

63. Sublette, *The World that Made New Orleans*, 4.

64. "Cuban Concert," *Daily Picayune* (February 11, 1894), 6; "The Cuban Circle," *Daily Picayune* (July 27, 1895), 12; "Circulo Cubano," *Daily Picayune* (July 28, 1895), 2; and "Cuban Clubs Keep Memories Sacred," *Daily Picayune* (November 28, 1896), 12.

city of Santiago, returning in April of 1899.[65] Nothing is known of their activities there, but they may well have been exposed to or even participated in local performances. Finally, Cuban musicians are known to have performed in New Orleans and many other US cities in 1889 and 1890 as part of a tour with the McCabe and Young Minstrels. A "Havana Sextet" accompanied the troupe for an entire season along the eastern seaboard and various midwestern states before arriving in New Orleans in February of 1890.[66] McCabe and Young hired even more Cuban musicians before touring the United States again, opening in New Orleans in October of 1891.[67]

Manuel John Mello (1887–1961), a cornetist of French and German heritage, is the only other early jazz artist known to have traveled to Cuba. His job with the Major Central Sugar Company led to travel on multiple occasions between Santa Clara, Cuba, and New Orleans, and reputedly to Oriente province as well. Such employment involved extended stays on the island.[68] As a young performer, Mello made a debut with a five-piece marching band, Big Five. He led an influential group, "Mello's Original Band," and also played in Perez's Imperial Orchestra and, beginning in 1899, the Onward Brass Band.[69] Mello helped lead and performed in Fischer's Sixth District Orchestra through about 1909 and in Jack Laine's influential Reliance Band beginning in about 1906.[70] Rose and Souchon note that he, like many others, was an admirer of Manuel Perez's sound and strove to imitate it.[71]

IMPROVISATION IN THE EARLY CUBAN DANZÓN

In acknowledging the many Hispanics involved in early jazz, Bruce Raeburn asserts that they "played a significant role in developing improvisational 'ear' music in New Orleans" because of their prominent role from the outset as performers, bandleaders,

65. John McCusker, "The Onward Brass Band and the Spanish American War," *Jazz Archivist*, 13 (1999), 24–35.

66. Lynn Abbott and Doug Seroff, *Out of Sight: The Rise of African American Popular Music, 1889–1895* (Jackson: University Press of Mississippi, 2003), 66–67. The minstrel troupe returned to Havana the following month, performing to an audience of 8,000 that included the Spanish governor.

67. Abbott and Seroff, *Out of Sight*, 69. Contact between US and Cuban musicians as part of exchanges involving blackface entertainment seems to have been considerable; Nancy González Arzola notes similar collaborations in Havana in 1890; see *Teatro Martí, Prodigiosa permanencia* (Havana: Ediciones Unión, 2010), 60. Lapique Becali mentions multiple US minstrel troupes that spent extended time in Cuba beginning in 1860, including the Christie Minstrels from New Orleans who arrived in 1862; see *Cuba colonial*, 204.

68. Information about Mello's employment comes from Daniel Vernhettes (personal email, November 26, 2011), who obtained it from reading notes on Mello's 1917 draft card. See also Stewart, "Cuban Influences on New Orleans Music," 14 and 20, and Manuel Mello oral history notes, Hogan Jazz Archive, Tulane University, 11.

69. Smith, "Caribbean Influences," 36.

70. Article clipping from the vertical files of the Hogan Jazz Archive at Tulane University, *Times-Picayune* (September 3, 1957), "Noise over Melody," no page. See also the Mello oral history notes from the Hogan archive, p. 7.

71. Al Rose and Edmond Souchon, *New Orleans Jazz. A Family Album* (Baton Rouge: Louisiana State University Press, 1967), 85.

and pedagogues.[72] He describes how ensemble players worked at establishing musical conversations between "front line" instruments such as the cornet and clarinet through the elaboration of lead sheet melodies in rehearsal. As will be seen, similar practices are found in danzón performance of the period.

Documentation exists of improvisatory practices not only in the Cuban danzón but also in its antecedent forms, the contradanza and danza. Hilario González, for instance, in discussing the repertoire of contradanza composer Manuel Saumell (1818–1870), mentions the frequent *floreos* (embellishments) and *especulaciones* (literally, speculations) associated with the repertoire.[73] He believes that the Cuban creole variant of the music developed in this way, out of improvised experimentation by (largely Afro-Cuban) performers in dance contexts. Similarly, Natalio Galán describes the B sections of most mid-nineteenth century danzas as longer than their corresponding A sections, primarily because they were improvised and/or elaborated.[74] He quotes S. E. Figueras de la Costa from the 1860s who references the "*algarabía infernal*" (infernal clamor) associated with the music; the author adds that, seemingly, each instrument "*va por su lado*" (heads off in its own direction), phrases that imply the presence of improvisation and/or heterophony. Galán notes that some published scores of nineteenth-century dance repertoire, such as Tomás Ruiz's "El dedo de Landaluze" from 1862, even include what seem to be open-ended two-measure vamp sections in the score, serving as the basis for improvisation as long as performers or dancers wished.[75] Galán believes these vamps were part of "official practice" of the time. They may well represent an early version of similar improvisatory segments found at the end of *sones* and danzones in twentieth-century repertoire.

Improvisation can be found in various segments of turn-of-the-twentieth-century danzones, but is most readily apparent in repeated A sections, as noted by Agüero and others.[76] Grenet, discussing what was already a defunct orquesta típica style by the 1930s, mentions that "the note of highest color [in the ensemble] was given by the cornet which as the *chantecler* of the band took over the introductions, imposing a dominance sustained by the artifice of its variations which were traced on the original melody, thus renewing the enthusiasm of the dancers to again enter the *parte*."[77] He describes clarinets and other instruments playing in their highest register during these moments in order to generate additional excitement.

A review of early danzón recordings confirms that the use of varied or improvised A themes helps build intensity through entire compositions. Usually, all ensemble

72. Raeburn, "Beyond the 'Spanish Tinge,'" 20.
73. Hilario González, "Manuel Saumell y la contradanza," in Manuel Saumell, *Contradanzas* (Havana: Letras Cubanas, 1981), 18.
74. Natalio Galán, *Cuba y sus sones* (Valencia: Pre-Textos, 1983), 166.
75. Galán, *Cuba y sus sones* 167.
76. Gaspar Agüero, "Consideraciones sobre la música popular cubana," *Revista de la Facultad de Letras y Ciencias*, Vol. 32 (1922), 41.
77. Emilio Grenet, *Popular Cuban Music. 80 Revised and Corrected Compositions Together with an Essay on the Evolution of Music in Cuba*, trans. R. Phillips (Havana: Secretary of Agriculture, 1939), 33.

instruments play the first repeated A segment together, complete with subdued cornet improvisations. During the next repeated iteration of A, clarinets and violins typically enter alone, without accompaniment from the cornet or the low horn. When the phrase repeats, however, low horns and the cornet re-enter, the cornet playing flashier improvisations, resulting in a climax of sorts that contrasts markedly with the sparser initial phrases. As Grenet implies, cornet performers in the orquesta típica apparently conceived of their role as discant instrumentalist, providing constantly new, complementary melodies to the principal themes played in variation by other instruments. Clarinets, violins, and lower horns complemented the lead cornet with heterophonic elaborations of the principal A theme, high sustained pitches, syncopated background figures, or other elements to the accompaniment of percussive ad-lib fills on the timbales.

It is often unclear exactly how much improvisation takes place during other segments of danzones on older recordings, largely because they do not repeat as frequently and are thus harder to evaluate. But it is fair to say that B themes tend to be softer and more lyrical, with less improvisation; they are often significantly longer than most A themes as well (16 or 32 mm. as opposed to 8), and may or may not be repeated. C or D segments, to the extent that limited recording time associated with Edison cylinders and 78 rpm records allowed for their inclusion, vary considerably in terms of their use of improvisation, but some include substantial amounts, both relatively free improvisation and varied interpretations of a single phrase. Sánchez de Fuentes seems to confirm this when he mentions that instrumentalists interpreted even the melodies of Italian opera arias found in many turn-of-the-twentieth-century danzones—often appearing in C or D segments—in a ragged, varied, or syncopated fashion.[78]

The first danzón piece analyzed in detail here, "La Patti negra" or "Black Patti," is interesting in various senses. It is one of the earliest surviving recordings of the music, dating from 1906, and both its title and one of its principal melodies reference US pop culture. It thus demonstrates that inter-influences between North American and Caribbean popular music extend back many years. Of course, North American cultural influences in Cuba were especially intense during the United States' four-year military occupation of the island at the turn of the twentieth century, and in subsequent years as North American business interests expanded there.

The Orquesta Valenzuela recorded "La Patti negra," as composed and arranged by trombonist and bandleader Raimundo Valenzuela. His ensemble ranked among the most popular danzón bands on the island at the time, as attested to by various critics.[79] Eduardo Sánchez de Fuentes went as far as to assert that Valenzuela contributed single-handedly to the mass popularization of the danzón within Cuba, owing to his talents as a performer and director.[80] Lamentably, Raimundo Valenzuela passed away in 1905, a year before his group's first opportunity to record, and leadership of

78. Eduardo Sánchez de Fuentes, *El folk-lore en la música cubana* (Havana: Imprenta El Siglo XX, 1923), 29.

79. See, for instance, Roig, *Apuntes históricos*, 14.

80. Sánchez de Fuentes, *El folk-lore*, 30.

the orchestra fell to his brother Pablo (1859–1926), a cornetist. The music of "La Patti negra" thus documents what the ensemble sounded like in broad strokes, but lacks the acclaimed trombone lines of its most famous member, renowned for their high range and technical difficulty.

It is significant that many of the members of the Valenzuela band had ties to Juan de Dios Alfonso's famous Orquesta Flor de Cuba of earlier decades. Raimundo Valenzuela, for instance, began his professional musical life as part of that group in 1864 and reorganized it as his own band in 1877 on de Dios Alfonso's death. The Orquesta Valenzuela thus had a well-established performance history by 1906, and their use of improvisation should be viewed as standard practice in Cuba, apparently pre-dating similar heterophonic textures in New Orleans. Pablo Valenzuela was already fifty-four at the time of the recording, a seasoned player. The earliest recordings by the Orquesta Valenzuela (such as "La Patti negra") were made in Havana and involved no direct exposure to New Orleans or other North American music through travel.[81] No recordings of New Orleans jazz existed at the time that they could have heard, and no New Orleans-based groups are known to have traveled to Cuba in the first years of the twentieth century.

"La Patti negra" takes its name from a well-known black US entertainer of the period, Matilda Sissieretta Joyner Jones (c.1868–1933), who adopted the stage name "Black Patti." She sang a variety of classical and popular repertoire beginning in the 1880s and developed a national and international reputation. In 1888 Jones toured the Caribbean together with an ensemble known as the Black Patti Troubadours and the Tennessee Jubilee Singers of Fisk University,[82] which undoubtedly contributed to her recognition among Cubans of the day. Incidentally, Black Patti created her stage name by riffing off the name of Italian opera singer Adelina Patti, who had herself toured the Caribbean, including Cuba and Puerto Rico, with Louis Moreau Gottschalk in 1856–1857.[83] So there are connections upon connections with Cuban, New Orleans, and European artists and musical forms to consider here, referenced within the same composition.

"La Patti negra," re-released commercially by Arhoolie Folklyric in *The Cuban Danzón. Before There Was Jazz 1906–1929*,[84] is available in the companion website; (🎧 Track 4.1) readers are encouraged to listen to it in conjunction with the analysis following. The B

---

81. It remains unclear whether recording sessions of the Orquesta Valenzuela in 1909 and 1913 took place in Havana or New York, as Columbia Records' data from that period is sketchy. But both Cristóbal Díaz Ayala and Dick Spottswood (personal emails, January 7, 2013) believe it unlikely that the label would have paid for a ten-piece orchestra to travel to New York to make a small number of recordings. Given that fact, and documentation of Columbia recording crews traveling to Puerto Rico during the same period, they believe all releases discussed here by the Valenzuelas, as well as other orchestras, were recorded in Havana.

82. Abbott and Seroff, *Out of Sight*, 28.

Specifically, they appear to have played British Guiana, Haiti, Jamaica, Panama, St. Kitts, and Trinidad and Tobago.

83. Francisco Echeverría, "El debut de la Patti en La Habana," *Clave. Revista cubana de música*, Vol. 11 (1988), 50–57.

84. This CD is still commercially available at www.arhoolie.com.

theme of the piece comes from a North American vaudeville tune written by African Americans Bob Cole and James Rosemond Johnson in about 1901. Both were well-known composers for the theater and members of the Black Patti Troubadours for a time. The overall structure of the danzón version of their song is roughly a rondo. As illustrated in Figure 4.3, there are three sections, but probably owing to the limited recording possibilities of Edison cylinders, the piece ends on C rather than returning to A or including additional sections.

When one first listens to these old pieces, it can be hard to differentiate the various simultaneous melodic lines, given the quality of the recording. For that reason, it is instructive to consider the third repetition of the "La Patti negra" A theme initially, featuring only clarinet and violins. This line can be heard in variation during each repetition of A and represents the "normative," principal melody of that section, but it is partially obscured during other iterations of A by low and high horn parts. It is hard to tell exactly how much the clarinet and violin lines vary in later repetitions for that reason. But a close listening to the A3 segment (0:56–1:09) of the recording reveals numerous minor discrepancies between what the violin and clarinet play together at any given time.

Compare Example 4.1, the line played by the clarinet, with Example 4.2, an approximation of the simultaneous line played on the violin, during the A3 segment where they are most audible. Taken together, the transcriptions provide a sense of the approach to heterophonic variation adopted by various instruments. Note that in these transcriptions, as in others in this chapter, the music has been written in 4/4, reflecting common contemporary practice, rather than 2/4, the more common time signature associated with danzones at the time.

Next, consider how the piece begins, with an initial statement of A (A1) played by the full ensemble, including prominent, relatively free variation of the melody heard on the cornet (Ex. 4.3). All A-theme transcriptions include chord symbols so that the

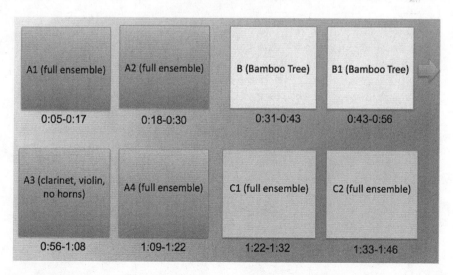

Figure 4.3: Raimundo Valenzuela, "La Patti negra" (ca. 1905). Formal structure.

Example 4.1: Raimundo Valenzuela, "La Patti negra." Melody of theme A as heard on the clarinet, 0:56–1:09.

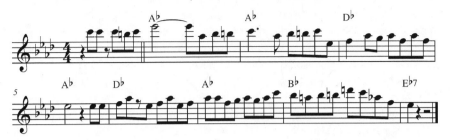

Example 4.2: Valenzuela, "La Patti negra." A variation of the same A-theme melody heard on the violin, 0:56–1:09, emphasizing constant motion and repeated notes.

various phrases can be easily compared. As you can see, only the chord structure and the occasional introductory lick or stock phrase tie most A-theme cornet melodies to those played by the rest of the ensemble, or to each other. A variant of the clarinet and violin melodies depicted in Examples 4.1 and 4.2 can be heard supporting the cornet during segments A1 and A2, as well as an additional melody played by trombone and lower horns; these horns fill out chords while simultaneously emphasizing the syncopated rhythms of the danzón clave pattern: a cinquillo followed by a series of less syncopated quarter or eighth notes. High, sustained notes on the clarinet at the end of the phrase (apparently a spontaneous variant) parallel the sound of early jazz in this part of the piece, as does the overall polyphonic texture.

Compare the cornet melody in A1 (Ex. 4.3) to the cornet line played over A2, the first repeat of A (A2, Ex. 4.4). As you can see, there is almost no relation between the two. The supporting clarinet and violin melody is more audible in this segment, especially as the cornet pauses for a moment in measure 4.

Following A1 and A2 come the two segments of B with the theme from "Under the Bamboo Tree." This segment is relatively pre-composed, though even here one can detect differences between the initial statement and the repeat, especially in the cornet line (see Exs. 4.5 and 4.6). The low horns and the percussion play more softly and emphasize the Afro-Caribbean cinquillo less in section B; much of the time they play backbeats on 2 and 4, for instance, and the güiro emphasizes downbeats rather than syncopations, giving the overall sound a US-style cakewalk or ragtime feel rather than a Cuban feel. This was apparently the intention. Incidentally, the original North

Example 4.3: Valenzuela, "La Patti negra." Cornet line played over section A1, 0:05–0:17.

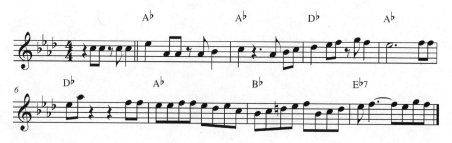

Example 4.4: Valenzuela, "La Patti negra." Section A2, 0:18–0:30.

Example 4.5: Valenzuela, "La Patti negra." B theme, initial statement by the cornet (0:31–0:43).

Example 4.6: Valenzuela, "La Patti negra." B theme, cornet, repeat (0:31–0:56).

Example 4.7: Valenzuela, "La Patti negra." Cornet line, section A4 (1:09–1:22).

American version of "Under the Bamboo Tree" features the classic cakewalk rhythm, an amphibrach followed by two eighth notes. An early version of the song featuring the cakewalk rhythm can be streamed from the Library of Congress website for purposes of comparison.[85]

As represented in the diagram of the musical form (Fig. 4.3), the B theme is followed by the clarinet and violin soli already discussed, A3. This in turn leads to the final repetition of A, A4, the "hottest" of the A repetitions. All instruments play louder, with clarinet and trombone emphasizing the high registers. As in the case of A2, the trumpet line in A4 (Ex. 4.7) is new and appears to be totally improvised, featuring more complex rhythmic elements.

The A4 segment in "La Patti negra" is followed by section C, with a new theme and harmony in the same key. When listening through it, one finds only relatively infrequent moments when cornet, violin, and clarinet play more or less the same line, at the beginning and end; most of the time they freely vary the theme together. Variation is so prominent here that it is difficult to distinguish a principal melodic idea for purposes of transcription. The use of high, sustained pitches in the clarinet, one aspect of such melodic play, is heard once again, especially during the repeat of the phrase. In the first half of the segment, the clarinet and violin emphasize arpeggios and looped phrases in their middle and low registers against the cornet, then return to their highest registers on the repeat. Along with A4, section C captures well the collective improvisatory exuberance of early jazz.

The "La Patti negra" recording raises questions about how the band may have altered typical aspects of performance in order to keep the overall recording under two minutes in length. But in the use of improvisation, the piece appears to be typical of its day. A close listening to dozens of other early danzones confirms that improvisation constituted a mainstay of the style. It is most apparent in repetitions of A themes, but is often found in C, D, or E themes as well. Of course, beginning in the 1910s

---

85. The Library of Congress version is of course by a white artist, Arthur Collins, as African Americans were not allowed to record music in the United States until about 1920. But it gives some feel for what the original piece may have sounded like: www.loc.gov/jukebox/recordings/detail/id/8393 (accessed on July 20, 2012). The main melodic theme begins at about 0:44. Molly Watson and other singers have recorded more recent remakes of the song as well.

Cuban danzones also began including a final open-ended vamp section (later known as a *guajeo* or *montuno*) influenced by the *son* and/or commercial rumba music of the comic theater. But it is the use of simultaneous improvisation or variation in earlier sections that most clearly parallels/anticipates the sound of New Orleans bands.

Following are transcriptions of a few trumpet lines taken from a different piece recorded by the Pablo Valenzuela orchestra in 1909, "Mamá Teresa," written by Raimundo Valenzuela and inspired by a Cuban vocal piece of the same name performed by Adolfo Colombo and Claudio García, also recorded in 1909. (❸ Track 4.2) Both this danzón and the song that inspired it can be found on the Harlequin release *Hot Music from Cuba 1907–1936*.[86] The principal A theme of "Mamá Teresa" is in a minor key, typical of many early danzones and possibly less so of early recordings by groups such as the Original Dixieland Jazz Band. And yet the approach to performance is largely the same as in "La Patti negra," with free improvisation provided by the cornet in A sections, sounding against varied normative melodies played by violin, clarinet, and low horns. In "Mamá Teresa" a low horn (apparently a tuba or *bombardino*) provides the bassline, something ostensibly more common in New Orleans repertoire than in the Cuban orquestas típicas though relatively frequent among early Cuban groups as well. One hears four distinct melodic ideas sounding at once during the A sections of this piece: the bassline, a trombone frequently harmonizing the main melody down a sixth, violins and clarinets playing the principal melody in heterophony, and Valenzuela's cornet improvising even more freely against the others. The overall form of the piece is AABAACAAD,[87] with B consisting of a sixteen-measure lyrical section divided into contrasting segments in major and minor keys, and D featuring the "Mamá Teresa" melody from the Colombo and García duet. The following transcriptions (Exs. 4.8–4.11) contrast the principal clarinet melody heard in the A section (Ex. 4.8) with distinct variations played by cornetist Pablo Valenzuela over A1, A2, and A6.

Similar improvisation can be found on virtually all Orquesta Valenzuela recordings. Those interested in further examples can compare iterations of the A theme in "El garrotín" from about 1913, apparently named after a turn-of-the-twentieth-century Spanish song form (this piece is also available on the Harlequin release mentioned earlier). One interesting aspect of the selection is that it was recorded on an unusually large twelve-inch disc and thus lasts over four minutes, as opposed to the usual two and a half.[88] For that reason its structure may provide better insight into typical danzón form at the time and/or how pieces might have been extended in live performance. In terms of cornet improvisations over A, the initial statements of

---

86. Harlequin HQCD 23 (1993).

87. As opposed to other chapters that analyze danzón form, Chapter 4 indicates all section repetitions in order to make clear which iterations are being discussed in the analysis (i.e., A4, A6, etc.).

88. Cristóbal Díaz Ayala, personal email communication, November 2011. He notes that nearly a third of all Cuban danzones recorded between 1907 and 1925 appeared on twelve-inch discs. By contrast, only about 4 percent of other genres of Cuban music appear on twelve-inch records, and very few US artists of the period either. The reason appears to be that the sectional form of the danzón required a longer recording time, and thus bandleaders requested the extended format of record company executives and technicians.

Example 4.8: Raimundo Valenzuela, "Mamá Teresa" (ca. 1909). Clarinet line heard in variation in all A sections.

Example 4.9: Valenzuela, "Mamá Teresa." Cornet line, A1 (0:00–0:14).

Example 4.10: Valenzuela, "Mamá Teresa." Cornet line, A2 (0:15–0:29).

Example 4.11: Valenzuela, "Mamá Teresa." Cornet line, A6 (1:59–2:11).

A1 and A2 (0:00–0:27) contrast markedly with the following repetition (A3, 1:47–2:12), for instance. The overall form of "El garrotín" is AABACAADAAD.

For additional comparison with the repertoire of a different group, consider a recording by the Orquesta Félix González, "Que volumen," from 1919.[89] This piece has never been commercially re-released, though it is available for streaming on the companion website to this book. (🖱 Track 4.3) Born in Madruga (Havana province), González was an ophicleide (*figle*) player and a member of Enrique Peña's group for a time before establishing his own band.[90] González is noteworthy both for his compositions and his significance as an educator; in 1915, before danzón instrumentalists had easy access to formal music training or union representation, he organized free classes for them and helped them organize collectively to find steady work.[91] As in earlier examples, the lead cornet of the González orchestra (Alfredo García) flirts with the principal theme played by the clarinet and violin in the first excerpt, then deviates from it more markedly in later repetitions of A.

Three representative cornet lines from "Que volumen" over A-theme segments are transcribed below (Exs. 4.12–4.14). The overall approach to improvisation on the cornet is quite similar to that of Pablo Valenzuela's group. Structurally, the piece consists of four sections presented in the following order: AABAACAAD. The D section is essentially a *son*-like "proto-vamp,"[92] with a four-measure repeated harmonic phrase punctuated with repeated riffs by the violin, clarinet, cornet, and lower horns. Interestingly, it appears that wind instruments other than the cornet improvise on the principal A-theme melody less in this ensemble than in the Orquesta Valenzuela, remaining more faithful to the pre-composed theme.

A similar approach to cornet improvisation can be heard on "Aprieta pero no pises" ("Squeeze but Don't Step on Me") from 1928, also by the Orquesta Félix González,[93] admittedly from a later date and one associated with distinct improvisational styles among many US performers. The cornetist does not have the flair of Pablo Valenzuela and solos less prominently (usually only on the repeat of A throughout rather than over both repetitions). But the same approach to discant performance is apparent as in earlier danzón recordings. The form of "Aprieta pero no pises" is AABBAACAAD, with D representing another *son*-like vamp, largely consisting of pre-composed repeated melodies. Compare especially the first two repetitions of A with A4 (1:00–1:13) and A6 (2:11–2:23).

89. Victor 78 #72381-2. Our thanks to the Green Library at Florida International University in the Díaz Ayala Cuban and Latin American Popular Music Collection for access to the recording.

90. Giro, *Diccionario enciclopédico*, Vol. 2, 151.

91. Ezequiel Rodríguez Domínguez, ed., *Iconografía del danzón* (Havana: Sub-Dirección Provincial de Música, 1967), 143–45.

92. We refer to the segment as a "proto-vamp" because it has many characteristics of improvisatory vamps associated with later *son* compositions, such as looped melodic phrases, yet appears to be completely pre-composed.

93. This track was re-released by Arhoolie in *The Cuban Danzón*; available at www.arhoolie.com.

Example 4.12: Félix González, "Que volumen" (ca. 1919). Cornet line, A1 (0:00–0:13).

Example 4.13: González, "Que volumen." Cornet line, A2 (0:14–0:24).

Example 4.14: González, "Que volumen." Cornet line A4 (0:59–1:08).

One might expect, given their stylistic similarities, that orquesta típica-style danzón and the early jazz bands performing within Cuba in the 1910s and 1920s might
have exchanged influences and contributed to each other's development directly in
various positive ways. However, literature from the period suggests that the relationship between the two styles was antagonistic or at least highly competitive and that
jazz bands contributed directly to a decline in the danzón's popularity through their
own ascendance. The extent of this conflict may be overstated owing to the increasingly nationalist orientation of Cuban cultural discourse at the time, but it rings at
least partially true. Of course, the orquesta típica ensemble itself had already become
obsolete among Cuban danzón dancers and performers by the 1920s who increasingly preferred the new *charanga francesa* format emphasizing flute, violins, and
piano. Charangas had a different, less boisterous and more delicate sound, not one
that lent itself as readily to collective improvisation. Certain moments of charanga
performance foreground improvisation on the flute, violin, and piano, such as the

final four measures of the repeated A section.[94] But for the most part the multiple violins and other strings tend to play compositions as written prior to the montuno section in order to function together as a cohesive unit.

In considering the lack of synergy between orquestas típicas and early jazz bands, remember that the repertoire of these jazz bands in Cuba did not sound much like hot New Orleans bands of the day, but rather more like "sweet jazz" such as that played by the Paul Whiteman orchestra, featuring lightly syncopated but primarily pre-composed material played from stock arrangements. A number of North American jazz bands, including Whiteman's, performed together with local jazz groups on the island beginning in the 1910s to entertain tourists and US expatriates; the extent of their presence is evident in the many groups photographed for the publication of the book *Cuba musical*.[95] Thus, it appears that early jazz repertoire as played in Cuba did not reflect the sort of collective improvisation associated with hot New Orleans bands or with the orquestas típicas and would not have contributed to the perpetuation of that style of performance. Jazz bands in various incarnations remained popular on the island through the 1950s, with Cuban artists altering their style gradually to reflect changes in the North American jazz scene. Jaime Prats is said to have founded the first jazz band in 1922 consisting entirely of Cuban performers.[96]

Ned Sublette notes that with the increasing popularity of jazz in Cuba over time, orquestas típicas themselves began to imitate the sound of North American jazz bands.[97] It is clear that at least some danzón orchestras in the 1910s did adopt modified instrumentation similar to that of jazz bands, and in that sense they might be considered the Cuban jazz scene's most direct antecedent (see Fig. 4.4). Both ensembles were similar; the addition of a banjo or saxophone in place of a couple of the lower horns, and the drum set instead of the timbales, was sufficient to allow danzoneros to emulate the jazz idiom.

The danzón appears to have been the first Cuban music to incorporate North American influences in an overt fashion.[98] Numerous examples can be found from the turn of the twentieth century of pieces inspired by prominent North Americans— such as "Jack Johnson" by the Orquesta Enrique Peña, in reference to a boxer—with titles in English ("Vedado Tennis Club" by the Orquesta Cubana Columbia), and/or that include themes taken from US popular culture ("Eskimo Pie" by the Orquesta Tata Pereira),[99] entirely aside from the "La Patti negra" piece discussed previously.

94. José Loyola, personal interview, November 30, 2011, Havana, Cuba. He notes that most Cuban musicians refer to the final four-measure section of the A section as the *paseo*.

95. Martín Calero et al., eds., *Cuba musical. Album-resumen ilustrado de la historia y de la actual situación del arte en Cuba* (Havana: Imprenta Molina y Cía, 1929). See also Cristóbal Díaz Ayala, *Los contrapunteos de la música cubana* (San Juan, Puerto Rico: Ediciones Callejón, 2006), 30.

96. Díaz Ayala, *Cuba canta y baila*, 130.

97. Personal email communication, November 6, 2011. Similar modifications in repertoire and orchestration took place among early *son* bands as well.

98. Acosta, *Descarga cubana*, 31.

99. Cristóbal Díaz Ayala, *Discografía de la música cubana, Vol. 1, 1898–1925* (San Juan, Puerto Rico: Fundación Musicalia), 112, 123, 128. See also Díaz Ayala, *Los contrapunteos*, 33.

Figure 4.4: Antonio María Romeu, performing here in a danzón ensemble with added saxophones and drum set, influenced by the vogue of US jazz music, 1920s. Photo courtesy of the Museo Nacional de la Música, Havana, Cuba.

Danzón repertoire also adopted harmonic and orchestrational elements from early jazz and other North American repertoire in the twentieth century, enriching its musical resources. Yet as mentioned, increasingly the strong interest in jazz among Cuban youth overshadowed the danzón. In the context of rising interest in the *son* and in boisterous musical styles from the United States such as the charleston, the relatively formal, staid dancing associated with danzones came to be perceived as antiquated. Grenet mentions 1916 as the moment this trend became obvious.[100] Castillo Faílde confirms that by that year even many Matanzas social clubs no longer included danzones in their dance programming, the only exceptions being El Pilar and the Liceo de Jesús Monte, with others opting for styles perceived as more modern.[101] Though music critics decried the danzón's decline and satirical images appeared in *La política cómica* exhorting Cubans to support their own music over imported genres,[102] danzones never regained their former national prominence. Only in their

100. Grenet, *Popular Cuban Music*, 32.
101. Osvaldo Castillo Faílde, *Miguel Faílde: creador musical del danzón* (Havana: Editora del Consejo Nacional de Cultura, 1964), 169.
102. See the image "La agonía del danzón," reproduced in Alejandro de la Fuente, *A Nation for All. Race, Inequality, and Politics in Twentieth-Century Cuba* (Chapel Hill: University of North Carolina Press, 2001), 181; and a similar unreferenced image, "El charleston

increasingly *son-* and mambo-influenced variants did they persist as a vital force into the mid-century.

AGAINST IMITATION: JAZZ AND DANZÓN IN TRANSNATIONAL DIALOGUE

After discussing in detail the historical ties between New Orleans and the Caribbean, Thomas Fiehrer summarized the views of an increasing number of scholars when he wrote: "In so far as it emerged from a society largely West Indian in religion, French in speech, Catholic in belief, European in its dominant tastes, contacts, and references, early jazz was certainly 'foreign' to America."[103] His work makes a compelling argument that researchers re-examine mainstream notions about jazz and its relation to music making in the United States. One might take Fiehrer's argument a step further and, rather than conceiving of early jazz as "foreign" or "North American," consider whether it is more appropriate to view music in the United States, the Caribbean, and Latin America as fundamentally part of the same hemispheric story. Enough evidence has been presented about common formal structures, melodic and rhythmic elements, performance practices, and of course centuries of sustained socioeconomic and political interaction to warrant new analytical frames. Specifically, this would involve a move away from research that prioritizes national cultural histories in favor of a broader lens. The danzón as a performance complex, and the specific examples examined here, speak to such inter-influences and transnational dialogues much more than to music making in any one location.

There is little doubt that early jazz performed in New Orleans is unique in terms of its swing, melodic inflection, and other factors; that it represents a significant break with past musical practice; and that a diversity of styles contributed to its emergence. Concert programs from the late nineteenth century make clear that local dance orchestras and brass bands played countless forms of popular music and may well have been influenced by local Afro-French drumming and other non-European traditions. Even so, the similarities in style and instrumentation between danzón and early jazz groups, together with the many Hispanics among early jazz performers, the frequent visits by Latin American groups to the area in the late nineteenth century, and the documented presence of danza and danzón performance in New Orleans force one to consider whether danzón represents one of the musical forms contributing directly to the formation of jazz. Cristóbal Díaz Ayala discussed the issue in a recent essay, asking: "Isn't it possible that dixieland bands copied Cuban [danzón] orchestras? That their music was the initial point of departure, from which jazz soon developed into its many varied modalities and styles? I have not found any

---

y el danzón," in Rodríguez Domínguez, *Iconografía*, 1964, 124. Both cartoons are rather racist, associating jazz with crudely stylized black performers (large lips, etc.) who make loud, unappealing music on sax or drum set. The danzón dancers depicted, by contrast, are exclusively white.

103. Fiehrer, "From Quadrille to Stomp," 29.

other type of orchestration in the United States or other countries in which [trumpet, clarinet, and trombone] feature so prominently against the rest of the orchestra."[104] Certainly early jazz groups performed in a diversity of instrumental formats that featured lead instruments other than those mentioned by Díaz Ayala, more so than is apparent today.[105] For this reason among others, it is unlikely that the influences from Cuba to New Orleans are as unidirectional as he suggests. Yet danzones deserve much greater prominence within jazz historiography.

An even more notable commonality than orchestrational similarities between danzón and early jazz is their approach to individual and group improvisation, as discussed. Improvisation was fundamental to the danzón, contributing much of the excitement to the listening and dancing experience, and its "front-line" performers combined their efforts polyphonically in a manner that closely parallels New Orleans players. There are no other prominent styles of music from the period in which improvisation and the use of simultaneous melodic material play so central a role. This suggests contact of some sort between musical forms and/or musicians in Havana and New Orleans, even if mediated through other Hispanic performers in most cases.

In discussing the origins of improvisational style among early New Orleans musicians, jazz scholars have compared distinct practices among the mostly non-literate uptown black population with that of musically literate Creoles and have speculated as to the interactions of such groups over time.[106] Two recent studies of jazz in New Orleans by Thomas Brothers and Charles Hirsch[107] have extended commonly held notions of this "melting pot" model in important ways, but neither has much to say about possible Latin American or Caribbean influences on New Orleans. The existence of improvisation within a literate form like the danzón suggests that early jazz practice may have emerged from multiple sources including those derived from local working-class African American culture, literate Creoles, and immigrant communities and/or international repertoire. This third possibility is not even recognized in most jazz research.

It remains unclear exactly how often danzones were performed or listened to in New Orleans of the 1880s and 1890s, by whom, or to what extent most early players

104. Cristóbal Díaz Ayala, "Influencias recíprocas entre el jazz y la música caribeña." Unpublished paper read at the IV Congreso Internacional de Música, Identidad y Cultura del Caribe, Santiago de los Caballeros, Dominican Republic, 2010, 4. The original text is the following: "¿No es posible que las bandas de dixieland copiaron a las orquestas cubanas? ¿Que ese fuera el punto inicial de lo que comenzó siendo dixieland y se convirtió rapidamente en el jazz en sus muchas modalidades y estilos? Yo no he podido encontrar ningún otro tipo de orquestación de los Estados Unidos u otro país, en que se produzca esta forma de relacionarse esos tres instrumentos sobre el fondo del resto de la orquesta."

105. Lawrence Gushee, liner notes to "Steppin' On the Gas: Rags to Jazz 1913–1927" (New World Records NW 269, 1977, 4).

106. Thanks to Alex Stewart for underscoring the importance of this issue; personal email communication, January 4, 2013.

107. Thomas Brothers, *Louis Armstrong's New Orleans* (New York: W.W. Norton, 2006); Charles Hirsch, *Subversive Sounds: Race and the Birth of Jazz in New Orleans* (Chicago: University of Chicago Press, 2007).

from the city were aware of the danzón tradition and its variants in Latin America. A great deal of research in that area remains to be undertaken, and on the extent of improvisation in danza and danzón performance among various Latin American groups in distinct time periods. It may be that approaches to danzón improvisation varied significantly among players from different countries or musical backgrounds; this appears to be the case even among Cuban bands.[108] The decidedly negative attitude of some Mexican performers in New Orleans such as Lorenzo Tio Sr. toward the emergent jazz idiom,[109] for instance, suggests that many preferred to work within a more literate musical tradition, or at the very least considered formal training and advanced technical skill a sine qua non of performance. The extent of improvisation in early Mexican danzones also requires further investigation; it may well have been substantial, given that prominent Cuban performers relocated to Mexico City, Mérida, Veracruz, and elsewhere, promoting the music there. Unfortunately, few Mexican danzones were recorded before 1925, owing largely to the political and economic upheaval surrounding the Mexican revolution.[110] However, little improvisation like that of the Cuban orquestas típicas is heard in Mexican danzones after 1930, only individual solos by particular groups imitating the instrumentation and style of big-band jazz. Finally, additional work is needed on the performance style of lower horn instruments in Cuban, Mexican, and other ensembles to determine how they compare with the improvisatory techniques found in more clearly audible high-register instruments. The bombardino seems to have been the favored instrument of improvisation in the Puerto Rican danza of the late nineteenth century, for instance, a form with close ties to the danzón in structural and stylistic terms (see Chapter 2).

It is increasingly apparent that music considered "Cuban," "Latin American," and even "North American" has developed out of an extended process of transnational dialogue and reinterpretation; the "Black Patti" example shows this trend clearly in terms of US influences in Cuba beginning in the mid-nineteenth century. Minstrels and other stage acts from the United States began touring Cuba in the 1860s, strongly influencing local entertainment, and Cuban performers collaborated on extended tours with US stage artists by the 1880s. At the turn of the twentieth century, the cakewalk, the two-step, the turkey trot, the charleston, and early jazz itself all had a strong impact in Cuba, influencing decades of performers, listeners, and dancers. Danzón band leaders were working two-step melodies and similar material into their compositions constantly as of 1900.[111] Entire books have been written

108. Early recordings by the Felipe Valdés orchestra, for instance, appear to feature improvisation less prominently than those by Valenzuela, González, or Enrique Peña's groups. It is also possible that the constrained act of recording dance music on 78 rpm records may have limited improvisational performance generally, and that certain pieces would have varied more in live events.

109. See Raeburn, "Beyond the 'Spanish Tinge,'" 31, footnote 17.

110. One of the few commercially available recordings available today is "El premio gordo" recorded by the Orquesta Babuco in 1910 and re-released on Arhoolie's *The Cuban Danzón. Before There Was Jazz*. It contains little if any overt improvisation.

111. Zoila Lapique Becali, *Cuba colonial. Música, compositores e intérpretes, 1570–1902* (Havana: Letras Cubanas, 2007), 326.

about the rapid growth of jazz performance on the island thereafter and the many bands that adopted such music as their own.[112] Cubans' attraction to North American popular music of the day was logical, given the many common African- and European-derived musical elements shared by both countries, their commercial and political ties, and the strong international influence of the North American music industry.

Interestingly, both the danzón and jazz traditions trended away from collective improvisation and the performance of simultaneous melodies after 1920. In Cuba, limited amounts of heterophony are evident in recordings by early twentieth-century charanga francesa bands (those of Antonio María Romeu, Ricardo Reverón, and others), as mentioned, but the music rarely approaches the degree of polyphony found in orquesta típica recordings. Just as the jazz tradition gradually came to be associated with the solos of individuals over set chord changes, danzoneros increasingly improvised individually within featured segments. Today, solo improvisation may still appear as an interlude within the formal initial structure of the danzón in dance contexts, or as free variation on the principal pre-composed themes of the piece, depending on the performer.[113] Yet more often since the 1930s it is found only in the final vamp at the end of pre-composed compositions, patterned after Orestes López's well-known *danzones de nuevo ritmo*.

Karl Miller argues in his book *Segregating Sound* that notions of racial difference in the United States have fundamentally shaped the way we categorize, listen to, and research music.[114] He suggests that preconceived categories promoted by the US music industry in the early twentieth century (i.e., blues, hillbilly music) have created artificial divisions between many musicians and forms of music making. Might something similar be said of our preconceived understanding of jazz in the present and its exclusive associations with the United States? Could notions among jazz researchers regarding the strong associations between jazz and US heritage have blinded them to the many hemispheric interrelations that gave rise to it? Or have nationalistic tendencies within the musical academy led to the conscious downplaying of such connections? It is noteworthy that the careers of individual musicians from the Caribbean region—beginning with Gottschalk and James Reese Europe and continuing in present-day performances by Gonzalo Rubalcaba, Michel Camilo, Tom

112. For instance, Leonardo Acosta *Descarga cubana: el jazz en Cuba 1900–1950* (Havana: Ediciones Unión, 2000); and *Otra visión de la música popular cubana* (Havana: Letras Cubanas, 2004).

113. Some orquesta típica groups that remain active in the twenty-first century such as the Orquesta Típica Tradicional de Santiago de Cuba incorporate free improvisation into their performances, typically featuring the cornet playing over pre-composed melodies. Flute players such as José Loyola continue to improvise over the principal themes of the danzón within the charanga format, though others such as instrumentalists in the Orquesta Siglo XX do not.

114. Karl H. Miller, *Segregating Sound. Inventing Folk and Pop Music in the Age of Jim Crow* (Durham, NC: Duke University Press, 2010).

McDermott,[115] and others—have not reflected the limitations of such discourses but instead have embraced connections between North American and Latin American music. Indeed, their experiments have resulted in some of the most vibrant recent compositions in jazz. Music historians and American studies scholars could benefit from a greater interest in such commonalities and transnational flows as well.

115. For instance, the Tom McDermott and Evan Christopher CD release *Danza* (STR CD 1009. New Orleans: STR Digital Records 2002) that features music popular at the turn of the twentieth century in Cuba, Brazil, and New Orleans. Michel Camilo's *Caribe* (Decca CD 468817, 2002), a work for solo piano, also beautifully combines elements of ragtime and jazz with Caribbean influences.

CHAPTER 5
Nostalgia, Affect, and Performativity in Contemporary Danzón Scenes

On the evening of April 4, 2009, Madruga, a small city between Havana and Matanzas, Cuba, hosts the largest public dance event of that year's Danzón Habana Festival. As the birthplace of numerous danzón legends, including José, Jesús, and Odilio Urfé, Félix González, and José Belén Puig,[1] organizers of the festival choose Madruga's Complejo Recreativo to present an orchestral *mano a mano* between a Cuban charanga (José Loyola's Charanga de Oro) and a Mexican danzonera (Felipe Fuentes's Danzonera Nuevos Aires del Danzón). This is one of the most highly anticipated events of the festival, officially dedicated to the danzón scene in Mexico City and attended by many of its dancers. By the time the two orchestras and the Mexican guests arrive by bus shortly before 8 PM, the Complejo is filled to capacity. Many locals as well as members of Amigos del Danzón clubs from Havana, whom the organizers have invited and transported, impatiently await the beginning of the dance. Eventually, charanga musicians make their way through the hall to set up on stage; after a few minutes they begin their first set with Abelardo Valdés's classic Cuban piece, "Almendra." As the familiar strains fill the air, members of the local Círculo Amigos del Danzón take over the area in front of the orchestra and display their dancing skill to the attentive and cheerful crowd. Older couples predominate; however, it is striking to see a few younger dancers, and even children, representing the club (Fig. 5.1). Regardless of their precarious financial circumstances, they all don their finest attire. Men wear spotless white shirts or neat (if rather outmoded) suits, and women simple but tasteful white or black dresses. As the music progresses, lissome men glide across the floor with refined and calculated motions; responsive to

---

1. Elena Pérez Sanjuro includes a fascinating account of how an influential music academy opened by chance in Madruga in 1894. An ailing music teacher, Domingo Ramos, founded the institution after moving to the area for treatment in nearby sulfur baths. He provided instruction to generations of poor children in the area, most of them black, and in the process established the careers of danzón performers who would be recognized nationally and internationally for decades. See Elena Pérez Sanjuro, *Historia de la música cubana* (Miami: La Moderna Poesía, 1986), 558–60.

Figure 5.1: Cuban dancers from the Círculo Amigos del Danzón at Madruga's Complejo Recreativo, 2009.

their partners' every touch of the hand or change in finger pressure, women let themselves be guided. The crowd cheers loudly and many others begin to dance as the charanga band plays their next piece. The distinct dancing style of the Amigos del Danzón, with their elegant but highly codified motion, contrasts with the more relaxed style of the general public. (📀 Video 5.1)

After two or three more numbers, the Charanga de Oro leaves the stage to make room for the Danzonera Nuevos Aires del Danzón. The overall sound of the music changes drastically to that of a wind ensemble, yet the dance floor remains packed. Trying to make a space for themselves in the middle of the crowd, a couple starts dancing in the characteristic Mexican danzón style which requires ample room to maneuver. The couple's elegant choreography catches the crowd's attention, and slowly people stop to watch them. The Mexican man moves his partner around himself; his torso stiff, with open turns that Cubans employ in traditional *son* but not in the danzón. He wears a striking orange guayabera and a white panama hat and his partner a long, flowered dress (Fig. 5.2). Many participants have never seen danzón performed in this way and marvel at the Mexican couple's style, erupting into an enthusiastic roar at their conclusion.

The event continues with the charanga and danzonera alternating sets throughout the night. The Danzonera Nuevos Aires del Danzón remains faithful to their core repertoire, but Charanga de Oro soon intersperses danzones with cha cha chás, *sones*, and timba/casino. The audience, unwilling to go home, keeps

Figure 5.2: Mexico City dancers at Madruga's Complejo Recreativo, 2009.

asking for more music, and as a result the orchestras keep playing until almost 4 AM.

This scene illustrates the sense of pride, wonder, and joy that the meeting between Cuban and Mexican danzón practitioners often generates. It also underscores some of the issues that characterize the current renaissance of danzón performance in Cuba and Mexico. The location of the event and the presentation by Madruga's Amigos del Danzón enthusiasts implicitly claim ownership of the tradition, while the flamboyant Mexican dance performance speaks to processes of appropriation and resignification that have characterized danzones interpreted abroad. The distinctive attire worn by the participants tells us of the special place such events hold in the lives of practitioners as well as the sense of nostalgia and tradition that surrounds the current revival. The dedication of the festival to Mexico City as well as the presence of a large group of Mexican dancers and musicians indicates the confluence and negotiation of desires behind the contemporary danzón scene. The ubiquitous presence of Amigos del Danzón members attests to their seminal role in the Cuban danzón's revitalization. The mano a mano itself suggests how practitioners see the danzón both as a space of encounter as well as a site for the performance of difference. Though not always explicitly recognized, the danzón's renaissance has resulted from a complex transnational dialogue. For all participants, the music and dance represent something very dear, especially in Mexico where the dedication of many contemporary enthusiasts borders on the religious.

NEW MODERNITIES AND THE DECLINE OF DANZÓN

Various social and artistic tendencies contributed to declining interest in the danzón among Cuban audiences beginning in the early twentieth century, not least of which was the broad popularity of international repertoire. With the Wars of Independence over, intense nationalist sentiment on the decline for a time, and foreign commercial interests expanding rapidly, Cuban audiences came to embrace a diversity of dance music styles from abroad. The tango, fox-trot, one-step, two-step, charleston, and a host of other forms competed for the public's attention and became quite popular, as documented in numerous sources.[2] The first decades of the twentieth century witnessed the constant presence of cosmopolitan entertainment in Cuba, with dancers and stage acts arriving from Italy, Russia, the United States, and elsewhere. Musicologists of the 1920s, especially, lamented the public's relatively tepid interest in the *habanera*, *canción*, danzón, and other more established forms. Eduardo Sánchez de Fuentes perceived the slow death of the danzón "in the multifarious claws" of North American popular song. He quoted José Cabruca Planas who discussed the angry protests heard from local dancers if danzones were played even in alternation with tangos, a fox-trot, or the two-step.[3] As of the late 1920s, few references to danzón performance appeared in periodical literature, though it retained a core fan base.

In contrast to the danzón, the Cuban *son* found increasing acceptance among all sectors of society in the 1920s; its skyrocketing popularity contributed at least as directly to the decline of the danzón as did foreign musical influences. *Sones*, with their incorporation of hand drumming, catchy call-response singing, street slang, and open-ended improvisatory vamps reflected the national embrace of working-class Afro-Cuban culture to a much greater extent than had been the case previously. Ned Sublette describes danzón events associated with elegant dress and refined movement as "a colonial-era form," and the *son* by contrast as "a product of [an] electrified, asphalted . . . post-Spanish, and increasingly black-proud Cuba."[4] Of course, after 1910 even groups that continued to play danzones generally incorporated elements of the *son* by emphasizing a final open-ended vamp, as discussed in Chapter 2. The many vocal variants of the danzón popular as of the 1920s—*danzonete*, *danzón cantado*, and others—reflect the strong influence of crooner repertoire from abroad, but also of *son*, as audiences came to prefer dance music with catchy vocal melodies over strictly instrumental accompaniment.

2. To cite only a few examples, the popularity of the two-step is mentioned in "Cosas de verano. Las matinees," *El Fígaro* 17, no. 28 (28 July 1901), 330–31; "Los bailes al menudeo," *La Política Cómica* 11, no. 554 (Sunday, 23 July 1916), 7, discusses dance schools in Havana for those interested in the one-step; issues from the same year note the popularity of fox trots and two steps as part of local stage entertainment, see "Troupe de bailarines," *La Política Cómica* 11, no. 558 (20 August 1916), 7.

3. Eduardo Sánchez de Fuentes, *El folk-lore en la música cubana* (Havana: Imprenta El Siglo XX, 1923), 41, 119.

4. Ned Sublette, *Cuba and Its Music. From the First Drums to the Mambo* (Chicago: Chicago Review of Books, 2004), 344.

Some musicologists cite the popularity of the cha cha chá in the mid-1950s as evidence of the ongoing influence of the danzón on popular culture. The cha cha chá might be viewed as a bridge form of sorts; its popularity led to the final disassociation of charanga repertoire from the danzón, though of course hybrid forms such as the danzón-cha remained popular for a time. The former's popularity appears to have signaled the final eclipse of the danzón rather than its perpetuation.[5] In many cha cha chás, only the use of charanga instrumentation constitutes a direct musical link to older forms like the danzón. Yet dancers often continued to perceive a connection between 1950s repertoire and earlier practice, in part because of the similar charanga sound and the fact that the same ensembles that had played danzón in the 1940s continued to play dance music in later years. The most important charanga bands of 1950s Cuba included the Orquesta América, the Orquesta Aragón, the Orquesta Fajardo, the Maravilla de Florida, the Melodías del 40, the Orquesta Sublime, and the Orquesta Sensación; of course, many others performed as well. "Bodas de oro" (Golden Weddings), a danzón-cha written in 1955 by Electo "Chepín" Rosell, represents one of the last danzón composition to become widely popular within Cuba.[6]

While the 1940s and 1950s witnessed the sharp decline of danzón performance in Cuba, it was precisely during those decades that a vigorous nightlife scene solidified in Mexico City around new dance clubs such as the Salón Los Angeles, Club Hipódromo, Fénix, Antillano, and California Dancing Club, as well as older establishments like the Smyrna Club, Salón Colonia, and Salón México.[7] The working classes' passionate embrace of this music in the 1930s led directly to the flourishing salon industry of later decades. From silver screen actors to politicians and sportsmen—especially boxers, the true Mexican stars of the day[8]—everybody who was somebody frequented the salones. During this period the tradition of the shout-out, ¡Hey familia! Danzón dedicado a . . . (Hey family! A danzón dedicated to . . .), was popularized as the standard formula to recognize celebrities attending the dancehall on any given evening.[9] Though the mambo and cha cha chá became fashionable during these decades as well, the danzón remained very popular; one could argue that through its

5. Aurelio Valdés, "El danzón en los veintiún años de revolución," *Bohemia* 72, no. 23 (6 June 1980), 10.

6. López-Nusia, "Contrapunto, polémica y danzón: habla Odilio Urfé," *Bohemia* 68, no. 44 [43] (October 29, 1976), 10.

7. Amparo Sevilla, *Templos del buen bailar* (Mexico City: CONACULTA, 2005), 121–22.

8. The prominence of boxers at the time is evident in the many danzones dedicated to idols like Luis Villanueva "Kid Azteca," Ricardo "El Pajarito" Moreno, José Becerra, Raúl "Ratón" Macías in the 1950s, as well as Vicente Saldívar and the Cuban-Mexican Ultiminio "Sugar" Ramos in the 1960s. Jesús Flores y Escalante mentions the prominent presence of boxers at the salones; see Jesús Flores y Escalante, *Salón México. Historia documental y gráfica del danzón en México* (Mexico City: Asociación Mexicana de Estudios Fonográficos, A.C., 2006 [1993]), 112.

9. Flores y Escalante argues that this shout-out was born in Veracruz's working-class neighborhoods in the 1910s and later adopted in the Mexico City salones in the 1920s and 1930s. See Flores y Escalante, *Salón México*, 59. Nevertheless, it was the shout-out's presence in many films of the Golden Age of Mexican cinema that made it a true emblem of 1940s and 1950s Mexican urban life and culture.

ubiquitous presence in Mexican films, radio, and in live performance at the time, the danzón first became a truly localized form. Many of the most popular Mexican danzón compositions, such as Amador "Dimas" Pérez's "Nereidas" (1932) (🔊 Track 5.1) or Tomás Ponce Reyes's "Salón México" (1958), were composed or popularized during these decades. Eventually, danzones found their way north of the US border in the repertoire of *orquesta* and *conjunto* ensembles led by Beto Villa, Isidrio López, Mike Ornelas, Leonardo "Flaco" Jiménez, and other Tejano performers.[10]

The 1950s and 1960s gave rise to a radical musical revolution: growing interest in rock 'n' roll throughout Latin America eventually distanced many individuals from the ballroom-style couple dances of earlier generations. Countless Cuban rock 'n'roll artists and bands appeared after 1955 (beginning with Jorge Bauer, Los Armónicos, Los Hotrockers, Los Llópiz, etc.), imitating the sounds of Elvis Presley, Bill Haley, and others.[11] At the same time, bands like Los Locos del Ritmo, Los Teen Tops, and Los Rebeldes del Rock started playing covers of US rock 'n' roll in Mexico, slowly displacing older styles as the favorite music of the young middle and upper classes.[12] The popularity of rock increased through the 1970s, at which time it constituted one of the most popular form of music in both countries among younger audiences, despite the fact that it lacked institutional support and often became a focus of attack on the part of local media and government. Rock music's emphasis on individual rather than couple dancing and unchoreographed movement as of the mid-1960s represented a radical departure from Cuban and Mexican social practices of the past.

In Mexico, the arrival of rock 'n' roll took place as the government attempted to modernize Mexico City's entertainment industry by opening to foreign investment. For the city's mayor Ernesto Uruchurtu (regent from 1952 to 1966), ballroom dance culture represented a token of the decadent past. He endeavored to weaken it by means of various moralistic policies, among them the prohibition of alcohol sales in dance establishments[13] and nighttime curfews that forced them to close early.[14] Uruchurtu's legislation dealt a deadly blow to the industry; out of more than twenty-six salons operating in Mexico City at the end of the 1950s, only four remained open by 1963.[15] The increasing broadcasting power of Telesistema Mexicano (later Televisa, the country's most influential TV network) provided Mexicans with an alternative to dance entertainment and also proved detrimental to the city's musical night life.

10. See, for instance, "Nereidas" on the release *Beto Villa. Father of Texas Orquesta, Vol. 1.* Arhoolie Records CD 9059. El Cerrito, CA: Arhoolie Productions, 2007; "La hiedra" and "Blanca estrella" [*sic*, "Blanca Estela"] on *Tejano Roots: Orquestas Tejanas.* Arhoolie Records CD 368. El Cerrito, CA: Arhoolie Productions, 1993; or "Juárez" on *The Best of Flaco Jiménez.* Arhoolie Records CD 478. El Cerrito, CA: Arhoolie Productions, 1999.

11. Humberto Manduley, *El rock en Cuba* (Bogotá: Atril Ediciones Musicales, 2001), 13–27.

12. Eric Zolov, *Refried Elvis. The Rise of the Mexican Counterculture* (Berkeley: University of California Press, 1999), 17–61.

13. Miguel Nieto, owner of Salón Los Angeles, personal interview, Mexico City, September 14, 2011.

14. Angel Trejo, *¡Hey, familia, danzón dedicado a...!* (Mexico City: Plaza y Valdés, 1992), 68.

15. Sevilla, *Templos del buen bailar,* 99.

Finally, the popularization of cumbia among the working classes as well as the arrival of *sonideros*[16] in the 1960s further fragmented the listening public. This left little room for the danzón, a practice broadly perceived by this point as anachronistic and confined to isolated dance scenes in Mexico City and Veracruz.

Protest song represented another musical component of Latin American heritage as of the 1960s that drew audiences away from dance venues. The phenomenon took inspiration from the widespread political unrest of the period, and—especially in Cuba—in revolutionary discourses surrounding the arts. The latter advocated attention to pressing social concerns and supported artistic experimentation of various sorts that avoided standard commercial formulas.[17] Many early Cuban protest (*nueva trova*) singers took inspiration from international artists such as Atahualpa Yupanqui and Bob Dylan. In the context of a socialist-leaning revolution, the danzón and related dances were frequently rejected as out of step with the times. Similarly, the rise of *la nueva canción latinoamericana* in Mexico provided a way for leftist Mexican youth to establish links with larger political endeavors inspired by the early success of the Cuban revolution.[18]

Ironically, the Cuban revolutionary government introduced legislation in 1960 to formalize the danzón's status as Cuba's national dance just as it was slipping into oblivion.[19] The move to recognize it as patrimony, while largely symbolic, resonated with a broader anti-imperialist agenda of the period that supported local forms of heritage as opposed to those from abroad. The proposed bill called for greater radio programming of the danzón, new LP releases, and mandated that the owners of jukeboxes include danzón recordings in every machine. Yet ultimately the initiative had little effect on resuscitating the music's popularity. As opposed to Mexico, where danzones remained at least a modest part of everyday musical life in the 1960s, danzones had virtually no place in Cuban popular culture. For the better part of two decades, danzones were effectively "museumized," divorced from mass culture and transformed from a living social practice into a static form of occasionally staged heritage.

The creation of the state-sponsored Piquete Típico Cubano (Fig. 5.3), a Cuban group devoted solely to the performance of turn-of-the-twentieth-century orquesta típica repertoire, resulted from the same governmental initiatives of the early 1960s described earlier. Odilio Urfé (1921–1988), a prominent member of the Consejo Nacional de Cultura (later the ministry of culture), successfully lobbied for the group's creation in 1963 as part of his drive to educate the public about historical forms of

---

16. Sonideros or *sonidos* are portable sound systems operated by a DJ/MC who animates events by playing recorded music. Historically, sonideros have focused on *música tropical*; most contemporary sonidos privilege cumbia music.

17. Robin Moore, *Music and Revolution. Cultural Change in Socialist Cuba* (Berkeley: University of California Press, 2006), 141–42.

18. Alejandro L. Madrid, *Music in Mexico. Experiencing Music, Expressing Culture* (New York: Oxford University Press, 2013), 111–16.

19. Osvaldo Castillo Faílde reproduces the proposed legislation in *Miguel Faílde: creador musical del danzón* (Havana: Editora del Consejo Nacional de Cultura, 1964), 251–53. However, he does not indicate whether the legislation was ever formally approved.

Figure 5.3: The Piquete Típico Cubano performing in Habana Vieja, with Amigos del Danzón dancers, 2008.

popular culture.[20] Founding members of the Piquete consisted of older performers who had played professionally in the 1920s and 1930s; many used period instruments such as the ophicleide or piston trombone. For the most part they played in festivals or formal academic contexts. As years passed they received occasional invitations to perform on radio and television as well, and for the soundtracks of historical films such as *La bella del Alhambra* (The Lovely Woman of the Alhambra Theatre, 1989). Since 2005 under the direction of cornetist Jorge Vistel, the Piquete has performed monthly at the José Martí museum in Havana and for dance events of the Círculos de Amigos del Danzón, discussed later.

The danzón came to the attention of the media once again in the 1970s during the centenary celebrations surrounding early compositions by Miguel Faílde, often heralded as the "inventor of the danzón." At the time, some journalists blamed international capitalist business practices for the danzón's demise,[21] but the actual causes related to the broader processes described previously. Whether they reflected the popularization of new types of entertainment, the fragmentation of markets under conditions of foreign investment, new socialist agendas, or young dancers' shifting tastes and practices, the decline of the danzón should be understood within larger

20. Ada Oviedo Taylor, "Piquete Típico Cubano," *Tropicana Internacional*, No. 30 (2008), 14.
21. At the very least, accusations of this sort surfaced in discourses surrounding the centenary celebrations of 1979. See Valdés, "El danzón," 10–13.

processes of modernization, exemplified both by capitalist and socialist economic endeavors.

BETWEEN OBLIVION AND TRADITION. THE DANZÓN'S RENAISSANCE IN CUBA

Odilio Urfé played a central role in attempting to revive the Cuban public's waning interest in danzones in the 1950s and 1960s. As a performer on flute and piano, a self-trained musicologist, and one with intimate connections to danzón performance through family ties, Urfé was a uniquely qualified advocate. He first studied music with his father José Urfé (the prominent danzón musician from Madruga mentioned earlier), played in the Orquesta Ideal beginning at age ten, and later was part of the ensembles of Cheo Belén Puig, the Orquesta Gris, and others.[22] In 1949, with the support of Fernando Ortiz and minister of education Raúl Roa, Urfé founded the Instituto Musical de Investigaciones Folklóricas (IMIF), the first Cuban institution of its kind, and used it as a means of organizing conferences, concerts, and mini-seminars in support of local expression.[23] In 1954 he sponsored the first Festival of Folkloric Music that included cash prizes for the best new danzón compositions.[24] That same year he oversaw the release of an LP in Mexico called *Historia del danzón*.[25] (● LP Jacket 5.1) Beginning in 1955 he offered sporadic lectures on danzón history at the University of Havana.[26]

Urfé was the first to organize sit-down danzón concerts with an educational focus. His initial effort in this regard involved the creation of the Charanga Nacional de Conciertos (CNC), a chamber ensemble devoted to interpreting dance and salon compositions written between 1870 and the early twentieth century (Fig. 5.4). It typically played once a month in Havana's Museo de Bellas Artes (Museum of Fine Art) beginning in the mid-1950s.[27] While perhaps accelerating the tendency to think of the danza, danzón, and related genres as relics of the past, the CNC undoubtedly had a positive educational impact. It also encouraged composers to write classical compositions inspired by the danzón, a trend that became more prominent in later decades

22. José Reyes Fortún, *Biobibliografía de Odilio Urfé* (Havana: Ediciones Museo de la Música, 2007), 17–19, 41.

23. Reyes Fortún, *Biobibliografía*, 21. After 1963, the IMIF became known as the Seminario de Música Popular and organized its activities even more towards didactic events rather than academic research.

24. Osvaldo Castillo Faílde, *Miguel Faílde. Creador musical del danzón* (Havana: Editora del Consejo Nacional de Cultura, 1964), 247–49.

25. *Historia del danzón*. Musart, M-114 (Mexico City), 1954 and re-released in 1960 in Cuba as *Antología del danzón* (ICAIC LP 1002).

26. Reyes Fortún, *Biobibliografía*, 22.

27. López-Nusia, "Contrapunto," 10, 12. Personnel for the ensemble as represented on recordings they made for the centenary of the danzón in 1979 included Aurelio Herrera (flute), Miguel Valdés (violin), Rafael Blanco (timbal), Gustavo Tamayo and/or Juan Febles (güiro), Iván Hernández (conga), Orestes Urfé (acoustic bass), and Odilio Urfé (piano).

Figure 5.4: Odilio Urfé's Charanga Nacional de Conciertos in performance, 1960s.

(see Chapter 7).[28] The CNC did not last long, as its most active years extended only into the 1960s. (🅔 LP Jacket 5.2) Yet CNC shows represented only one facet of many innovative concert events associated with the early revolution. Composer Gilberto Valdés directed the Gran Orquesta Típica Nacional in 1959, specializing in danzones and featuring singer Paulina Álvarez.[29] The Charanga Típica Cubana (apparently a separate iteration of the CNC) continued playing "elevated" versions of the danzón as chamber music.[30] (🅔 LP Jacket 5.3) The Orquesta Provincial de Cultura staged danzón concerts in 1961 and the Orquesta Típica Habanera and Charanga Típica Cubana performed as part of the First National Festival of Popular Cuban Music in 1962.[31]

28. Gonzalo and Armando Romeu arranged charanga dance repertoire for symphony orchestra on occasion, which the CNC interpreted. José Loyola, personal interview, Havana, Cuba, November 30, 2011.

29. Radamés Giro, *Diccionario enciclopédico de la música de Cuba*, Vol. 1 (Havana: Letras Cubanas, 2007), 49.

30. Natalio Galán, "Charanga Típica Cubana," *La Gaceta de Cuba* 2, no. 13 (February 1963), 21. This ensemble featured Orlando "Cachaíto" López on bass, Odilio Urfé on piano, Aurelio Herrera on flute, and Miguel Valdés on violin, as well as percussionists. Reyes Fortún (*Biobibliografía*, 42) notes that the CTC played sporadically through 1981.

31. Valdés, "El danzón," 11. Well-known performers/groups took part in the 1962 event including Paulina Álvarez, Barbarito Diez, Arcaño y sus Maravillas, the Orquesta Típica Santiaguera, the Orquesta Enrique Jorrín, and the Orquesta Aragón. Moore, *Music and Revolution* (176–77) provides background on the festival, the other styles of music it featured, and public reactions to it.

As mentioned, danzón performance of all sorts declined markedly in Cuba from the mid-1960s through much of the 1970s. Virtually no literature on them appears in press of the period, and few recordings were made. Some of this decline relates to an overall slump in music and record production owing to a national economic crisis, which led eventually to massive intervention by the Soviet Union. The few danzón compositions of the period appear to have been commissioned by state organizations to accompany official events. They include Pedro Gómez's "El danzón es siempre joven" ("The Danzón Is Forever Young"), dedicated to 26th of July celebrations marking the anniversary of the revolution; "Desembarco del Granma" ("Disembarking from the Granma") by Luis Felipe Vargas Lefebre, celebrating the arrival of Fidel Castro's insurgents in Cuba from Mexico in 1956; and "En Cubana" by Ramón Navarro Simón, dedicated to the fiftieth anniversary of the national Cuban airline.[32]

Toward the end of the 1970s, the centenary of Miguel Faílde's first widely recognized performances of the danzón resulted in renewed concert activity and a mobilization of older dancers still attached to the it. New LP compilations appeared and a short documentary film on the music's history.[33] Odilio Urfé traveled both to Mexico City and to the United States to discuss the danzón, speaking on the radio and as part of university events.[34] The popular television show *Para bailar* featured danzones in a renewed attempt to engage the public.[35] In Matanzas, Manuel Bofill Luis reorganized the Orquesta Típica Miguel Faílde.[36] Prominent articles appeared in magazines such as *Bohemia* and *Revolución y Cultura* discussing the danzón's legacy. A dizzying succession of centenary concerts, exhibitions, and commemorations took place in January and February of 1979 in Havana's Museum of Fine Arts, National Music Museum, and Karl Marx Theater; Matanzas's Sala White; and in Madruga, Guantánamo, and elsewhere; the jazz fusion group Irakere, jazz trombonist Juan Pablo Torres, and classical composers Eddy Galtán and Tony Taño wrote new danzones for the occasion.[37]

32. Valdés, "El danzón," 12.

33. The LPs included *Arcaño y sus Maravillas* (Areíto LD-3486, EGREM, 1975), *La Charanga Nacional de Concierto* (Areíto LD-3486, EGREM, 1975), the two-volume release *Charanga Nacional de Concierto* (EGREM LD-3715 and 3716, 1979), and *La Charanga Típica Cubana de Concierto* (Guamá LDG-2000, 1980). The film short directed by Oscar Valdés is entitled simply *Danzón* (Havana, ICAIC, 1979, 31 mins.).

34. Reyes Fortún, *Biobibliografía*, 29–30.

35. Santos Ulloa, "El danzón: cien años de vida," *Bohemia* 71, no. 7 (February 16, 1979), 13.

36. Martha Navarro, "Quienes siguen o desempolvan la obra de Miguel Faílde," *Girón* (Thursday, December 23, 1989), no page (files, Biblioteca Gener y Del Monte, Matanzas). Bofill continued to perform with the ensemble until 1994 when the group disbanded once again. Yet another incarnation of the Orquesta Típica Miguel Faílde formed more recently under the direction of Faílde's great grandson Ethiel Fernández Failde, as discussed in Chapter 7.

37. For information on events in Havana, see the unsigned article "Concierto especial por el centenario del danzón" *Trabajadores* (January 25, 1979), 5. Tania Quintero's article "Centenario del danzón," *Bohemia* 71, no. 4 (January 26, 1979), 24 mentions the organizing committee, events planned nationally, and the new compositions. Other artists participating included Frank Emilio, Zenaida Romeu, the José Urfé string quartet from the Instituto Superior de Arte, the Charanga Típica Cubana directed by Guillermo Rubalcaba, and the Orquesta Típica Habanera directed by Horacio Benilde Morales. Discussion of photo and music score exhibitions appears in Arnaldo Morales, "Inauguran hoy en Bellas Artes exposición sobre el danzón," *Trabajadores* (January 30, 1979), 5.

Through these celebrations and into the following decade of gradual revitalization, Guillermo Rubalcaba (b. 1927) proved an increasingly important musical figure. Born into a family of danzoneros in Pinar del Río, Rubalcaba played piano in the Charanga Típica Cubana de Concierto in the 1960s and in 1973 formed his own ensemble, the Charanga Rubalcaba. (● LP Jacket 5.4) It continues to perform and to collaborate with prominent artists. In the 1980s the Charanga Rubalcaba was one of only a few ensembles to record new danzones (on the *Vivencias* LP, featuring Barbarito Diez and Tito Gómez). Rubalcaba's career more than that of any other danzonero has spanned the period of early revolutionary effervescence, decline, and slow revival.

To the extent that the danzón has once again become part of Cuba's living cultural heritage, credit is due largely to the determination of elderly individuals across the country who love the dance and have struggled to support it over the past thirty years. In many cases, they face an uphill battle against frequently indifferent and invariably overtaxed cultural institutions. The Círculos de Amigos del Danzón (Associations of Friends of the Danzón), as they are known, typically lack adequate spaces in which to organize events, sound equipment for concerts, the economic means to attract live bands, or funding for outreach, travel, education, or promotion. One poignant situation that speaks to this issue was encountered during an interview with Círculo president Ageo Martínez Alayo in Santiago de Cuba. He met us in the dilapidated shell of a structure without a roof or even complete walls that he and friends hoped to convert into a finished dance space, yet lacked the materials to complete. Nevertheless, Amigos del Danzón groups such as Martínez Alayo's continue to agitate for recognition, in some cases with notable results, because the music means so much to them. A prominent dancer in Matanzas, Bertila Portillo, confessed that our interview with her and subsequent dancing brought her to tears a few hours later. In part, the visit reminded her of happier times when she had danced regularly with her now-deceased husband. And in part our concern for the danzón made her hopeful that conditions for enthusiasts would improve in the future.

As part of centenary celebrations surrounding the danzón events of 1979 and 1980, the UNEAC (Union of Cuban Writers and Artists) institutions in Matanzas and Havana famously organized a Baile de 100 Parejas (Dance of 100 Couples). The event, accompanied by live music and staged in the René Fraga Moreno Park in the Simpson neighborhood of Matanzas, featured dancers and danzón-related personalities from across Cuba as well as Mexico.[38] (● Picture 5.1) It received heavy coverage in the media and served to re-energize the danzón dance community. The Baile de las 100 Parejas was the final event in a series of activities across the country organized by Casas de Cultura, Círculos Sociales Obreros, and Centros Culturales that selected couples to participate.[39] Prior to the Baile, the dancers had largely lost touch with one another. During the centenary celebrations and in their aftermath, a few residents of Matanzas determined that they would work to maintain the danzón's public profile. On January 5, 1980, eleven founding members established the Asociación Provincial

38. Ildelfonso Acosta, personal interview, Matanzas, Cuba, December 2, 2011.
39. José B. Navia, personal interview, Matanzas, Cuba, December 10, 2006.

Amigos de Danzón Miguel Faílde Pérez and began organizing occasional dances in the Sala White (formerly the Club de Matanzas). They intended to "rescue and revitalize" the danzón tradition, as well as to create danzón schools for children, organize community events, and promote the historical study of the music.[40] Eventually the group liaised with the Dirección de Cultura in Matanzas, and later in the decade scheduled regular meetings with them. Initially through personal contacts and later by means of government cultural institutions, members of the Círculo established communication with other danzón dancers and encouraged them to organize similar institutions across the country. As the result of such efforts, a modest number of Amigos del Danzón clubs came into existence within the year. By the late 1980s, the ministry of culture formally recognized them all and established a national organization linking them together.

The Amigos del Danzón phenomenon expanded slowly at first; by 1986, for instance, the central Matanzas Círculo listed approximately seventy active members. In occasional newspaper coverage, representatives called for more presentations of the danzón on radio and television, noting the recent loss of a weekly show on station Radio 26, and lamented the conversion of Miguel Faílde's former residence into industrial storage space.[41] They continued to struggle for recognition and resources, and dance events organized in the Sala White slowly attracted a broader public.[42] By 1987, the Matanzas Círculo began planning joint events with related civic institutions in Madruga, Santa Cruz, Aguacate, and other nearby municipalities.[43] Their cause generated more interest among government agencies as of that year, owing in part to the realization that it could help attract Mexican tourists to the island. In October, Matanzas's Círculo received an invitation to take part in annual Semana de la Cultura events and notification that INTUR (the state tourism agency) and the ministry of culture would organize and fund bi-weekly danzón dances with music provided by the Banda de Conciertos de Matanzas.[44] Danzón enthusiasts began taking part regularly in national Amateurs' Movement concerts and events as well.

In April of 1988, Matanzas hosted its first Encuentro Nacional de Danzoneros with the support of government cultural institutions. Participants enjoyed performances of live music by the Orquesta Siglo XX, the Orquesta Típica Miguel Faílde, and other groups but continued to voice concern over a lack of institutional support

40. Asociación Provincial Amigos de Danzón Miguel Faílde Pérez, "Estatutos" Unpublished manuscript (dated January 15, 1980), 3; property of current president Aurelio Fernández Yáñez.

41. Martha Navarro, "Crecen las aspiraciones entre amigos del danzón," *Girón* (Tuesday, March 25, 1986), no page (archives, Biblioteca Gener y Del Monte, Matanzas). Thankfully, the decision to appropriate Faílde's home for commercial purposes was later reversed and a modest danzón museum created there. But a fire in the new millenium devastated the building and most of the museum's collection; the space remains uninhabitable.

42. Jesús Soto Acosta, "El danzón no ha muerto," *Juventud Rebelde* (Friday, March 28, 1986), no page (archives, Biblioteca Gener y Del Monte, Matanzas).

43. Martha Navarro, "Ni para viejos ni para nuevos, el danzón es para todos," *Girón* (Sunday, January 4, 1987), no page (archives, Biblioteca Gener y Del Monte, Matanzas).

44. Martha Navarro, "Rinde cuenta el círculo Miguel Faílde," *Girón* (Friday, October 16, 1987), no page (archives, Biblioteca Gener y Del Monte).

and the need to educate the public about the danzón.[45] Local residents increased their outreach efforts, for instance by offering dance lessons to orphans and foster children in the Flor de la Sierra house.[46]

Following the advent of formal state recognition, the creation of annual danzón festivals in Cuba in 1989 (discussed later), and more determined attempts to teach the dance to children and youth—the first Encuentro Nacional de Niños Danzoneros took place in 2000[47]—the revival movement has expanded more rapidly. As of 2011, approximately twenty-five Círculos de Amigos del Danzón exist in Matanzas alone, and 224 across the island.[48] A majority of the Círculos' membership is made up of *gente de la tercera edad* (those in the "third stage" of life, over sixty years of age) who become active in the danzón scene after retiring and finding themselves with more free time.[49] Participating in this endeavor provides them with social support and a powerful sense of personal accomplishment. However, not all the members of the circles are elderly. It is now commonplace to feature groups of children or adolescents at festivals or participating in local dances.

While more visible than in the past, Cuban danzoneros still represent a small group and have struggled mightily for modest victories. Members of the central Matanzas Círculo had nowhere to schedule dances for years after the Sala White closed for reparations about 1990, for instance. State organizations eventually offered them an old shoe factory in disrepair as an alternate site; members began carrying out garbage, scraping debris from the walls, and reconstructing the building entirely on their own since cultural agencies provided no labor, materials, or funding. The new dancehall finally opened about a decade later (see Fig. 5.5). Despite the years of hard work the Matanzas Círculo members invested, their case represents one of the most fortunate since most other groups have no permanent physical location to call their own.[50]

An Amigos del Danzón event held in the La Víbora neighborhood of Havana on December 4, 2011 (Fig. 5.6), provides insights into the importance of local events for participants, and also the extent to which the danzón continues to negotiate a place among many other musical styles within the community. The afternoon gathering began about 4:30 PM at a Casa de Cultura (a cultural center); local residents arrived dressed in their best attire—indeed, they adhered to a strict dress code—and greeted each other warmly. Snacks, punch, and rum were available for purchase; most

45. The unsigned article, "Encuentro nacional de danzoneros," *Girón* (Wednesday, March 9, 1988), no page [archives, Biblioteca Gener y Del Monte, Matanzas]) provides information on the various state organizations supporting the event. See also Martha Navarro, "Pronto un encuentro con los seguidores del danzón" (Friday, April 8, 1988), no page; and Martha Navarro "Como en sus mejores tiempos volvió el danzón a la tierra de Faílde," *Girón* (Wednesday, April 20, 1988), no page.

46. Yolanda del Solar Guirola, "Retoños de hoy; relevos [de] mañana," *Girón* (Sunday, May 1, 1988), no page (archives, Biblioteca Gener y Del Monte, Matanzas).

47. José B. Navia, personal interview.

48. Asociación Provincial Amigos de Danzón Miguel Faílde Pérez, "Estatutos," 4.

49. Armando Valdés Abreu, personal interview, Havana, November 28, 2011.

50. Tania Chappi, "Hasta la Reina Isabel . . ." *Bohemia* 103, no. 13 (July 1, 2011), 14–16.

Figure 5.5: Dancehall of the Asociación Provincial Amigos del Danzón "Miguel Faílde." Matanzas, Cuba, 2011.

attendees consumed the rum with gusto and thus the crowd became livelier as time went on. Recorded music played through a small sound system to accompany the dancing. Initial pieces consisted of instrumental and vocal danzones from the mid-twentieth century, but before long other styles of music were heard in the mix as well, such as modern *son*/salsa.[51] As the more contemporary repertoire was played, couples began separating from one another and dancing individually, some incorporating moves from *rumba guaguancó* or even *Santería* worship with distinct hip, shoulder, and arm movements. Perhaps because the dance fell on the saint's day for Santa Barbara (Changó), invited vocalist Juan Torres sang during the final hour of the gathering over pre-recorded backtracks of modern dance music, primarily those of the Orquesta Revé, and at several points incorporated Yoruba-derived religious chants into the improvised vocals of the montunos. Thus, the stylistic contrast between how the peña began (sedately, traditional) and how it ended (exuberant, in dialogue with Afro-diasporic religious forms) could not have been more striking. In Cuba of the twenty-first century, it appears that even hard-core danzón fans feel the need for more "liberated" forms of expression to accompany their social gatherings

51. Shifting musical styles and concluding dances with more modern music is common practice in Cuban peñas de danzón, as seen in the mano a mano between the charanga and danzonera in Madruga. This happens only rarely during contemporary Mexican events, which tend to feature danzones exclusively.

Figure 5.6: Peña del danzón in La Víbora, Havana, organized by the Círculo Amigos del Danzón, 2011. The photo depicts early dancing to a traditional danzón.

alongside classic repertoire. They recognize that the danzón represents only one facet of their heritage and that it must share space within a broader musical reality.

BETWEEN TRADITION AND LIVING PRACTICE: THE DANZÓN'S RENAISSANCE IN MEXICO

. . . eres un danzón en domingo . . . tú eres México (. . . you are a Sunday danzón . . . you are Mexico)
      —Federal Government Publicity for the Bicentennial of Mexico's Independence

On February 22, 2010, the Festival Nacional Danzonero de Monterrey concluded with a joint concert by Danzonera SierraMadre and the Chamber Orchestra of Nuevo León University's Music Department. Critics and the public alike considered the concert's orchestral arrangements of classic Mexican and Cuban danzones conducted by Cuban Daniel Guzmán a huge success. A standing ovation brought the combined ensembles back to the stage to play "Almendra" as an encore. That piece's final montuno proved particularly exciting as members of the danzonera let themselves go, transforming the piece into an extended jam session with virtuosic flute, trombone, and piano solos supported by the orchestra. The concert crowned a weekend of activities for danzón aficionados from all over the country who had enjoyed choreographed group presentations, a gala dinner featuring a dance competition, dance and music workshops, and a meeting of danzón promoters sponsored by the Veracruz-based Centro Nacional para la Investigación y Difusión del Danzón, A.C. (CNIDDAC, the most prestigious danzón organization of its kind in the country).

The Monterrey festival provides insights into the growing contemporary danzón scene in Mexico, one that is now visible beyond Mexico City and Veracruz where the danzón remained alive as a social practice after its decline elsewhere in the 1960s. Activities in Monterrey are especially significant, as they underscore the passion and commitment of a new generation of promoters. Monterrey had never been known for danzón performance, not even in the 1940s or 1950s. It is thus striking to witness escalating northern interest in the genre, sustained primarily through the efforts of professionals aged thirty to forty-five. Miguel Velasco and Maru Ayala, for instance, founded the influential dance troupe El Patio del Danzón in 2004.[52] They revolutionized a more traditional dance scene that enthusiasts Edmundo Ruiz Torres, Gloria Lerma, and dance teacher Arturo Salinas started five years earlier after discovering the dance through María Novaro's film *Danzón* (1991).[53] By developing media contacts for the local promotion of danzón culture, becoming more involved with CNIDDAC in Veracruz, organizing an annual festival, and eventually founding the Consejo Mexicano para la Divulgación del Danzón, A.C., Ayala and Velasco helped establish Monterrey as a vibrant part of Mexico's danzón scene.

Perhaps Ayala and Velasco's most significant contribution was the creation of Danzonera SierraMadre, the first ensemble of its kind in northern Mexico and one of the few in the country interested in the tradition of improvisation in danzón repertoire. SierraMadre's instrumentation includes old-style timbales modeled after nineteenth-century Cuban percussion and blends violins with a variety of wind instruments (two trumpets, trombone, clarinet, and flute). Thus, their sound is more reminiscent of early orquesta típica groups than present-day Mexican ensembles that foreground large saxophone and trumpet sections (see Chapter 2). The SierraMadre's recordings of older Cuban and Mexican repertoire under Daniel Guzmán are unique among Mexican promoters and establish links with projects beyond Mexico.[54] The vibrancy of Monterrey's new danzón community, the enthusiasm it has generated among younger performers, its historically informed performance, and international ties exemplify the transformation that the country has experienced in the last twenty years.

The increased profile of the danzón in concert halls as well as public squares across Mexico motivated federal authorities to market it unabashedly as a symbol of Mexican identity during the country's bicentennial of independence (note the slogan at

52. See https://sites.google.com/site/patiodeldanzon/.
53. Edmundo Ruiz Torres, personal interview, Monterrey, Mexico, February 8, 2009.
54. This is especially true of Daniel Guzmán's recording of classic danzones for orquesta típica and charanga with students from the Rotterdam Conservatory. See *Orquesta Cuba. Contradanzas and Danzones.* Rotterdam Conservatory Orquesta Típica and Charanga Orchestra. Nimbus Records, CD NI 5502. Charlottesville, VA: Nimbus Communications International, 1996.

the beginning of this section). How did a salon dance that seemed destined to disappear in the 1960s become the object of festivals, exhibitions, and public dances nationwide by 2010? As in the case of Cuba, the process was gradual and involved primarily grassroots efforts. During the 1970s and early 1980s, a small but fragmented Mexican danzón scene remained alive thanks to the managers of a few large Mexico City dancehalls (California Dancing Club, Salón Colonia, Salón Riviera), and other groups of dance enthusiasts such as Club Inspiración (Mexico City) and Bailadores de Danzón Hoy y Siempre (Veracruz); the popularity of bands like Acerina y su Danzonera, Danzonera Dimas, Felipe Urbán y su Danzonera; and the enthusiasm of individual couples and instructors.[55] Yet the danzón remained marginal; only a few events attracted the attention of large audiences and attained regional or national recognition. Exceptions included Salón Colonia's "Centenario del Danzón" dance competition in honor of the hundredth anniversary of Miguel Faílde's "Las Alturas de Simpson," held in September 1979;[56] and the First Danzón Festival Veracruz, Mexico-Cuba held in November 1987. At the time, the Cuban and Mexican scenes had so little contact with one another that Cuban artists featured at the event (Guillermo Rubalcaba, Pedro Hernández, Barbarito Diez) expressed their amazement that the danzón still retained a devoted following in Mexico.[57]

The Mexican danzón scene of this period was characterized by factionalism and rival claims to authenticity. One of the more notorious controversies took place in 1989 during a dance competition organized by Patricia Aulestia de Alba entitled "¡Viva el Danzón!" in which an outcry over the jury's decision forced organizers to select a different winner. Scandals of this nature appear to have been fueled by differences of opinion over how to interpret danzón choreography. The event led to the formation of Escuela de Baile Fino de Salón (School of Refined Ballroom Dancing),[58] an institution devoted to reinvigorating the danzón through a systematized teaching method influenced by other ballroom styles—tango, ballroom dancing, fox-trot—and in fact it eventually borrowed many of their steps and mannerisms. Although this was not the first Mexican danzón academy to be established, its creation marked the beginning of a new trend. From this point onward, dance academies rather than

55. Legendary dancers include Manuel M. Rosales "El Gallito," Jesús Ramírez "El Muerto," Carmen López Matus "La Naris," and Enrique Romero from Mexico City; and Natalia Pineda Burgos, Sigfrido Alcántara, Eutiquio Madrigal, Miguel Bada, and Yolanda García from Veracruz.

56. Jesús Flores y Escalante, *Imágenes del danzón. Iconografía del danzón en México* (Mexico City: Asociación Mexicana de Estudios Fonográficos, A.C., 2006 [1994]), 164–65.

57. According to Jara Gámez et al., on that occasion Hernández declared, "Certainly, the danzón was born in Cuba but is now danced in Mexico. We have abandoned it . . . and for that reason we offer it to you with love!" ("Ciertamente en Cuba nació el danzón y hoy se baila en México; nosotros lo hemos abandonado un poco, y por todo ello ¡se los cedemos con amor!") See Simón Jara Gámez, Aurelio Rodríguez "Yeyo," Antonio Zedillo Castillo, *De Cuba con amor . . . el danzón en México* (Mexico City: CONACULTA, 2001), 192. Note that Cuban performers from the mid-1960s through the mid-1980s had limited opportunity to travel abroad, which undoubtedly contributed to their ignorance of Mexican danzón performance.

58. Jara Gámez et. al, *De Cuba con amor*, 172.

dancehalls became the primary centers of danzón instruction. The rise of academies, in turn, supported the creation of regional and national festivals where members could publicly demonstrate their skills. Dance schools became the front line of an overt project to reinvent the danzón as a refined dance style, obscuring its past ties to prostitution and low-class urban life.[59]

In 1989, Rosa Abdalá (1940–1996) and a group of danzoneros from Veracruz founded Tres Generaciones del Danzón Veracruzano (Three Generations of Veracruz Danzón), another organization central to the restructuring of the contemporary Mexican danzón scene. Abdalá became involved with the danzón at a late age, only after she separated from her husband of twenty-two years.[60] As with many other danzoneros, Abdalá's dancing allowed her to rekindle a personal passion and a sense of independence that had remained dormant during her married life. The organization formed as a splinter group of Bailadores de Danzón Hoy y Siempre, Veracruz's first danzón association; members separated following disagreements regarding the role of younger dancers within the collective. While older members preferred to foreground their own skills, Abdalá thought one of the club's primary goals should be teaching younger generations about the danzón in order to ensure its survival. Tres Generaciones thus emerged with this central mission.[61] Organizers also expressed a desire to preserve the "rhythmic purity of traditional danzón, avoiding its 'degeneration' by imitating rhythms foreign to Veracruz's musical culture"[62] as new dance styles like salsa and cumbia became popular. The project thus discursively and practically reframed the danzón as *jarocho* (from Veracruz), justified to an extent given the music's long history in the city. The move may have led to a greater sense of pride and recognition of local heritage. But it also tended to transform local danzón music from a living and continuously changing social practice into a fixed "tradition," much as had taken place in Cuba two or three decades earlier.

In the years following its creation, Tres Generaciones established itself as the leading danzón group in Mexico. They presented formal shows and choreographies but also emphasized danzón workshops and lessons for children and adolescents in Veracruz and in the states of Aguascalientes, Chiapas, Guerrero, Guanajuato, Jalisco, Nuevo León, Querétaro, Quintana Roo, San Luis Potosí, Oaxaca, Puebla, Tabasco, and Tamaulipas. Tres Generaciones frequently appeared on local and national TV shows and represented Mexico at cultural events in Argentina, Brazil, Canada, Cuba, France, Germany, Japan, the United States, and Venezuela. Their constant activity resulted in a prominent national and international reputation. Tres Generaciones (Fig. 5.7) served as a model for new groups throughout the country and has also helped establish networks linking existing danzón scenes. The group's ability to develop strong national alliances provided them with the infrastructure upon which

59. Flores y Escalante harshly criticizes this trend, calling its advocates "snobs." See Flores y Escalante, *Imágenes del danzón*, 65.
60. Rafael Figueroa Hernández, *Tres Generaciones del danzón veracruzano* (Veracruz: CNIDDAC, 2008), 19.
61. Miguel Bada, personal interview, Veracruz, Mexico, December 16, 2008.
62. Figueroa Hernández, *Tres Generaciones* 23.

Figure 5.7: Group Tres Generaciones rehearsing a choreography. Veracruz, 2009.

Miguel Zamudio Abdalá founded the CNIDDAC in 1998, two years after his mother Rosa passed away.

Fundamental to the cohesion and growing popularity of danzón scenes in early 1990s Mexico was María Novaro's film *Danzón*. The movie is not a documentary about the danzón scene per se, but it does offer glimpses of the dance as a background to dramatic action. More important, it disseminated glamorous representations of the dance, associated it with a young, attractive heroine, and exposed the public to a subculture most knew little about. Novaro's collaboration with Mexico City's Club Inspiración and Veracruz's Tres Generaciones allowed the film to both celebrate older danzón performers and to encourage the efforts of a new generation. As Edmundo Ruiz Torres of Monterrey confirms, the movie inspired many new converts who began taking lessons and adopted the danzón as an essential part of their lives. María Rojo, the star of the movie, played an increasingly pivotal role in the national danzón revival. By accepting invitations to dozens of high-profile events she became the new face of a danzón scene most had previously associated only with the elderly.

The popularity of Novaro's film stimulated an increasing number of danzón-related activities in the early 1990s, from the creation of new danzón clubs and schools to the publication of books about the dance—Angel Trejo's *¡Hey, familia, danzón dedicado a . . .!* (1992) and Jesús Flores y Escalante's *Salón México* (1993) and *Imágenes del danzón* (1994) among them—to the establishment of festivals. Thus, the

Figure 5.8: Choreographic presentation at the First Festival Nacional Danzonero, Monterrey, 2009.

Academia Nacional del Danzón, an organization created with the preservation of the danzón as its goal, began in 1993—with María Rojo designated its godmother—and the first Muestra Nacional del Danzón appeared a year later, a festival based on staged choreographic presentations, such as those in Figure 5.8, that inspired many imitators.[63]

A series of danzón couple dancing competitions in Mexico City's Plaza de la Ciudadela in October and November of 1995 led to the formal establishment of La Plaza del Danzón on January 27, 1996 (see Fig. 5.9). This square provides a space for groups to teach the danzón on weekdays, with support from Mexico City's municipal government, and for hundreds of danzoneros to gather for free dances on Saturdays.[64] The idea of turning public squares into danzón spaces is not new but derives from a tradition established in Veracruz in the 1980s. There, civic leaders, entrepreneurs, and local danzoneros collaborated to establish danzón evenings at the Zócalo, the Parque Zamora, and the Plazuela de la Campana. (🔊 Video 5.2) (🔊 Video 5.3) The creation of public danzón spaces outdoors accelerated in the new millenium; by 2012, the Alameda Sur, the Parque de los Venados, and the Parque de los Cocodrilos hosted popular free weekly danzón afternoons in Mexico City, and the idea spread to other

63. See Chapter 6 for additional information about muestras, and links to video footage on the book's companion website.
64. Rosalinda Aceituno, personal interview, Mexico City, September 17, 2011.

Figure 5.9: Plaza del Danzón Event on a Saturday afternoon, Mexico City, 2011.

cities throughout the country including Guadalajara, Oaxaca, Cuernavaca, Tijuana, and Monterrey.

Although not devoted solely to the danzón, the Federación Mexicana de Baile y Danza Deportiva, A.C. (FMB) was created in 1998 with the aim of "planning, organizing, standardizing, regulating, supervising, and evaluating dancers."[65] The federation consists of civic groups interested in unifying dance associations, dance promoters, and dancers in an attempt to develop "a methodological unity for their activities."[66] Many danzoneros soon affiliated with the organization, especially dance instructors, and found in it means of validating their personal projects and developing a common style of teaching. Thus, the federation promoted the homogenization of the danzón. Also founded that year, the CNIDDAC's goal was to solidify cultural alliances among danzoneros throughout the country as a means to oversee and systematize danzón learning. In a sense, the mission of the CNIDDAC dovetailed with that of Tres Generaciones del Danzón Veracruzano (and in fact they frequently collaborated) but redirected such efforts nationally. Through the CNIDDAC, many local scenes began featuring workshops taught by experienced members of Tres Generaciones. When the CNIDDAC eventually organized a national danzón competition

65. "Estatuto y Reglamento del Estatuto de la Federación Mexicana de Danza y Baile Deportivo, A.C.," www.femexbaile.com/noticias/imagenes/estatuto.pdf (accessed April 20, 2012).
66. "Estatuto y Reglamento."

in Veracruz whose goal was to attract danzoneros from every corner of the country, regional muestras organized by groups associated with the center became the perfect forum for preliminary rounds of elimination.

In this way, the CNIDDAC became the preeminent institution of its kind in Mexico, training new danzón instructors, coaching promoters on the intricacies of securing state and private funding for their initiatives, teaching them how to organize events, and helping to devise new and creative ways to disseminate the danzón. One of the keys to the success of the CNIDDAC network is the freedom it allows local groups to develop scenes that highlight local histories even as they adhere to the center's normative dancing method. For instance, in Oaxaca, organizers highlight the role of the local wind band tradition in the perpetuation of the danzón, while in Chiapas the long-standing practice of danzones played by marimba ensembles takes central stage.[67] These regional scenes, along with the aforementioned case of Monterrey, are good examples of the aggressive and enterprising initiatives promoted by the CNIDDAC.

Economically, the danzón renaissance has at least two aspects. On the one hand, it encourages the development of formal commercial enterprises and institutions supporting the needs of danzoneros. New salones have opened (most of them only ephemerally), for instance, as well as stores specializing in danzón shoes and dance attire. New academies and schools are created constantly; musicians found new orchestras and revive old ones. Those in the music industry re-release old recordings and produce new CDs. On the other hand, the danzón renaissance encourages the growth of an informal economy, reflecting trends within all developing nations of the region.[68] At every danzón event one can acquire pirated copies of old and new danzón recordings, home videos of last week's muestra—which proliferate due to teachers' desire to know the steps and choreographies other schools are using—and pirated movies that feature danzón segments.

While the institutionalization of the danzón has increased the visibility of Mexican danzoneros and helped them reinvigorate older scenes by attracting new aficionados, it has also had a negative impact. The creation of free danzón events in large

67. Some performers in the Oaxaca area have ties to Mexico City, such as timbalero Abel Jiménez Luis and his Banda Santa Cecilia de Teotitlán del Valle. Jiménez Luis studied with Acerina and played in the Orquesta Dimas and other Mexico City orchestras before moving to Oaxaca City. See Francisco Ponce, "Maestro Abel Jiménez Luis. Un pilar del danzón en Oaxaca," *Oaxaca Profundo*, no. 93 (2011), 10–11. Other Oaxaca City bands with no ties to the capital play danzón as well. They include the Banda de Música del Estado de Oaxaca that holds weekly concerts in the city's central plaza; the Marimba del Estado de Oaxaca; the Banda Príncipe; and the Orquesta Primavera. Smaller towns throughout Oaxaca state continue to support municipal wind bands that also include danzones in their repertoire. This is established practice, as evidenced by the church archives of San Bartolo Yautepec containing over 140 danzón scores dated from 1900 to 1950. It appears that the transcontinental railroad built through Oaxaca prior to the creation of the Panama Canal facilitated the spread of Caribbean cultural forms to the entire region.

68. For a compilation of studies about informal economies, see Alejandro Portes, ed., *The Informal Economy: Studies in Advanced and Less Developed Countries* (Baltimore, MD: Johns Hopkins University Press, 1989).

public squares proved catastrophic for newer establishments and for the few dance-halls that had remained open through the years of the danzón's decline. As Miguel Nieto, owner of Salón Los Ángeles affirms, many salones proved unable to compete against government-organized events offered free to the public.[69] Thus, the legendary Salón Colonia and Salón Ribera had to close their doors, while ventures like Salón Atzín and the newly recreated Salón México lasted only a short time. Other venues reinvented themselves in order to attract more diverse audiences. Nieto, for instance, transformed Salón Los Ángeles into a cultural center of sorts, as well as renting it as a theater or private ballroom for dances and parties.[70] Javier Cruz Sánchez, manager of Salón Sociales Romo, opened his space to many other dance styles. Yet both of these entrepreneurs still host regular danzón functions once or twice a week. According to Nieto and Cruz Sánchez, their support for the danzón derives more from loyalty to their clientele and their own love of the scene rather than the minimal profits such efforts generate.[71]

The proliferation of local and national muestras and festivals has also had detrimental side effects within the danzón community. Dance academies encourage the memorization of collective choreographies for such events and the adoption of standardized moves and sequences even among couples dancing individually. As a result, schools contribute to a rather constrained and unspontaneous approach to dance, as analyzed further in Chapter 6. Some aficionados resent this phenomenon and express their dissatisfaction with a practice they feel betrays the history of danzón couple dancing in the salones;[72] they view group choreographies, however impressive visually, as adopting exaggerated movements that "deform" the dance's essence.[73]

The homogenization of the danzón has created antagonisms between the Veracruz and Mexico City scenes that exacerbate historical center-periphery tensions between the two cities. Older jarocho danzoneros have argued for decades that the cerrado (closed, non-flamboyant) dancing style seen in Veracruz's Parque Zamora or Zócalo through the early 1990s was more authentic than the embellished style associated with Mexico City, replete with elements from ballroom dance. Yet as danzoneros from Mexico City move to Veracruz and/or as veracruzanos slowly adopt dominant modes of performance at muestras and festivals, the older veracruzano choreography

69. Nieto, personal interview.
70. Nieto, personal interview.
71. Javier Cruz Sánchez, manager of Salón Sociales Romo, personal interview, Mexico City, November 18, 2009.
72. Enrique Guerrero Rivera, "Grupos de danzón ó ¿cuerpo de baile?" *Mini Boletín Danzonero*, 19. Danzoteca 3, www.wix.com/danzonerox/danzoteca3/temporal#!__bicentenario (accessed on April 23, 2012).
73. Luis Pérez Simpson, "Pina Bausch, coreografía y danzón," *Mini Boletín Danzonero*, 7. Danzoteca 3, www.wix.com/danzonerox/danzoteca3/temporal#!__bicentenario (accessed on April 23, 2012). For a larger discussion about these issues, see also the formal answer to Pérez Simpson's article in which Saul Torres blames the CNIDDAC for creating and supporting these choreographic practices. See Saul Torres, "Respuesta de Saul Torres," *Mini Boletín Danzonero*, 7. Danzoteca 3, www.wix.com/danzonerox/danzoteca3/temporal#!__bicentenario (accessed on April 23, 2012).

is disappearing; only a handful of couples still practice it at weekly Zócalo events.[74] Many jarocho danzoneros consider the decline of local traditions that set them apart from others a cultural affront.[75] In contemporary Veracruz, struggles over danzón performance not only contribute to the center-periphery tensions mentioned; they also constitute a very personal matter of identity that generates passionate discussion.

Civic associations like the Academia Nacional del Danzón, CNIDDAC, and the FMB, along with municipal authorities, have collectively contributed to the transformation of the danzón into a codified practice, something that practitioners believe needs to be preserved in its present form. Ironically, institutions such as these, created with the noble goals of rescuing the danzón, have contributed to present-day dogmas and mythologies about the style. Examples of the former include the prescribed musical models and unalterable dancing steps used in the choreographies that form the backbone of dance academy performance. Civic and municipal agencies have thus fundamentally altered the Mexican "danzón tradition" through the adoption of elements of the tango and other ballroom dances, and an avoidance of the "corrupting" influences of newer dance trends and styles. Their efforts have both preserved elements of earlier social practice and transformed them. Thus, it is not surprising to see mass choreographies at Mexico City's Monumento a la Revolución (Monument to the Revolution) or in Plaza Ixtapaluca that attempt to establish a Guinness Book of World Records category for the largest number of couples dancing the danzón. Such demonstrations reflect in part a desire to definitively appropriate the danzón and to suggest that its rightful home is now Mexico rather than Cuba.[76] Use of the danzón to express Mexican pride was not possible in the late 1950s and 1960s when the style's links to prostitution, working-class culture, and immorality continued to tarnish its image. However, its reinvention as a refined ballroom tradition after 1990 helped transform the danzón into a symbol of nostalgic national culture and early modernity.

NOSTALGIA AND THE REVIVAL OF DANZÓN IN CUBA AND BEYOND

The rise of festival activity surrounding danzones in Cuba coincided with a gradual opening to tourism and related investment after decades of limited contact with capitalist countries. Especially after the dissolution of the former Soviet Union in 1989 and the sudden end of its economic subsidies to Cuba, tourism provided desperately

74. Chapter 6 offers a more detailed discussion of these dancing styles.

75. Bada, personal interview; Eutiquio Madrigal, personal interview, Veracruz, Mexico, January 31, 2009; Natalia Pineda Burgos, personal interview, Veracruz, Mexico. February 11, 2009.

76. Rosalinda Valdés, coordinator of the "1000 Parejas Bailando Danzón" event at Monumento a la Revolución, quoted in "1000 parejas mexicanas bailan por un record de danzón," *Terra Noticias*, http://noticias.terra.es/2008/sucesos/1027/actualidad/1000-parejas-mexicanas-bailan-por-un-record-guinness-de-danzon.aspx (accessed on April 30, 2012).

needed jobs and income.[77] The state-run tourist industry has taken various approaches to attracting foreigners since that time: the promotion of academic tourism, for instance, involving invitations to conferences on music and other topics; or cultural exchanges in which visitors take drumming lessons, learn songs and dances, attend festivals, or tour the country to view performances of various kinds. The travel industry also frequently invokes Cuba's mystique as a center of nightlife prior to 1959. Whether one considers venues of the mid-twentieth century recreated for present-day visitors such as the Gato Tuerto or Las Vegas Club; references to past artists through names such as the "Salón Rosado Beny Moré" in Havana; the resuscitation of performance groups of earlier decades (the Septeto Habanero, the Conjunto Chappottín); the expansion of activities in iconic 1940s–1950s establishments like the Tropicana; or the use of the Tropicana name to sell popular music magazines,[78] one finds constant evocations of the era. Memories of the past generated for tourists (or commercial music sales) tend to avoid references to political, historical, or other potentially controversial themes and instead suggest that visitors will find a timeless haven of music making in Cuba, an authentic source of Latin rhythms. The shaping of Cuba's past in this way has coincided with enhanced government sponsorship of danzón performance as well.

In tandem with the tourist renaissance and building on grassroots interest in the danzón in Cuba and Mexico, representatives of the UNEAC in Havana and Matanzas collaborated to create the first national CubaDanzón festival. José Loyola Fernández and Ildelfonso Acosta spearheaded the effort. As head of the music section in Havana's UNEAC through much of the 1980s, Loyola had the authority to realize high-profile initiatives. And as a flutist and composer who had played in charangas since an early age, he identified strongly with the danzón. Initiating a conversation with Acosta, his counterpart in Matanzas, Loyola noted that Matanzas had no annual festival that featured its unique regional heritage. The two worked together to stage a major danzón event in December of 1989 (high season for tourism in the Caribbean), with programming staged in Matanzas, nearby Varadero Beach, and Cárdenas, with support from the National Music Museum, multiple concert venues, Círculos de Danzón across the island, and other institutions.[79] As in the case of virtually all UNEAC-sponsored events, a series of academic presentations by musicologists accompanied the concerts and dances. Loyola and Acosta took advantage of their classical background by scheduling danzón concerts with the Matanzas Symphony that featured guest appearances by well-known popular artists (Richard Egües, Félix Reyna, Guillermo Rubalcaba, Orestes Urfé, etc.).[80] Virtually every established charanga orchestra took part in the 1989 festival—twenty-one in all.[81] The event lasted four days and

77. Moore, *Music and Revolution*, 226–32.
78. Specifically, *Tropicana International*, a magazine intended for tourist consumption.
79. José Loyola, personal interview, Havana, November 30, 2011.
80. Omar Vázquez, "Síntesis de los valores culturales de Matanzas," *Granma* (Tuesday December 26, 1989), 4.
81. Martha Navarro, "Cubadanzón '89 en Matanzas, Cárdenas y Varadero," *Girón* (Tuesday, December 19, 1989), no page (archives, Biblioteca Gener y Del Monte); Ildelfonso Acosta, *Cuerdas de la memoria* (Matanzas: Ediciones Matanzas, 2004), 80.

featured a national danzón dance competition—organized in collaboration with the Círculos del Danzón—and dance and music master classes, in addition to the concerts.[82] Despite bad weather in outdoor locations, problems with lighting and sound, and the need to constantly rush from one venue to another to follow the program, it represented an impressive accomplishment.[83]

Organizers hoped to stage such a festival annually but revised their plans following the breakup of the Soviet Union and the onset of Cuba's economic crisis (a contingency Cuban authorities labeled the "Special Period"). The second CubaDanzón took place two years later (December 1991), a modest affair with only a few orchestras participating and a short roster of events.[84] After this, no danzón festivals were scheduled for some time. In part this reflected the deepening repercussions of the Special Period, and in part friction between cultural organizations in Havana and Matanzas. Acosta stepped down as musical director of the UNEAC in the early 1990s, and the new leadership did not work as well with those in Havana. Officials in Matanzas wanted full control of the festival and related programming decisions, though of course they needed Havana's resources. Eventually, Loyola decided to let Matanzas officials plan the festival themselves without his support. In response, the Matanzas UNEAC initially suspended all such activities, but by 1998 began to schedule CubaDanzón once again.[85] Their events did not always have national projection, but slowly became more ambitious as the economy improved.

In 2004, Cuba's danzón festivals entered a new phase as both Havana and Matanzas scheduled separate events each year, resulting in an implicit competition of sorts. Matanzas offered visitors numerous iconic locations central to danzón history that they could visit, as well as nearby beach resorts, while Havana boasted much more infrastructure and attracted visitors through the extent and variety of its other cultural offerings. Loyola designed the independent Havana festival, naming it "Danzón Habana" to distinguish it from Matanzas's CubaDanzón. He believed Havana should have its own event since it also had been important to the history of the danzón, and since many artists and groups associated with the music were based there.[86] Danzón Habana, with greater resources to draw from, planned their festival in conjunction with state tourist organizations from the outset and attracted significant numbers of foreigners as a result, somewhat to the consternation of CubaDanzón organizers. As opposed to Matanzas celebrations that featured many free or low-cost events, those

82. Ildelfonso Acosta, personal interview, Matanzas, Cuba, December 2, 2011.

83. Martha Navarro, "La última noche de Cubadanzón '89," *Girón* (Tuesday, December 26, 1989), no page (archives, Biblioteca Gener y Del Monte).

84. Charo Guerra, "Será en diciembre el Cubadanzón '91," *Girón* (Thursday, August 1, 1991), no page (archives, Biblioteca Gener y Del Monte, Matanzas); Acosta, *Cuerdas*, 80.

85. Dagoberto Arestuche Fernández, "El danzón vive, ¡Viva el danzón!," *Girón* (November 26, 1998), 6; Hugo García, "Cuba Danzón," *Juventud Rebelde* (November 20, 1999), no page (archives, Gener y del Monte); Dagoberto Arestuche Fernández, "Cubadanzón-2001, vivir y recorder," *Girón* (Thursday, August 2, 2001), no page (archives, Biblioteca Gener y Del Monte); Fernando Valdés Fré, "CubaDanzón en su VI edición," *Girón* (Thursday, November 20, 2003), no page (archives, Biblioteca Gener y Del Monte).

86. José Loyola, interview.

in Havana were conceived in conjunction with foreign currency ticket sales (costing roughly 50 CUC or US$70.00 a person) that provided access to multiple performances staged in hotels and theaters. The first Danzón Habana coincided with the debut of Loyola's all-star charanga ensemble, La Charanga de Oro. With veteran performers such as Eladio "Pancho" Terry on *chéquere*, flautist Policarpo "Polo" Tamayo of the Orquesta Neno González and Ritmo Oriental, as well as the full institutional backing of the UNEAC, they immediately garnered press attention within Cuba and received contracts to tour internationally.[87]

As of 2009, budget cutbacks to the UNEAC across the island resulted in a rationalization of the dueling festivals; Havana and Matanzas now offer events in alternating years rather than during the same year. Habana Danzón continues to dwarf Matanzas's CubaDanzón in the diversity of its programs, the number of orchestras taking part, the presence of danzón-related activities on television and other media, and its coordination with nearby regional performance centers in Madruga, Bejucal, and elsewhere. Recent festivals in both cities have been dedicated to particular regions or cities in Mexico (Oaxaca, Veracruz, the Yucatán, etc.) with the intention of attracting more visitors from those locations. Younger couples have participated more actively in all recent festivals, perhaps resulting from the ongoing educational efforts of Amigos del Danzón groups and/or the higher profile of danzón activities within the country overall.[88]

The revival projects of danzoneros in Cuba and Mexico have allowed danzón culture to spread beyond these countries. In some cases, foreigners have fallen in love with the dance and brought it back to their countries of origin. In others, Cuban or Mexican dancers and musicians have traveled and established danzón scenes in new locations. Holland may be one of the most notable cases. Cuban conductor Daniel Guzmán Loyzaga visited that country and created a Cuban music workshop within the World Music Department of the Rotterdam Conservatory. His teaching emphasized the danzón and eventually led to the production of *Contradanzas y Danzones*. *Orquesta Cuba* (2000), a recording of historical Cuban danzones for orquesta típica and charanga played by an ensemble consisting largely of conservatory students.[89] In 2004, Piroska Delouw and Samuel Molly, a Dutch couple involved in danzón and other Cuban dance performance since the mid-1990s, won first prize at the CubaDanzón competition. Soon after, they founded CubaDanzón Holanda, an organization devoted to teaching, promotion, and research related to the dance.[90] In the United States, the Bay Area-based Orquesta La Moderna Tradición promotes the charanga danzón repertory in northern California;[91] Aaron Bussey and Laura Sánchez

87. Rela Misi, "Charanga de Oro: La nueva revelación de la música cubana," *Música Cubana*, no. 1 (2005), 28–33.

88. Giselle Bello, "IX Festival Internacional Cubadanzón 2006," *Girón* (Thursday, November 23, 2006), no page (archives, Biblioteca Gener y Del Monte).

89. Daniel Guzmán Loyzaga, personal interview, Monterrey, Mexico, February 19, 2010.

90. See the website for Fundación Cuba Danzón Holanda: www.cubadanzon.nl/sp/Fundacion/Fundacion.htm (accessed on May 2, 2012).

91. See the website of Orquesta La Modern Tradición at www.danzon.com/eng/schedule/schedule.htm (accessed on May 2, 2012).

teach Mexican-style danzón dancing at Salón México, their dance academy in San Antonio, Texas;[92] Mano a Mano, a New York-based non-profit organization, also offers regular Mexican danzón lessons,[93] and they and other Mexican danzoneros have recently received invitations from Casa de la Ciudad de México in Chicago to perform and conduct workshops in that city. In Leeds, England, musicologist and flutist Sue Miller founded La Charanga del Norte in 1998, an ensemble dedicated to the performance of Cuban music, especially danzón and related styles like cha cha chá and mambo.[94] Some of her danzones ("Isora Club," "Ritmo alegre," "Arrepentirse") have been released on the CDs *Our Mam in Havana* (2008) and *Look Back in Charanga* (2010).

DANZÓN, NOSTALGIA, AND MASCULINITY ON THE MEXICAN DANCE FLOOR

In December 19, 2008, Milpa Alta, a suburb of Mexico City, hosted a regional end-of-the-year Muestra de Danzón. This type of presentation showcases local, regional, and even national groups and schools in elaborate choreographies. The muestra in Milpa Alta followed a standard format: groups dancing one after the other over a period of roughly four hours, with a few breaks in which the Danzonera Jóven de México del "Chamaco" Aguilar played additional live music and the audience could dance as well. For these events, the style of dress among performers tends to be similar: men wear matching suits or guayaberas and women wear identical dresses, usually custom made for the occasion. The well-coordinated choreographies are impressive, reflecting the months each group devotes in preparation for public display, but at times they strike the viewer as stiff and artificial. In Milpa Alta, one performance stood out from the others, however: that of a group from Pachuca, Hidalgo, called Bella Época. Although their routine was also rigid, their choreography was not only about dancing; it was also a theatrical representation of 1940s–1950s Mexico City nightclub life, and especially of a type of bygone masculinity in which the male dancers' bravado and colorful zoot suits rekindled the persona of the *pachuco* (Fig. 5.10).

Grupo Bella Época's infatuation with the pachuco is not exceptional, but reflects a growing trend in Mexico. The revival of the character originated in Mexico City, but now men from around the country dress as pachucos while dancing danzón. Their presence is noticeable at muestras and at the weekly Plaza del Danzón gatherings in Mexico City's Ciudadela. They attend either as individuals or as part of larger groups—Bella Época (Belle Époque), Pachucos Hoy y Siempre (Pachucos Now and Forever), or Pachucos, Tarzanes y Rumberas—in which the zoot suit is mandatory dress and a courteous but domineering masculinity is expected of participants. The

---

92. The website of Salón México is www.salonmexico.20m.com/index.html (accessed on May 2, 2012).

93. Consult their website, Mano a Mano. Mexican Culture without Borders: www.manoamano.us/en/danzon.html (accessed on May 2, 2012).

94. See the Charanga del Norte site, www.charangasue.com/ (accessed on May 2, 2012).

Figure 5.10: Pachucos from Grupo Bella Época at the Muestra del Danzón. Milpa Alta, Mexico, 2008. Courtesy of Ekaterina Pirozhenko.

nostalgic, retro-reinterpretation of pachuco culture found in contemporary Mexico articulates a particular constellation of masculine values and desires. Perhaps most important, it allows for their expression in a modern society that, in its quest for gender equality, finds such values more and more objectionable. As Elizabeth Guffey puts it, the pachuco orientation allows those adopting danzón subculture to "come to terms with the modern past" in a uniquely masculine way.[95]

The pachuco is a dandy character imported into Mexico from 1940s Chicano culture, related to other prominent urban character types throughout Latin America.[96] In that decade and in the 1950s, the pachuco—along with the danzón and mambo— became a ubiquitous presence in Golden-Age Mexican film. From the cabaret dramas of Rodolfo Acosta to the iconic comedies of Germán Valdés "Tin Tan," the pachuco symbolized a new type of urban cosmopolitan masculinity (Fig. 5.11). From the earliest years of Mexican film, rural characters like the *charro* (cowboy) embodied the attributes and values expected of Mexican men. In contrast, pachucos represented an aberrant masculinity, one consigned to villains like those played by Acosta, or to clowns like Tin Tan.

95. Elizabeth E. Guffey, *Retro. The Culture of Revival* (London: Reaktion Books: 2006), 9.
96. The close links between the similar figure of the *malandro* in Rio de Janeiro and music/dance has been noted by Cláudia Matos in *Acertei no milhar: malandragem e samba no tempo de Getúlio* (Rio de Janeiro: Paz e Terra, 1982). In Buenos Aires, the *compadrito*'s ties to early tango are well established. See, for instance, Simon Collier et. al., *Tango* (London: Thames and Hudson, 1995), 38; and Marta Savigliano's discussion in *Tango and the Political Economy of Passion* (Boulder, CO: Westview Press, 1995) beginning on p. 61.

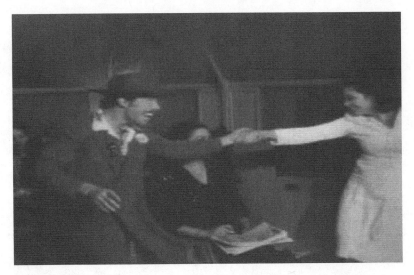

Figure 5.11: Germán Valdés "Tin Tan" as a pachuco in *El hijo desobediente* (1945).

In 1950s Mexico, the pachuco was understood as a man raised or living in the United States who had lost touch with his Mexican cultural heritage and whose hypermasculinity represented a hostile reaction to the discrimination experienced there. In *El laberinto de la soledad* (1950), Octavio Paz describes him as

> a helpless Mexican—without support or values—who affirms his differences with the world. A pachuco has lost his heritage: language, religion, customs, and beliefs. He is left only with an exposed body and soul, helpless before everyone's eyes. His costume protects him and, at the same time, distinguishes and isolates him: it both hides and exhibits. . . . The pachuco suit is not a uniform or a ritualistic dress. It is simply a fashion trend. Like all fashion trends, it consists of novelty . . . and imitation.[97]

Paz's critique of pachucos and their ambiguous relation to Mexican national identity of the 1940s–1950s corresponds to their representations in film. As Sergio de la Mora explains, the pachuco on screen, who speaks a hybrid mix of Spanish and English, displays a proto-metrosexual attitude (that of a man highly concerned with his personal appearance) and is "caricatured as narcissistic and vulgar and marked as not

---

97. ". . . el mexicano desvalido—huérfano de valedores y de valores—afirma sus diferencias ante el mundo. El pachuco ha perdido toda su herencia: lengua, religión, costumbres y creencias. Sólo le queda un cuerpo y un alma a la intemperie, inerme ante todas las miradas. Su disfraz lo protege y, al mismo tiempo, lo destaca y aísla: lo oculta y lo exhibe. . . . El traje del pachuco no es un uniforme ni un ropaje ritual. Es simplemente una moda. Como todas las modas está hecha de novedad . . . e imitación." Octavio Paz, *El laberinto de la soledad* (Mexico City: Fondo de Cultura Económica, 1986), 14.

Mexican. . . . [H]is extravagant zoot suits make him a spectacular figure and renders his style of masculinity curiously unmanly."[98] It is striking that in the contemporary revival of the pachuco among danzón practitioners not only are the negative connotations of the character ignored but the figure is reimagined as the quintessential Mexican male.

Mexico City dancer Jesús Juárez "El Cebos" initiated the pachuco trend among danzoneros in the 1980s when he began organizing regular pachuco-costumed meetings in his house. El Cebos explains:

> I was feeling depressed, so I got together my friends, the best dancers, and we started the Tarzans and Pachucos Club. I used to be a pachuco [in the 1950s], and one day I felt like wearing my old zoot suit that was in the back of a closet. I said to myself "I will use it." Everyone thought it was strange. "What? El Cebos dressed like a pachuco?" But little by little the trend grew. I started with twelve pachucos and now there are hundreds.[99]

The phenomenon became so popular that by 2008 El Cebos began celebrating pachuco meetings in one of Mexico City's large traditional danzón halls, Salón Los Ángeles. The boom of pachuco events and competitions has made retro attire a common part of all present-day danzón events. José Jesús Vargas, a member of the Tarzans, Pachucos, and Rumberas club, comments on the movement:

> It is important to attract young people, but also the "old guard." Because many of the couples that used to go out to salons . . . their partners have died, either men or women, and they've let themselves go, they get depressed. They stop wearing their party clothes. No, that can't be! We invite them to wear those clothes again, to dress nicely. . . We should not cast aside the people who struggled so much for [the new danzón movement].[100]

Many older danzoneros consider the dance floor a space that allows them to become something special for a brief period. This is an acute need in a society that has rendered them invisible and replaced their cherished cultural manifestations with modern musical trends favored by younger generations.

Most contemporary dancers associate the pachuco with a set of specific values that they imagine to have existed in the past but that are no longer in evidence in the modern world. These include elegance, chivalry, and honor. El Cebos notes that pachucos of the past dressed well. "A gabardine suit with a thousand stripes and Cuban-style two-tone shoes. Nobody dressed as classy as the real pachucos."[101] Even younger pachuco enthusiasts like Mario Morales, who first became acquainted with

---

98. Sergio de la Mora, *Cinemachismo. Masculinities and Sexuality in Mexican Film* (Austin: University of Texas Press, 2006), 57–58.
99. Jesús Juárez Flores "El Cebos," personal interview, Mexico City, February 22, 2009.
100. José Jesús Vargas, personal interview, Mexico City, February 15, 2009.
101. El Cebos, personal interview.

them by watching his grandfather, refer to such values as central to the pachuco/danzón experience:

> Chivalry and elegance are now lost in the [danzón]. It used to be a very glamorous dance. Everything started with a ritual at home, taking a shower and dressing up, using cologne, putting on clean clothes, shiny shoes, making a well delineated moustache, [putting on] a clean hat, a tie. All of these details make you project a certain personality. . . . Ladies also wore their best dresses and tried to stand out by dancing with the best dancers. This glamour is now lost.[102]

While El Cebos and Morales highlight elegance and chivalry as fundamental features of the pachuco, José Guadalupe Olivares ("Pepe el Elegante") emphasizes that a pachuco demonstrates through his demeanor and dance prowess that he has the right to dress elegantly and thus gains the respect of his fellow dancers:

> You cannot just dress like a pachuco, you have to earn it in dance competitions. You win the right to wear your hat, your shoes, your suit, your hat feather. . . . When a pachuco gets on the dance floor he is allowed to dance wherever he wants because he has earned it. People open a space for him. Why? Because a pachuco does not get into petty fights, he shows his merit by dancing. He can dance in front or on the side of the orchestra, anywhere he likes because he has earned that right.[103]

The concept of theatrics and performance is implicit in commentary by El Cebos, Morales, and Pepe el Elegante. They dress up in order to project elegance but also recognize the pachuco as a representation, a construct (see Fig. 5.12). Testimony by another young pachuco, Armando Sánchez "El Suavecito," similarly acknowledges the importance of costume and role-playing to the pachuco revival: "Why do I dress like this? Because it is our attire, it is what makes us what we are. . . . If one day I come without a hat people would say 'That guy is a mess. Who is that guy?' . . . No, if you take it off, you are finished. You create a character for yourself, you create the situation."[104]

Clearly, honor and sophistication figure prominently among the attributes that dancers claim (or reclaim) through pachuco performance, virtues that modern working-class life largely neglects. But they are not the only values that the pachuco construct embodies, as it also emphasizes dominance, control, and machismo. El Suavecito, known for his flirtatious personality and flamboyant dancing, states: "I am not a pachuco, I am a pimp! [laughing] It all depends on how you want to think about it. Anyone can have one woman, but if you decide to have three or four [like me] you have to be careful, you need to be very smart, know

102. Mario Morales, personal interview, Mexico City, January 24, 2009.
103. José Guadalupe Olivares, "Pepe el Elegante," personal interview, Mexico City, January 24, 2009.
104. Armando Sánchez "El Suavecito," personal interview, Mexico City, January 24, 2009.

Figure 5.12: A Mexican pachuco couple received the "Elegance Prize" at the 2011 Danzón Habana Festival.

where and how to do it."[105] El Suavecito's attitudes are not universally shared among pachucos, but the type of domineering man El Suavecito represents, one who boasts unabashedly about female conquests or control over women, contributes strongly to the pachuco mystique.

Jesús "El Comandante" Terrón (see Fig. 5.13), a relative newcomer to the danzón scene, embodies all of the masculine attributes mentioned by the interviewees here. Terrón is a former police detective who claims to have successfully participated in countless crime investigations and detentions locally and internationally, including collaborations with Interpol. He defines himself as "a tenacious, brave, and honest guy . . . a very prominent policeman . . . [and] a legend on the force."[106] A dancer since his youth, Terrón (now in his late seventies) found in the danzón a way of continuing

105. Sánchez, personal interview.
106. Jesús Terrón "Comandante Terrón," personal interview, Mexico City, February 26, 2009.

his lifelong passion. He has established himself not only as a prominent figure in the Mexico City scene but also as a promoter of dance events. These include a series of competitions that featured new danzones dedicated to him by Felipe Urbán y su Danzonera, Danzonera Veracruz, Danzonera Azul y Oro, Danzonera La Playa, Acerina y su Danzonera, Danzonera Jóven de México del Chamaco Aguilar, and other orchestras.[107] (🌐 Video 5.4) The shows not only enhanced the profile of the danzón in Mexico City but they also converted Terrón into a celebrity, the embodiment of masculinity. As one enthusiast claimed, "Commander Terrón exudes elegance, a regal presence. He has what many of us lack, he knows how to wear a suit. . . . He arrived on the scene and gave new life to the danzón."[108] The comment suggests that many members of the danzón scene perceive Terrón as a role model.

The most salient feature of Terrón's character is his celebrated status as a womanizer. In "¿Dónde estás, Terrón?," the piece dedicated to him by the Danzonera Veracruz, the lyrics claim: "*Querido por las mujeres /así es Don Jesús Terrón*" [Loved by women / that is Don Jesús Terrón]. Indeed, Terrón makes no secret of his lifestyle. "Obviously I am a very special guy. I have three families with children and there is a cordial relationship among all of them. They love me very much and . . . they allow me to act as I do, so I continue."[109] Terrón's charismatic personality follows in the tradition of the *caudillo* masculinity common to much of Latin America. He is a danzón caudillo, one whose actions are said (at least by men) to benefit the community while enhancing the myths surrounding his persona. Although he does not always dress like a pachuco, Terrón embodies the same domineering masculine values and aura that working-class danzoneros long for and envy.

The pachuco construct allows danzoneros to acquire a personality on the dance floor that transcends the limitations of their everyday lives. The danzón scene offers them not only a music from the past that they can identify with but also a space for them to regain a sense of self-worth they imagine lost with the advent of late twentieth-century modernity. Theirs is a type of restorative nostalgia that relives the past through the imagining of figures and/or moments from that past.[110] By becoming pachucos they embody particular values, making their participation in danzón events a performative utterance.

In evaluating the revival of the pachuco, it is important to consider the role of Mexican media, and especially television with its constant reruns of films from Golden-Age Mexican cinema. Generations of Mexicans grew up watching such films, identifying with their iconography, and reading particular values into the past. This has certainly influenced how younger generations view the pachuco. Mexican cinema of earlier decades has also served as inspiration for a number of more contemporary

107. These danzones were presented during a series of events at Mexico City's Salón Atzín between January 18 and February 15, 2009. The jury selected as the winning composition "Jesús Terrón, el tremendo" ["The Incredible Jesús Terrón"] by Felipe Urbán y su Danzonera. See "Dedican danzón a jefe de Dantes," *Metro* (Sunday, February 22, 2009), 7.

108. Anonymous danzón aficionado, interviewed in an unreleased documentary about El Comandante Terrón.

109. Terrón, personal interview.

110. Svetlana Boym, *The Future of Nostalgia* (New York: Basic Books, 2001), 41.

Figure 5.13: Newspaper article dedicated to Commander Jesús Terrón.

movies set in the 1930s and 1940s. *La vida conyugal* (1993), *La reina de la noche* (1994), *Los vuelcos del corazón* (1996), *Salón México* (1996), *Luces de la noche* (1998), and *Arráncame la vida* (2008) all use the danzón, cabaret night life, and/or pachuco culture to delineate the landscape of Mexican urban life, thus perpetuating the central role of music and dance in contemporary representations of the mid-twentieth century.

Guillermo Ortiz Pichardo is a young filmmaker who recently produced a short based on Arturo Márquez's classical composition Danzón No. 2 (see Chapter 7). The film nostalgically recreates Mexico City of the 1940s and references the types of masculinity and gender values celebrated by contemporary pachucos.[111] Ortiz Pichardo adapts his film to the formal structure of Márquez's musical score, conceived in sonata form. During the first theme, the story alternates between images of young people dancing at a club and a woman getting dressed and preparing to go out. The agitated second theme introduces a male character who pursues the woman; she runs from him. The development section presents a flashback in which we learn that the two characters had met and fallen in love in the past. The recapitulation returns to the present; the man finds the woman on a dark street and the two dance sensually together before another flashback reminds the woman of his infidelity. A heated argument follows, accompanied by the agitated second theme, which continues as the woman flees again and seeks refuge in a club. Ortiz Pichardo evokes the city, the night life, the dress codes, and the gendered attitudes of Golden-Age movies. His effort is not informed by firsthand knowledge of the era; he is too young to have lived through it. Instead, his film might be characterized as reflective nostalgia, a fantasy that does not presume fidelity to a mythical past but rather invokes it in order to mediate with history and inform the future.[112] The film short celebrates a time when ideas about Mexico, Mexicanness, and gender roles seemed stable and fixed—or at least when films made us believe as much—and has appeared at a moment when these ideas seem to have lost their political valence. Ortiz Pichardo himself acknowledges that he has "always been fascinated with the 1940s. They were an age of many changes, when a lot of nationalist ideas crystallized."[113] And in fact he references nationalism through the use of color in the film. Each adaptation of the three large sections of *Danzón No. 2* feature specific colors: red during the exposition, white during the development, and green during the recapitulation. Thus, visually the film presents a slowly unfolding Mexican flag in the background. *Danzón No. 2* received mixed reviews in national and international film festivals;[114] however, the Mexican danzón community embraced it enthusiastically and the CNIDDAC gave it the Rosa Abdalá Gómez Award for promotion of the danzón.

---

111. Ortiz Pichardo's short film is available at www.youtube.com/watch?v=zTO_tllxCYw&feature=related (accessed April 17, 2012). The making of the short is discussed at www.youtube.com/watch?v=P_FILYz9Y5Y&feature=related (accessed April 17, 2012).

112. Boym, *The Future of Nostalgia*, 49.

113. Guillermo Ortiz Pichardo, personal interview, Mexico City, September 22, 2011.

114. It appeared in film festivals in Mexico, Cuba, and Spain but did not receive any awards.

The nostalgia that informs the film projects desires and anxieties of the present onto the past and conceives the latter as a moment when everything made sense. Tellingly, Ortiz Pichardo's idealized representations of the past circulate even as notions of Mexico are challenged by talk of a failed state and the lack of cohesive cultural forms that might otherwise have served as symbols of national pride.[115] The current crisis in government intersects with notions of masculinity, as past models of a paternalistic and domineering single-party government are now questioned by the advance of democratic values and egalitarian gender relations. One might suggest that with the chauvinistic male subject under attack, nostalgia offers the promise of a return to familiar categories. It is a space that allows for the reimagination of the past in the present. The danzón is also perceived as a symbol of national unity transcending individual aspiration, as expressed in rhetoric surrounding the centenary and the massive choreographic displays at the Monumento a la Revolución.

The resignification of pachucos from a threat to Mexican identity into virile national symbols indicates that nostalgic memories perform cultural work and that they are organized according to the needs of the present. Nostalgia for an idyllic past provides a way of making sense of life experiences in troubled times. Pachucos demonstrate not only that the very objects of collective nostalgia are frequently media creations[116] but that nostalgic images and discourses constantly interweave moments of reflection with anxiety and a desire for its resolution.

MODERNITY, NOSTALGIA, AND HERITAGE IN EARLY TWENTY-FIRST-CENTURY DANZÓN

As a result of migration, displacement, and urbanization, nostalgia has become a quintessentially modern sentiment and the danzón's recent history in Mexico reflects this. Danzón in that context is, as Arjun Appadurai puts it, "an object with patina, a perpetual reminder of the passage of time as a double-edged sword."[117] On the one hand, its present-day incarnations in Mexico have brought about the demise of the salón culture where it initially thrived. On the other, the transformation of danzón into national heritage has provided practitioners with a powerful cultural

115. Since 2008, US governmental reports, the US military, and the media have advanced the idea that Mexico may be a failed state due to its increasing drug violence, government corruption, and social insecurity. See *The Joint Operating Environment. Challenges and Implications for the Future Joint Force* (Suffolk, VA: United States Joint Forces Command, 2008), 36; Gardenia Mendoza Aguilar, "Parts of Mexico show signs of 'Failed State,'" *New American Media* (September 24, 2010), http://newamericamedia.org/2010/09/parts-of-mexico-show-signs-of-failed-state.php (accessed April 18, 2012); Gary J. Hale, "A 'Failed State' in Mexico. Tamaulipas Declares Itself Ungovernable" (Houston: James A. Baker III Institute for Public Policy-Rice University, 2011).

116. Fred Davis, *Yearning for Yesterday: A Sociology of Nostalgia* (New York: Free Press, 1979), 22.

117. Arjun Appadurai, *Modernity at Large. Cultural Dimensions of Globalization* (Minneapolis: University of Minnesota Press, 1996), 76.

and affective resource, even though it may be externally manipulated. Danzón revivals in both Cuba and Mexico demonstrate the complex ways in which nostalgic fantasies articulate personal affect within larger national discourses, often in circular flows in which one set of practices acquires meaning in relation to the other. The economic and historical circumstances contributing to the danzón's renaissance over the last thirty years inform the ways that danzoneros and cultural brokers from both countries relate to each other. The presence of Mexican dancers at the Baile de las 100 Parejas, the musical mano a mano in Madruga, the implementation of a prize for Mexicans at the CubaDanzón Festival, the mass dance spectacle at Mexico's Monumento a la Revolución, and the resignification of the pachucos as a model of Mexican masculinity all suggest that the construct of danzón as heritage results from complex dialogues across borders.

It is almost impossible not to read the Cuban danzón renaissance against the strong sense of nostalgia for pre-revolutionary Cuban culture to which Wim Wenders's *Buena Vista Social Club* contributed in the mid-1990s. The film depicts Cuban society as frozen in the past, and Cuban music similarly as a relic of the same age. Wenders ignores the vibrancy of much contemporary Cuban music (*timba*, reggaeton, etc.) and fails to provide a historically informed view even of Cuba's past musical practices. However, the Buena Vista phenomenon has created opportunities for Cuban musicians to profit by catering to expectations generated by Wenders's project. Similarly, the Cuban tourist industry takes advantage of North American and European nostalgia for pre-revolutionary Cuba in the same way that recent Cuban danzón festivals capitalize on Mexican idealizations of the past.

The claiming of the danzón as Mexican heritage may strike some as uninformed or historically inaccurate. But of course all forms of heritage are consciously constructed and speak to the needs of social groups in the present. Ultimately, the origin of cultural forms is largely irrelevant to their experience as tradition.[118] From such a perspective, Cuban attitudes toward a heavily European-influenced danzón genre that they perceive as exclusively "theirs" deserve at least as much scrutiny. Notions of tradition have progressed from Enlightenment-era views that characterized it as a national essence, to those of early anthropologists who described it as the unproblematic handing down of acquired human knowledge, to more modern periods that characterize it as an at least partially conscious shaping of practices in the present toward particular ends. The danzón until recently might have been characterized as a form of residual culture, a dance music of the past existing on the margins of contemporary society.[119] More recently, through the intervention of musicians, dancers, state agencies, and others, it has become en emergent practice once again, associated with new values, processes, and relationships, and altered substantially in response to the demands of new social contexts.

118. Richard Handler and Jocelyn Linnekin, "Tradition, Genuine or Spurious," *Journal of American Folklore* 97, no. 385 (1984), 273–90.

119. Raymond Williams, *Marxism and Literature* (New York: Oxford University Press, 1977), 122.

CHAPTER 6

Cachondería, Discipline, and Danzón Dancing

Contemporary Cuban and Mexican danzón dancing styles are fairly different from one another, and each national style also consists of numerous regional variants. However, the national styles share basic traits—all Cuban styles count motion in a similar way, for instance, and all Mexican styles start on the downbeat—making it possible to broadly speak of a style of *danzón cubano* and a style of *danzón mexicano* that are at odds. If one has mastered one of the two styles and attempts to dance with a partner who is only familiar with the other, the chances of having a pleasing experience are rather low; each dancer would be moving on different beats of the measure. These differences are central to the distinct codes adhered to by danzoneros in Cuba and Mexico. Indeed, danzón dancing styles are highly codified, and competence in codes or structures constitutes a very important aspect of how all participants experience movement. Needless to say, the many dancing styles one witnesses at social events as well as festivals throughout Cuba and Mexico have not always looked as they do today; they are the result of ongoing processes of development informed by a wide variety of cultural, social, and even political values.

This chapter combines ethnography, oral history, discourse analysis, and a study of choreography itself to examine the similarities and differences between contemporary and historical Cuban and Mexican danzón dancing. It explores how dance relates to a variety of notions of difference that have developed in transnational dialogue. A central focus of the discussion is how the pleasures of dancing provide individuals with a space for both challenging and reproducing mainstream discourses about gender and race, depending on the context. Finally, the chapter analyzes how different styles of danzón dancing have gained social meaning and how they allow danzoneros to reimagine themselves, their bodies, and their cultural surroundings.

[T]he woman is in the man's embrace, allowing her flexible body to be tightly squeezed. Their breath intertwines, they become one magnetic gaze: rocking, swinging, rubbing, vanishing in delightful thoughts and desires, intoxicated with the danzón's pitches, saturated with harmony and sensuality.[1]

This short description of danzón dancing, published in 1886 in the Cuban newspaper *El Eco de Galicia*, reflects an inclination to associate the danzón with eroticism that has been evident since its inception. Such connotations have positively or negatively inflected the music and dance according to the moral discourses of specific historical moments. Sensuality is central to the danzón dancing experience; the particular ways practitioners as well as critics have spoken and written about it provide the basis for a theoretical discussion about the performativity of pleasure. In dance as well as in sex, desire and enjoyment lie both in the body that entices and in the body that seduces, in the body that guides and in the body that knows how to follow, in the body that frees itself within the sounds and rhythms of music and in the body that recognizes how to channel that freedom through culturally sanctioned movement.

This relationship between dancing, sexuality, and bodily pleasure informs how dancers experience the danzón even today. Raúl Martínez González, *güirero* with Cuba's Orquesta Siglo XX, suggests that the danzón allows for a type of intimate contact regardless of whether you are meeting your dance partner for the first time. "Even if I do not know her, when I am dancing with her I am smelling her hair, touching her hands . . . it is very sexual."[2] The recurrence of sensuality in talk about the danzón is especially evident among Mexicans. In his novel, *Los años con Laura Díaz* (1999), for instance, Mexican writer Carlos Fuentes describes one character's longing to dance with her lover in the following terms: "I already see myself glued to him—she continued in her best dreamy tone—cheek to cheek, dancing on a single brick, as danzón should be danced, almost without moving your body, just your feet, and your feet keeping the slow, flavorful, *cachondo*, rhythm. Hey family, I want to really live!"[3] Fuentes's fictional account is

1. ". . . la mujer en brazos del hombre: dejándo oprimir fuertemente su flexible talle: confundiéndose los alientos: envolviéndose en una misma magnética mirada: meciéndose, columpiándose, rozándose, aniquilándose en el deleite del pensamiento y en el deleite del deseo: embriagándose con las notas saturadas de armonía y de sensualismo del danzón . . ." in *El Eco de Galicia* (November 28, 1886). Quoted in Nancy González Arzola, *Teatro Martí. Prodigiosa permanencia* (Havana: Ediciones Unión, 2010), 51. This description of danzón dancing was part of a campaign against the perceived immorality of the dance at the end of the nineteenth century in Cuba.

2. Raúl Martínez González, personal interview, Havana, Cuba, September 29, 2011.

3. "Ya me veo pegada a él–continuó con su mejor aire de ensoñación–, de cachetito, bailando sobre un ladrillo, como se debe bailar el danzón, sin mover apenas el cuerpo, sólo los pies, los pies llevando en ritmo lento, sabroso, cachondo. Ey familia ¡Voy a vivir!" in Carlos Fuentes, *Los años con Laura Díaz* (Mexico City: Alfaguara, 1999), 279–80. The term *cachondo* references sensuality; it is discussed in note 6. "Hey family" refers to the popular manner danzón orchestra leaders would call attention to and dedicate the upcoming danzón to someone in the audience. Eg. "Ey familia, danzón dedicado a . . ." [Hey family, danzón dedicated to . . .].

not that different from the responses of female and male *danzoneros* when asked what they liked about dancing danzón. José, a dancer in his sixties from the group Danzoneros de la Ciudadela (a Mexico City group), simply noted: "The music is very sensual. The dance implies sensuality. It is about dancing with your partner and being in synch step by step, beat by beat, cadence to cadence, rhythm to rhythm; that's very sensual."[4] Luisa, another dancer from the same group in her forties, was even more explicit: "to me it is a very sensual, erotic, and expressive dance . . . you can feel your partner's movements . . . you feel like . . . *híjole* [gosh], I do not know, I call it an *alegrasmo* [happy-orgasm] because it feels so nice to be able to let yourself go with the music and feel the rhythm in your body . . . I am telling you, it has a cadence, it is sensual, erotic . . . Ay! Beautiful, pleasant, *cachondo*. How do I feel the danzón? It is like saying to my partner "enjoy me, honey!"[5]

Recent film representations of the danzón also tend to focus on the sensuality of the dancing body, particularly the female body. In María Novaro's *Danzón* (1991), actress María Rojo plays a working-class woman and danzón dancer who goes through a process of personal liberation as she searches for her lost dancing partner. Numerous sequences of the film show danzón dancing in Mexico City and Veracruz, but especially noteworthy is an almost fetishistic shot of Rojo's naked feet as she practices a basic step of Mexican danzón, the *cuadro* [box], on a sandy Veracruz beach (Fig. 6.1). The association of Rojo's dancing body with the sensuality of the danzón was so strong after the release of the movie that she was later called to act in Rubén Gámez's experimental film *Tequila* (1992) and José Luis García Agraz's *Salón México*

Figure 6.1: Close-up of María Rojo's feet dancing in *Danzón* (1991).

4. José, personal interview, Mexico City, December 3, 2008. With the exception of famous dancers or musicians, the names of the interviewees have been changed to maintain their anonymity.
5. Luisa, personal interview, Mexico City, December 3, 2008.

(1996), a remake of the 1949 classic. Each of these works features long, voyeuristic shots of Rojo's sensual movements.

After the 1991 release of *Danzón*, the Mexican danzón movement adopted Rojo as a type of symbol. In fact, Rojo's association with the danzón's *cachondería* [lust, sensuality][6] not only defined much of her own post-*Danzón* work but it also helped solidify the very link between danzón and sensuality by providing an image of a young, attractive female body engaged with the dance in a scene dominated by older practitioners, and in the process making it appealing for younger couples. By exemplifying how the dancers' discourse about danzón's canchondería feeds the imagination of filmmakers and moviegoers, which in turn informs the danzón revival, Rojo's involvement demonstrates the complex nature of the construction of desire in relation to dance, its representation by practitioners, and what outsiders expect from those practitioners.

Clearly, in the popular representation of the dance in Mexico as well as in the mind of hardcore danzoneros there, to dance danzón is all about cachondería. Cachondo is a recurring adjective when danzoneros are asked about their decision to stick with this genre instead of more modern styles of Latin dance. The danzón, with its slower cadence, is all about subtlety, gallantry, chivalry, and what these attitudes keep silent; it is as much about what is untold as what is expressed. As such, the dance is very different from more modern and extroverted Latin genres like salsa or lambada that require a type of vigorous physicality. Danzón dancers replace this with the restrained enjoyment of the slow-moving body. While salsa and lambada are the youthful dances of a more sexually open generation, the danzón represents the incarnation of older discourses about the body and gender relations. Dancing danzón is about the disciplining of desire and the reinforcement of traditional gender privileges, but also about negotiating one's right to pleasure. This chapter takes the notion of cachondería as a theoretical space in which two contrasting ideas about pleasure and enjoyment intersect: the Adornian notion of *Genuß* or *plaisir* (an uncritical pleasure that reproduces conditions of social oppression or discursive repression/inequality), and the Lacanian concept of *jouissance*, the temporary emancipation of the body from mainstream discourses about gender and sexuality.[7] It is precisely the complex codes that regulate dance and discipline dancers' desires, the expression of their pleasure, that temporarily strengthen danzoneros' social control over their bodies; it allows individuals to reclaim their bodies, though often reproducing stereotypes about female bodies as sexual objects. Danzón dancing demonstrates the tension between social and individual claims over people's bodies; its cachondería represents the mystery of the corporeal in the emotional, the intersection between the social and subjective realms, between what is

6. Cachondería is an elusive term; the word, as Mexicans use it, has no exact translation into English. Cachondería is about subdued lust, and the subtle expression of desire is central to the construction of identifications that characterize danzón.

7. See Theodor W. Adorno, *Ästhetische Theorie* (Frankfurt: Suhrkam, 1970), 26–27; and Néstor Braunstein, *El goce. Un concepto lacaniano* (Buenos Aires: Siglo XXI, 2006), 20.

expected from individuals and what they long for. That is the beauty of embodied culture, the emotions that lie in the almost secretive language of dance. In order to investigate tensions between the reproduction of discourse and the reclamation of individual bodies, it is important to explore the relational ways in which cachondería emerges as dancing bodies perform themselves. Such performance within particular social and emotional structures demonstrates the fundamentally intertwined nature of contestation and conformity.

CACHONDERÍA AND THE LOCATION OF PLEASURE IN MEXICAN DANZÓN DANCING

Danzón descriptions in contemporary Mexico tend to emphasize the interaction of bodies as the location of sensual pleasure and the ability of dance to free the body from ideological constraints. Fuentes's description and the responses from other interviewees in Mexico City confirm this. Either as an expression of an individual or a couple's sensuality, the pleasure in danzón dancing seems to be located in the body. And certainly, the body is a locus of sensuality, but not the only one; cachondería invariably emerges in the dialogues between social context and personal affect. A consideration of the contexts of danzón performance in Mexico and Cuba is central to such analysis because contexts are performed by dancing bodies as much as they inform bodies how to enjoy dancing. One does not dance in the same manner in all spaces nor among different people or publics.

Cachondería is not only located in the emotions we feel as we move or communicate with our partner, they are also located in the understanding of how well we and those around us know appropriate dancing codes, and whether those around us realize how well or poorly we understand those codes. The desire created by the other's gaze is fundamental in the production of both social and individual pleasure. In danzón and other forms of dancing there is a voyeuristic element in the production of sensuality and cachondería; the gaze of the other helps to generate desire for the dancing body as well as to develop a sense of awareness and sensual friction in the dancer being observed, admired, and desired.

One illustration of the multifaceted sites of pleasure and meaning is found in the story of Nelly Juárez ("Nelly de Veracruz"), a frequenter of Mexico City dance halls (Fig. 6.2). When asked about how she started dancing danzón, she replied:

> When I started . . . well I did not know how to do it. The women who did know would look at me to see what I would do at the end of a danzón, because it is very important to finish correctly. I would make mistakes and end up with my feet like this [not aligned with each other], and they would laugh at me. And once I said to myself "one day I will dance in front of them and they will admire me. I will [keep improving] and they will be stuck with the same [steps]; I will surpass them." . . . Now, I use different steps they do not know and they congratulate me. . . . When you are aware that people are looking at you it forces you to get better. . . You dance and you

Figure 6.2: Nelly de Veracruz dancing at Mexico City's Salón Atzín, 2009.

think they are not looking, but they are actually looking at you to see if they learn something or whether you make a mistake; [they look at you] either to criticize or congratulate you.[8]

In Nelly's account it is evident that the gaze of other participants is a determining factor not only in shaping one's dancing skills but also in displacing cachondería from the satisfaction of simply dancing with one's partner into the rewarding distinction associated with the disciplining of one's body. Nelly's statement shows that the pleasures of danzón dancing are multi-sited; they are located in the act of "showing off" and causing admiration as much as in moving the body. This realization may help us re-orient dance inquiry toward the relationship between the social and cultural relations that individuals articulate and perform in their everyday lives. When considering cachondería we should distinguish between a variety of modalities. Such

8. Nelly Juárez "Nelly de Veracruz," personal interview, Mexico City, February 15, 2009.

discrimination takes into account the social and emotional structures that are performed, reproduced, and challenged by the dancing body but that also frame its emotions. (Video 6.1)

DANZÓN, DESIRE, AND OTHERNESS: CUBA AND MEXICO

Nelly de Veracruz's account of learning the codes of the danzón and disciplining her body in order to be admired by her fellow female dancers reminds us that, as Slavoj Žižek suggests, the quintessential question of desire is not "what do I want?" but rather "what do others want from me?"[9] It is important to keep in mind that every desire is accompanied by anxieties, and therefore that anxieties also lie at the core of the dynamics that reproduce desire. As desires and anxieties inform notions of self and pleasure as well as discourses of "otherness" and racialization, they remain central to the identity of the dancing body, and, as discussed later, in the definition of body politics via transnational dialogues. It is not the same, for instance, to dance in massive public squares such as the Plaza del Danzón, or as part of a group at one of many public exhibitions organized in Mexico City districts, or at a dancehall such as Sociales Romo with Danzonera Acerina playing in the background, or in Veracruz's Callejón de la Campana to the beat of Manzanita's *guerrilla*,[10] or to compete at the annual Concurso Nacional de Danzón [National Danzón Competition]. In Cuba, it is not the same to dance in Havana's La Víbora neighborhood at the weekly Amigos del Danzón event, at formal exhibitions during the biennial CubaDanzón festival in Matanzas, or on Friday mornings at José Martí's house with the Piquete Típico playing nineteenth-century-style danzones. These different spaces change how dancers move and also how they are looked at as they move; something different would be expected from them in each location. In this dialogue between voyeurism, sensuality, and self-awareness, between Genuß, jouissance, desire, anxiety, and geography, the body becomes a contested space for the definition of "selves" and "others."

Desire, geography, normalization, and codification interweave in a conceptual counterpoint that informs notions of sensuality in relation to the body. Žižek's formulation of desire suggests that people develop notions of sensuality not only in relation to their own bodies but also in relation to others. As such, their sexualized or repressed bodies (depending on the context), as well as the perception of others' bodies in their own discourses of difference, are fundamental in shaping the libidinal imagination. In the case of Cuban and Mexican danzón, many stereotypes and contradictions lie at the core of their respective representations of each other. Issues of admiration, authenticity, as well as local pride and chauvinism, occupy a central place in such representations.

9. Slavoj Žižek, *El acoso de las fantasías*, trans. Clea Braunstein Saal (Mexico City: Siglo Veintiuno, 1999), 19.

10. *Guerrilla* is a term used by local danzoneros in Veracruz to refer to a reduced music ensemble—one that includes the bare number of instruments necessary to play a danzón and still maintain its stylistic musical features.

Participation in the 2007 Danzón Habana Festival provided an opportunity for the authors to interview Cuban dancers, event organizers, and cultural promoters, as well as to examine the event in detail as a performative enunciation. During the week-long festival, it became clear that Mexico occupied a central place in the Cuban understanding of danzón today (at least within the institutionally sanctioned danzón experience that is the Danzón Habana Festival); Mexican aficionados presented exhibitions, choreographies, and musical performances as part of the official program and the organization awarded a special prize to honor the best non-Cuban dancing couple (specially created to recognize Mexicans).

Although Cuban dancers recognize Mexican danzón dancing as "very different," they often admit to a particular fascination with it. Ángela Aldana Linares, head of the local Havana Amigos del Danzón circle, explained: "Mexicans are spectacular dancers. When they dance we just look at them in amazement."[11] Ageo Martínez Alayo, leader of the danzón movement in Santiago de Cuba adds: "Mexicans have their own Mexican danzón . . . and we are grateful that Mexicans cultivate [it]."[12] The frequent laudatory phrases of this nature, interest in learning about the Mexican dance style, and the dedications of recent festivals to Mexican danzón scenes have established the centrality of Mexico in Cuba's contemporary danzón renaissance. Curiously, Cubans' talk of a "Mexican danzón style" does not recognize the existence of at least two distinct danzón traditions in Mexico, *danzón floreado* [embellished danzón] and *danzón cerrado* [closed-couple danzón], and variants within each. The specifics of these variants are discussed later in the chapter.

If Mexican danzón has a central place in the Cuban imagination, the place of Cuba for the Mexican dancers' own imaginary is no less important. This was clear during a conversation with Mina Arreguín and Benjamín Bautista, Mexican winners of the 2005 Danzón Habana competition, who had been invited to be part of the 2007 competition jury:

> Mina: Cubans look like they are enjoying themselves. They do not count [dance steps or beats of the music], they are not as rigid [in terms of body posture]. There is more improvisation in their movement. It is really a pleasure to look at them dancing.

> Benjamín: Yes, in Mexico everyone dances, counts out steps, and suffers . . . here, they dance and enjoy it.[13]

For Mina and Benjamín, Cuban dancers embody a sense of authenticity and originality that Mexican dancers aspire to understand and emulate. In their account, bodily pleasure becomes the site for authenticity that seems to escape the Mexican danzón experience. Mexican dancers' pilgrimages to Havana and their participation in the festival represent attempts to observe and experience the sense of authenticity

11. Ángela Aldana Linares, personal interview, Havana, Cuba, December 12, 2006.
12. Ageo Martínez Alayo, personal interview, Havana, Cuba, March 22, 2007.
13. Mina Arreguín and Benjamín Bautista, personal interview, Havana, Cuba, March 22, 2007.

they ascribe to Cubans. For Cubans, on the other hand, the broad popularity of danzón in Mexico is simultaneously a source of cultural pride, a contradiction (how could Cuba's national dance be alive and well in Mexico while it is almost defunct as a social practice in their own country?), and a form of potential revenue in the form of cultural tourism.

Not all representations that Cubans and Mexicans perpetuate of each other derive from tolerance, acceptance, or admiration. Many times, misguided expectations and anxieties influence such discourses. During the closing ceremony of the 2007 Danzón Habana Festival, for instance, a Mexican group from Guadalajara presented an exhibition of Mexican danzón to an almost all-Cuban audience. As the couple performed a highly codified, choreographed, and rather rigid *danzón de exhibición* to the music of Electo Rosell's classic danzón-chá "La reina Isabel," a young Cuban couple in the audience laughed and commented "*¡Están en llamas!*," which translates roughly as "They're going down in flames!" The comment was informed by the obvious choreographic differences between Cuban and Mexican dancers and cross-cultural (mis) readings of them. Such differences are particularly clear in the Mexican exhibition danzón style that emphasizes an extreme sense of control over posture, movement, and use of space. For Cubans, used to less restricted styles of danzón and a certain freedom of interaction among couples on the dance floor, as well as relatively loose hip movement, the Mexican style appeared repressive. It did not help that the music played was a Cuban danzón-chá, a form danced in a specific way by Cubans that was apparently unfamiliar to the Mexicans on stage. For Cubans expecting to see cha cha chá-influenced dancing in the montuno segment associated with very familiar music, this was an unfulfilling experience. Mexican bodies do not do what Cubans expect to the beat of a danzón-chá. This is apparent in the following sections that consider the specifics of Mexican and Cuban danzón choreographies.

If Cubans occasionally disparage Mexican dancers' understanding of the danzón, Mexicans sometimes also misunderstand the Cuban body, perceiving it as "uncontrolled," and projecting upon it their own anxieties about ethnic and racial difference. When asked about the differences between Cuban and Mexican dancing styles, "El Suavecito" [The Smooth One], a danzón teacher from Mexico City's Plaza del Danzón, he responded:

The most *chingones* [bad-ass] dancers are here [in Mexico City], not in Cuba. . . . Bring the Cubans on and everyone will see how we kick their asses. . . . We have technique, I am not sure who created it, but it is like this: [starts dancing by himself] close, open [the embrace], *entrar* [start] and finish [he dances according to the danzón sections]. Cubans start and then keep on going like that [shakes his hips], because Cuban women move their asses very well. But the *entrada* should be here, not there [imitates the movement]. Can you see? Am I in synch with the music? [imitates Cuban dancing] Do you know what I mean? That's the big difference between Cubans and Mexicans. Cubans have very good music, but dancers . . . well, the best are here![14]

14. Armando Sánchez "El Suavecito," personal interview, Mexico City, January 24, 2009.

El Suavecito's statement is rich with key elements in discourses of "otherness" and the civilization-barbarism dichotomy that often accompanies them. Particularly interesting are the notions of discipline and unruliness that underlie El Suavecito's description of Cuban dancers. While in his view Mexicans feature a technique that characterizes a "civilized" body, Cuban dancers are "undisciplined," "unable" to follow the music, and adopt movements associated with the black "barbaric" body, especially the hips. El Suavecito's disciplined/unruly dichotomy and the racialization implied in this description suggest that anxiety is as strong an impulse as desire in the construction of difference. Depending on the context, in Mexican danzón mythology the "freely moving" Cuban dancers may equally embody authenticity and individual creative expression or unruliness and disorder.

The meanings of danzón at the beginning of the twenty-first century are dialogically produced in acts of cultural translation between Cuba and Mexico. Local meanings of the dance derive from a regional process that often essentializes the "other" but that urgently needs it and thus refers to it in order to define the "self." Such trans-border relationships are not new, but indeed lie at the core of the danzón diaspora throughout the Gulf of Mexico during the twentieth century, informing and catalyzing local constructions of race, nationality, and modernity. An analysis of the similarities and differences in danzón dancing demonstrates a range of acts of discipline, codification, and racialization that inform the construction of such discourse.

A RITMO O A MELODÍA. DANZÓN DANCING FROM SANTIAGO DE CUBA TO HAVANA

In his novel, *Las criadas de La Habana* (2001), Pedro Pérez Sarduy includes a description of Cuban danzón at a ball sponsored by La Bella Unión, a black recreational organization from Güines, near Havana, in the 1950s. Marta, a black working-class character, describes the dance:

> To dance danzón was not easy at all. You cannot go around jumping and wildly moving [*desparramando*] your body all over the place here and there as if it were a mambo; no, everything was based on turns [*giros*], pauses, grace during the promenades [*pasillos*] and such things.[15]

Pérez Sarduy's description suggests that the kind of danzón danced in Cuba toward the end of the 1950s was seen by dancers as highly codified. Danzoneros needed to restrain their movements and control the more uninhibited motions that characterize Afro-Cuban styles like rumba or conga. Clearly, danzón enforced a type of discipline as well as implying familiarity with a very specialized code (at the very

---

15. "Bailar danzón no era nada fácil. No todo el mundo sabe bailar danzón. No se podía estar dando muchos salticos y desparramando el cuerpo por aquí o por allá como si fuera un mambo, sino que todo era a base de giros, pausas, gracia en los pasillos y esas cosas" in Pedro Pérez Sarduy, *Las criadas de La Habana* (San Juan, PR: Editorial Plaza Mayor, 2001), 16.

least, the ability to identify when to pause and when to start dancing again once the pasillo or *paseo* was over) that was not necessary present in other, more "unruly" forms. Pérez Sarduy quotes the lyrics of "Negro de sociedad," a cha cha chá by the Orquesta América, to further emphasize that dancing among black Cubans was informed by anxieties and desires for distinction similar to those of their Mexican counterparts: *No negrita, no / no bailes más la conga así / No negrita, no / mira que soy de sociedad / porque si me ven / bailando como en El Manglar / toda mi argumentación de negro fino se me va a caer* (No, dear black girl / don't dance the conga like that / No, dear black girl / you see, I belong to high society / because if they look at me / dancing like I am in the Manglar neighborhood / my whole premise of being a refined black guy will collapse).[16] Evidently, danzón among Cubans also frequently served (and serves) as a vehicle through which to express the disciplined and controlled movements of a "civilized" body as opposed to the "natural" ways of undisciplined and unsophisticated blacks (i.e., living in marginal neighborhoods and dancing the conga in street processions).

Danzón dancing in Cuba has changed considerably throughout the twentieth century. From the choreographic *piezas de cuadro* of the mid-nineteenth century to the *son*-infused style of the 1910s, to the hybrid danzón-mambo and danzón-chá from the 1940s and 1950s, musical changes have consistently reflected new trends on the dance floor. For instance, Bertila Portillo, an eighty-three-year-old Cuban dancer, remembers that in the 1950s her contemporaries would introduce cha cha chá steps during the final section of a danzón-chá, a practice that is forbidden today among orthodox dancers and during competitions, yet common practice among others.[17] The development of danzón in Cuba took place in relation to its function as a social dance. As part of its current renaissance on the island, the Amigos del Danzón clubs offer lessons and promote the dance among teens and children; thus, older practitioners are able to transmit the style of the 1950s to a younger generation. They gather to socialize on Saturday or Sunday afternoons.

Although danzón dance style tends to be rather homogeneous throughout Cuba, one can differentiate between two basic substyles, *bailar a ritmo* (to dance following the recurrent underlying rhythmic pattern, usually marked by the bass line, beginning on beat 4 of the 4/4 measure) or *bailar a melodía* (to dance following the melody, beginning on beat 1 of the 4/4 measure).[18] The two styles can be found throughout the island, but dancers associate them with specific locations. Local connoisseurs consider *bailar a ritmo* the most "authentic" form and a distinctive feature of choreography from Santiago de Cuba, while *bailar a melodía* is frequently considered a "corruption" of the

16. "Society" in the lyrics of "Negro de sociedad" could refer to the type of cultural and recreational organizations for blacks common in Cuba before the 1959 revolution (such as La Bella Unión), or to a "higher" social status. At any rate, it denotes a type of distinction. See Juan Gualberto Gómez's comments about dance and refinement in black *sociedades de color* (Chapter 3, note 131).

17. Bertila Portillo, personal interview, Matanzas, Cuba, December 2, 2011.

18. The terms *bailar a ritmo* and *bailar a melodía* are used by Cubans in general, although there are some different local variants, especially in Santiago de Cuba.

Santiago style that developed in Havana.[19] Such disputes over authenticity reproduce long-standing tensions between Santiago de Cuba (the former capital of the country) and Havana as rival sites of *cubanidad* [Cubanness].

The *a melodía* style was most prevalent among Cubans competing at CubaDanzón in 2007 and 2009. However, organizers of the competition did not make a distinction between them and kept *a melodía* and *a ritmo* couples competing against each other in the same category. Curiously, some dancers did not realize they were dancing one style or the other, reflecting the less formalized approach to dance pedagogy in Cuba. When queried about their *a ritmo* approach to dance, which seemed at odds with that of most others in the dance floor, one couple from Sancti Spíritus replied "Oh! I do not know about all that, we just dance."[20]

Cuban danzón today involves closed couple dancing; partners stay in each other's arms throughout a given piece, avoiding any separation or opening of the frame except during the paseo section (see Fig. 6.3). The embrace is the same in both *a ritmo* and *a melodía* styles; partners stand very close together, sometimes even leaning on each other, allowing for momentary contact between their chests, groins, and thighs. Yet overall movement is delicate and restrained, with virtually no shoulder or arm movement and little hip movement relative to other local forms of dance. The man's right hand is placed relatively high, on the shoulder blade of the woman, while the woman's left hand is placed on the right shoulder of the man, even as it continues to grip a closed *abanico* (fan). The man folds his left hand gently over the fingertips of the woman's right hand and together they raise them, with the hands well above the man's eye level. The style emphasizes the dominant role of the man, who leads most of the choreography in indicating to the woman where and how to move by means of understated hand signals and arm or body pressure.

Both *a ritmo* and *a melodía* styles are characterized by sequences of steps in groupings of three, performed over a four-beat segment of the music. *A ritmo* dancers begin to move on the fourth beat of music and continue on the second and third beats (4-234-234-234, etc.), pausing on the first beat and thus creating a sense of syncopation that very often coincides with musical accentuations on the fourth beat by the bass or the timbales. (🔊 Video 6.2) *A melodía* performers, by contrast, start on the first beat and continue to move on the second and third beats, while pausing on the fourth beat (123-123-123-, etc.). (🔊 Video 6.3) *A melodía*

---

19. During dance lessons with members of the Círculo Amigos del Danzón "Electo Rosell" from Santiago de Cuba, it became clear that santiagueros emphasize motion beginning on the fourth beat. However, they refer to their style as *bailar con la música* [dancing with the music] instead of *bailar a ritmo*, and describe the style that starts on the beat as *bailar atravesado* [dancing off-beat], an alternative to *bailar a melodía*. Their choice of terms may seem contradictory since, in fact, *bailar atravesado* refers to a style that starts on the downbeat of the measure and *bailar con la música* refers to a style that starts on the upbeat. The reason for this discrepancy is that Cuban dancers rarely count beats, instead guiding their dancing by the structure of the syncopated bass line. For them the emphasis of that bass line, usually on beat 4, constitutes the beginning of the musical phrase; beginning a dance sequence on beat 1 means being off-beat.

20. Anonymous couple at the 2009 Habana Danzón, personal conversation, Havana, Cuba, April 2, 2009.

Figure 6.3: Cuban couples competing at the 2009 Danzón Habana Festival.

counting is similar to the counting of today's standard salsa, with an emphasis on strong-beat movement that simplifies the overall experience by largely avoiding syncopation.[21]

There are two basic steps or gestures in Cuban danzón, common to both the *a ritmo* and *a melodía* subgenres; *giros* [circular turns] mentioned in Pérez Sarduy's novel, and the *cajita*/cuadro [little box] or *cuadro lateral* [lateral box]. In both gestures, steps are counted in groupings of three, as explained previously. In giros, the couple moves together in circles or partial circles, generally to the woman's right and the man's left. In executing a cajita/cuadro, the couple starts moving to the woman's right side and the man's left side, separating the feet with a step to the side, closing them on two, the man moving forward with his left foot and the woman moving backward with her right foot on three, and separating their feet on a diagonal (the man moving forward with his right foot, the woman backward with her left) on beat four.[22] Although sometimes one sees couples do the cuadro by itself, they most often perform a combination of giro and cuadro, with both dancers turning in a circle as they mark the shape of the square with their feet. A sketch of the cajita/cuadro as performed a melodia can be represented by the following graphic, where "F" stands for a step forward, "Rt" indicates a step forward to the right, "Lf" a step sideways and

21. This is a generalization; in practice, *a melodía* dancers may at different moments emphasize the upbeat or even shift to *a ritmo* style.

22. Examples of these basic steps can be seen in video example 6.2.

to the left, "B" a step backward, and "Lt" means a step backward and diagonally to the left. The second line of the graphic indicates which foot is used for any given step, left or right.

A melodia   ‖: Lf F Rt – | B Lt Lf – :‖
                    (L R L   R L R)

The *a ritmo* style is similar, though the emphasis of the steps shifts so that movement begins and ends on the fourth beat of the measure rather than the first:

A ritmo   ‖: – F Rt B | – Lt Lf Lf:‖
                  (R L R   L R L)

Although overall movement is strongly codified and controlled, the Cuban style allows for some rhythmic sway of the hips and a polycentric motion that characterizes much Afro-Caribbean dancing, particularly Cuban *son* and its local variations. In this style, the hips and legs create a cadenced movement with the upper body moving in the opposite direction or (more characteristic of danzón) staying still. Thus, the upper body, hips, legs, and feet are sources of a counterpoint of independent movements. This independence is central in the Mexican imagination of the Cuban dancing body as "free" and the epitome of cachondería and enjoyment as mentioned earlier by Mina and Benjamín (the Mexican dancers at the Habana Danzón festival), but also as an expression of the unruliness criticized by El Suavecito.

As mentioned in Chapter 2, the danzón is usually organized in rondo form (ABACAD),[23] and both Cuban and Mexican danzón steps and figures follow the musical structure. In contemporary practice, the A theme is known as a paseo or pasillo in which couples refrain from dancing. Cuban dancers most often walk around the dance floor greeting others during the paseo, arm in arm with their partner. Men keep their left arm behind their back, while women hold an abanico with their right. In the Mexican style, couples stand still in front of the orchestra during the paseo, watching the performers, though women also fan themselves. Cubans refrain from dancing for the duration of the paseo and its repetition. In Mexico, since danzoneras often do not repeat the A section, dancers have learned to start dancing right after it is played through, which may mean that they dance during its repeat if the orchestra chooses to play it. Sections B and C involve relatively restrained dancing, while the D section consists of a montuno or final vamp that allows for more choreographic freedom within the formality of the style.[24]

Cuban danzón dancing shows the complex ways in which the dancing body articulates contradictory desires and anxieties; at the same time, it provides an avenue for cachondería. On the one hand, as evidenced in Pérez Sarduy's literary account, the danzón provided Afro-Cubans with an act that would discipline their bodies in conformity

23. The refrain, being the only repeated musical section, is usually the easiest to remember.
24. Mexican dancers refer to the B section as *tradicional* (traditional) and the C section as *romántica* (romantic).

with mainstream racist notions of the "naturally" wild and "unruly" black body. The kind of gratification experienced within this context would have to be described as an instance of uncritical pleasure that reproduces the civilization-barbarism dichotomy in relation to an external gaze (because if they look at me / dancing like I am in El Manglar). However, the dancer's ability to introduce and validate a number of black bodily and performative practices into mainstream Cuban culture (syncopated motion, polycentric dance, call and response vocals, use of timelines like the cinquillo clave, famous black orchestras themselves, etc.), should be understood in terms of a symbolic challenge to hegemony.

Talking to Cuban promoters and dancers, one gets the idea that some of their greatest satisfaction derives from the revival of a "national dance" that declined markedly in popularity right after the triumph of the Cuban revolution in 1959. Hayron Portillo Álvarez, a young dancer from Matanzas, says: "The danzón has disappeared from people's houses, from the streets, from parties. . . People either do not know it or have a false impression of it and do not dance it anymore."[25] In that sense, the efforts of the networks of Amigos del Danzón clubs in Cuba, as Ángela Aldana Linares states, focus on "keeping the danzón alive, keeping it from being forgotten."[26] From this perspective, the satisfaction of dancing derives in part from a re-inscription of a forgotten practice in the body's memory—although within the dominant discourse of national belonging—and offers sites for a cachondería that both reproduce and challenge hegemony. Evidently, these two types of pleasure intertwine in the performances of the Cuban body-nation and of the black Cuban body and its racialized memory.

BAILANDO SOBRE UN LADRILLO. DANZÓN DANCING FROM VERACRUZ TO MEXICO CITY

There are two main styles of danzón dancing in Mexico, *danzón lírico* (learned empirically through experience on the dance floor) and *danzón académico* (learned in schools or academies), and numerous substyles. Traditionally, danzón lírico (Fig. 6.4) tends to privilege the continuous embrace of the couple; it is also known as *danzón cerrado* [closed danzón], although sometimes couples exit the closed position to allow turns. (● Video 6.4) In this sense, danzón lírico is more similar to Cuban styles. In Mexico, danzoneros usually associate danzón cerrado with Veracruz and the traditional danzón style of *salones* [dancehalls] of 1940s and 1950s Mexico City. Danzón académico, on the other hand, tends to privilege the opening of the embrace, allowing individuals to do turns and at moments even dance independently from the partner, a style also known as *danzón floreado*. (● Video 6.5) It is this style that most people identify as characteristically Mexican, as it differs greatly from closed Cuban dancing. However, most old and young danzoneros acknowledge the danzón floreado to be a rather recent development. As *veracruzano* Tomás Riande Uscanga explains: "In the old

25. Hayron Portillo Álvarez, personal interview, Matanzas, Cuba, December 10, 2006.
26. Ángela Aldana Linares, personal interview, Havana, Cuba, December 12, 2006.

Figure 6.4: Danzón lírico couple at Veracruz's Zócalo, 2009.

times, danzón used to be danced closed style and without a pause, without the rest [during the paseo sections]. My father used to go to the Salón Villa del Mar, and he said that back then people danced cheek to cheek. . . . I first learned to dance danzón lírico, without the rests or the cuadro."[27]

Antonio Moreno's *Santa* (1931), the first Mexican sound film, offers a brief description of what Mexican danzón dancing might have been like toward the end of the 1920s when the dance first became truly popular in Mexico City. When asked to describe the danzón, Santa, the film's main character, replies in a seductive tone: "You get very close, you know? In the first part you have to do a lot of turns, almost in the same place. And in the second one you have to move your hips."[28] This description is taken, almost verbatim, from the novel by Federico Gamboa that inspired the film.[29] Although the book describes danzón dancing from the early twentieth century, it is interesting that Moreno kept the same description,

27. Tomás Riande Uscanga, personal interview, Veracruz, Mexico, February 4, 2009.

28. In Antonio Moreno's *Santa* (1931).

29. "You press your body really close to your man, like so, see? In the first part there are lots of turns that you do almost in place, like so, see? Then, in the second part, you have to really relax your waist and let your hips go, like you're about to faint with pleasure and so you avoid your partner's advances by slipping from side to side and forward and back, like so . . ." See Federico Gamboa, *Santa. A Novel of Mexico City*, trans. and ed. John Charles Chasteen (Chapel Hill: University of North Carolina Press, 2010), 78.

which coincides with what dancers do in the film. In the absence of other ethno-graphic evidence it is difficult to determine how danzón was danced in Mexico during the late 1920s and early 1930s. Nevertheless, since it is ubiquitous in later Mexican movies, one can at least indeed confirm that, as Tomás Riande Uscanga stated, the dancing of the 1930s, 1940s, and 1950s was quite different from most contemporary practice. Emilio Fernández's *Salón México* (1949) pays particular at-tention to the dancer's footwork and shows that the step many today consider to be the essence of the danzón—the cuadro—was in fact largely absent from Mexi-can danzón repertory at that time. With minor variations, the continuous closed embrace mentioned by Riande Uscanga and described in *Santa* abound in Mexican films from the 1940s, as exemplified in scenes from *Campeón sin corona* (1946) and *Rey del barrio* (1949). A rare exception can be found in *Ustedes los ricos* (1948), where we see Pedro Infante doing *son cubano*-like turns while dancing to "Nere-idas."[30] At any rate, based on available film sources and the information gathered from dancers, it appears that the overall danzón dancing style in Mexico during the late 1920s, 1930s, and 1940s was very similar to the closed dance work of Cuban styles.

Accounts from older practitioners also call into question the genesis of other elements of Mexican danzón style taken for granted now, especially the cuadro. Mrs. Natalia Pineda Burgos, one of the forces behind the resurgence of danzón in Veracruz in the early 1980s, suggests it was around that time, with the growing pres-ence of danzón clubs and later schools and academies, that the box became a central aspect of Mexican danzón practice:

In 1982 in the Parque Zamora, when schools and groups first formed, people started teaching the cuadro. Before that there were not so many [places danzón was danced], in fact [it] was practically forgotten, but in 1982 people started with the *cuadrito* [little box], and they said "move that way or move this way." They did not get the cuadro from Mexico City but rather from Cuba. . . . Nowadays they dance using cuadro choreography, but in a disorderly fashion, too flamboyant. They took it from a book from Cuba that mentions something about a box step, and they started doing it. I never taught [the cuadro], I do not like it. People who learn how to dance the cuadro keep doing it all the time. It is useless that way, it looks ugly. If you pay attention and analyze those people's moves, you will notice they cannot do anything else. We teach based on how we dance. I would take you,

30. We should be careful when looking at films as sources of historical dance practices, since on many occasions the style was modified for practical reasons. Rafael Figueroa Hernández argues that in movies, danzoneros never stop during the refrain because it was impractical to have people standing on the dance floor doing nothing at a given moment (unpublished lecture presented at the Congreso Internacional de Danzón, Mexico City, March 27, 2008). Although we agree one cannot completely trust films as sources of his-torical dance practices, there are general aspects of the style that can be inferred from comparing how dancers are represented in films in a given time period, especially in con-junction with interviews by practitioners and literary descriptions.

and with the music I would start teaching you how to dance, and you would end up dancing the danzón well. And then you would improve it on your own . . . but not [just with] the cuadrito![31]

It is difficult to determine when and where Mexicans started to use the box as basic step, but this and other testimonies indicate that its adoption by dancing schools and groups in Veracruz and Mexico City at the end of the 1970s or early 1980s contributed to its popularization.

Manuel M. Rosales "El Gallito" was a legendary Mexican dancer and teacher who began winning danzón competitions as early as the 1930s. He states that the danzón's cuadro is the same used in other ballroom dances like the fox-trot, slow waltz, or blues.[32] However, it would be a mistake to assume that he was already using this step in the Mexican salones of the 1930s. Rosales studied ballroom dancing techniques at the Arthur Murray Dance Studio. The experience changed his vision of danzón dancing, as he realized that "in terms of dancing technique we [Mexicans] were still in our infancy (estábamos en pañales)."[33] It is safe to assume that some time after his experience in the United States—presumably years later—the box became a standard in Rosales's studio. Regardless of the presence of these dance academies, danzón lírico remained the prevalent style among Mexican danzoneros until the decline of the style as a social dance in the 1960s; it was not until then that the spaces for learning danzón moved from the salon to studios and schools like Rosales's.

The advent of danzón schools, although fundamental to the music's survival in Mexico, also disciplined bodies, codified the dance, and established or reinforced the central mythology about Mexican danzón: the importance of the box, the use of short step sequences ending in rests, and the notion that danzón should be danced sobre un ladrillo [on a single brick] as described in Carlos Fuentes's novel earlier in this chapter. The box pattern became standard in the Mexican scene as schools attempted to authenticate their practices in dialogue with international ballroom repertoire, yet still looked to Cuba as a source of authenticity. Although the idea of dancing on a single brick in Mexico goes back at least to the late 1940s, decades before the box step became standard practice (indeed even earlier in Cuba), many contemporary danzoneros believe the phrase suggests that the box step is the basis

31. Natalia Pineda Burgos, personal interview, Veracruz, Mexico, February 11, 2009. This fact seems to be corroborated by Mexican films. Although the danzón is ubiquitous in the history of Mexican movies, the earliest film in which we have found danzoneros executing the box step is Paul Leduc's Frida, naturaleza viva, from 1983. This was precisely a year after the moment Burgos claims it began to be taught at the Zamora Park. The danzoneros who appear in Leduc's movie were members of Club Inspiración, a legendary club at the core of the dance's revival in the early 1980s. Eight years later the club would also make an appearance in María Novaro's cult movie Danzón.

32. Jesús Flores y Escalante, Imágenes del danzón. Iconografía del danzón en México (Mexico City: Asociación Mexicana de Estudios Fonográficos, A.C., 1994), 92.

33. Flores y Escalante, Imágenes del danzón. Rosales does not mention exactly when he studied at the Arthur Murray Dance Studio, but the studio did not show an interest in teaching Latin dances until after World War II.

of danzón movement. However, the phrase originally referred only to the close embrace adopted by couples and the small space needed for their dancing ("you have to do a lot of turns, almost in the same place").

Danzón académico as taught in schools and groups is a type of danzón that involves frequent opening of the dancers' embrace so they can execute turns or to allow dancers brief moments of individual freedom in which they are not forced to lead or follow their partners. Depending on the skill and creativity of the dancers, these moments may feature improvisation and even virtuosic displays; however, in most instances the movements are prepared and choreographed in advance. Danzón académico style assumes a precise relationship between musical structure and dancing gestures; it thoroughly prescribes when and how dancers should start dancing in relation to the musical structure as well as when and how they should come to a rest during the pasillos or refrains. Danzón académico (Fig. 6.5) is also explicit about how the couple should behave during refrains, as mentioned earlier. In order to stay in synch with the musical structure and make sure they start and stop dancing at the appropriate moments, dancers are encouraged to count measures constantly. Counting, as explained earlier

Figure 6.5: Danzón académico dancers practicing at Mexico City's Plaza del Danzón, 2009.

by Benjamín Bautista ("in Mexico they dance, count, and suffer"), is a fundamental aspect of the Mexican danzón experience; it is the system that allows dancers to avoid committing mistakes such as starting at the wrong moment or missing the cadences at the end of the B and C sections and therefore missing the correct moment to stop dancing as the refrain returns.

Today, there are two ways of counting in Mexican danzón dancing, either by beats or steps. Most teachers teach step counting, but in both cases dancers start to move on the downbeat (as is done in the lírico style as well).[34] Dancers who adopt step counting count in groups of eleven, since eleven steps are taken over four measures. This longish sequence of prescribed steps is reminiscent of ballroom tango, which may have served as the inspiration for the reinvention of Mexican danzón choreography in the mid-twentieth century. The man begins stepping on the left foot, the woman on the right. Constant foot alternation is the norm; the basic pattern looks like this over four 4/4 measures:

$$\|: 1 - 2\ 3 \mid 4 - 5\ 6 \mid 7 - 8\ 9 \mid 10 - 11 - :\|$$

The eleventh step brings the two feet together, as at the beginning. Teachers who privilege the relationship between musical forms and dance prefer to teach counting beats. In this case, dancers count in groups of eight beats consisting of a half note each, with subdivisions to represent movement on the quarter notes in between:

$$\|: 1 - 2\ \text{and} \mid 3 - 4\ \text{and} \mid 5 - 6\ \text{and} \mid 7 - 8 - :\|$$

The dashes after 1, 4, 7, and 10 (when counting steps) or 1, 3, 5, and 7 (when counting beats) are moments when the dancer remains still. In either case the count could be conceived in several smaller groupings of three steps, beginning on the downbeat and coming to a final pause at the end of the sequence—whether on step 11 or beat 8—when dancers bring their feet together and stand in front of each other before beginning a new gesture on the 1 of the next sequence.

All basic steps taught in danzón académico—such as cuadro, *columpio* (swing), *salidas laterales* (lateral movement), and *giros* (turns)— are executed so as to fit within these groupings, which results in a rather fragmented dancing style conceived in four-measure segments. The box step, for instance, uses the basic footwork as described, but in the form of a square. The step sequence for men is represented below, where "F" stands for "step forward," "Rt" indicates a step forward to the right, "Lf" a step backward and to the left, "B" a step backward, and "T" means "bring feet together." The second line indicates which foot is used for any given step, left or right:

$$\|: F - Rt\ T \mid B - Lf\ T \mid F - Rt\ T \mid B - T - :\|$$
$$(L\quad R\ L\quad R\quad L\ R\quad L\quad R\ L\quad R\ L)$$

---

34. It is difficult to establish when Mexican danzón started to emphasize the downbeat (or if it was ever danced in syncopation as in Cuban *a ritmo* style).

The box sequence for women involves opposite movements, starting backward with the right foot:

‖: B – Lf T | F – R T | B – Lf T | F – T – :‖
(R   L R   L   R L   R   L R   L   R)

In the columpio, the basic step sequence is executed in a rocking motion, partially forward and partially back. Each grouping of three steps, performed sequentially over steps 2-3-4 and 5-6-7 of the following diagram, thus changes direction in the middle. The man's version of the sequence (starting forward rather than back) can be represented graphically as follows. It begins on the left foot, and continues in alternation:

‖: F – F T | B – B T | F – F T | B – T – :‖
(L   R L   R   L R   L   R L   R   L)

The woman's pattern is the opposite, starting backward:

‖: B – B T | F – F T | B – B T | F – T – :‖
(R   L R   L   R L   R   L R   L   R)

Dancers employ a slightly shorter ten-step foot sequence, the *remate* (conclusion or cadence), at the end of each of the major danceable musical segments of the danzón, the B, C, and D sections. The remate is virtually identical to the basic step, except that the final eleventh step (or seventh beat if counting groupings of eight beats) is eliminated. Instead, dancers bring their feet together immediately after taking step ten on the downbeat of the final measure of their four-measure sequence:

‖: 1 – 2 3 | 4 – 5 6 | 7 – 8 9 | 10 – – – :‖
or
‖: 1 – 2 and | 3 – 4 and | 5 – 6 and | 7 – – – :‖

The inclusion of this sequence explains why for Mexican danzón dancers it is important to constantly focus on the music and know exactly where they are, not only within the larger musical structure of a single danzón but also within each section of that structure: losing their place will result in missing the crucial remate cadence.

Probably one of the reasons the cuadro, columpio, and other four-measure step sequences taught in danzón schools became so pervasive among Mexican dancers is that their predictability provides dancers with a sense of security. Yet this regularity, with continual pauses and cadences, forces the flow from one sequence to the other to be constantly interrupted, as mentioned. Such fragmentation contrasts with the longer and smoother choreographic gestures one finds among danzón lírico practitioners. This is precisely what individuals like Natalia Pineda Burgos criticize about académico performers, since they believe that privileging individual step sequences conditions the dancer to always execute the same movements in a rather tedious fashion.

Central to Mexican danzón style, particularly in danzón académico, is not only what dancers do or how they move, but also what is absent, what they are not allowed to do. Such prohibitions are justified on the basis of a desire for elegance and typically exclude elements considered shameful or awkward. When contemporary Mexican dancers define the danzón they are quickly to state that it is a type of *baile fino de salón* (refined salon dance). Such a description is part of a conscious project to erase the connection between the danzón and prostitution or underclass life, perhaps African heritage as well, and make it a site for the performance of distinction. One of the fundamental rules of Mexican danzón is that the dancer's feet always glide without lifting from the floor.[35] Danzón lírico dancers frequently reject this technique, but it remains an essential convention of danzón académico, as teachers claim it is not "elegant" to lift the feet from the floor or "walk";[36] by contrast, lírico dancers (as well as many Cuban dancers) often lift their feet from the floor. The criticism that Nelly de Veracruz experienced when she started dancing ("they would laugh at me") were precisely the result of adopting some stylistic aspects of lírico style (with its lifting of feet, absence of rests, and overall free-flowing attitude) into an académico context. Those observing her did not interpret her movements as free but rather as undisciplined.

Another fundamental aspect of Mexican danzón style, particularly in danzón académico, is the absence of hip movement. In the Mexican style, the polycentric motion of Afro-Caribbean dances is transformed into a monocentric motion that characterizes most Mexican dance. Danzón teachers are very specific about this, favoring a still posture that avoids not only hip but also shoulder movement because it is perceived as inelegant, suitable for salsa or cumbia but not danzón. Needless to say, the *quebrada* (break), a breaking of the hips in which the bodies of the dancers come into full contact and common to many Latin dances,[37] is discouraged among Mexican académico practitioners. Nevertheless, regardless of the attempt to render it invisible, this move shows up in a whitewashed manner as part of a couple of steps, especially one called *la cucaracha* (the cockroach). Much like a *quebrada*, the cucaracha starts with the couple moving to one side and suddenly returning to their previous position. But here, no hip motion is evident and the male dancer does not really pull the female dancer back to the center; instead, they both change direction by shifting the weight of their bodies with their feet in a manner that resembles the killing of a cockroach—hence the name of the step. If the Cuban closed embrace brings the dancing partners very close to each other, allowing for occasional rubbing, the Mexican styles, particularly académico but also lírico, stress a separation of four fingers or more of distance between partners. These features, as well as the shift of motion from the

35. Sigfrido Alcántara enumerates the basic rules for "decent" danzón dancing—the type of *baile fino de salón* that contemporary dancers strive to emulate and judges expect in competitions. Alcántara stresses the distance maintained between dancers, their elegant clothing, and restricted hip motion. See Angel Trejo, ¡*Hey, familia, danzón dedicado a . . .!* (Mexico City: Plaza y Valdés, 1992), 47–49.

36. This practice is very similar to movement in academic tango, where dancers are encouraged to *gatear* [walk like a cat] or glide on the dance floor.

37. See John Charles Chasteen, *National Rhythms, African Roots. The Deep History of Latin American Popular Dance* (Albuquerque: University of New Mexico Press), 19–20.

upbeat (as in Cuban a ritmo style) to the downbeat and an avoidance of movements of the body, speak to how discipline and codification in the Mexican danzón render blackness invisible, part of a larger discursive strategy to make it disappear from the body-politics of the nation-state, as discussed in Chapter 3.

STAGING THE DANZÓN. DANCING FOR THE OTHER

The rise of the académico style in Mexico also meant the transformation of a purely social dance form into an exhibitionistic practice. *Danzón de exhibición* or *danzón coreográfico* is arguably today's most popular style in Mexico. (🔵 Video 6.6) Most schools and groups teach danzón through group choreographies; such routines are usually presented at the many *muestras* (collective demonstrations) organized both locally and nationally. The exhibición style allows new enthusiasts to master basic moves and practice them with a partner without the anxiety of having to lead or follow independently, skills that require much more practice. It also provides a sense of community among group members. For many dance groups, the presentations represent the highlight of their year. They prepare for months, perfecting moves, coordinating the collective routine, making field trips to search for the right fabric for their dresses, ordering custom-made matching shoes, etc. Indeed, part of the satisfaction in danzón coreográfico lies in becoming an object of collective admiration. The formal staging of dance for an external gaze is fundamental to the sense of pride and pleasure among practitioners. It is precisely in this context that the closing cadences of danzón académico, with partners standing side by side and raising their arms, make sense: they are truly meant as show-off moments that put on display the dancers' precision and the beauty of their attire.

Although most choreographies consist of chained combinations of basic danzón steps with added variations or embellishments, some groups do push the boundaries of the permissible. At a danzón muestra in the Milpa Alta suburb of Mexico City, a group from the city of Pachuca presented a choreography that had one of the male dancers standing on a brick while other couples danced around him, performing unconventional moves such as *el tornillo* (the screw), in which one of the dancers lowered his or her body until he or she sat on one heel while a partner moved around and simultaneously rotated him or her with one hand. This kind of step, as well as individual moves performed by dancers who perform freer, open footwork, is what many call *danzón de fantasía* (fantasy danzón) or *danzón acrobático* (acrobatic danzón). (🔵 Video 6.7) In such a choreography, dancers attempt to create an extraordinary presentation based on but not restricted to the fundamental steps of danzón académico. One may find elements from the cuadro or the columpio interspersed with highly embellished turns and movements borrowed from salsa, Cuban *son*, tango, or fox-trot that defy convention. Often, dancers lift their feet off the floor or even jump and carry their partners in movements that resemble the aerial turns of lindy hop or swing more than traditional danzón. Clearly, danzón de fantasía is meant for the stage, or at least an imaginary stage; it is prepared for others to observe and admire as a combination of tradition and innovation that dazzles the eye.

Ideas from the danzón de fantasia have filtered into the individual practices of creative and uninhibited dancers. Tomás Riande Uscanga is a good example of someone who adopts fantasía style when performing in the public square (zócalo). Riande Uscanga is certainly one of the most spectacular dancers active in the Veracruz scene, in striking contrast to both the many académico and occasional cerrado dancers that still attend. His style incorporates elements from tango, salsa, and even flamenco learned through his experience as a dance teacher in the Veracruz public school system:

> Now, I dance in a very embellished and ornate way. Right after finishing the cuadro I point the tip of my foot upwards. So, I embellish the danzón, something I did not do before; it started happening little by little. I have been polishing this style for many years. A lot of people do not like how I dance, they say it is not true danzón; but I don't do danzón cerrado, I do danzón de fantasía.[38]

Although, danzón académico/floreado has recently become more prominent among younger jarocho (native of Veracruz) dancers and newcomers from Mexico City, and is more visible as the older generation slowly retires from the dance floor, Veracruzanos still favor rather conservative choreography. This is understandable, given that the idea of danzón tradition and Veracruz are so intricately connected in the Mexican imagination—a fact used strategically by veracruzanos to define themselves as "authentic." In this context, Riande Uscanga's dancing style is not only noticeable but is indeed a threat to local hegemony and discourse.

Disapproving attitudes toward danzón de fantasia are not unique to the Veracruz context; they are also common around the country. Many conservative performers feel that the danzón de fantasia has opened itself to too many external influences that overpower or erase what they consider the form's "essence." Roberto Salazar Hernández, an older dancer from Mexico City, argues: "There are many teachers who do not deserve to be teachers. They have destroyed the danzón by making it too acrobatic. The authentic style is the danzón clásico (classic or lírico)."[39] Such opinions have been noted by the board of the CNIDDAC during meetings at the 2009 Festival Nacional Danzonero in Monterrey. CNIDDAC events function as a normative space that reinforces the dominance of danzón académico practice while discouraging the innovations featured in danzón de fantasía. In this context, the danzón as developed and staged by performers like Riande Uscanga displays a body that rejects the reproduction of normative movement. However, for foreigners who enjoy the more energetic salsa, tango, and flamenco moves, Riande Uscanga's style fulfills expectations as to how a "passionate" Latin body should dance. His style also shows the complex ways in which insubordination and conformity intertwine in the cachondería of Mexican danzón.

38. Tomás Riande Uscanga, personal interview.
39. Roberto Salazar Hernández, personal interview, Mexico City, February 22, 2009.

Figure 6.6: Dance students from Cuba's Instituto Superior de Arte present a danzón choreography at the 2009 Danzón Habana Festival.

While the staging of danzón in Mexico displays both the normalization of choreographed danzón and the defiance of danzón de fantasía in moves and attire that transcend everyday life, Cuban dance events privilege everyday social practice. Cuban danzón, both in competition and in exhibition, depicts danzón in commonplace settings. When Cubans participate in CubaDanzón or Danzón Habana Festivals, they get on the stage and essentially do what they do during their regular Amigos del Danzón gatherings. Nothing particularly extraordinary takes place, there are no coordinated collective routines, and although dancers may wear elegant outfits—generally men wear suits and women one-piece dresses—there are no specially designed matching costumes; their representations are simulacra of how the danzón was practiced in salones de sociedad. Couples rarely rehearse, even prior to competitions. Only when an official dance troupe from the Instituto Superior de Arte or the Ballet Nacional (Fig. 6.6) is invited to the festival does one witness a stylized show that departs from everyday norms. (🌐 Video 6.8)

RESTRICTION AND ENHANCEMENT IN THE BOX OF DESIRE

Codification and restriction provide danzón dancing with its character while enhancing silent desires, the cachondería of moving bodies. Within the conventions of Mexican danzón, individual bodies are disciplined as choreographies unfold within the specific parameters of racial and ethic erasure promoted by the nation-state. Indexes of blackness are rendered invisible or disguised and are expunged from memory. Mexican discourses of *mestizo* national belonging require the transfer of blackness into the "other," thus creating a type of loss-desire dynamic. In this process, what the "self" loses is transferred into the "other"—here, the "unruliness" and "uncivilized" body movements of black performers—which in turn generates a type of desire for that which has been lost, the "uninhibited freedom" and "authenticity" of such movements. These contradictions lie at the intersection of the racial discourse that erases blackness in Mexico and the presence of blackness in the desire and nostalgia projected onto Cuba and the Cuban body. Contradictions are also articulated by dancers as they move and reproduce or question the presence or absence of African-derived aesthetic elements. As Luisa, my classmate from the Danzoneros de la Ciudadela group, explains it, "yes, the proximity . . . I mean, yes, there's always a space [between the dancers], it is always four fingers wide . . . but the proximity is wonderful."[40] We could read this proximate sensuality as the pleasure of holding another's body close in a society that has traditionally discouraged bodily contact, the result of repressive Catholic values. In this sense, the "alegrasmo" that Luisa referred to earlier represents a type of pleasure that frees her body from repressive discourses and empowers her to enjoy sensations often denied. However, as mechanisms for the performance of memory—"acts of transfer," as Diana Taylor would put it—danzón dancing, its pleasure, and enjoyment also make evident a desire for the very practices that hegemony attempts to render invisible. The words and silences that make blackness invisible in Mexico are challenged by embodied behavior that exceeds the possibilities of these discourses.[41]

The recognition of the Cuban body as a source of authenticity that Mina Arreguín and Benjamín Bautista express when talking about Cuban dancing ("It is really a pleasure to look at them dancing," "here, they dance and enjoy it") speaks of a desire developed out of an association in Mexico and elsewhere between the black body, nature, and freedom. (◉ Video 6.9) It is as if the absence of the disciplining that Mexican dancers go through makes the (frequently blacker) Cuban body closer to nature. The essentialization that accompanies Mexican desire for the Cuban dancing body inverts the value system in the civilization-barbarism dichotomy as understood by black Cuban dancers. For them, it is precisely what they see as the refined movements of the danzón that allow them to claim being *negros de sociedad*. Interestingly, the sense of freedom or unruliness ("Cuban women move their asses very well") that Mexicans project onto Cuban dancers is not recognized in the Mexican bodies that practice danzón lírico. This suggests that such a discourse is essentially devised for differentiation, not for the creation of unity.

Danzón dancing styles show the body as a contingent site where contradictory discourses of "otherness," desires, and anxieties are negotiated through cachondería; through the dialogical relation between uncritical aesthetic pleasure and impudent enjoyment. The intimate cuadro, that "box of desire" imagined and reimagined transnationally throughout the danzón's history, is the perfect metaphoric space to witness and explore such behavior.

40. Luisa, personal interview, Mexico City, December 3, 2008.
41. See Diana Taylor, *The Archive and the Repertoire. Performing Cultural Memory in the Americas* (Durham, NC: Duke University Press, 2003), 15.

CHAPTER 7
Danzón Musings beyond the Dancehall

November 8, 2011. Fulton Recital Hall, University of Chicago. Three performers take the stage. The flute of Alejandro Escuer fills the dimly illuminated auditorium with atonal melodies. They enter into playful counterpoint with Rodrigo Sigal's carefully selected computer-generated sounds. Simultaneously, José Luis García Nava captures images of the performers and audience, manipulates them with his computer, and projects them onto a screen behind the musicians. The concert's exploration of sound and light is an interactive multi-sensorial experience that challenges conventional boundaries between music, space, and performer. Images alternate between pure abstraction and barely recognizable representations, between continuously morphing geometric shapes and pixilated forms derived from the flute player's hands and facial gestures. Audience members experience this visual display together with the sounds of Escuer's standard flute and newly invented flute-like instruments, the noise of industrial objects like electric drills or aluminum cans, the computer-generated timbres mentioned previously, and various dancelike percussion grooves. The three performers featured at the concert are members of Lumínico, a project whose artistic strategy involves the improvised fusion of pre-composed classical repertoire, computer composition, and Latin American traditional music with avant-garde performance techniques. All elements interact with one another in a seamless multimedia experience.[1] Their show comments obliquely on contemporary life through largely subtle or abstract referents. Yet toward the middle of the performance, the graphics and sounds change dramatically as recognizable images of downtown Mexico City fill the screen and a quirky, sample-based electronic danzón-chá fills the hall.[2]

The images and sound in the danzón segment derive from *Ciudad de México–Capital en movimiento* (2010), a promotional video clip about Mexico City created independently of Lumínico for the Expo 2010 Shanghai by Luis Mandoki and Mariana Rodríguez, with

1. More information about Lumínico can be found in their website, www.luminico.org/ (accessed on May 4, 2012).
2. Luis Mandoki and Mariana Rodríguez's *Ciudad de México–Capital en movimiento*, with music by Alejandro Castaños can be seen at www.youtube.com/watch?feature=player_embedded&v=3I17uqtQq-w (accessed on May 4, 2012).

music by Mexican composer Alejandro Castaños (b. 1978). Asked about the incorporation of this video and music into an otherwise abstract art music presentation, Sigal responded, "We used it during last year's tour to have something more normal in the middle [of the concert, and to include a segment] that, besides being Mexican, would give Escuer a chance to rest."[3] Lumínico's use of the video showcases Mexican identity within a larger cosmopolitan artistic project. The film's affective representation of place involves the juxtaposition of Mexico City imagery with an adaptation of the danzón, a style that producers and audiences alike now immediately associate with the city's urban life. Castaños explains:

> From the beginning we talked about having a very local element [within the Shanghai video presentation on Mexico], but something that was not a commonplace. The danzón seemed like the best choice . . . this kept us away from more standard rhythms like cumbia, salsa, or mariachi [variants]. We needed [the presentation] to include contemporary elements. Yet we did not want the accompanying music to be a danzón literally; [instead, we wanted a sound] closer to what Nortec has done with *norteña* music [by transforming the style electronically], although we retained some basic formal elements of the danzón. The script was about "a day in Mexico City." It worked well to use the slow part of the danzón for the morning segment, to speed up [the same music] during the midday segment, and to incorporate the livelier montuno for the evening images.[4]

Castaños's transformation of the danzón through electronics helped create a cosmopolitan representation of Mexico City for an international audience. And the video's cosmopolitan representation of locality also made it a perfect fit for the needs of Lumínico.

This is one of many instances in which composers and artists have used the danzón to develop a sonic identity for their works in Mexico, Cuba, and throughout the hemisphere. From classical music to jazz and vocal genres, from traditionalist to modernist projects, distancing danzones from the dance hall and reinventing them elsewhere has allowed composers to establish new audiences for them and new channels of communication for well over a century. Such experimentation extends the danzón as performance complex beyond a dialogue with stylistically related dances to include much more diverse musical traditions derived from Europe and the Americas, both elite and popular. This chapter explores some of the ways concert composers have taken inspiration in the danzón and how they have referenced it intertextually or reconfigured it within a variety of historical, cultural, and social circumstances, giving it new meaning and forms of circulation. Far from trying to flatten cultural difference in describing the wide variety of ways Latin American composers have appropriated the danzón, we show how these practices result from individuals engaging in global cultural dialogues while responding to specific local circumstances. Danzones have allowed musicians to

---

3. Rodrigo Sigal, electronic communication, April 27, 2012.
4. Alejandro Castaños, electronic communication, May 2, 2012.

resignify a wide variety of histories of colonization, emancipation, nation building, migration, and community bonding through music while reimagining their identities and place in the world in the process.

FROM NINETEENTH CENTURY BORROWINGS TO NEOCLASSICAL RECREATIONS

A diverse concert repertory for solo piano inspired by danzón-related forms such as the *contradanza*, *danza*, and *habanera* flourished during the second part of the nineteenth century. It can be divided into three categories: arrangements of popular dance tunes; original salon compositions that "artify" and/or stylize dance forms while staying largely faithful to their stylistic and formal features; and original compositions that incorporate elements of dance repertoire but that are not meant to be heard as such. The piano version of Raimundo Valenzuela's "El negro bueno" analyzed in Chapter 2 as well as the pieces published in *J. Jacinto Cuevas* fall into the first category. They are basically piano reductions of popular orchestral dance music. The salon contradanzas and danzas for piano by Cuban composers like Manuel Saumell (1817–1870) and Ignacio Cervantes (1847–1905) fall into the second category. They borrow the conventional binary form and/or basic habanera accompaniment pattern (see Ex. 2.1) of pieces danced by all social classes at the time. However, the compositions feature more harmonic variety than most dance repertoire and are technically challenging. Puerto Rican composers Manuel Gregorio Tavárez (1843–1883), Juan Morel Campos (1857–1896), and José Ignacio Quintón (1881–1925) adapted the same artful style of salon composition to the *danza puertorriqueña*. Similar pieces became popular in Mexico. Composed by Felipe Villanueva (1862–1893), Juventino Rosas (1868–1894), and Ernesto Elorduy (1854–1913), as well as early twentieth-century musicians like Alfredo Carrasco (1875–1945) and Manuel M. Ponce (1882–1948) and virtually identical in style to their Caribbean counterparts, they were nevertheless labeled *danzas mexicanas*. Competing claims to local variants of the danza and contradanza speak of the broad circulation and popularity of such music throughout the Caribbean region, and to the interconnected nature of nationalist schools of composition, however ostensibly independent.[5]

New Orleans composer Louis Moreau Gottschalk (1829–1869) and later Ponce produced the first concert music inspired by the contradanza, danza, and related forms, representative of the third category mentioned. Both composers spent many years in Cuba for different reasons; Gottschalk visited for extended periods as a touring artist between 1854 and 1860 while Ponce took up residence as a political exile of sorts from 1915 to 1917. Elements of Cuban popular music soon found their way into both composers' works. The habanera rhythm, for instance, is evident in

---

5. Peter Manuel discusses the circulation of these forms throughout the Caribbean in *Creolizing Contradance in the Caribbean* (Philadelphia: Temple University Press, 2009). For a study of the danza mexicana, see Joel Almazán Orihuela, "La danza habanera en México (1870–1920)," PhD Dissertation, Centro de Investigación y Docencia en Humanidades del Estado de Morelos (2010).

pieces like Gottschalk's *El cocoyé*, Op. 80 (1853), *Danza*, Op. 33 (1857), and *Souvenir de la Havane* (1859); and Ponce's *Malgré tout* for solo piano (1900) and "Trópico" from *Cuatro piezas* for solo guitar (1932). Both individuals also took inspiration from the danzón, particularly its cinquillo (Ex. 2.1). Gottschalk features the rhythm in the middle section of his *Danza*, and Ponce throughout his *Suites cubanas* (1914–1916), in pieces composed while living on the island like *Elegía de la ausencia* (1917) (◉ Score 7.1), and later in "Rumba" from *Cuatro piezas*. Generally, Ponce uses the cinquillo for coloristic purposes in an almost orientalist vein that resonates with larger cultural tendencies in Mexico at that time; particularly, the aesthetics of *modernista* and *posmodernista* poets.[6] However, in *Guateque* for solo piano (1916) Ponce goes beyond the mere coloristic use of Cuban elements to compose an actual danzón. Although he does not label *Guateque* as such, its formal structure (ABACA); the organization and length the of its phrases (the A part is made of a repeated eight-measure phrase while the B and C sections are more extended); the pervasive use of cinquillo in the refrain; and the more lyrical, clave-based melodies in the B and C sections make it very similar to danzones popular in Mexico in the 1910s and 1920s.[7] Although it is debatable whether Ponce's *Guateque* should be considered concert or salon music—a discussion linked to the porous border between popular and art music among Latin American composers of the period[8] and reflected in the varied dynamics informing appropriations of the danzón at different times and places—it is certainly one of the earliest examples of a stylized rondo-form danzón written by a Mexican concert music composer.

6. For an account of Ponce's relationship to modernista and posmodernista aesthetics, see Alejandro L. Madrid, *Sounds of the Modern Nation. Music, Culture, and Ideas in Post-Revolutionary Mexico* (Philadelphia: Temple University Press, 2009), 82–110.

7. Ponce's interest in the danzón is evident in an article in which he refers to it as "su majestad el danzón . . . rey de los bailes populares cubanos" ("his majesty, the danzón . . . the king of popular Cuban dances"). See Manuel M. Ponce, "Manuel M. Ponce en nuestra casa. 'Plática' sobre la música popular cubana," *Revista de Revistas* (January 21, 1917), 15.

8. Throughout the history of Latin America one witnesses constant instances of inter-penetration between traditional, popular, and "art" music: from the shared elements between late renaissance and baroque music in the *son* traditions of Cuba, Mexico, Venezuela, and elsewhere, to the popular music and dance elements in nineteenth-century salon repertory such as danza, *bambuco* (as briefly described in Chapter 3), *pasillo*, and the many local waltz and polka traditions in the region, to the continuous presence of popular music practices and elements in the work of twentieth-century nationalist, modernist, and even avant-garde art music composers (for example, Heitor Villa-lobos [1887–1959], Silvestre Revueltas [1899–1940], Alberto Ginastera [1916–1983], Leo Brouwer [b. 1939], or Gabriela Ortiz [b.1964]), to the popular music of artists who continuously move back and forth between the "classical" and popular music worlds (such as Ástor Piazzolla [1921–1992], Egberto Gismonti [b. 1947], or Eugenio Toussaint [1954–2011]). See among other publications Antonio Corona Alcalde, "The Popular Music of Veracruz and the Survival of Instrumental Practices of the Spanish Baroque," *Ars Musica Denver* 7, no. 2 (1995), 39–68; Peter Manuel, "From Scarlatti to 'Guantanamera': Dual Tonicity in Spanish and Latin American Musics," *Journal of the American Musicological Society* 55, no. 2 (2002), 311–36; Ketty Wong, *La música nacional. Identidad, mestizaje y migración en Ecuador* (Havana: Casa de las Américas, 2012), 53–110; Marc Gidal, "Contemporary 'Latin American' Composers of Art Music in the United States: Cosmopolitans Navigating Multiculturalism and Universalism," *Latin American Music Review* 31, no. 1 (2010), 40–78.

The same exoticism observed in Ponce's "Cuban" music informs the works of Julián Carrillo (1875–1965), George Gershwin (1898–1937), and others who composed musical postcards after visiting Cuba for short periods or listening to recordings. Carrillo's *Impresiones de La Habana* (1929) and Gershwin's *Cuban Overture* (1932) both took inspiration from the island's dance music including the danzón, weaving recognizable melodies from popular music of the day into their compositions. Some Cubans took a similar approach in their symphonic works; Amadeo Roldán (1900–1939), for instance, quoted a fragment of Antonio María Romeu's danzón "Africa" in the third movement of his *Tres pequeños poemas* (1926). And Darius Milhaud (1892–1974) may have initiated this trend, by (ironically) including a fragment of a melody from Romeu's danzón "Ojos triunfadores" ("Triumphant Eyes") in *Saudades do Brasil* (*Yearning for Brazil*, 1921).[9] These appropriations took place in dialogue with larger "nationalist" and "orientalist" musical trends of the time that promoted the borrowing of local sonic elements within traditional Western European musical forms and genres.[10]

Other composers adopted the danzón's cinquillo in order to create abstract concert music that did not seek to establish overt connections between sound and geography. This is the case of Ponce's Sonata for cello and piano (1922). The piece opens with a cello melody played over piano chords that repeat the cinquillo incessantly; here, as Ricardo Miranda explains, the rhythm provides "intensity to the theme . . . framed by romantic harmonies completely foreign to its original context."[11] Ponce uses this rhythmic pattern again during the middle section of "Nocturno," the second movement of his symphonic poem *Chapultepec* (1921–1934). Strings play the figure during a crescendo to create a dramatic mood against which the oboe, clarinet, horn, and violins play an expressive melody.

The decontextualization of the cinquillo is even more striking in works by experimental composers of the time. One could easily overlook the relationship of the rhythm to the danzón when it appears in futuristic works such as Edgard Varèse's percussion masterpiece *Ionisation* (1929–1931); but in fact Varèse established a close friendship with Cuban composers like Amadeo Roldán (1900–1939)—whose Afro-Cuban percussion scoring, especially from *La rebambaramba* (1928), he studied

9. Ezequiel Rodríguez Domínguez, "El maestro del café de la Diana," *Revolucion y Cultura*, no. 51 (October 1976), 25.

10. Works like Antonin Dvořák's *Slavonic Dances*, Op. 72, Bedřich Smetana's *Má vlast*, Isaac Albéniz's *Suite española*, Op. 47, and Manuel de Falla's *Noches en los jardines de España* exemplify the European nationalist trend; while pieces like Claude Debussy's *Pagodes*, Maurice Ravel's *Boléro*, and Igor Stravinsky's *Piano-Rag-Music* exemplify the orientalist appropriation of non-European musics at the end of the nineteenth century or beginning of the twentieth century. The rhetoric behind these endeavors inspired a variety of nationalist musical movements throughout Latin America based on the adoption of elements from local heritage into European forms. Appropriations of the danzón at the time should be analyzed in the context of both these trends as well as the complex class and ethnic implications of the continual dialogue between high- and lowbrow musical practices in the region.

11. Ricardo Miranda, *Ecos, alientos y sonidos: ensayos sobre música mexicana* (Xalapa and Mexico City: Universidad Veracruzana and Fondo de Cultura Económica, 2001), 229.

carefully before embarking on *Ionisation*[12]—and Cuban musicologist Alejo Carpentier (1904–1980), with whom he collaborated as early as 1927 in Paris.[13] During a moment of strong pan-American sentiment among artists and composers that led to the creation of the Pan American Association of Composers (PAAC), the incorporation of sounds and rhythms from traditional repertoire of the hemisphere was not uncommon.

Danzones strongly influenced the artistic career of Alejandro García Caturla (1906–1940), though in a manner different from that of other composers of his day. García Caturla's trajectory as an artist began with sustained involvement in popular music in which the danzón figured prominently; this affected his sensibilities in a general way. Several authors have noted that his heavy reliance on percussion and brass in orchestral compositions derives from a familiarity with dance music; Alejo Carpentier insists more specifically that the essence of his compositional style derives from performance of the danzón.[14] Similarly, US popular music and dance represented a strong influence. His cousin José Gastón Caturla had a jazz band in Remedios that he often performed with. In 1921 he joined another jazz band there, and after moving to Havana to pursue a law degree in 1922 he formed his own university jazz band (Caribe).[15]

García Caturla demonstrated surprisingly eclectic musical tastes from an early age, listening to opera and other classical pieces but also expressing strong interest in Kongo drumming, *bembés*, and similar African-derived repertoire. Such openness to Afro-Cuban culture represented a radical departure from the norms of middle-class Cuban society. The increasingly central place of African-derived music in his compositions as of the late 1920s, at least as a loose source of inspiration, converted him into a figurehead of the controversial *afrocubanismo* movement during the last dozen years of his life. Along with Amadeo Roldán, García Caturla became a member of the PAAC in the late 1920s and established professional contact with Henry Cowell, Nicolas Slonimsky, Manuel M. Ponce, Carlos Chávez, and others.[16] The influence of African-American traditional and popular repertoire on his modernist works after 1927 has a parallel in the works of many contemporary European composers.[17]

12. Graciela Paraskevaídis, "Edgard Varèse and his Relationships with Latin American Musicians and Intellectuals of His Time," *Contemporary Music Review* 23, no. 2 (2004), 9.

13. Christina Taylor-Gibson, "The Music of Manuel M. Ponce, Julián Carrillo, and Carlos Chávez in New York, 1925–1932," PhD Dissertation, University of Maryland at College Park (2008), 207.

14. Alejo Carpentier, *La música en Cuba* (Mexico City: Fondo de Cultura Económica, 1946), 320. See also Radamés Giro, ed., "Caturla," *Diccionario enciclopédico de la música en Cuba*, Vol. 1 (Havana: Letras Cubanas, 2007), 222.

15. Giro, *Diccionario enciclopédico de la música en Cuba*, Vol. 1, 221.

16. Early correspondence between Caturla and many of these figures has been collected in María Antonieta Henríquez, ed., *Alejandro García Caturla. Correspondencia* (Havana: Editorial Arte y Literatura, 1978). See especially pp. 37–50.

17. Robin Moore, *Nationalizing Blackness. Afrocubanismo and Artistic Revolution in Havana, 1920–1940* (Pittsburgh: University of Pittsburgh Press), 193–94.

García Caturla played more danzones between the mid-1910s and early 1920s than any other music style. Some of his first compositions as a teenager were danzones such as "El piano de Colín" ("Colín's Piano") and "El cangrejito" ("The Little Crab").[18] He practiced piano in a local dancehall in Remedios, El Gran Maceo (The Great Maceo), and thus heard the latest danzón hits from the capital.[19] After moving to Havana, García Caturla supported himself in part through extended solo piano performances in silent movie theaters where danzones featured prominently. He performed in the Campoamor Theater, the Oriente, the Norma, the Cerro Garden, and other venues, often alternating with danzón orchestras.[20]

None of García Caturla's danzón compositions have been reprinted in published editions, but a number of them exist in manuscript collections of Havana's museums and libraries. "Tócala con limón" ("Play It with Lime") from 1923 is representative of the piano repertoire Caturla played to accompany silent film. (❷ Score 7.2) The piece is striking in various ways. Its introduction consists of a through-composed sixteen-measure phrase, not the repeated eight measures common to danzones. While highly sectional, the music includes few rhythmic cadences, suggesting that the composer never intended it to be danced. Perhaps most noteworthy, the initial sections of the piece (A, B, C, and D) include no cinquillo or other overt reference to the characteristic rhythms that help define the danzón. Its melodies and bass line differ little from US ragtime and related piano styles of the day, and this music appears to have influenced García Caturla's compositional style. Only the final "otra" (section E) and coda of "Tócala con limón" incorporate a variant of cinquillo clave, primarily in the right-hand melody, while the bass line provides a relatively straight accompaniment, a quarter note followed by two eighth notes. A fragment of the "otra" with claved melodies is reproduced in Example 7.1.

Caturla composed the danzón "Tu alma y la mía" ("Your Soul and Mine") in 1923 as well but arranged it for small orchestra or jazz band, probably his own group. Thus, it demonstrates the ways that the composer's interest in Cuban and North American music influenced one another. The score includes alto and tenor saxophone parts in addition to piano and the more standard orquesta típica lineup of flute, clarinet, cornet, trombone, violin, and bass. Structurally, "Tu alma" is typical of danzones; it consists of a repeated eight-measure A section, a sixteen-measure B section, three additional extended "otras" (the first two upward of twenty measures each, the last one possibly a vamp over which to improvise), and a coda. The A and B themes, especially, adopt a surprisingly dense texture in a minor key, with flashy sixteenth-note runs written for flute, clarinet, and alto sax that continue virtually without a break. Cornet, trombone, and tenor sax play lower supporting melodies in contrary motion. The cinquillo and other Afro-Caribbean rhythmic cells appear only infrequently in

18. Juan Antonio Pola, "Aproximación a lo popular en Caturla en el 80 aniversario de su natalicio," in *Caturla el músico, el hombre*, ed. Radamés Giro (Havana: Ediciones Museo de la Música, 2007), 141.

19. María Antonieta Henríquez, *Alejandro García Caturla* (Havana: Ediciones Unión, 1999), 31.

20. Henríquez, *Alejandro García Caturla*, 35.

Example 7.1: Alejandro García Caturla, "Tócala con limón" (1923). Final "otra" segment with right-hand cinquillo melodies.

these sections, as in much of "Tócala con limón," and thus the overall sound of the music is distinct from most popular danzones of the 1920s (see Ex. 7.2). By contrast, sections C and D adopt slower, lyrical melodies in major keys featuring the cornet and flute, with background arpeggiation provided by the clarinet and supporting lines in cinquillo clave played on the piano, tenor sax, and trombone. The principal melodies of these segments sound much like US popular music of the day as well, despite the low cinquillo phrases (❸ Score 7.3).

While García Caturla primarily made only oblique timbral and instrumental reference to the danzón in later compositions, other composers dialogued with the music more overtly, especially in Mexico. An early invocation of the danzón's formal structure and other characteristic elements is found in "Con aire de danzón," the second movement from *Sonatina* for piano (1934) by Mexican composer José Pomar (1880–1961). Along with Silvestre Revueltas (1899–1940), Pomar founded Mexico's Liga de Escritores y Artistas Revolucionarios (LEAR), a communist organization committed to fighting fascism and supporting worker's rights through revolutionary art. His political views contributed directly to his development as an artist, especially toward the end of his life when he took inspiration from urban working-class culture even while adopting a decidedly non-functional harmonic language.[21] Clearly, aesthetic and social concerns inform Pomar's use of the danzón, one of the most popular dances in 1930s Mexico. However, in "Con aire de danzón" Pomar did not compose a popular-sounding piece as previous composers had. Instead, he used the danzón's structure and rhythmic foundation to evoke the dance abstractly while combining it with contrapuntal melodies and mild dissonance.

"Con aire de danzón" is organized in rondo form (ABACA). The A section consists of two-part counterpoint that features the Cuban cinquillo. The cinquillo never repeats consistently in alternation with straight quarter or eighth notes as in popular danzones; instead, Pomar writes through-composed melodies that incorporate it freely. The tonality of section A fluctuates between D minor and D major, sometimes presenting Phrygian gestures. The B section is highly chromatic and dissonant, although it also revolves around D as a tonal center. At the beginning and the

21. Eduardo Contreras Soto, "Un reencuentro con Pomar," *Heterofonía* 33, no. 124 (2001), 136.

Example 7.2: Alejandro García Caturla, "Tu alma y la mía" (1923). Excerpt from the B theme, demonstrating fast contrapuntal lines and infrequent use of the cinquillo.

end of B, Pomar employs a variant of the cinquillo rhythm repeatedly in the left hand (Ex. 7.3).

This rhythm and the harmonic motion provide the music with its drive and tonal character. The overall contrapuntal texture, the compositional techniques employed (the alternation of melodic material between the right and left hands in the second part of the A section and the use of a Picardy third in the final cadence, typical features

Example 7.3: José Pomar, Sonatina for piano (1934). Movement III, "Con aire de danzón," mm. 18–21.

of baroque music)[22] and the organization of the piece (its adoption of an established form) adhere to the aesthetics of neoclassicism, typical of Western art music composers during the first half of the twentieth century.[23]

One of the most popular concert pieces inspired by the danzón during the first half of the twentieth century is *Danzón cubano* for two pianos (1942) by Aaron Copland (1900–1990). Composed on commission from Claire Reis and the League of Composers, the work reflects some of the music Copland heard during multiple trips to Cuba in 1941. They were part of a larger tour of the Americas sponsored by the US State Department and the Office for the Coordination of Commercial and Cultural Relations between the American Republics (OCCCRBAR). In the context of the Roosevelt administration's Good Neighbor policy, its attempt to rehabilitate the US's bruised reputation in Latin America, and pursuit of hemispheric unity during a period of crisis (World War II), the composer's mission was to establish networks for cultural exchange. Copland's history of contact with Latin American composers through the PAAC helped paved the way for this effort.

Although Copland acknowledges that the danzones he heard in Cuba in 1941 inspired *Danzón cubano*, he did not intend his work to sound like a typical danzón but rather, as Elizabeth Crist suggests, "an abstraction."[24] In the preface to the score of the piece's orchestral version, Copland provides clarification as to how he understood this music:

> The danzon is a well-known dance form in Cuba and other Latin-American countries. It is not a fast dance, however, and should not be confused with the rhumba, conga or samba. It fulfills a function rather similar to the waltz in our own dance [repertoire], providing contrast for the more animated numbers. Usually constructed in two parts which are thematically independent, the special attraction of the danzon is a certain naïve sophistication, alternating in mood between passages of rhythmic precision and a kind of sentimental sweetness.[25]

22. Tierce de Picardie or Picardy third is a compositional device by which a major chord unexpectedly replaces the standard minor chord in a final minor cadence. It is a common compositional device in Baroque music.

23. A detailed formal analysis of Pomar's Sonatina can be found in Emilio Casco Centeno, "Análisis de la Sonatina para piano de José Pomar," *Heterofonía* 35, no. 134–35 (2006), 109–28.

24. Elizabeth B. Crist, *Music of the Common Man. Aaron Copland during the Depression and War* (New York: Oxford University Press, 2005), 67.

25. Aaron Copland, *Danzón cubano*. Full Score (New York: Boosey & Hawkes, 1949), preface.

Example 7.4: Aaron Copland, *Danzón cubano* (1942), mm.1–4. First iteration of the recurring A theme.

Copland's description of the danzón is less than precise but provides clues as to the kinds of music he may have heard in Cuba. The fact that he characterizes the danzón as a tranquil genre alternating between rhythmic precision and sentimental sweetness suggests that *danzones de nuevo ritmo* with their lyrical B (or B and C) themes and more rhythmic montuno may have been the source of his inspiration. Oddly, Copland does not mention rondo form but rather describes danzones as composed of two independent sections. It may be that the danzones he heard were in the truncated style of Arcaño's nuevo ritmo (ABAC), which he interpreted as consisting of a multi-part A section (ABA) and a second section made up of the montuno (C), the latter clearly different due to its more animated character. The fact that Copland visited Cuba in the early 1940s when Arcaño's was the dominant danzón sound supports this view. However, the recurrent use of the opening motive of *Danzón cubano* throughout the piece (Ex. 7.4) could be interpreted as a stylized reference to the recurring A theme in rondo-form danzones, suggesting he may have also heard more traditional pieces.

Danzón cubano consists of two parts, coinciding with Copland's characterization. His adaptation is eminently percussive—indeed, its melodies consist mostly of short, syncopated phrases reminiscent of earlier primitivist compositions—with specific recurring patterns found in both segments. The patterns in section A (especially his use of the amphibrach, notated in Ex. 2.1, and its variations) appear occasionally in danzones but cannot be considered their most characteristic feature. It is in section B that Copland introduces the more typical cinquillo and the tresillo (also notated in Ex. 2.1); the recurrent use of these patterns in melodies as well as in prominent bass lines sets section B apart from A and gives the former a vaguely montuno-like character at times, as for instance in the solo piano sequence that opens the section. However, Copland frequently combines characteristic Afro-Caribbean rhythms with irregular metric changes and accents that, as Neil Butterworth suggests, are "symptomatic of Copland's style."[26] Copland's *Danzón cubano* thus evokes

26. Neil Butterworth, *The Music of Aaron Copland* (London: Toccata Press, 1985), 96. One might say the same of contemporaries of Copland like Mexican composer Carlos Chávez. Both appear to have been influenced by Stravinsky in this sense.

the danzón in a highly abstract fashion. His impressions were based on limited exposure to the dance at a specific moment in time, informed by the inter-Americanist atmosphere of US politics in the 1940s and the neoclassical aesthetic that dominated Western art music composition.

A number of mid-twentieth century Cuban composers referenced the danzón in a similar fashion, especially those working under the aegis of the Grupo de Renovación Musical (Group for Musical Renovation). Students of José Ardévol (1911–1981) based at the Conservatorio Municipal de Música de La Habana established the group in 1942, seeking to build on the efforts of early *afrocubanista* composers such as García Caturla and Roldán, and to continue challenging the Cuban art music scene. Members included Virginia Fleitas (1916–1966), Harold Gramatges (1918–2008), Hilario González (1920–1996), Argeliers León (1918–1991), and Julián Orbón (1925–1991), among others. They combined a cosmopolitan vocabulary acquired from their mentor with formal and stylistic elements adopted from traditional Cuban music in at least some compositions.[27] Argeliers León's interest in Cuban folklore and popular culture eventually led him to become an influential ethnomusicologist; however, early in his career, these concerns crystallized in the creation of a number of art music compositions based on local models. His Danzón No. 1 (1945) and Danzón No. 2 (1945), both for solo piano, are good examples of the group's attempt to work at the intersection of local identity and cosmopolitan aesthetics.

León's Danzón No. 1 strictly follows the danzón's rondo form (ABACAD) as well as rhythms based on danzón clave. Sections A, B, and C consist of repeated eight-measure phrases, while D is a longer segment divided into smaller repeated units of ten, four, and ten bars each. Danzón No. 2 also features an ABACAD form, but the organization of measures within each section is irregular. The A section is divided into two segments of ten and eleven bars, respectively; the B section into two segments of seven and five measures; the C section into segments of nine and eighteen bars, and the D section into three parts of eight, four, and seventeen bars. The 2/4 time signature typical of danzones remains unchanged throughout the piece.

Both of León's danzones feature the contrapuntal writing characteristic of much neoclassical music but also make use of cadences and phrases found in popular danzones. The pieces' melodies are mainly diatonic, giving the music a sense of tonal centricity despite a predominance of whole-step or greater intervals and the presence of pandiatonic chord clusters, mildly dissonant counterpoint, and non-functional harmonies. The tonal center of Danzón No. 1 is C, emphasized melodically at the cadence of section A and throughout the D section. However, León presents a clear C major harmony only at the beginning of section D; at other cadential moments, such as the end of the A section and the end of the piece, he makes the harmony more ambiguous through the use of non-harmonic pitches, either the sixth degree of the

---

27. Edgardo Martín, *Panorama histórico de la música cubana* (Havana: Universidad de La Habana, 1971), 132. The pieces discussed here bear a certain resemblance to that of afrocubanista composers of the 1920s and 1930s. However, for many years most members of the Grupo de Renovación Musical (GRM) avoided the incorporation of local musical references, considering such an approach aesthetically limiting. Danzón-inspired works of the 1940s thus represent something of an anomaly within the GRM's overall orientation.

Section	A		B		A´					
Subsection	a	a´	b	b´	a´´		a´´´			
Motive	a1 a2 a1 a3				a1 a4 a5 a4 a6					
Tonal center	G		C G		G C G C					G
mm	1 5 9 13		17 20		25 29 31 33 35 36					

Figure 7.1: Harold Gramatges, "Danzón" from *Suite cubana para niños* (1956). Formal structure.

scale to create ambiguity or the second and seventh degrees to create more pandiatonic clusters (as in the final chord of the piece). The absence of a functional chord progression and the presence of harmonies with added seconds or sevenths create an austere, modernist atmosphere that contrasts with the piece's popular references.[28]

Other members of the Grupo de Renovación Musical wrote danzones in a related style. Harold Gramatges's "Danzón," the first movement of his *Suite cubana para niños* for piano (1956), is one such example. Using similar harmonic and contrapuntal practices, Gramatges manages to develop a less dissonant texture and create more tonal variety within a piece only thirty-six bars long. "Danzón" does not follow rondo form; instead, it features an ABA' structure with a sixteen-bar A section, an eight-bar B section, and a 12-bar A' section. Gramatges provides a sense of variety and contrast through clever organization of material in the A section. He divides A into two eight-measure parts, a and a'; and he further divides each of them into four-measure motives, a1 and a2 for the a part, and a1 and a3 for the a' part. The final section, A', presents the a1 motive followed by a two-bar a4 motive, a two- bar a5 motive, and a repetition of the a4 motive that leads to the closing a6 motive (see Fig. 7.1). This structure allows Gramatges to provide a type of four-bar ritornello (a1) that appears twice within the A section and once at the beginning of the A' section, while offering a4 as an element of variety that lingers in the listener's ear. His approach provides the short piece with all the formal contrast of a longer rondo-form danzón.

The tonal, harmonic, and structural practices in concert danzones by Argeliers León, Harold Gramatges, José Pomar, and others are similar. Yet there are differences between the interpretation of Latin American composers and those of Copland or Gershwin. The former hold more closely to the structures and rhythms associated with the danzón and related musics, reflecting a more profound understanding of traditional idioms and a more overtly nationalist orientation as well, a desire to foreground the local in combination with selected modernist techniques. North American composers, by contrast, reference the danzón and Cuban music only obliquely by means of isolated rhythmic or melodic elements, thus creating works that are decidedly more North American than Latin American, regardless of their labeling.[29]

28. In the recorded versions of both pieces included in the CD *Argeliers León. Grupo de Renovación Musical*, the pieces are accompanied by percussion, adding rhythmic drive and an accessible referent to the listener. See *Argeliers León. Grupo de Renovación Musical* CD/DVD/CDROM 151. Havana: Instituto Cubano de la Música, 2009. The accompanying CD ROM includes a copy of the score.

29. While beyond the scope of this study, it should be noted that Cuban composers wrote many danzones to accompany modern dance choreographies in the post-1959 period. Cuba's ballet troupes first experimented along these lines in 1978 with the premiere

Figure 7.2: Arturo Márquez in his studio in Tepoztlán, Morelos, Mexico, 2011.

DANZÓN AS CONCERT MUSIC IN THE LATE TWENTIETH- AND EARLY TWENTY-FIRST CENTURY

Mexican composer Arturo Márquez (b. 1950, Fig. 7.2) is probably the contemporary academic composer most closely associated with the danzón. The phenomenal international success of his Danzón No. 2 (1994) for symphony orchestra has made it a symbol of contemporary Mexican art music and converted Márquez into one of the most popular Latin American composers of the new millennium. However, the simple melodies and catchy rhythms that contributed to the success of Danzón No. 2 conceal the work of a sophisticated artist; Márquez is a master of thematic derivation, structure, and

of Gustavo Herrera's *Dan-son* in the García Lorca Theater. Rodrigo Prats provided original music to accompany the work (see *Cuba en el ballet* 9, no. 3 [September–December 1978], 47). Herrera's choreography derived entirely from ballet traditions rather than the danzón itself, though the music conformed to traditional norms. *Dan-son* became part of the Ballet Nacional's standard repertoire for years; members performed it both within Cuba and while touring abroad. A short clip of the original choreography can be viewed on youtube as part of the documentary *Cuatro joyas: Josefina*, on the career of Josefina Méndez. See www.youtube.com/watch?v=iF1tRuSHa0k&feature=plcp; the clip begins at 3:27. Santos Ulloa mentions later performances of the work within Cuba in "El danzón: cien años de vida" (*Bohemia* 71, no. 7 [February 16, 1979], 12). Discussion of performances abroad appears in *Cuba en el ballet* 3, no. 1 (January–March 1984), 10, 21, and a feature on the professional career of Gustavo Herrera in the same issue, 16–30.

orchestration whose musical language synthesizes years of avant-garde experimentalism and a long-standing love for Mexican popular music and US jazz.

Márquez's early compositional training took place at Mexico's National Conservatory of Music under Héctor Quintanar, Joaquín Gutiérrez Heras, and Federico Ibarra, and with Jacques Castérèd in Paris.[30] Throughout the 1980s, with a dissonant music style that made use of aleatoric principles as well as collaborations with visual artists, Márquez helped guide a young generation of composers that kept avant-garde experimentalism alive in Mexico. In the late 1980s he continued studies of composition at the California Institute of the Arts with Morton Subotnick and Mel Powell. There, Márquez was exposed to neo-tonal compositional languages fusing world music and jazz with modernist techniques, an experience that dramatically changed his aesthetic vision. Upon his return to Mexico he began to incorporate elements of popular Mexican music into concert works, especially the bolero and the Mexican *son*.[31] In 1992, Márquez composed Danzón No. 1 for pre-recorded tape and optional saxophone (the first piece in a long series inspired by the danzón) in collaboration with a dance company called Mandinga. Danzón No. 1 is a minimalist composition based on a melodic/harmonic phrase that repeats with minor variations in a continuously modulating harmonic sequence, each iteration featuring different instrumental combinations. Although the style is somewhat different from the rest of his danzones, Danzón No. 1 already presents many of the elements that characterize Márquez's later works: clear tonal centers, modulation to distant keys, and a principle of melodic construction based on the use of repeated rhythmic cells or motives. These generate a familiar melody that seems nevertheless to constantly unfold. After composing Danzón No. 1, Márquez started frequenting Salón Colonia; fascinated with the sound of Danzonera Acerina and Carlos Campos's orchestra, he slowly became a regular of Mexico City's danzón scene.[32]

Márquez composed Danzón No. 2 during his tenure as a fellow with Mexico's Fondo Nacional para la Cultura y las Artes, infusing the work with his newly discovered musical passion. The political backdrop that informed the work was the 1994 Zapatista uprising in Chiapas, Mexico, a protest against neoliberal policies and systematic policies of discrimination against indigenous peoples. As in the case of many artists and intellectuals at the time, Márquez supported the Zapatistas' demands for equality, and in particular their anti-colonialist stance. His use of the danzón thus operates as a dual declaration of principles. On the one hand it articulates the renovation of Márquez's own musical language, his move away from the avant-garde and the creation of a more direct link with audiences through the incorporation of elements from popular music. On the other, it stands as a symbol of hope, political renovation, and a marker of local heritage.

Márquez's Danzón No. 2 and Danzón No. 3 (1994), the latter for flute, guitar, and orchestra, are his most popular works. They represent the crystallization of a musical

30. Eduardo Soto Millán, ed., *Diccionario de compositores mexicanos de música de concierto*, Vol. 2 (Mexico City: CONACULTA, 1998), 77.

31. Arturo Márquez, personal interview, Tepoztlán, Morelos, Mexico, September 21, 2011.

32. Márquez, personal interview.

Example 7.5: Arturo Márquez, Danzón No. 4 (1996). Excerpt of theme A with cinquillo variants as played by the oboe, mm. 22–25.

Section	Introduction		Exposition		Development				Recapitulation		
Theme	A		B C		A A+B	C	B		B	C	
Instruments	Fg Ob Fl+Cl		Vln Crn		Winds	Trb Pno			Winds Sax (Tutti)		
Main Keys	Am Fm Cm C#m		Em Bm		Fm Cm	Fm Cm			Bm	Gm	A
mm		45	67 82		105 131	244 263			274	302	320

Figure 7.3: Márquez, Danzón No. 4. Formal Chart.

language based on the thorough appropriation of danzón elements. Both pieces incorporate classical structure: sonata-allegro form with concertante elements. Cinquillo-based melodies unfold throughout the piece in constantly modulating harmony, together with the lush orchestration that characterizes Márquez's tonal music. The same language has filtered into most of Márquez's music thereafter, including compositions that do not openly evoke the danzón. Like all of his danzón-inspired works, Danzón No. 2 and Danzón No. 3 avoid rondo form since, as he explains, that form is meant for dancing and his danzones are intended to be listened to.[33]

Danzón No. 4 (1996) for chamber orchestra combines attributes found in Danzones No. 2 and No. 3 with a more sophisticated manipulation of the cinquillo in melodies of continuously shifting meter. The piece is constructed from three themes that are closely related by means of shared rhythmic cells. The first melody, from the introduction, shifts between 5/8 and 4/8 meters. However, by interlocking segments of the cinquillo that emphasize the pattern's syncopation in the 5/8 section and using cinquillo variants in the 4/8 section, Márquez manages to invoke the danzón's claved rhythm even within this irregularity. Example 7.5 shows the oboe melody as it appears in measures 22–25, though groupings in the 5/8 bars have been reorganized to put in evidence the cinquillo-based syncopation.

Of all Márquez's compositions, Danzón No. 4 bears the closest formal resemblance to a popular danzón based on the continuous juxtaposition of its three contrasting themes (A, B, and C), yet they appear within a loose sonata-allegro form (Fig. 7.3). Played by the bassoon, continued by the oboe, and finally taken up in a dialogue between the flute and clarinet, the A theme calmly unfolds throughout the first sixty-eight measures (Ex. 7.5). This is the only presentation of the A theme as such, although elaborations of its melodic and rhythmic material appear in the development section. Particularly interesting is Márquez's harmonic language which emphasizes minor mode-dominated sequences (with a few internal exceptions); the piece's only structural point tonicized in a major mode is the final cadence on measure 320 (See Fig. 7.3).

Márquez's tonal exploration of the danzón provided many other Mexican composers with justification for openly embracing tonality and popular music, and specifically the

33. Márquez, personal interview.

danzón, as sources of inspiration in what critics have labeled the "postmodern turn" in Mexican concert repertoire.[34] Chicago-based composer and musical director of Sones de México Víctor Pichardo (b. 1961), Oaxaca-based Carlos Salmón (b. 1967), Veracruz guitarist and composer Ernesto García de León (b. 1952), and Mexico City-based Luis Trejo León (b. 1968), all grew up listening to the danzón and have composed short works inspired by it.[35] However, the case of Brian Banks (b. 1964), a US composer living in Mexico, demonstrates how Márquez's appropriation of the danzón has influenced art music composers from abroad. Banks composed a danzón as part of his Serenata No. 1 "Legados imaginarios" ("Imaginary Legacies," 2008) for chamber ensemble. Each of the movements of the work pays homage to a composer whose music has influenced him. The first two movements, "Goes Dancing at" and "Elegantly Melancholic," honor George Harrison, Lou Harrison, and klezmer musician Henry Sapoznik; the last movement, "Tiempo de danzón," is dedicated to Márquez. However, more than derived from Márquez, Banks's composition is modeled after the music of Acerina y su Danzonera[36] and adheres to the rondo form and phrase structure of traditional danzones. For all of these composers, the sound of the danzón references urban Mexican culture, not Cuban culture. As such it appeals to them as insiders involved in danzón-related scenes or as outsiders attracted to the musical style for purely aesthetic reasons.

Borrowing from the danzón or taking it as a cultural referent has not been unique with contemporary tonal composers but is also common among avant-garde musicians of different nationalities, as was the case in past decades. New York–based Cuban composer Tania León (b. 1943) and Mexican composer Juan Trigos (b. 1965) have both adopted elements of the danzón in aesthetically challenging works. León has written many pieces in dialogue with Cuban styles: of African influence she heard as a child in the Cayo Hueso neighborhood of Havana (e.g., *Batá*, 1985; *Kabiosile*, 1988; *Carabalí*, 1991). Recent compositions for piano have incorporated elements of the danza and contradanza, as for instance *Homenatge* (2012), in memory of Catalan composer Xavier Montsalvatge (1912–2002) and *Going, Gone* (2012), inspired by Stephen Sondheim's "We Had a Good Thing Going." Her most substantial piece influenced by danzones is the 2006 composition *Toque* (Rhythm) for chamber orchestra, a dense and technically difficult yet playful composition inspired by the 1938 danzón classic "Almendra." As León notes in the score, "Almendra" is so well known that most Cubans recognize its principal themes after only a few notes.[37] She plays with such familiarity by using a recurring motive played by the piano in the original version of "Almendra" at the beginning of the montuno (Ex. 7.6). Her citation of this material appears first in measures 22–31 of the score

34. Aurelio Tello, "La creación musical en México durante el siglo xx," in *La música en México. Panorama del siglo xx*, ed. Aurelio Tello (Mexico City: Consejo Nacional para la Cultura y las Artes and Fondo de Cultura Económica, 2010), 542–50.

35. Their works include Trejo León's *Chiaparimba II* (1999) for Mexican marimba and electronics, and *Danzón "Hea"* (2001) for chamber ensemble; Pichardo's *Danzonete* (2002) for violin and piano; García de León's "Como un danzón" from *Fantasía tropical*, Op. 66 (2007) for chamber ensemble; and Salmón's *Los danzoneros* (2009) for violin and piano.

36. Brian Banks, personal interview, Cholula, Puebla, Mexico, July 18, 2009.

37. Tania León, *Toque* (New York: Peer Music, 2006), 1.

Example 7.6: Abelardo Valdés, "Almendra." Piano motive from the montuno.

Example 7.7: Tania León, *Toque* (2006). Piano excerpt, mm. 26–31, based on the montuno motive from "Almendra."

(see Ex. 7.7). Shortly thereafter, the acoustic bass makes references to a montuno-style bassline in a similar fashion (e.g., mm. 33–35, 38–41). Both motives then disappear for a time, but reappear in variation.

León's use of "Almendra" motives are far from straightforward, as she fragments them, shifts their rhythmic orientation, transposes them, and plays them against newly composed, non-tonal material unrelated in any way to the danzón (e.g., Ex. 7.7). The latter includes passages played on the marimba, djembe, log drum, castanets, and other instruments. Yet one recognizes the quotations, both because of their relatively straightforward presentation at the outset and because of their incorporation of characteristic intervals and rhythms. *Toque* loosely references the danzón's rondo form as well, given the use of "Almendra" motives as a recurrent theme that alludes to a repeating A section;[38] and through the instrumentation of the chamber ensemble (B-flat clarinet, alto sax, piano, violin, acoustic bass, two percussionists) that roughly approximates the format of an orquesta típica. Yet the complexity of the superimposed rhythmic/melodic elements, the use of polytonality, the incorporation of frequently shifting meters (4/8, 5/8, 2/8, etc.), and of slaps, flutters, trills, slides, and other extended performance techniques, mark the composition as decidedly experimental.

Juan Trigos initiated composition studies with Jesús Villaseñor at Mexico City's Instituto Cardenal Miranda and continued with Franco Donatoni at the Civica Scuola di Musica in Milan in the 1980s. Although his early works followed Donatoni's modernist compositional procedures, he soon developed a personal language that combined the technical rigor of the post-serial European tradition with veiled references to localized popular music. In the fourth movement of his opera *DeCachetitoRaspado* (*CheekTo-StubbledCheek*, 1999), Trigos uses danzón-related rhythms (cinquillo and cha cha chá

38. Tania León, telephone interview, May 9, 2012.

permutations and cinquillo-based percussion improvisation) as well as formal references to the multi-section danzón form and montuno in conjunction with a highly modernist yet engaging musical language. Trigos's use of the danzón has helped him develop a musical aesthetic that he dubs "abstract folklore." It is aimed at "project[ing] the rhythmic vitality of popular dance without resorting to literal quotations and avoiding their dilution . . . with 'cultured' and modernist elements."[39] Thus, the danzón in *DeCachetitoRaspado* exemplifies his attempt to develop a personal, stylistically unified, and cosmopolitan musical language while retaining oblique referents to Mexican popular culture.

Márquez, Banks, León, and Trigos approach the danzón from very different national, ethnic, racial, and class perspectives, which necessarily inform their use of the music. For Márquez, recurring use of the danzón allowed him to assume a political stance at a highly volatile moment in Mexican history; for Banks, it gave him an opportunity to pay homage to both the classical and popular music traditions of his adopted country; for León, it was a means of re-identifying with her black/Cuban heritage while living abroad; and for Trigos, it was an almost kitsch way to celebrate Mexican urban working-class culture from the lens of his upper-class upbringing. However, regardless of such differences, all references to the danzón discussed suggest a common desire to develop an artistic language that engages meaningfully with popular music. For each composer this tendency marks a shift from the musical aesthetics they trained in and adopted early in their careers. In some cases, borrowing elements from the danzón or obliquely referencing it in concert music provides an opportunity to refashion their own artistic identity; in other cases it adds a sense of depth and a marker of local heritage to their cosmopolitan experimentation.

CROSSOVERS, FUSIONS, AND LATIN JAZZ

Composers have arranged traditional danzones for symphony orchestra for a wide variety of reasons. Among them, one tendency has been to appeal to consumers of popular music by fusing the danzones with a variety of styles outside the classical tradition such as popular vocal music and jazz. The danzón's easily recognizable stylistic features and largely instrumental character lend themselves to such experimentation. Recent Boston Pops–style arrangements of danzones by Cuban musicians Gonzalo Romeu and Daniel Guzmán Loyzaga have been particularly successful within the context of Mexico's contemporary danzón renaissance. Their work with the Filarmónica de la Ciudad de México and the Orquesta de Cámara de la Universidad Autónoma de Nuevo León, respectively, has influenced other local orchestras.[40] Jazz musicians have also

39. Ricardo Zohn-Muldoon, liner notes for *DeCachetitoRaspado*. Quindecim Recordings QP089. Mexico City: Quindecim, 2002.

40. See Gonzalo Romeu, *Danzones de Cuba y México, Vol. 1* (CP07. Mexico City: Caibarién, 2007). Guzmán Loyzaga's orchestral arrangements have not been released commercially but his arrangements for Danzonera SierraMadre appear in *Siéntate* (without catalogue number. Monterrey, Mexico: Consejo Mexicano para la Divulgación del Danzón, 2012).

used danzones as a means of crossing over into the realm of light classical composition. New York–based Cuban jazz saxophonist Paquito D'Rivera (b. 1948) has composed a number of works inspired by the danzón for the concert stage including *Danzón* for clarinet, cello, and piano (1998), *Gran danzón* for flute and orchestra (2002), and *Invitación al danzón* for clarinet, cello, and piano (2008). Subsequently transcribed for a variety of instrumental ensembles and championed by world-class musicians/groups like Marina Piccinini, Leonard Slatkin, Yo-Yo Ma, and the Turtle Island String Quartet, D'Rivera's works have been warmly received by diverse audiences.

Although classical renditions of popular danzones in this vein have appeared only recently, fusions of danzón and jazz have a long history among Cuban artists. Indeed, early danzón performance itself involved considerable improvisation, as discussed in Chapter 4, making clear distinctions between the two repertoires difficult. North American popular culture influenced Cuba strongly following the US military occupation, and in the 1920s many of the same individuals playing or writing danzones, such as Alejandro García Caturla or Moisés Simons, also performed in jazz bands. In the 1940s and 1950s, Cuban musicians continued to develop individual styles that reconciled elements of local music with jazz idioms, much in the same way as their counterparts in New York (Mario Bauzá, Noro Morales, etc.) did. Of those in Cuba, Frank Emilio Flynn (1921–2001) stands out as an influence on subsequent performers. An admirer of Saumell, Cervantes, and Lecuona, Flynn began his professional musical life in a danzón orchestra and performed contradanzas, danzas, and danzones throughout his career, recording many of them.[41] In the 1940s he formed Loquibambia, a group that helped pioneer the jazz-influenced bolero movement known as *filin*. He was a founding member of the Club Cubano de Jazz in the 1950s that invited US musicians to play in Havana, and also in that decade formed the Quinteto Instrumental de Música Moderna together with percussionist Tata Güines and others. The repertoire of the latter ensemble, one of the first devoted exclusively to Latin jazz in Cuba (as opposed to others that played primarily US repertoire or Cuban dance repertoire with stylistic influences from big-band jazz), served as a model for later projects spearheaded by Emiliano Salvador, the Orquesta Cubana de Música Moderna, Irakere, and others.[42]

Jesús "Chucho" Valdés (b. 1941) has long demonstrated an interest in fusing danzones and related repertoire with jazz.[43] In the early 1970s he arranged the Saumell contradanza "Los ojos de Pepa" ("Pepa's Eyes") for performance with Irakere.[44] The piece's

41. Michael P. Belfiore, biographical post in www.musicianguide.com/biographies/1608003264/Frank-Emilio-Flynn.html (accessed on June 6, 2012).

42. For additional background information on the Orquesta Cubana de Música Moderna or the early history of Irakere, see Robin Moore, *Music and Revolution* (Berkeley: University of California Press, 2006), 117–19.

43. Chucho Valdés's interest in danzones may have been inspired in part by his father, pianist Bebo Valdés (1918–2013), who also experimented with the fusion of jazz elements and local Cuban musical forms. One recent example of Bebo Valdés's danzón-style renditions of boleros can be found on the Grammy-winning CD *Bebo y Cigala* (RCA Victor, 2004), in pieces such as "Inolvidable" and "Se me olvidó que te olvidé."

44. *Irakere Vol. 1. Selección de éxitos 1973–78.* Areito cassette C-4003. Havana: EGREM, 1980.

tempo in the Irakere version is rapid (roughly 240 bpm) and follows rounded binary form. Valdés's Fender Rhodes piano plays alone, then accompanied by cinquillo clave on the güiro; the repeat of A is followed by a brief funk section with distorted electric guitar fills. Flute and saxophone feature on a reprise of the piece; later the piece segues to a funk- and jazz-infused jam with accompanying guitar and piano improvisations. Irakere's experiments with the contradanza appeared at roughly the same time as compositions in a similar vein by Emiliano Salvador (1951–1992), and inspired later efforts by José María Vitier (b. 1954) and others.[45]

Valdés has also composed jazz-inflected danzones. "Valle de Picadura" represents an example from the late 1960s dedicated to the state-driven agricultural efforts of the early revolutionary period. The overall form of the piece is ABCAD; it contrasts segments of jazz ballad (A) with two other themes in a jazz idiom accompanied by danzón clave (B and C), then returns to A before segueing to a slow son-style montuno and instrumental solos. Valdés's more recent danzón compositions include his adaptation of Richard Rodgers/Lorenz Hart's "My Funny Valentine" (2000) and his own "Danzón" (2010), both performed with his quintet, the Afro-Cuban Messengers.[46] "My Funny Valentine" alludes to the danzón in its incorporation of an introductory ballad segment set to danzón clave and continued use of the same rhythm throughout the presentation of the song itself (ABA), apparently inspired by the structure of the danzón cantado (see Chapter 2). It forgoes rondo form and instead follows the ABA structure as a vehicle for solos, supported by danzón rhythms. The more recent "Danzón" is less conventional; it juxtaposes compositional segments in a standard jazz style with others reminiscent of traditional danzón. The introduction is reminiscent of a jazz ballad with alto sax on the main melody. A danzón segment follows featuring only piano and güiro, then a segue to a new and longer jazz ballad segment in binary form. Valdés sets the B theme of the ballad to danzón clave, follows it with a new theme also accompanied by danzón clave, a return to the first half of the principal jazz theme played strictly as a jazz ballad, and finally a segue to a cha cha chá–style montuno with solos. Valdés thus seeks little reconciliation between the danzón and jazz conventions in this composition, but more often extends and varies the sound of the jazz standard with danzón interludes.

45. Contradanza compositions by Salvador and Vitier are available commercially on *Danzones All Star*. Desarrollos Artísticos CD LEGCD-11517. Mexico City: Discos Continental, 2005. Both composers' works sound much like the Claude Bolling *Suite for Flute and Jazz Piano Trio*, fusing elements of jazz and classical music and featuring flute as the principal melodic instrument. However, Vitier's contradanzas from the early 1990s tend to be shorter and pre-composed while Salvador's (from 1972) emphasize extended jazz improvisations. José María Vitier and his older brother Sergio (b. 1948) have also composed danzones, primarily for film scores and as repertoire for the ensemble Grupo ORU. His works tend to combine elements of traditional Cuban music with classical repertoire. Especially noteworthy are José María's danzones for José Luis García Agraz's *Salón México* (1996), the remake of Emilio "Indio" Fernández's classic film *Salón México* (1949).
46. "My Funny Valentine" appears on *Live at the Village Vanguard* (Blue Note CD 7243 5 20730 2 3. Los Angeles: EMI Music, 2000); "Danzón" appears on *Chucho's Steps* (Four Quarters Records CD 1823. New York: Four Quarters Records and Entertainment, 2010), which won the 2011 Grammy for best Latin jazz album.

The 1980s gave rise to new jazz-influenced compositions by Emiliano Salvador and Gonzalo Rubalcaba, both of whom remained faithful to the traditional structure of the danzón even as they expanded the parameters of the music in other ways. Salvador studied composition with Leo Brouwer and others, participated in the Grupo de Experimentación Sonora (GES)[47] together with various *nueva trova* artists, and served as Pablo Milanés's arranger and musical director for many years. Influenced by McCoy Tyner, Thelonious Monk, and Cecil Taylor, he attempted to find a vocabulary that reconciled jazz piano style with traditional Cuban dance music, especially that of Peruchín Justiz and Dámaso Pérez Prado.[48] In pieces such as "Para luego es tarde" ("The Sooner the Better")[49] one hears music in a danzón-cha style (influenced by Arcaño's nuevo ritmo, ABAC) in which conventional harmonies have been expanded substantially, often with abrupt modulations or contrasting harmonic sequences within a single segment; in which the second half of the introductory A theme becomes a vehicle for free piano improvisation in a North American "swung" style; and in which mambo flute/horn lines within the montuno adopt rhythms and intervals more reminiscent of bebop or the jazz fusion of Chick Corea than traditional Cuban music.

Jazz artist Gonzalo Rubalcaba (b. 1963) has composed danzones even more consistently than Salvador or Valdés, owing in large part to his extended family replete with *danzoneros* and thus heavy exposure to the genre from an early age.[50] He is part of an increasing number of Cuban jazz artists who now reside abroad, either in other parts of the Caribbean or in the United States, and who therefore interact more directly with the international jazz mainstream. After collaborating with renowned Cuban groups including the Orquesta Cubana de Música Moderna, the Orquesta Aragón, and Los Van Van, Rubalcaba formed his own Latin jazz ensemble, Grupo Proyecto, in 1983.[51] He soon performed with them in major international jazz festivals and recorded CDs, resulting in the acquisition of many prizes including two Grammy awards. Rubalcaba left Cuba for the Dominican Republic in 1992 and moved to the United States in 1996, continuing a productive performance career. His most substantive project involving the danzón, *Mi gran pasión* (My Great Passion, 1988), was conceived while still in Cuba. He intended the recording to revive/renovate the

47. A compositional collective under the artistic direction of Leo Brouwer that composed music for television and film. See Jaime Sarusky, *Grupo de Experimentación Sonora del ICAIC. Mito y realidad* (Havana: Editorial Letras Cubanas, 2005).

48. Sarah Towne, "Emiliano Salvador's 'Puerto Padre': One Man's Jazz." Master's thesis, City University of New York (2009), 45; Radamés Giro, "Emiliano Salvador," *Diccionario enciclopédico de la música cubana*, Vol. 4, 119–120.

49. This song is available on the *Danzones All Star* release mentioned earlier. It first appeared on Salvador's LP release *Puerto Padre* in 1988 and subsequently on CD (Yemayá Records YY9428, 2003).

50. Gonzalo Rubalcaba's father Guillermo (b. 1927) has been an influential artist for many years and continues to lead a charanga, as mentioned in Chapter 5; his uncle José Antonio Rubalcaba directs Pinar del Río's Orquesta Metropolitana, also known for danzón performance. Gonzalo's grandfather Jacobo Rubalcaba (1895–1960) led an orquesta típica as of the 1910s and composed many famous danzones as well.

51. Giro, *Diccionario*, Vol. 4, 90–91.

form in a manner similar to Astor Piazzolla's *nuevo tango* initiative of the mid-twentieth century or Paco de Lucía's experiments with flamenco.[52]

Rubalcaba's stylistic approach to jazz-danzón fusion draws heavily from one of his composition teachers at the Conservatorio Amadeo Roldán in Havana, Pedro Hernández, and in fact the piece "Recordando a Tschaikowsky" ("Remembering Tchaikovsky") attributed to Rubalcaba is only a slightly modified version of Hernández's "Carnegie Hall" recorded decades earlier by Antonio Arcaño's ensemble.[53] Rubalcaba plays danzones on *Mi gran pasión* with a small jazz combo—piano, bass, drum set, horns—rather than a charanga and creates arrangements that feature jazz-inflected instrumental lines (typically on flugelhorn, trumpet, and sax) supporting flute and piano melodies. His work is less harmonically daring than Salvador's and draws directly from popular *son*/mambo dance traditions in the final montunos, though the jazz influence on his piano style is unmistakable. His pieces tend to be heavily citational, appropriating both classical European melodies and US popular song, in a fashion similar to the danzones-chá played by Arcaño y sus Maravillas. "Recordando a Tschaikowsky" is noteworthy not only for including a theme from the second movement of Tchaikovsky's fifth symphony in section C, but for shifting to triple meter in section B, something heard occasionally in early twentieth-century danza and danzón repertoire.[54] Both this piece and the CD's title track, "Mi gran pasión," follow the same overall structure ABACAD, where A and B are newly composed, C presents a musical citation (in the latter case the Jerome Kern/Otto Harbach hit "Smoke Gets in Your Eyes" from 1933), and D a montuno. Given the prominence of the Kern melody in this piece, one wonders whether the "great passion" referenced in the song's title is the danzón, US pop music and jazz, or both. Similar to Chucho Valdés's works discussed earlier, Rubalcaba shifts the rhythmic accompaniment to a shuffle beat in section C but in all other sections maintains danzón clave. Such rhythmic shifts take place during the C themes of "Príncipe niño" ("Child King") and "Concierto en Warsovia" ("Concert in Warsaw") as well, the latter incorporating a melody from Richard Addinsell's *Warsaw Concerto*.

Though not technically part of the Latin jazz tradition, many New York-based charanga bands—La Orquesta Broadway, La Orquesta Duboney, La Orquesta Novel, Joe Quijano's orchestra, La Sociedad 76 Orquesta, and others—included at least a few danzones in their active repertoire beginning in the 1960s and many fused them with salsa, jazz, or other elements. Eddie Palmieri has a long history of interest in danzones as well. Pieces his charanga has recorded include "La gioconda" (1962), an adaptation of a piece originally recorded by Belisario López in the 1940s that itself appropriated melodies from Amilcare Ponchielli's popular opera *La Gioconda* (1876);

52. Anonymous liner notes to *Mi gran pasión* (Messidor CD 15999-2, 1988).
53. Hernández's "Carnegie Hall" appears on the CD *Grandes orquestas cubanas: Arcaño y sus Maravillas*. Areito CD 0034. Havana: EGREM, 1992.
54. Two pieces recorded by Odilio Urfé in the 1950s and re-released on the Smithsonian Folkways Records CD *The Cuban Danzón: Its Ancestors and Descendants* (FE 4066, 1982) incorporate the same shift to triple meter halfway through: "La revoltosa" from 1:13" to the end and "El ñáñigo," also from 1:13" to the end.

"Una rosa española" ("A Spanish Rose," 1973) that fuses an adaptation of the Beatles' "You Never Give Me Your Money," sung in Spanish by Lalo Rodríguez, with improvisations over a cha cha chá–based montuno; and "Ritmo alegre" ("Happy Rhythm," 1981) featuring Cheo Feliciano on lead vocals, an adaptation of an Antonio Arcaño recording from the 1940s. "Ritmo alegre" is especially eclectic, juxtaposing Bobby Collazo's bolero "Tenía que ser así" ("It Had to Be Like That") in a harmonically lush big-band style similar to Carlos Campos's Mexican danzones-chá with a salsafied adaptation of Gonzalo Asencio's *rumba guaguancó* "Consuélate como yo" ("Console Yourself Like Me"). Pieces such as these make evident the extent to which experimentation across stylistic boundaries has characterized danzón performance from the outset, even among popular band leaders.

Notable danzón-jazz experiments of the 1990s include the title track of Arturo Sandoval's *Danzón* (*Dance On*) CD.[55] Sandoval defected from Cuba in 1990 and hit the ground running with numerous tours and recording projects such as a tribute album to Clifford Brown, and collaborations with US jazz artists. *Danzón* was his first CD produced in the United States to feature largely Cuban rather than North American material, apparently in an effort to capitalize on his unique background as an immigrant and to appeal to enthusiasts of Latin jazz. The release includes a wide variety of jazz-influenced Cuban music and a danzón featuring Puerto Rican flautist Dave Valentín and Panamanian pianist Danilo Pérez. Sandoval's "Danzón" is conceived as a fusion of charanga and big-band jazz ensembles. He arranges the traditional eight-measure repeated A theme first for a small ensemble of flute, piano, bass, and timbales. But on the repeat, an extended horn section (trumpets, trombones, saxes) plays the same material. Structurally, "Danzón" is innovative in that it extends the music's traditional rondo form with additional segments. At the conclusion of theme A, Sandoval inserts an eight-measure interlude for big band consisting of a series of rhythmically accented melodies over modal harmonies and sustained pedal tones (0:31–0:47) before segueing to the B section. A always includes danzón clave and the B section does initially. The latter segment actually consists of four distinct themes: an initial lyrical melody on trumpet, a six-measure big-band segment similar to the extension between A and B, a more driving repeated riff on horns over a cha cha chá beat, and a second, longer big-band jazz interlude (0:48–1:43). This is followed by a repeat of A and finally an extended montuno with open solos, also featuring big-band-style mambo breaks as well as solos emphasizing quartal harmonies, multiphonics, sequences of chromatic melodic fragments, and other innovative techniques.

New York–based Elio Villafranca has experimented with fusions of the danzón in a similar jazz combo format, combining that ensemble with a classical string quartet in a manner somewhat reminiscent of Antonio Arcaño's radio orchestra with extended string section from the 1940s. Villafranca's scoring for strings is lush and replete with jazz-influenced sonorities (flat nine chords, minor ninth chords, etc.). He orchestrates "Danzón Chao" (2008), dedicated to Israel "Cachao" López, in a highly varied fashion so as to highlight the flute and piano alone, the string quartet,

55. GRP Records CD GRD-9761, New York, 1994.

Example 7.8: Elio Villafranca, "Danzón Chao" (2008). Four-measure ostinato bassline reminiscent of Israel "Cachao" López's danzones de nuevo ritmo.

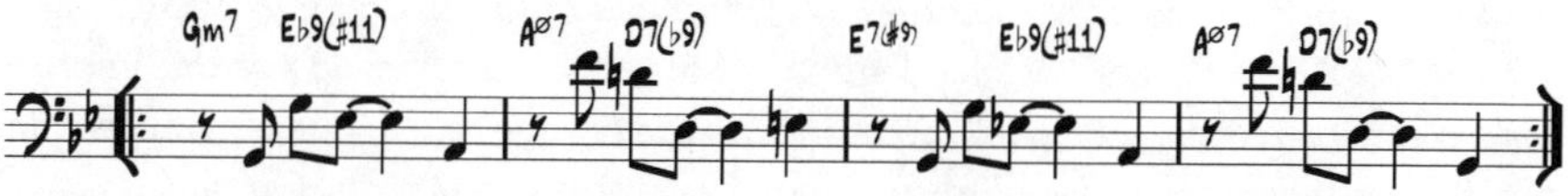

and the jazz combo in alternation. In later segments the drum set plays danzón clave on the ride cymbal rather than on the toms to add variety. Villafranca's writing is generally sparse and allows the bassline to be heard prominently; in the montuno it serves as the foundation for extended solos on flute and piano. The centrality of the four-measure melodic bass line (Ex. 7.8) and the use of an extended montuno vamp with prominent string *guajeos* (repeated melodic riffs) reference Cachao's influence on the mid-twentieth century danzón.[56] (● Video 7.1)

Villfranca also created a film score for the independent film *Mirror Dance* (2005), by Frances McElroy and María Teresa Rodríguez, based on the danzón and its antecedent forms. The documentary considers the lives of identical twin ballerinas, Margarita and Ramona de Saá, who performed together in the Ballet Nacional and then separated from one another for decades following the Cuban revolution. The principal theme song of the film score, "Calle Paula," is scored for string quartet, two clarinets, piano, bass, and drum set. It seamlessly combines the cinquillo, danzón clave, and the rounded binary form of the danza with extended jazz improvisations.[57]

Saxophonist, composer, and percussionist Yosvany Terry is another New York–based jazz artist who, like Rubalcaba, was influenced by the danzón from an early age; his father, Eladio "Don Pancho" Terry (b. 1940) founded the famous charanga Maravillas de Florida and now plays in José Loyola's Charanga de Oro (see Chapter 5). Eladio Terry incorporated Afro-Cuban traditional instruments and rhythms into charanga repertoire for years, a practice that eventually led his son to experiment along the same lines.[58]

In May of 1995, Cuban trumpeter Jesús Alemañy and British producer Joe Boyd invited Yosvany Terry to collaborate on a new Cubanismo[59] project celebrating musical interconnections between Cuba and New Orleans. He agreed, and the artists traveled to

56. A live performance of "Danzón Chao" can also be viewed at www.youtube.com/watch?v=a2H7suNWP8g (accessed on June 14, 2012).

57. More information on the film is available at www.pbs.org/independentlens/mirrordance/film.html. Live performances of "Calle Paula" with accompanying modern dancers can be viewed at www.youtube.com/watch?v=flHrs53kRms (accessed June 22, 2012).

58. Eladio Terry plays violin but also the *chéquere*, the latter a practice maintained by his sons Yosvany and Junior who freely combine Afro-Cuban religious music and even traditional dances into their jazz fusion presentations. See, for instance, the "Ye-de-gbe" recording project discussed at www.yosvanyterry.com.

59. Cubanismo was initially a Cuban jazz collective that had the good fortune to begin recording in 1995, just before the onset of the Buena Vista Social Club phenomenon. Capitalizing on the popularity of the Wenders film, they released several CDs and toured widely for years. Since 2000, the group has performed more *timba*-influenced dance music than Latin jazz, apparently in an attempt to become marketable once again.

that city, working with local musicians for a month and eventually releasing the CD *Mardi Gras Mambo*[60] with multiple arrangements and an original composition by Terry, the danzón-inspired "It Do Me Good." The CD includes music in a variety of styles highlighting US-Cuban musical fusions. Time spent in New Orleans made a strong impression on Terry and other Cuban collaborators who had never realized the extent of history, cuisine, and artistic forms New Orleans shared with other parts of the Caribbean.

Highly eclectic, "It Do Me Good" begins with a short segment of traditional devotional praise singing to the Yoruba deity Elegguá over *chéqueres* and conga drums, inspired by Eladio Terry's fusion compositions; it is intended to highlight the Afro-Latin connections between Cuba and New Orleans.[61] The work continues with the danzón's traditional A segment arranged for flugelhorn on the lead melody, then segues into a cha cha chá beat for the verse with an introductory scat solo by African American vocalist Topsy Chapman. Chapman and co-collaborator John Boutté[62] later sing a duet in English over the accompaniment, then fall silent to let the flugelhorn play a subdued instrumental interlude over danzón clave. The second half of the piece consists of solos over a slightly faster *son*-like groove, interspersed with mambo horn fills, vocal choruses in English ("Good. . . it do me good"), and a coda consisting of a variant of the danzón A theme. Reminiscent of the Latin-soul fusions associated with the boogaloo era as described by Juan Flores,[63] the Terry composition demonstrates a striking degree of hybridity. Two years later the composer arranged a danzón-influenced composition by Jesús Alemañy himself called "Danzón Daulema" on the Cubanismo CD *Malembe*.[64] This piece is noteworthy for its adaptation of the melody to Jimmy Van Heusen's "Darn That Dream" as a danzón-style interlude, an extended conga percussion solo, and musical quotations from the Beatles' "Eleanor Rigby." Examples such as these deviate almost completely from traditional danzón form and instead freely juxtapose discrete segments or rhythmic elements of the danzón with others of Caribbean or North American derivation. More recent compositions by Terry for the progressive jazz group Columna B such as "Danzón Eve" adopt non-traditional harmonies and unusual rhythmic shifts, yet fuse danzón elements with US funk and Latin pop melodies ("Corazón enamorado" and "Me voy pa'l pueblo" in the case of "Danzón Eve") in roughly the same fashion.[65]

60. Hannibal CD HNCD 1441, Rycodisc Ltd., 2000.

61. Yosvany Terry, telephone interview June 1, 2012. The Elegguá segment is given its own title and track number on the CD, but Terry intended it to be part of the following piece.

62. For more information on these artists, see www.johnboutte.com (accessed on June 14, 2012) and www.topsychapman.com (accessed on June 14, 2012).

63. Juan Flores, "'Cha-Cha with a Backbeat': Songs and Stories of Latin Boogaloo," in *Situating Salsa. Global Markets and Local Meaning in Latin Popular Music*, ed. Lise Waxer (New York: Routledge, 2002), 75–100.

64. Hannibal Records/Rykodisc, 1997.

65. Columna B was a jazz project that began while Terry still lived in Havana; his collaborators included Roberto Carcassés (piano), Descemer Bueno (bass), and Dafnis Prieto (drum set), all of whom now live in the United States. "Danzón Eve" was recorded on the CD *Enclave* (Mas CD009. Barcelona: Mas i Mas Records, 2010).

Many other jazz fusion artists could be mentioned who continue to take inspiration from the danzón in original compositions. This tendency is pronounced not only among those based in the United States, but also in Cuba where references to local heritage serve as an important form of marketing for those desirous of drawing international attention. Timbales player Amadito Valdés (b. 1946) is one such individual. He has been attracted to jazz since childhood, introduced to big-band repertoire through his father (Amadito Valdés Sr., 1907–1996) who played saxophone in the Tropicana nightclub alongside Bebo Valdés and accompanied US jazz vocalists such as Sarah Vaughan. Amadito Jr. formed jazz bands of his own beginning in the mid-1960s, but (ironically) first gained broad international recognition through his performances of ultra-traditional Cuban dance music in the film *Buena Vista Social Club*. In 2002 he released the first CD of his own, the Grammy-nominated *Bajando Gervasio* (Walking Down Gervasio Street)[66] that incorporates jazz-style improvisations and orchestrational techniques into traditional Cuban repertoire, including numerous danzones.

Flautist Orlando Valle "Maraca" (b. 1966) collaborated with Valdés on *Bajando Gervasio* and has released multiple CDs that feature at least one danzón each. A classically trained artist, Maraca joined Irakere for a time before launching a solo career. His releases are amazingly eclectic, usually including Afro-Cuban religious repertoire and timba-inspired dance tunes alongside relatively "straight" renditions of traditional danzones, boleros (frequently incorporating danzón clave), or original danzón compositions. Maraca's 1995 release *Fórmula 1* contains the Abelardo Valdés classic "Almendra" in a relatively traditional setting, for instance, as well as a bolero-danzón entitled "Danzón para Celine." The latter is essentially an instrumental version of pieces discussed in the vocal danzón section later in the chapter (i.e., that use danzón rhythms to accompany popular song), though its montuno includes free blues-inflected improvisation. *Tremenda rumba* from 2002 features "Danzón barroco," a composition whose early sections foreground baroque-style melodies and whose montuno incorporates elements from the baroque period (pedal tones, melodic sequences, mordents, trills and other ornamentation) into free flute improvisation.

Inspired by the work of Valdés, Rubalcaba, Terry, and Maraca, a younger generation of Cuban jazz musicians trained at Havana's Escuela Nacional de Arte (ENA) and Instituto Superior de Arte (ISA) continues the tradition of borrowing from the danzón. Especially noteworthy is the work of pianist Dayramir González (b. 1983), whose first CD, *Dayramir & Habana EnTRANCe* (2007),[67] includes two danzón-chá-inspired tracks, "Complaciendo peticiones" ("Granting Requests") and "Kimb's Blue Eyes." Both combine formal elements of standard jazz practice—use of a head theme followed by a jam session leading to a repeat of the theme at the end of the track—with elements of the danzón: the first part of the theme is accompanied by cinquillo, the second part by cha cha chá rhythms that provide a foundation for improvisation. A piano solo presents the main theme first, before the ensemble joins in. González chose the danzón as the basis of this piece because it is "among the musics that most

66. Pimienta Records 245-360-551-2, 2002.
67. Cinquillo Colibrí CD097. Havana: Instituto Cubano de la Música.

identifies Cubans throughout the world."[68] This is especially salient since he now lives in Boston and plays for international rather than local audiences. Clearly, the crafting of identity, both as a representation of self and nation, remains one of the powerful motivations behind many musicians' interest in the style.

Some new danzón compositions have resulted from the rise of the festivals discussed in Chapter 5. CubaDanzón activities in Matanzas inspired Miguel Faílde's great-great-grandson, flautist Ethiel Fernández Failde (b. 1991), to revive the Orquesta Típica Miguel Faílde, for instance. In 2008 the orchestra consisted entirely of performers aged fifteen to nineteen who first played publicly in the 2009 festival.[69] Most members currently pursue advanced music degrees at the Conservatorio de Música in Matanzas, at the ENA or ISA on the outskirts of Havana, or perform in the Matanzas Symphony Orchestra. They strive to make their music appealing to younger audiences—for instance, by increasing the tempo of their repertoire, adding additional percussion or other instruments to the standard orquesta típica format, interspersing danzones with styles such as the cha cha chá or mambo in live performances, or by fusing the danzón itself with more contemporary forms.[70]

Fernández Failde performs newly composed danzones whenever possible, relying primarily on a network of friends and colleagues to provide such repertoire. Matanzas's Ildefonso Acosta wrote an original work for the group called "Danzón para Ethiel" (2010), conceived as a danzón escenográfico or elaborated stage danzón. Among other elements, it includes multiple choral refrains (alternating with solo passages featuring various instruments) that all the group's instrumentalists are expected to sing, and a section at the end involving simultaneous solos for trumpet, trombone, and flute. Havana-based Alejandro Falcón (an ISA graduate, like Dayramir González) also composed a work for the Faílde ensemble entitled "Monserrate" (2010). It includes quotations of Mozart (his "Rondo alla turca") in early sections, then transitions to an up-tempo, salsa-like montuno with a piano solo.[71] The piece premiered at the 2011 CubaDanzón festival to considerable controversy. Many applauded it and danced with abandon, but the president of the Asociación Nacional del Danzón at the time, Caridad Rodríguez Cervantes, took exception with the tempo of the montuno and criticized the group. Her comments and subsequent public debates at the festival underscore ongoing disagreement within Cuba about how best to perpetuate/renovate the danzón tradition.

Fernández Failde and his collaborators struggled from the outset to gain formal recognition for their orchestra and thus institutional support and a full-time salary for all participants. Matanzas's state empresa (musical management agency) has been reluctant to incorporate them despite the fact that the province does not have a

68. Dayramir González, personal interview, Havana, Cuba, December 16, 2009.

69. Ethiel Fernández Failde, personal interview, Matanzas, Cuba, December 1, 2011.

70. Additional background information on the group can be accessed at www.atenas .cult.cu/content/el-danz%C3%B3n-ra%C3%ADz-melodica-de-ayer-para-bailadores-de-ma%C3%B1ana (accessed on June 14, 2012); and http://ethielfailde.wordpress.com/monografias (accessed on June 14, 2012).

71. A video clip of the Orquesta Miguel Faílde playing "Monserrate" is available at www.youtube.com/watch?v=WsseysCgjyc (accessed on June 14, 2012).

single orchestra devoted exclusively to danzón performance. As a result, the new Orquesta Típica Miguel Faílde often performs free of charge; this was the case even in the high-profile CubaDanzón festival 2011 in which all other groups received substantial compensation. The Orquesta's many expenses related to rehearsal space, transportation, the copying of music, the borrowing or renting of instruments for performance as necessary, and so on thus fall entirely on individual members. Fernández Faílde notes the difficulty of convincing trained performers to commit to his project under such circumstances even if they support its mission. He continues to battle bureaucratic restraints in the hopes of receiving a consistent salary, making a CD, and touring nationally and/or internationally with his group, to date with limited success.[72]

Other noteworthy danzón fusion projects include those of Roberto Juan Rodríguez who combines Latin jazz, klezmer influences, and Cuban rhythms, especially those derived from the danzón. Tracks like "El danzón de Moisés" ("Moses's Danzón"), "Danzonete hebreo" ("Hebrew Danzonete"), "Paseo del Prado" ("Prado Boulevard"), "Danzonete Emanuel," and "El sabor del Shabat" ("Shabbat Flavor") feature prominent cinquillo patterns, Phrygian or Freigish scales, and guajeo-driven improvisatory jams that at times sound like danzón, Latin jazz, or klezmer music.[73] Rodríguez's compositions reflect his own background as a Cuban raised in Miami and immersed in the culture of that city's two largest diasporic communities, Cuban and Jewish (the latter from both Eastern Europe and Cuba). His interest in klezmer repertoire results from this experience, but also from John Zorn's Radical Jewish Culture recordings for the Tzadik label (the same label released Rodríguez's CDs).[74] Rodríguez's unique fusions underscore the centrality of constructs of identity behind many contemporary reinventions of the danzón.

DANZÓN THROUGH THE LENS OF *NUEVA TROVA* AND SOCIALLY COMMITTED SONG

As mentioned in Chapter 2, the danzón has long been in dialogue with vocal music. Many pieces from the nineteenth and early twentieth centuries incorporated lyrics, either final repeated choruses or in some cases entire verses sung over earlier sections of the piece. In the late 1920s and beyond, *danzonete* and *danzón cantado* performers fused vocal works with the danzón constantly though the repertoire was still intended for dancing. Beginning in the 1970s, artists associated with Cuba's

72. As of the summer of 2012 the group had been contracted consistently to perform only once a month with pay. However, Fernández Faílde notes that the current head of cultural affairs in Matanzas, Carlos Torrent, has expressed verbal interest in offering them additional support (electronic communication, June 25, 2012).

73. These tracks have been released on *El danzón de Moisés*. Tzadik Records TZ7158, 2005; *Baila! Gitano baila!* Tzadik Records TZ7189, 2005; *Timba talmud*. Tzadik Records TZ8140, 2009.

74. For more information about Roberto Juan Rodríguez's fusion projects visit www .robertojuanrodriguez.com/home.html (accessed on June 17, 2012).

nueva trova (political song) movement began to write danzón-inspired music, but in contexts intended for listening only. Much like classical composers and Latin jazz artists, proponents of socially committed song searched actively for new sounds and innovative ways of fusing past practices with music of their own creation, inspired at least in part by the ideological imperatives of the 1959 revolution. Some ensembles such as Grupo Manguaré have performed actual danzones within larger concert programs intended for listening rather than dancing; Alejandro García "Virulo" (b. 1955) also used traditional danzones as a sonic backdrop for comic sketches discussing early twentieth-century Cuban history.[75] However, the most typical way nueva trova performers have dialogued with the danzón is through the incorporation of its percussion patterns into other styles of music. Most of the resulting works are not danzones in a strict sense, yet allusions to the style remain overt.

Several first-generation *trovador* artists/groups aside from Virulo and Manguaré experimented with the danzón, even as they simultaneously incorporated influences from other traditions. Pablo Milanés (b. 1943) recorded Eduardo Ramos's "Siempre te vas por las tardes" ("You Always Leave in the Afternoon") on his 1979 album *Aniversario*, for instance;[76] the song employs danzón rhythms in the accompaniment played only on conga drums. Danzón clave is heard from the outset over an instrumental, jazz-influenced introduction (A) dominated by electric keyboard and soprano sax; this is followed by a sung verse (B), and a repeat of both A and B, the latter with new lyrics. The song then segues into a cha cha chá–style montuno in which a vocal chorus alternates with sax improvisations. A few years later, Silvio Rodríguez (b. 1946) recorded "El dulce abismo" ("The Sweet Abyss") on *Tríptico vol. 2*.[77] It plays with the stylistic linkages between danzón and vocal repertoire of the early twentieth century (*vieja trova*) that also frequently includes danzón clave. Rodríguez's piece begins with vocals supported by acoustic guitar and a pair of claves playing the danzón clave rhythm; subsequently *tres*, piano, and güiro are added to the texture. While the Milanés recording is similar to danzón-chas of the 1940s and 1950s, Rodríguez departs more substantially from established practice. His use of danzón clave and traditional instruments reference shared heritage in a general sense, even though the guitar-based format distances the overall sound from traditional danzones. The song's lyrics are also rather unconventional, metaphorically alluding to travel, adventure, and the importance of striving toward one's aspirations or vision.

Many examples of recent experiments with danzón elements on the part of second- and third-generation trovadores exist as well. Amaury Pérez (b. 1953) released "Danzón deseo" in 1987, a ballad that incorporates variants of the danzón clave played

75. Manguaré recorded an original instrumental danzón by Pancho Amat called "Danzón de Campos," dedicated to the group's flautist, Jorge "Fumanchú" Campos. It first appeared on the LP *Regálame tus manos* from 1985 (Areito LD-4284, re-released in Mexico on the Discos NCL label, NCL-LP0076, 1986). Virulo's use of the danzón can be heard on the LP release *Historia de Cuba* (Havana, Areito LD-3471, n.d.).

76. Havana: Areíto/EGREM LD-3805. The song has been re-released on the *Serie Milenium 21* CD (Universal Música Latino, 1999).

77. The LP first appeared in 1984. It is now available on CD (Ojalá CDO-0007. Havana: Ojalá Records, 2004).

on high hat and a variety of synthesizer drum pads to create a decidedly modernistic romantic song.[78] In 1996, Xiomara Laugart (b. 1960) recorded José Antonio Quesada's "Hoy mi Habana" ("My Havana Today") using traditional danzón percussion (timbales, güiro, congas) as accompaniment to a sultry ballad.[79] Many similar pieces written by contemporary trovadores remain unrecorded owing to the difficulties of securing record contracts in Cuba generally, a situation exacerbated by the Special Period of the 1990s and its aftermath, and the ongoing US embargo. Yet over the past decade, David Torrens, Ariel Díaz, Liuba María Hevia, Boris Larramendi, and others have continued to release compositions referencing danzones in a variety of ways, often in conjunction with nostalgic reflections on the city of Havana.[80] Heidi Igualada (b. 1964), for instance, has demonstrated a sustained interest in danzón-influenced accompaniment to popular song. In pieces such as "Canción del viento" ("Song of the Wind"), "Sobreviviendo" ("Surviving"), and "Flor de luna" ("Moon Flower," dedicated to "the Havana of my grandparents") she freely mixes elements of danzón, tango, and jazz ballads.[81] Igualada admits a fascination with the danzón, though notes that because of its dated associations in Cuba audiences prefer to listen only to the occasional piece in that style: "Unfortunately [the danzón] represents a[n artistic] risk these days, though [my pieces] have been warmly received in small doses . . . No one would ever try to present an entire concert of sung danzones [to a nueva trova audience, though], let alone try to get the audience dancing to them!!!"[82]

Canto nuevo was the Mexican response to Cuban nueva trova in the late 1970s and 1980s. The movement included local Mexican musicians and singers like Oscar Chávez, Marcial Alejandro, Eugenia León, and the group Mexicanto, as well as South American exiles like the Argentineans Carlos Díaz "Caíto," Liliana Felipe, and Carlos Porcel de Peralta "Nahuel." Although Mexican canto nuevo musicians did not adopt the danzón at the height of the movement in the 1980s, the danzón renaissance of the 1990s inspired at least one visible danzón-based project, the CD *Que devuelvan* (1996). This recording brought together singer Eugenia León and the Danzonera Dimas to perform a set of politically charged songs written by Liliana Felipe (with lyrics by her partner, performance artist Jesusa Rodríguez) that touch upon everything from the corruption in President Salinas de Gortari's administration ("Que devuelvan" ["Let

78. "Danzón deseo" is on *De vuelta*, an LP that apparently appeared in multiple Latin American countries more or less simultaneously. The Argentina release is on EMI LP 58027. Buenos Aires: Fonarte Latino, 1987.

79. "Hoy mi Habana" was released on *La Habana entera* (Bis Music B148. Havana: Bis Music, 1996).

80. Ariel Díaz's unrecorded composition is called "Danzón de cuna." Liuba María Hevia recorded "Ausencia" as a vocal duet with Silvio Rodríguez on the CD *Del verso a la mar* (Eurotropical, 1999), which in concert she typically interprets as a danzón. Boris Larramendi's composition "Aquel danzón" has been posted to the web at http://conciertocubano. wordpress.com/2012/05/26/tragedy/ (accessed June 26, 2012).

81. "Canción al viento," arranged by Teresita de Jesús Rodríguez, was recorded on the *Serenata* CD (Havana: Unicornio UN-CD7014, 2002). "Sobreviviendo" (arr. Pepe Ordás) and "Flor de luna" (arr. José Antonio Miranda) appear on *En la línea de mi mano* (Cinquillo Colibrí CD 120. Havana: Instituto Cubano de la Música, 2008).

82. Heidi Igualada, electronic communication, May 21, 2012.

Them Give Back"]) to AIDS awareness ("Ana Luisa") to classism in Mexican society ("A su merced" ["For Your Favor" or "At Your Mercy"]).[83] Felipe's interest in the danzón began after hearing the Danzonera Dimas at Salón Colonia and by noticing the similar histories between this music and the tango—both being working-class musics appropriated by the bourgeoisie.[84] By obliquely referencing urban working-class culture associated with the danzón, the songs in *Que devuelvan* further emphasize the popular humor and irony that Felipe draws upon for her songs.

More recent invocations of the danzón by Mexican pop musicians include Aleks Syntek's danzón-chá–inspired "Historias de danzón y de arrabal" ("Histories of the Danzón and the Slums") with an accompanying video that also underscores the relationship between the danzón and Mexican working-class culture by incorporating imagery from 1940s Mexican *rumbera* and cabaret films.[85] Especially noteworthy are rock-ska band La Maldita Vecidad y Los Hijos del Quinto Patio's invocation of the danzón and pachuco culture in "Kumbala" and "Pachuco,"[86] and Control Machete's danzón-infused rap "Danzón" in collaboration with pianist Rubén González and bassist Orlando "Cachaíto" López from the Buena Vista Social Club project. The latter piece presents three repeated sections organized as ABABCBC plus a montuno finale. The A theme is instrumental and features danzón clave. The piano plays its main melody the first time; when it repeats after the B section, a solo flute improvises over the same harmonic sequence. Control Machete raps over B, using the danzón as a metaphor of the cultural flows that gave rise to it and the struggles of the people who embrace it. The band suggests that, like these cultural flows, the danzón will live forever. The C section, also sung, borrows the words "sóngoro cosongo" from Afro-Cuban poet Nicolás Guillén as a sort of refrain.[87] The song finishes with a montuno that features piano improvisations. "Danzón" was released on *Artillería pesada, presenta . . . Control Machete* (1999), the band's most commercially successful CD.[88] An accompanying video contrasts images of urban life in Havana with those of Control Machete singing at a train depot in Mexico, and closes with glimpses from a recording session with members of the rap band, their Cuban guest artists, and the lead singer of the popular Mexican rock band Café Tacvba.[89] Use of the danzón by one

83. Eugenia León and Danzonera Dimas, *Que devuelvan*. El Hábito CDFL-1312. Mexico City: Ediciones El Hábito, 1996.

84. Liliana Felipe interviewed by Ivanna Costa. See "Vacas sagradas de Liliana Felipe," www.rock.com.mx/lilianafelipe.html (accessed on January 3, 2013).

85. The video is available at www.youtube.com/watch?v=fG8Im8EuCH0 (accessed on June 19, 2012).

86. La Maldita Vecindad y Los Hijos del Quinto Patio, *El Circo*. Mexico City: SONY B000005LEN, 1991. These songs, as well as the name of the band, invoked 1940s–1950s Mexican popular culture related to the danzón through film precisely at the moment when the pachuco trend became popular among danzoneros.

87. See Nicolás Guillén, *Sóngoro cosongo y otros poemas* (Madrid: Alianza Editorial, 2006).

88. *Artillería pesada, presenta . . . Control Machete*. Universal 314 538 944-2. Miami: Universal, 1999.

89. The video is available at http://www.youtube.com/watch?v=_P5oS9Kfnuc (accessed on June 19, 2012).

BIBLIOGRAPHY

Abbott, Lynn and Doug Seroff. *Out of Sight: The Rise of African American Popular Music, 1889–1895*. Jackson: University Press of Mississippi, 2003.

Acosta, Ildelfonso. *Cuerdas de la memoria*. Matanzas: Ediciones Matanzas, 2004.

Acosta, Leonardo. *Descarga cubana: el jazz en Cuba 1900–1950*. Havana: Ediciones Unión, 2000.

———. *Otra visión de la música popular cubana*. Havana: Letras Cubanas, 2004.

———. "On Generic Complexes and Other Topics in Cuban Popular Music." *Journal of Popular Music Studies*, Vol. 17, No. 3, 227–54, 2005.

———. "The Rumba, the Guaguancó, and Tío Tom." In *Essays on Cuban Music. North American and Cuban Perspectives*, ed. Peter Manuel. New York: University Press of America, 49–74, 1991.

Adorno, Theodor W. *Ästhetische Theorie*. Frankfurt: Suhrkam, 1970.

Agüero, Gaspar. "Consideraciones sobre la música popular cubana." *Revista de la Facultad de Letras y Ciencias*, Vol. 32, 33–49, 1922.

Alemán Agusti, Arsenio J. "José Demetrio Alemán Rodríguez. El creador de la primera orquesta de Santiago de las Vegas." www.santiagodelasvegas.org/Jose%20Aleman%20La%20Primera%20Orquesta%20de%20Santiago%20de%20las%20Vegas.pdf (accessed February 12, 2009).

Alén, Olavo. *Combinaciones instrumentales y vocales de Cuba*. Havana: Dirección General de Servicios Técnicos Docentes, 1973.

———. *Géneros musicales de Cuba. De lo afrocubano a la salsa*. San Juan, Puerto Rico: Editorial Cubanacán, 1992.

Alfonso López, Félix Julio. "Las narrativas del béisbol en la construcción del nacionalismo cubano: 1880–1920." In *Perfiles de la nación*, ed. María del Pilar Díaz Castañón. Havana: Editorial de Ciencias Sociales, 123–53, 2004.

Almazán Orihuela, Joel. "La danza habanera en México (1870–1920)." PhD Dissertation, Centro de Investigación y Docencia en Humanidades del Estado de Morelos, 2010.

Altamirano, Ignacio Manuel. *Crónicas de la semana*. Mexico City: Ediciones de Bellas Artes, 1969 [1869].

Anderson, Margaret L. "Whitewashing Race: A Critical Perspective on Whiteness." In *White Out: The Continuing Significance of Racism*, ed. Ashley W. Doane and Eduardo Bonilla-Silva. London: Routledge, 21–34, 2003.

Aparicio, Frances. *Listening to Salsa. Gender, Latino Popular Music, and Puerto Rican Cultures*. Middletown, CT: Wesleyan University Press, 1998.

Appadurai, Arjun. *Modernity at Large. Cultural Dimensions of Globalization*. Minneapolis: University of Minnesota Press, 1996.

Armas Lara, Marcial. *Origen de la marimba, su desenvolvimiento y otros instrumentos músicos*. Guatemala City: National Government Publication, 1970.

Asociación Provincial Amigos de Danzón Miguel Faílde Pérez. "Estatutos." Unpublished manuscript dated January 15, 1980; property of President Aurelio Fernández.

Bacardí y Moreau, Emilio. *Crónicas de Santiago de Cuba*, Vol. 4, 2nd ed. Madrid: Breogán, 1973.

Balbuena, Bárbara. *El casino y la salsa en Cuba*. Havana: Letras Cubanas, 2003.

Ballester López, Amparo María. "Antonio Maceo y la Mansión de Nicoya." http://verbiclara .wordpress.com/2011/12/06/antonio-maceo-y-la-mansion-de-nicoya/ (accessed June 28, 2012).

Basail Rodríguez, Alain. "Imagen y nación: narrativas de identidad en la prensa: Cuba, 1878–1895." In *Perfiles de la nación*, ed. María del Pilar Díaz Castañón. Havana: Editorial de Ciencias Sociales, 77–121, 2004.

Bauman, Richard. *Verbal Art as Performance*. Prospect Heights, IL: Waveland Press, 1977.

Béhague, Gerard. *Music and Black Ethnicity: The Caribbean and South America*. New Brunswick: Transaction, 1995.

Berger, Monroe. "Letters from New Orleans." *Annual Review of Jazz Studies*, Vol. 7, 62–67, 1994–95.

Berlin, Edward A. "Ragtime." In *Grove Music Online*. Section 1, Stylistic Conventions. 2007 (accessed January 10, 2012).

Bermúdez, Egberto. "From Colombian 'National' Song to 'Colombian Song,' 1860–1960." *Lied und populäre Kultur / Song and Popular Culture*, No. 53, 167–259, 2008.

Blesh, Rudi. "Scott Joplin: Black American Classicist." In Scott Joplin, *Scott Joplin. Collected Piano Works*. New York: New York Public Library, 1971, xiii–xl.

Bojórquez Urzaíz, Carlos E. *La emigración cubana en Yucatán, 1868–1898*. Mérida, Mexico: Imagen Contemporánea, 2000.

Boletín de Instrucción Pública. Mexico City: Tipografía Económica, 1907.

Bordreaux, Peggy C. "Music Publishing in New Orleans in the Nineteenth Century." Master's Thesis, Louisiana State University, 1977.

Borneman, Ernest. "Creole Echoes." *Jazz Review*, Vol. 2, No. 8, 13–15, 1959.

———. "Creole Echoes: Part II." *Jazz Review*, Vol. 2, No. 10, 26–27, 1959.

Bourdieu, Pierre. *Outline of a Theory of Practice*. New York: Cambridge University Press, 1977.

Boym, Svetlana. *The Future of Nostalgia*. New York: Basic Books, 2001.

Braunstein, Néstor. *El goce. Un concepto lacaniano*. Buenos Aires: Siglo XXI, 2006 [1990].

Bremer, Fredrika. *Cartas desde Cuba*. Havana: Editorial Arte y Literatura, 1995.

Briceño, Enrique Martín. "Ecos del Yucatán porfiriano: el semanario musical *J. Jacinto Cuevas*." In *Guía y joyas de los archivos de Mérida*, ed. Maureen Ransom Carty. Mérida: Instituto de Cultura de Yucatán, 2005.

Brothers, Thomas. *Louis Armstrong's New Orleans*. New York: W.W. Norton, 2006.

Brown, Julie. "Introduction. Music, History, Trauma: Music and Race, 1883–1933." In *Western Music and Race*, ed. Julie Brown. New York: Cambridge University Press, xiv–xxii, 2007.

Browning, Barbara. *Infectious Rhythm. Metaphors of Contagion and the Spread of African Culture*. New York: Routledge, 1998.

Buffington, Robert. "La 'Dancing' Mexicana. Danzón and the Transformation of Intimacy in Post-Revolutionary Mexico City." *Journal of Latin American Cultural Studies*, Vol. 14, No. 1, 87–108, 2005.

Butler, Judith. *Excitable Speech. A Politics of the Performative*. London: Routledge, 1997.

Buttersworth, Neil. *The Music of Aaron Copland*. London: Toccata Press, 1985.

Cable, G. W. *Jazz Dance. The Story of American Vernacular Dance*, ed. Marshall and Jean Stearns. New York: Da Capo, 1994 [1964].

Calero, Martín and José y Leopoldo Valdés Quesada, eds. *Cuba musical. Album-resumen ilustrado de la historia y de la actual situación del arte musical en Cuba*. Havana: Molina y Compañía, 1929.

Campbell, Reau. *Campbell's New Revised Complete Guide and Descriptive Book of Mexico*. Chicago: Robert O. Law, 1899.

Campos, Rubén M. *El folklore musical en las ciudades. Investigación acerca de la música mexicana para cantar y bailar*. Mexico City: Secretaría de Educación Pública, 1930.

———. *El folklore y la música mexicana*. Mexico City: Secretaría de Educación Pública, 1928.

Caro Cocotle, Guadalupe. "La música de las pelonas. Nuevas identidades femeninas del México moderno, 1920–1930." PhD Dissertation, Universidad Nacional Autónoma de México (in process).

Carpentier, Alejo. *La música en Cuba*. Mexico City: Fondo de Cultura Económica, 1946.

Carrington, Ben. *Race, Sport, and Politics. The Sporting Black Diaspora*. London: Sage, 2010.

Carty, Maureen Ransom. *Guía y joyas de los archivos de Mérida*. Mérida: Instituto de Cultura de Yucatán, 2005.

Casanova Olivia, Ana Victoria. "Güiro o guayo." In *Instrumentos de la música folklórico-popular de Cuba*, Vol. 1, ed. Victoria Eli Rodríguez et al. Havana: Editorial de Ciencias Sociales, 156–65, 1997.

Casco Centeno, Emilio. "Análisis de la Sonatina para piano de José Pomar." *Heterofonía*, Vol. 35, No. 109–128, 2006.

Castaneda, Jose. "Tampeekoe." *Jazz Archivist*, Vol. 13, 9–11, 1998–99.

Castillo Faílde, Osvaldo. *Miguel Faílde. Creador musical del danzón*. Havana: Editora del Consejo Nacional de Cultura, 1964.

Chapple, Steve and Reebee Garofalo. "Black Roots, White Fruits: Racism in the Music Industry." In *Rock 'n' Roll Is Here to Pay: The History and Politics of the Music Industry*, ed. Steve Chapple and Reebee Garofalo. Chicago: Nelson-Hall, 1977.

Chapple, Steve and Reebee Garofalo, eds. *Rock 'n' roll Is Here to Pay: The History and Politics of the Music Industry*. Chicago: Nelson-Hall, 1977.

Charters, Samuel B. *Jazz: New Orleans, 1885–1963*, rev. ed. New York: Oak Publications, 1963.

Chase, Gilbert. *America's Music. From the Pilgrims to the Present*. New York: McGraw-Hill, 1955.

Chase, Malcolm and Christopher Shaw. "The Dimensions of Nostalgia." In *The Imagined Past. History and Nostalgia*, ed. Malcolm Chase and Christopher Shaw. Manchester: Manchester University Press, 1–17, 1989.

Chasteen, John Charles. *National Rhythms, African Roots. The Deep History of Latin American Popular Dance*. Albuquerque: University of New Mexico Press, 2004.

Collier, Simon, Artemis Cooper, María Susana Azzi, and Richard Martin. *Tango*. London: Thames and Hudson, 1995.

Contreras Soto, Eduardo. "Un reencuentro con Pomar." *Heterofonía*, Vol. 33, No. 124, 135–38, 2001.

Córdoba, María de los Ángeles and Natalí Méndez Díaz. "El género en la música: una aproximación a su estudio." *Clave*, Año 12, No. 1–3, 90–103, 2010.

Corona Alcalde, Antonio. "The Popular Music of Veracruz and the Survival of Instrumental Practices of the Spanish Baroque." *Ars Musica Denver*, Vol. 7, No. 2, 39–68, 1995.

Cook, Pam. *Screening the Past. Memory and Nostalgia in Cinema*. New York: Routledge, 2005.

Crist, Elizabeth B. *Music of the Common Man. Aaron Copland during the Depression and War*. New York: Oxford University Press, 2005.

Cunin, Elisabeth, ed. *Mestizaje, diferencia y nación. Lo "negro" en América Central y el Caribe*. Mexico City: INAH, 2010.

Dávila, Arlene. *Latino Spin. Public Image and the Whitewshing of Race*. New York: New York University Press, 2008.

Davis, Fred. *Yearning for Yesterday: A Sociology of Nostalgia*. New York: Free Press, 1979.

de Céspedes, Benjamín. *La prostitución en La Habana*. Havana: Establecimiento Tipográfico O'Reilly, 1888.

de la Fuente, Alejandro. *A Nation for All. Race, Inequality, and Politics in Twentieth-Century Cuba*. Chapel Hill: University of North Carolina Press, 2001.

de la Mora, Sergio. *Cinemachismo, Masculinities and Sexuality in Mexican Film*. Austin: University of Texas Press, 2006.

de León Granda, Mercedes. "Lo cubano, en música. Un problema de estilo o de género." *Clave*, Año 12, No. 1–3, 56–59, 2010.

de Ximeno y Cruz, Dolores María. *Memorias de Lola María*. Havana: Letras Cubanas, 1983 [1928].

Deschamps Chapeaux, Pedro. *El negro en la economía habanera del siglo xix*. Havana: UNEAC, 1971.

Díaz Ayala, Cristóbal. *Cuba canta y baila. Discografía de la música cubana. Primer volumen: 1898–1925*. San Juan, Puerto Rico: Fundación Musicalia, 1994.

———. "Influencias recíprocas entre el jazz y la música caribeña." Unpublished paper presented at the IV Congreso Internacional de Música, Identidad y Cultura del Caribe, Santiago de los Caballeros, Dominican Republic, 2010.

———. "La invencible charanga." *Encuentro*, Vol. 26–27, 295–308, 2002–3.

———. *Los contrapunteos de la música cubana*. San Juan, Puerto Rico: Ediciones Callejón, 2006.

Díaz Ayala, Cristóbal and Richard Spottswood. Liner notes to *Hot Music from Cuba 1907–1936*. Harlequin HQ CD 23. West Sussex, England: Interstate Music, 1993.

———. Liner notes to *The Cuban Danzón. Before There Was Jazz*. Arhoolie Folklyric CD 7032. El Cerrito, CA: Arhoolie Productions, 1999.

Díaz Castañón, María del Pilar, ed. *Perfiles de la nación*. Havana: Editorial de Ciencias Sociales, 2004.

Díaz y de Ovando, Clementina. *Invitación al baile. Arte, espectáculo y rito en la sociedad mexicana (1825–1910)*, Vols. I and II. Mexico City: UNAM, 2006.

Doane, Woody. "Rethinking Whiteness Studies." In *White Out: The Continuing Significance of Racism*, ed. Ashley W. Doane and Eduardo Bonilla-Silva. London: Routledge, 3–18, 2003.

Doane, Ashely W. and Eduardo Bonilla-Silva, eds. *White Out: The Continuing Significance of Racism*. London: Routledge, 2003.

Doheny, John. "The Spanish Tinge Hypothesis: Afro-Caribbean Characteristics in Early New Orleans Jazz Drumming." *Jazz Archivist*, Vol. 19, 8–15, 2006.

Dollero, Adolfo. *Cultura cubana. La provincia de Matanzas y su evolución*. Havana: Imprenta Seoane y Fernández, 1919.

Duff, David, ed. *Modern Genre Theory*. New York: Longman, 2000.

Echeverría, Francisco. "El debut de la Patti en La Habana." *Clave. Revista cubana de música*, Vol. 11, 50–57, 1988.

Egüez Guevara, Pilar. "Colonial Anxieties over Sex and Race: Regulating 'Public' Spaces and the *Escuelitas de Baile* in 19th Century Havana." Unpublished manuscript. Center for Latin American and Caribbean Studies, University of Illinois Urbana Champaign, 2008.

Eli Rodríguez, Victoria. "Cuban Music and Ethnicity: Historical Considerations." In *Music and Black Ethnicity: The Caribbean and South America*, ed. Gerard Béhague. New Brunswick: Transaction, 91–108, 1995.

Eli Rodríguez, Victoria et al. *Instrumentos de la música folklórico-popular de Cuba*, Vol. 1. Havana: Editorial de Ciencias Sociales, 1997.

Eli Rodríguez, Victoria and María de los Ángeles Alfonso, eds. *La música entre Cuba y España. Tradición en innovación*. Madrid: Fundación Autor, 1999.

Eli, Victoria and Zoila Gómez García, *Música latinoamericana y caribeña*. Havana: Editorial Pueblo y Educación, 1995.

Eng, David. *Racial Castration. Managing Masculinity in Asian America*. Durham, NC: Duke University Press, 2001.

Estrada, Abelardo. "Estudio de un libro, su autor, y el ámbito de ambos." In Laureano Fuentes Matons, *Las artes de Santiago de Cuba*. Havana: Letras Cubanas, 9–109, 1981 [1893].

Estrada, Hall. "The Sensuous Habanera." *Cuban Heritage*, Vol. 1, No. 1, 21–29, 1987.

Fabbri, Franco. "A Theory of Popular Music Genres: Two Applications." In *Popular Music Perspectives*, ed. David Horn and Philip Tagg. Göteburg: A. Wheaton, 52–81, 1982.

Farren, Katrina McNeely. "Narrative Identity in Paul Ricoeur and Luce Irigaray: The Circularity between Self and Other." PhD Dissertation, Michigan Technological University, 2010.

Featherstone, Mike, Scott Lash, and Roland Robertson. *Global Modernities*. London: Sage, 1995.

Fernández, María Antonia. *Bailes populares cubanos*. Havana: Editorial Pueblo y Educación, 1976.

Fernández, Nohema. "La contradanza y Manuel Saumell." *Latin American Music Review*, Vol. 10, No. 1, 116–34, 1989.

Fernández de Latorre, Ricardo. *Historia de la música militar de España*. Madrid: Ministerio de Defensa, 1999.

Ferrer, Ada. *Insurgent Cuba. Race, Nation, and Revolution, 1868–1898*. Chapel Hill: University of North Carolina Press, 1999.

Fiehrer, Thomas. "From Quadrille to Stomp: The Creole Origins of Jazz." *Popular Music*, Vol. 10, No. 1, 21–38, 1991.

Figueras, Francisco. *Cuba y su evolución colonial*. Havana: Imprenta Avisador Comercial, 1907.

Figueroa Hernández, Rafael. *Tres generaciones del danzón veracruzano*. Veracruz, Mexico: CNIDDAC, 2008.

Flores, Juan. "'Cha-Cha with a Backbeat': Songs and Stories of Latin Boogaloo." In *Situating Salsa. Global Markets and Local Meaning in Latin Popular Music*, ed. Lise Waxer. New York: Routledge, 75–100, 2002.

Flores y Escalante, Jesús. *Imágenes del danzón. Iconografía del danzón en México*. Mexico City: Asociación Mexicana de Estudios Fonográficos, 1994.

———. *Salón México: historia documental y gráfica del danzón en México*. Mexico City: Asociación Mexicana de Estudios Fonográficos, 1993.

Friedenthal, Albert. *Musik, Tanz und Dichtung bei den Kreolen Amerikas*. Berlin: Hausbücher-Verlag Hans Schnippel, 1913.

Frith, Simon. *Performing Rites: On the Value of Popular Music*. Cambridge, MA: Harvard University Press, 1998.

Fontela, C. and M. Silva, eds. *Galicia-Cuba: un patrimonio cultural de referencias y confluencias*. A Coruña: Ediciós do Castro, 2000.

Fornäs, Johan. "The Future of Rock: Discourses that Struggle to Define a Genre." *Popular Music*, Vol. 14, No. 1, 111–25, 1995.

Fuentes, Carlos. *Los años con Laura Díaz*. Mexico City: Alfaguara, 1999.

Fuentes Matons, Laureano. *Las artes de Santiago de Cuba*. Havana: Letras Cubanas, 1981 [1893].

Gabriel, John. *Whitewash. Racialized Politics and the Media*. London: Routledge, 1998.

Galán, Natalio. "Charanga Típica Cubana." *La Gaceta de Cuba*, Año 2, No. 13, 13, 21, 1963.

———. *Cuba y sus sones*. Valencia: Pre-Textos, 1983.

Gamboa, Federico. *Santa: A Novel of Mexico City*, trans. John Charles Chasteen. Chapel Hill: University of North Carolina Press, 2010.

Garcia, David F. "Going Primitive to the Movements and Sounds of Mambo." *Musical Quarterly*, No. 89, 505–23, 2007.

García Díaz, Bernardo. "La migración cubana a Veracruz. 1870–1910." In *La Habana / Veracruz, Veracruz / La Habana. Las dos orilla*, ed. Bernardo García Díaz and Sergio Guerra Vilaboy. Xalapa, Mexico: Universidad Veracruzana, 297–399, 2002.

García Díaz, Bernardo and Sergio Guerra Vilaboy, eds. *La Habana / Veracruz, Veracruz / La Habana. Las dos orillas*. Xalapa, Mexico: Universidad Veracruzana, 2002.

Gelbart, Matthew. *The Invention of "Folk Music" and "Art Music": Emerging Categories from Ossian to Wagner*. Cambridge, UK: Cambridge University Press, 2007.

Gidal, Marc. "Contemporary 'Latin American' Composers of Art Music in the United States: Cosmopolitans Navigating Multiculturalism and Universalism." *Latin American Music Review*, Vol. 31, No. 1, 40–78, 2010.

Giro, Radamés. *Diccionario Enciclopédico de la música cubana*, Vols. 1–4. Havana: Letras Cubanas, 2007.

Giro, Radamés, ed. *Caturla el músico, el hombre*, ed. Radamés Giro. Havana: Ediciones Museo de la Música, 2007.

———. *Panorama de la música popular cubana*. Havana: Editorial Letras Cubanas, 1995.

Goffin, Robert. *La Nouvelle-Orléans, capitale du jazz*. New York: Édicions de la Maison française, 1946.

Gómez Cairo, Jesús. "Acerca de la interacción de géneros en la música popular de Cuba." *Boletín Música*, No. 83–84, 19–30, 1980.

———. "Dos enfoques sobre géneros de la música cubana: Odilio Urfé y Argeliers León." *Clave*, Año 12, No. 1–3, 28–49, 2010.

González, Fernando. Liner notes to the Arturo Sandoval CD *Danzón (Dance On)*. GRP Digital Master CD GRD-9761, 1994.

González, Hilario. "Manuel Saumell y la contradanza." In Manuel Saumell, *Contradanzas*. Havana: Letras Cubanas, 5–21, 1981.

González Arzola, Nancy. *Teatro Martí. Prodigiosa permanencia.* Havana: Ediciones Unión 2010.

González Bello, Neris and Liliana Casanella. "La timba cubana: un intergénero contemporáneo." *Clave*, Vol. 4, No. 1, 2–9, 2002.

González Hechevarría, Roberto. *Crítica práctica*. Mexico City: Fondo de Cultura Económica 2002.

González Moreno, Liliana. comp., "Género, forma, lenguaje, estilo y demás complejidades." *Clave*, Año 12, No. 1–3, 104–25, 2010.

Goodman, Walter. *The Pearl of the Antilles or An Artist in Cuba.* London: Henry S. King, 1873.

Grenet, Emilio. *Popular Cuban Music. 80 Revised and Corrected Compositions Together with an Essay on the Evolution of Music in Cuba*, trans. R. Phillips. Havana: Secretary of Agriculture, 1939.

Gruson, Bart. Liner notes to *Cuba. Contradanzas and Danzones*. Rotterdam Conservatory Orquesta Típica. Nimbus Records CD NI 5502. Charlottesville, VA: Nimbus Communications International, 1996.

Guerra y Sánchez, Ramiro. *Historia de la nación cubana*, Vol. 7. Havana: Editorial Historia de la Nación Cubana, S.A, 1952.

Guffey, Elizabeth E. *Retro. The Culture of Revival*. London: Reaktion Books, 2006.

Guillén, Nicolás. *Sóngoro cosongo y otros poemas*. Madrid: Alianza Editorial, 2006.

Gupta, Akhil and James Fergusen. "Beyond 'Culture': Space, Identity, and the Politics of Difference." *Cultural Anthropology*, Vol. 7, No. 1, 6–23, 1992.

Gushee, Lawrence. Liner notes to "Steppin' On the Gas: Rags to Jazz 1913–1927." New World Records NW 269, 1977, 4.

———. "The Nineteenth-Century Origins of Jazz." *Black Music Research Journal*, Vol. 14, No. 1, 1–24, 1994.

———. *The Pioneers of Jazz. The Story of the Creole Band*. New York: Oxford University Press, 2005.

Gutierrez S., Edgar J. *Fiestas: once de noviembre en Cartagena de Indias. Manifestaciones artísticas, cultura popular, 1910–1930*. Medellín: Editorial Lealón, 2000.

Hale, Gary J. "A 'Failed State' in Mexico. Tamaulipas Declares Itself Ungovernable." Houston: James A Baker III Institute for Public Policy-Rice University, 2011.

Hall, Stuart. "Introduction: Who Needs 'Identity'?" In *Questions of Cultural Identity*, ed. Stuart Hall and Paul du Gay. London: Sage, 1–17, 1996.

———. "Race, Articulation and Societies Structured in Dominance." In *Black British Cultural Studies: A Reader*, ed. Houston A. Baker et al. Chicago: University of Chicago Press, 16–60, 1996.

———. "The Local and the Global: Globalization and Ethnicity." In *Culture, Globalization, and the World-System: Contemporary Conditions for the Representation of Identity*, ed. Anthony D. King. Minneapolis: University of Minnesota Press, 19–40, 2007.

———. "What Is the 'Black' in Black Popular Culture?" In *Black Popular Culture*, ed. Michelle Wallace and Gina Dent. Seattle, WA: Bay Press, 21–33, 1992.

Hallorans, O., ed. *Guarachas cubanas. Curiosa recopilación desde las más antiguas hasta las más modernas*. Havana: Librería La Principal Editora, 1882.

Handler, Richard and Jocelyn Linnekin. "Tradition, Genuine or Spurious." *Journal of American Folklore*, Vol. 97, No. 385, 273–90, 1984.

Hannerz, Ulf. "The World in Creolisation." *Africa: Journal of the International African Institute*, Vol. 57, No. 4, 546–59, 1987.

Hanks, William F. "Discourse Genres in a Theory of Practice." *American Ethnologist*, Vol. 14, No 4, 668–92, 1987.

Hazard, Samuel. *Cuba with Pen and Pencil*. Hartford, CT: Hartford Publishing, 1871.

Helg, Aline. *Our Rightful Share. The Afro-Cuban Struggle for Equality, 1886–1912*. Chapel Hill: University of North Carolina Press, 1995.

Henríquez, María Antonieta. *Alejandro García Caturla*. Havana: Ediciones Unión, 1999.

Henríquez, María Antonieta, ed. *Alejandro García Caturla. Correspondencia*. Havana: Editorial Arte y Literatura, 1978.

Hernández, Gisela and Olga de Blanck, eds. *Ignacio Cervantes: Cuarenta danzas*. Havana: Ediciones de Blanck, 1959.

Hernández Cuevas, Marco Polo. *African Mexicans and the Discourse on Modern Nation*. Lanham, MD: University Press of America, 2004.

Herzfeld, Michael. *Cultural Intimacy. Social Poetics in the Nation-State*. New York: Routledge, 2005.

Hirsch, Charles. *Subversive Sounds: Race and the Birth of Jazz in New Orleans*. Chicago: University of Chicago Press, 2007.

Hitchcock, Wiley H. *Music in the United States: A Historical Introduction*. Englewood Cliffs, NJ: Prentice Hall, 1974.

Holt, Fabian. *Genre in Popular Music*. Chicago: University of Chicago Press, 2007.

Ibarra, Domingo. *Colección de bailes de sala y método para aprenderlos sin ausilio de maestro*. Mexico City: Tipografía de Nabor Chávez, 1862 [1858].

Iglesias, Ada. "Un músico del pueblo." *Actas del folklore*, Año 1, No. 4, 13–15, 1961.

Iglesias Utset, Marial. *A Cultural History of Cuba during the U.S. Occupation, 1898–1902*, trans. Russ Davidson. Chapel Hill: University of North Carolina Press, 2011.

Inda, Jonathan Xavier and Renato Rosaldo. "Tracking Global Flows." In *The Anthropology of Globalization. A Reader*, ed. Jonathan Xavier Inda and Renato Rosaldo. Malden, MA: Blackwell, 3–46, 2008 [2002].

Inda, Jonathan Xavier and Renato Rosaldo, eds. *The Anthropology of Globalization. A Reader*. Malden, MA: Blackwell, 2008 [2002].

Jara Gámez, Simón, Aurelio Rodríguez "Yeyo," and Antonio Zedillo Castillo. *De Cuba con amor. El danzón en México*. Mexico City: CONACULTA, 2001.

Johnson, Gaye Teresa. "'Sobre Las Olas': A Mexican Genesis in Borderlands Jazz and the Legacy for Ethnic Studies." *Comparative American Studies*, Vol. 6, No. 3, 225–40, 2008.

Jones, LeRoy. *Blues People*. New York: Apollo Editions, 1963.

Joplin, Scott. *Scott Joplin. Collected Piano Works*. New York: New York Public Library, 1971.

Junius Hart Company. *Catalogue of Musical Publications*. New Orleans, LA: Junius Hart [Historic New Orleans Collection], 1894.

Kinzer, Charles E. "The Tios of New Orleans and Their Pedagogical Influence on the Early Jazz Clarinet Style." *Black Music Research Journal*, Vol. 16, No. 2, 279–302, 1996.

Kun, Josh. *Audiotopia. Music, Race, and America*. Berkeley: University of California Press, 2005.

Laird, Ross and Brian Rust. *Discography of OKeh Records, 1918–1934*. Westport, CT: Greenwood, 2004.

Lane, Jill. *Blackface Cuba, 1840–1895*. Philadelphia: University of Pennsylvania Press, 2005.

———. "Black/Face Publics. The Social Bodies of *Fraternidad*." In *Critical Theory and Performance*, ed. Janelle G. Reinelt and Joseph R. Roach. Ann Arbor: University of Michigan Press, 141–55, 2007.

Lapique Becali, Zoila. *Cuba colonial. Música, compositores e intérpretes, 1570–1902*. Havana: Ediciones Boloña, 2007.

———. *Música colonial cubana. Tomo 1 (1812–1902)*. Havana: Letras Cubanas, 1979.

Largey, Michael. "Haiti: Tracing the Steps of the Méringue and Contredanse." In *Creolizing Contradance in the Caribbean*, ed. Peter Manuel. Philadelphia: Temple University Press, 209–30, 2009.

Leal, Rine. *Breve historia del teatro cubano*. Havana: Letras Cubanas, 1980.

———. *La selva oscura, Vol. 2, De los bufos a la neocolonial.* Havana: Editorial Arte y Literatura, 1982.

Leal, Rine, ed. *Teatro bufo siglo XIX. Antología tomo II.* Havana: Editorial Arte y Cultura, 1975.

León, Argeliers. *Del canto y del tiempo.* Havana: Editorial Letras Cubanas, 1984.

Linares, María Teresa and Faustino Núñez. *La música entre Cuba y España.* Madrid: Fundación Autor, 1998.

Lipsitz, George. *Time Passages. Collective Memory and American Popular Culture.* Minneapolis: University of Minnesota Press, 1990.

Lomanno, Mark. "Topics on Afro-Cuban Jazz in the United States." Master's Thesis, Rutgers University, 2007.

Lopes Cançado, Tania Mara. "An Investigation of West African and Haitian Rhythms on the Development of Syncopation in Cuba Habanera, Brazilian Tango/Choro and American Ragtime (1791–1900)." PhD Dissertation, Shenandoah University, 1999.

López, Alfonso. "Las narrativas del béisbol en la construcción del nacionalismo cubano: 1880–1920." In *Perfiles de la nación,* ed. María del Pilar Díaz Castañón. Havana: Editorial de Ciencias Sociales, 124–53, 2004.

López Cano, Rubén. "Favor de no tocar el género: géneros, estilo y competencia en la semiótica musical cognitiva actual." In *Voces e imágenes en la etnomusicología actual,* ed. Josep Martí and Silvia Martínez. Madrid: Ministerio de Cultura, 325–37, 2004.

López Mayorical, Mariano, ed. *La polémica de "La Marimba": el poema más discutido de todas los tiempos, consagrado antes de llegar al bronce esculpido en monumento.* Guatemala City: Editorial José de Piñeda Ibarra, 1978.

Lowenthal, David. "Nostalgia Tells It Like It Wasn't.'" In *The Imagined Past. History and Nostalgia,* ed. Malcolm Chase and Christopher Shaw. Manchester: Manchester University Press, 1989.

Lugo-Ortiz, Agnes. "Material Culture, Slavery, and Governability in Colonial Cuba: The Humorous Lessons of the Cigarette Marquillas." *Journal of Latin American Cultural Studies,* Vol. 21, No. 1, 61–85, 2012.

Madrid, Alejandro L. "El continuo proceso de intercambio cultural. Leo Brouwer y *La espiral eterna* (1971)." *Pauta. Cuadernos de teoría y crítica musical,* Vol. XVI, No. 66, 67–77, 1998.

———. *Music in Mexico. Experiencing Music, Expressing Culture.* New York: Oxford University Press, 2013.

———. "Retos multilineales y método prolépsico en el estudio posnacional del nacionalismo musical." In *Discursos y prácticas musicales nacionalistas (1900–1970): España, Argentina, Cuba, México,* ed. Pilar Ramos López. Logroño: Universidad de La Rioja, 2012.

———. *Sounds of the Modern Nation. Music, Culture, and Ideas in Post-Revolutionary Mexico.* Philadelphia: Temple University Press, 2009.

———. "The Sounds of the Nation: Visions of Modernity and Tradition in Mexico's First National Congress of Music." *Hispanic American Historical Review,* Vol. 86, No. 4, 681–706, 2006.

———. "Transnational Cultural Translations and the Meaning of Danzón across Borders." In *Performance in the Borderlands,* ed. Ramón H. Rivera-Servera and Harvey Young. New York: Palgrave Macmillan, 37–57, 2011.

———. "Transnational Musical Encounters at the U.S.-Mexico Border: An Introduction." In *Transnational Encounters. Music and Performance at the U.S.-Mexico Border,* ed. Alejandro L. Madrid. New York: Oxford University Press, 1–18, 2011.

———. "Why Music and Performance Studies? Why Now? An Introduction to the Special Issue," *Trans. Revista Transcultural de Música,* No. 13, 2009. www.sibetrans.com/trans/a1/why-music-and-performance-studies-why-now-an-introduction-to-the-special-issue (accessed July 20, 2012).

Madrid, Alejandro L., ed. *Transnational Encounters. Music and Performance at the U.S.-Mexico Border.* New York: Oxford University Press, 2011.

Malcomson, Hettie. "La configuración racial del danzón: los imaginarios raciales del Puerto de Veracruz." In *Mestizaje, diferencia y nación. Lo "negro" en América Central y el Caribe,* ed. Elisabeth Cunin. Mexico City: INAH, 267–98, 2010.

————. "New Generations, Older Bodies: Danzón, Age and 'Cultural Rescue' in the Port of Veracruz, Mexico." *Popular Music*, Vol. 31, No. 2, 217–30, 2012.

————. "The 'Routes' and 'Roots' of Danzón. A Critique of the History of a Genre." *Popular Music*, Vol. 3, No. 2, 263–78, 2011.

Manduley, Humberto. *El rock en Cuba*. Bogotá: Atril Ediciones Musicales, 2001.

Manuel, Peter. "Cuba: From Contradanza to Danzón." In *Creolizing Contradance in the Caribbean*, ed. Peter Manuel. Philadelphia: Temple University Press, 51–112, 2009.

————. "From Scarlatti to 'Guantanamera': Dual Tonicity in Spanish and Latin American Musics," *Journal of the American Musicological Society*, Vol. 55, No. 2, 311–36, 2002.

————. "Introduction: Contradance and Quadrille Culture in the Caribbean." In *Creolizing Contradance in the Caribbean*, ed. Peter Manuel. Philadelphia: Temple University Press, 1–50, 2009.

————. "The Dominican Republic. Danza and the Contradanced Merengue." In *Creolizing Contradance in the Caribbean*, ed. Peter Manuel. Philadelphia: Temple University Press, 155–87, 2009.

Manuel, Peter, ed. *Creolizing Contradance in the Caribbean*. Philadelphia: Temple University Press, 2009.

————. *Essays on Cuban Music. North American and Cuban Perspectives*. New York: University Press of America, 1991.

Manuel, Peter and Edgardo Díaz Díaz, "Puerto Rico: The Rise and Fall of the Danza as National Music." In *Creolizing Contradance in the Caribbean*, ed. Peter Manuel. Philadelphia: Temple University Press, 113–54, 2009.

Marrero, Gaspar. *La Orquesta Aragón*. Havana: Editorial José Martí, 2008 [2001].

Martí, José. *Biblioteca popular martiana no. 4. La cuestión racial*. Havana: Editorial Lex, 1959.

Martín, Edgardo. *Panorama histórico de la música cubana*. Havana: Universidad de La Habana, 1971.

Martínez-Alier, Verena. *Marriage, Class, and Colour in Nineteenth-Century Cuba*. Ann Arbor: University of Michigan Press, 1974.

Martínez Rodríguez, Raúl. "La música bailable en el siglo XIX en Matanzas." Booklet published for the centenary of the danzón. Matanzas: Consejo Nacional de Cultura, 1979.

————. *Para el alma divertir*. Havana: Letras Cubanas, 2004.

Martínez Furé, Rogelio. "Tambor." *Essays on Cuban Music. North American and Cuban Perspectives*, ed. Peter Manuel. New York: University Press of America, 25–48, 1991.

Martré, Gonzalo. "La migración musical cubana (1930 a 1950)." *Batey. Una revista cubana de antropología social*. www.revista-batey.com/index.php?option=com_content&view=article&id=40&Itemid=41 (accessed July 20, 2012).

Matos, Cláudia. *Acertei no milhar: malandragem e samba no tempo de Getúlio*. Rio de Janeiro: Paz e Terra, 1982.

Mayer Serra, Otto. *Panorama de la música mexicana*. Mexico City: El Colegio de México, 1941.

McCusker, John. "The Onward Brass Band and the Spanish American War." *Jazz Archivist*, Vol. 13, 24–35, 1999.

Mendoza, Vicente T. *El romancero español y el corrido mexicano. Estudio comparativo*. Mexico City: Universidad Nacional Autónoma de México, 1997 [1939].

————. *La canción mexicana. Ensayo de clasificación y antología*. Mexico City: Fondo de Cultura Económica, 1982 [1961].

Mendoza Aguilar, Gardenia. "Parts of Mexico Show Signs of 'Failed State,'" *New American Media* (September 24, 2010) http://newamericamedia.org/2010/09/parts-of-mexico-show-signs-of-failed-state.php (accessed April 18, 2012).

Meintjes, Louise. "Paul Simon's *Graceland*, South Africa, and the Mediation of Musical Meaning." *Ethnomusicology*, Vol. 34, No. 1, 37–73, 1990.

Miller, Karl H. *Segregating Sound. Inventing Folk and Pop Music in the Age of Jim Crow*. Durham, NC: Duke University Press, 2010.

Miller, Marilyn Grace. *Rise and Fall of the Cosmic Race. The Cult of Mestizaje in Latin America*. Austin: University of Texas Press, 2004.

Miller, Sue M. "Flute Improvisation in Cuban Charanga Performance: With a Specific Focus on the Work of Richard Egües and Orquesta Aragón," Vol. 1. PhD Dissertation, University of Leeds, 2011.

Miranda, Ricardo. *Ecos, alientos y sonidos: ensayos sobre música mexicana*. Xalapa and Mexico City: Universidad Veracruzana and Fondo de Cultura Económica, 2001.

Moliner Castañeda, Israel. *El Teatro Principal de Matanzas*. Matanzas: Ediciones Matanzas, 2007.

———. *José Silvestre White y Laffite. Folleto homenaje en el 60o. aniversario de su muerte*. Matanzas: Dirección Sectorial de Cultura OPP, 1978.

Moore, Robin D. *Music and Revolution. Cultural Change in Socialist Cuba*. Berkeley: University of California Press, 2006.

———. *Music in the Hispanic Caribbean. Experiencing Music, Expressing Culture*. New York: Oxford University Press, 2010.

———. *Nationalizing Blackness. Afrocubanismo and Artistic Revolution in Havana, 1920–1940*. Pittsburgh: University of Pittsburgh Press, 1997.

———. "The *Teatro Bufo*: Cuban Blackface Theater of the Nineteenth Century." In *Performativity, Power, and the Poetics of Being: Soundscapes from the Americas*, ed. Donna Buchanan. London: Ashgate, forthcoming.

Moreno Chicharro, Francisco. *Cuba y su gente. Apuntes para la historia*. Madrid: Establecimiento Tipográfico de Enrique Teodoro, 1887.

Moreno Farginals, Manuel, ed. *Africa in Latin America: Essays on History, Culture, and Socialization*. New York: Holmes and Meier, 1984.

Moreno Rivas, Yolanda. *Historia de la música popular mexicana*. Mexico City: CONACULTA, 1989.

Moreno Villarreal, Jaime. *Fracciones*. Mexico City: La Máquina de Escribir, 1980.

Música guatemalteca para piano: antología histórica, siglos XIX–XXI. Guatemala City: Universidad de San Carlos de Guatemala, Dirección General de Investigación, Centro de Estudios Folklóricos, 2008.

Negus, Keith, *Music Genres and Corporate Cultures*. London: Routledge, 1999.

Ochoa, Ana María. "Género, tradición y nación en el bambuco." *A Contratiempo*, No. 9, 35–44, 1997.

Olavarría y Ferrari, Enrique. *Reseña histórica del teatro en México*, Vols. 2–3. Mexico City: La Europea, 1895.

Omi, Michael and Howard Winant. *Racial Formation in the United States*. New York: Routledge, 1994.

Orovio, Helio. *Cuban Music from A to Z*. Durham, NC: Duke University Press, 2004.

———. *Diccionario de la música cubana*, 2nd ed. Havana: Letras Cubanas, 1992.

Orozco, Danilo. *Nexos globales desde la música cubana con rejuegos de son y no son*. Havana: Ediciones Ojalá, 2001.

———. "Procesos socioculturales y rasgos de identidad en los géneros musicales con referencia especial a la música cubana." *Latin American Music Review*, Vol. 13, No. 2. 158–78, 1992.

———. "Qué e(s)tá pasando, ¡Asere! . . . Detrás del borroso 'qué sé yo y no sé qué' en la génesis y dinámica de los géneros musicales," *Clave* 12, No. 1–3, 60–89, 2010.

Ortiz, Fernando. "La cubanidad y los negros." *Estudios Afrocubanos*, No. 3, 3–15, 1939.

———. *Los instrumentos de la música afrocubana*, 5 Vols.. Havana: Publicaciones de la Dirección de Cultura del Ministerio de Educación, 1952-1955.

Padrón Díaz, Sigryd. "Galicia en el baile nacional cubano: el danzón." In *Galicia-Cuba: un patrimonio cultural de referencias y confluencias*, ed. C. Fontela and M. Silva. A Coruña: Ediciós do Castro, 405–16, 2000.

Palmié, Stephan. "Ackee and Saltfish vs. Amalá Con Quimbombó." *Journal de la Société des Américanist*, Vol. 91–92, 89–122, 2005.

Pareyón, Gabriel. *Diccionario enciclopédico de música en México*, Vols. 1 and 2. Guadalajara: Universidad Panamericana, 2007.

Paraskevaídis, Graciela. "Edgard Varèse and His Relationships with Latin American Musicians and Intellectuals of His Time." *Contemporary Music Review*, Vol. 23, No. 2, 3–17, 2004.

Paz, Octavio. *El laberinto de la soledad*. Mexico City: Fondo de Cultura Económica, 1986.

Pedelty, Mark. *Musical Ritual in Mexico City: From the Aztec to NAFTA*. Austin: University of Texas Press, 2004.

Pérez Cuza, Yianela. "El dancismo en Santiago de Cuba en la segunda mitad del siglo XIX." Unpublished manuscript. 2012.

Pérez Sanjuro, Elena. *Historia de la música cubana*. Miami: La Moderna Poesía, 1985.

Pérez Sarduy, Pedro. *Las criadas de La Habana*. San Juan, PR: Editorial Plaza Mayor, 2001.

Perna, Vicenzo. *Timba. The Sound of the Cuban Crisis*. London: Ashgate, 2005.

Pichardo, Esteban. *Diccionario provincial casi razonado de vozes y frases cubanas*. Havana: Editorial de Ciencias Sociales, 1985 [1836].

Pola, Juan Antonio. "Aproximación a lo popular en Caturla en el 80 aniversario de su natalicio." In *Caturla el músico, el hombre*, ed. Radamés Giro. Havana: Ediciones Museo de la Música, 141–44, 2007.

Ponce, Francisco. "Maestro Abel Jiménez Luis. Un pilar del danzón en Oaxaca." *Oaxaca Profundo*, No. 93, 10–11, 2011.

Ponce, Manuel M. *Escritos y composiciones musicales*. Mexico City: Cultura, 1917.

Pond, Steven. *Herbie Hancock's* Head Hunters: *The Making of Jazz's First Platinum Album*. Ann Arbor: University of Michigan Press, 2005.

Portes, Alejandro, ed. *The Informal Economy: Studies in Advanced and Less Developed Countries*. Baltimore, MD: Johns Hopkins University Press, 1989.

Pulido Llanos, Gabriela. "Las mil y una rumbas. Cuatro cubanas en México." *Dimensión Antropológica* 15, Vol. 44, 99–132, 2008.

Quintana, José Luís "Changuito" and Chuck Silverman. *Changuito. A Master's Approach to Timbales*. New York: Manhattan Music Publishing, 1998.

Radano, Ronald "Hot Fantasies: American Modernism and the Idea of Black Rhythm." In *Music and the Racial Imagination*, ed. Ronald Radano and Philip V. Bohlman. Chicago: University of Chicago Press, 459–82, 2000.

Radano, Ronald and Philip V. Bohlman. "Introduction. Music and Race, Their Past, Their Presence." In *Music and the Racial Imagination*, ed. Ronald Radano and Philip V. Bohlman. Chicago: University of Chicago Press, 1–56, 2000.

Radano, Ronald and Philip V. Bohlman, eds. *Music and the Racial Imagination*. Chicago: University of Chicago Press, 2000.

Raeburn, Bruce Boyd. "Beyond the 'Spanish Tinge': Hispanics and Latinos in Early New Orleans Jazz." In *Eurojazzland: Jazz and European Sources, Dynamics, and Contexts*, ed. Luca Cerchiari, Laurent Cugny, and Frank Kerschbaumer. Lebanon, NH: Northeastern University Press, 21–46, 2012.

Ramírez, Serafín. *La Habana Artística. Apuntes por la historia*. Havana: Imprenta del E. M. de la Capitanía General, 1891.

Ramos López, Pilar, ed. *Discursos y prácticas musicales nacionalistas (1900–1970): España, Argentina, Cuba, México*. Logroño: Universidad de La Rioja, forthcoming.

Ramsey, Guthrie P. *Race Music. Black Cultures from Bebop to Hip-Hop*. Berkeley: University of California Press, 2003.

Reyes Fortún, José. *Biobibliografía de Odilio Urfé*. Havana: Ediciones Museo de la Música, 2007.

Roberts, John Storm. *The Latin Tinge. The Impact of Latin American Music on the United States*. New York: Oxford University Press, 1999 [1979].

Robertson, Roland. "Glocalization: Time-Space and Homogeneity-Heterogeneity." In *Global Modernities*, ed. Mike Featherstone, Scott Lash, and Roland Robertson. London: Sage, 25–44, 1995.

Robreño, Eduardo. *Como lo pienso lo digo*. Havana: UNEAC, 1985.

Rodríguez, Iraida. *Artículos de costumbres cubanos del siglo XIX*. Havana: Editorial Arte y Literatura, 1974 [1854].

Rodríguez Domínguez, Ezequiel. *Iconografía del danzón*. Havana: Sub-Dirección Provincial de Música, 1967.

Ricoeur, Paul. "Narrative Identity." *Philosophy Today*, Vol. 35, No. 1, 73–81, 1991.

———. *Time and Narrative Vol. 1*. Trans. Kathleen McLaughlin and David Pellauer. Chicago: University of Chicago Press, 1982.

Río Prado, Enrique. *La Venus de bronce: una historia de la zarzuela cubana*. Havana: Ediciones Alarcos, 2010.

Rivera-Servera, Ramón H. "Musical Trans(actions): Intersections in Reggaetón," *Trans. Revista Transcultural de Música*, No. 13, 2009. www.sibetrans.com/trans/a62/musical-transactions-intersections-in-reggaeton (accessed July 20, 2012).

Rivera-Servera, Ramón H. and Harvey Young, eds. *Performance in the Borderlands*. New York: Palgrave Macmillan, 2011.

Roig, Gonzalo. *Apuntes históricos sobre nuestras bandas militares y orquestas*. Havana: Molina y Compañía, 1936.

Rose, Al and Edmond Souchon, *New Orleans Jazz. A Family Album*. Baton Rouge: Louisiana State University Press, 1967.

Sachs, Curt. *World History of the Dance*. New York: W.W. Norton, 1937.

Saldívar, Gabriel. *Historia de la música en México*. Mexico City: Secretaría de Educación Pública, 1934.

Samson, Jim. "Genre." *Grove Music Online*, 2011. www.oup.com/online/us/grovemusic/?view=usa (accessed August 9, 2012).

Sánchez de Fuentes, Eduardo. *El folk-lore en la música cubana*. Havana: Imprenta El Siglo XX, 1923.

———. "El danzón." *Social*, Vol. 13I, No. 12, 32, 77, 83, 1928.

———. *Folklorismo. Artículos, notas y críticas musicales*. Havana: Imprenta Molina y Cía, 1928.

———. *La música aborigen de América*. Havana: Imprenta Molina y Cía, 1938.

Sánchez Castillo, Julio César. *Producción marimbística de Guatemala*. Guatemala City: Impresos Industriales, 2001.

Sandroni, Carlos. "Rediscutindo gêneros no Brasil oitocentista: tangos e habaneras." In *Música popular na América Latina: pontos de escuta*, ed. Ana María Ochoa and Martha Ulhoa. Porto Alegre: UFRGS, 175–93, 2005.

Santos, John. Liner notes to *The Cuban Danzón: Its Ancestors and Descendents*. Folkways LP #FE 4066. New York: Folkways Records and Service Corp. 1982.

Sarusky, Jaime. *Grupo de Experimentación Sonora del ICAIC. Mito y realidad*. Havana: Editorial Letras Cubanas, 2005.

Savigliano, Marta. *Tango and the Political Economy of Passion*. Boulder, CO: Westview Press, 1995.

Saxton, Alexander. "Blackface Minstrelsy and Jacksonian Ideology." *American Quarterly*, Vol. 29, 3–28, 1975.

Schafer, William J. *Brass Bands and New Orleans Jazz*. Baton Rouge: Louisiana State University Press, 1977.

Scherzer, Joel. *Explorations in the Ethnography of Speaking*. Cambridge, MA: Cambridge University Press, 1989.

———. *Kuna Ways of Speaking: An Ethnographic Perspective*. Austin: University of Texas Press, 1983.

Schuller, Gunther. *Early Jazz: Its Roots and Musical Development*. New York: Oxford University Press, 1968.

Seigel, Micol. "Beyond Compare: Comparative Method after the Transnational Turn." *Radical History Review*, Vol. 91, No. 1, 62–90, 2005.

Sevilla, Amparo. *Los templos del buen bailar*. Mexico City: CONACULTA, 2003.

Skidmore, Thomas. *Black into White. Race and nationality in Brazilian thought*. New York: Oxford University Press, 1974.

Smith, Pamela J. "Caribbean Influences on Early New Orleans Jazz." Master's Thesis, Tulane University, 1986.

Solernou Martínez, Angélica Ma. "Panorama histórico-musical de Santa Clara, 1689–1898." Paper presented at the VII Coloquio Internacional de Musicología Casa de las Américas, March 21, 2012.

Solís, Cleva. "En torno a una poesía del danzón." *Islas. Revista de la Universidad Central de Las Villas*, Vol. 2, No. 1, 23–32, 1959.

Soloni, Félix. "El danzón y su inventor, Miguel Faílde. Notas históricas." In *Cuba musical. Album-resúmen ilustrado de la historia y de la actual situación del arte musical en Cuba*, ed.

José Calero Martín y Leopoldo Valdés Quesada. Havana: Molina y Compañía, 1039–41, 1929.

Soto Millán, Eduardo, ed. *Diccionario de compositores mexicanos de música de concierto*, Vol. 2. Mexico City: CONACULTA, 1998.

Spotswood, Richard K. *Ethnic Music on Record, Vol. 4. Spanish, Portuguese, Philippine, Basque*. Champaign: University of Illinois Press, 1990.

Spottswood, Dick. *Lost Sounds. Blacks and the Birth of the Recording Industry, 1890–1919*. Urbana: University of Illinois Press, 2004

Stearns, Marshall and Jean, *Jazz Dance. The Story of American Vernacular Dance*. New York: Da Capo, 1994 [1964].

Stevenson, Robert. "The Latin Tinge, 1800–1900." *Inter-American Music Review*, Vol. 2, No. 2, 73–102, 1980.

Stewart, Jack. "Cuban Influences on New Orleans Music." www.arhoolie.com/titles/7032c .shtml (accessed January 17, 2007).

———. "The Mexican Band Legend: Myth, Reality, and Musical Impact: A Preliminary Investigation." *Jazz Archivist*, Vol. 6, No. 2, 1–14, 1991.

———. "The Mexican Band Legend—Part II." *Jazz Archivist*, Vol. 9, No. 1, 1–17, 1994.

———. "The Mexican Band Legend—Part III." *Jazz Archivist*, Vol. 20, 1–10, 2007.

———. "The Original Dixieland Jazz Band's Place in the Development of Jazz." *Jazz Archivist*, Vol. 19, 16–25, 2006.

Stokes, Martin. *Ethnicity, Identity, and Music: The Musical Construction of Place*. Oxford, UK: Berg, 1994.

———. "Music and the Global Order." *Annual Review of Anthropology*, Vol. 33, 47–72, 2004.

Suárez y Romero, Anselmo. "El baile." In *Artículos de costumbres cubanos del siglo XIX*, ed. Iraida Rodríguez. Havana: Editorial Arte y Literatura, 239–49, 1974 [1854].

Sublette, Ned. *Cuba and Its Music. From the First Drums to the Mambo*. Chicago: Chicago Review Press, 2004.

———. *The World that Made New Orleans. From Spanish Silver to Congo Square*. Chicago: Lawrence Hill, 2008.

Sutton, Allan. *Cakewalks, Rags, and Novelties. The International Ragtime Discography (1894–1930)*. Denver, CO: Mainspring Press, 2003.

Szwed, John. *Crossovers: Essays on Race, Music, and American Culture*. Philadelphia: University of Pennsylvania Press, 2005.

Szwed, John F. and Morton Marks. "The Afro-American Transformation of European Set Dances and Dance Suites." *Dance Research Journal*, Vol. 20, No. 1, 29–35, 1988.

Talavera, Mario. *Miguel Lerdo de Tejada; su vida pintoresca y anecdótica*. Mexico City: Editorial Compás, 1958.

Taylor, Diana. *The Archive and the Repertoire. Performing Cultural Memory in the Americas*. Durham, NC: Duke University Press, 2003.

Taylor-Gibson, Christina. "The Music of Manuel M. Ponce, Julián Carrillo, and Carlos Chávez in New York, 1925–1932." PhD Dissertation, University of Maryland at College Park, 2008.

Tello, Aurelio. "La creación musical en México durante el siglo XX," in *La música en México. Panorama del siglo XX*, ed. Aurelio Tello. Mexico City: Consejo Nacional para la Cultura y las Artes and Fondo de Cultura Económica, 2010.

Tello, Aurelio, ed. *La música en México. Panorama del siglo XX*. Mexico City: Consejo Nacional para la Cultura y las Artes and Fondo de Cultura Económica, 2010.

The Joint Operating Environment. Challenges and Implications for the Future Joint Force. Suffolk, VA: United States Joint Forces Command, 2008.

Thomas, Susan. *Cuban Zarzuela. Performing Race and Gender on Havana's Lyric Stage*. Urbana: University of Illinois Press, 2009.

Torres, Dora Ileana. "Del danzón cantado al chachachá." In *Panorama de la música popular cubana*, ed. Radamés Giro. Havana: Editorial Letras Cubanas, 193–218, 1995.

Towne, Sarah. "Emiliano Salvador's 'Puerto Padre': One Man's Jazz." Master's Thesis, City University of New York, 2009.

Trejo, Ángel. *¡Hey familia, danzón dedicado a . . .!* Mexico City: Plaza y Valdés, 1992.

Tucker, Mark. "Jazz." In *Grove Music Online*, Section 1, Definitions, and 2, Jazz and the New Orleans Background. 2007 (accessed January 10, 2012).

Turino, Thomas. "Are We Global Yet? Globalist Discourse, Cultural Formations and the Study of Zimbabwean Popular Music." *British Journal of Ethnomusicology*, Vol. 12, No. 2, 51–79, 2003.

Ulhoa, Martha. "Pertinência e musica popular-Em busca de categorías para análise da musica brasileira popular." www.hist.puc.cl/iaspm/pdf/Ulloa.pdf (accessed on July 31, 2012)

Urfé, Odilio. "Music and Dance in Cuba." In *Africa in Latin America: Essays on History, Culture, and Socialization*, ed. Manuel Moreno Farginals. New York: Holmes and Meier, 170–88, 1984.

———. "Paternidad verdadera del mambo y el chachachá." *Carteles*, Año 39, No. 36, 14–15, 73, 129, 1958.

Vela, David. *La marimba; estudio sobre el instrumento nacional*. Guatemala City: Editorial José de Pineda Ibarra, Ministerio de Educación Pública, 1962.

Velázquez, María Elisa and Ethel Correa, eds. *Poblaciones y culturas de orígen africano en México*. México City: Instituto Nacional de Antropología e Historia, 2005.

Vernhettes, Daniel. "Buddy Bolden, 1877–1931." In *Jazz Puzzles*. Paris: Jazz'Edit, 29–58, 2012.

Villaverde, Cirilo. *Cecilia Valdés*. Barcelona: Linkgua Ediciones S.L., 2008 [1882].

Vinson III, Ben and Bobby Vaughn. *Afroméxico*. Mexico City: Fondo de Cultura Económica, 2004.

Wade, Peter. *Race and Ethnicity in Latin America*. London: Pluto Press, 1996.

Washburne, Christopher. "The Clave of Jazz: A Caribbean Contribution to the Rhythmic Foundation of an African-American Music." *Black Music Research Journal*, Vol. 17, No. 1, 59–80, 1997.

Waxer, Lise, ed. *Situating Salsa. Global Markets and Local Meaning in Latin Popular Music*. New York: Routledge, 2002

Williams, Raymond. *Marxism and Literature*. New York: Oxford University Press, 1977.

Winant, Howard. "White Racial Projects." In *The Making and Remaking of Whiteness*, ed. B. Rasmussen. Durham, NC: Duke University Press, 97–112, 2001.

Witmer, Ruth "Sunni." "Cuban *Charanga*: Class, Popular Music, and the Creation of National Identity." PhD Dissertation, University of Florida, Gainesville, 2011.

Wong, Ketty. *La música nacional. Identidad, mestizaje y migración en Ecuador*. Havana: Casa de las Américas, 2012.

Work, John Wesley. "Jazz." In *Harvard Dictionary of Music*, 2nd ed., ed. Willi Apel. Cambridge, MA: Harvard University Press, 440–44, 1972.

Žižek, Slavoj. *El acoso de las fantasías*. Trans. Clea Braunstein Saal. Mexico City: Siglo Veintiuno, 1999.

Zolov, Eric. *Refried Elvis. The Rise of the Mexican Counterculture*. Berkeley: University of California Press, 1999.

ARCHIVES

Agrasánchez Film Archive. Harlingen, Texas, USA.

Archivo Provincial Vivac. Matanzas, Cuba.

Biblioteca del Centro Nacional de las Artes. Servicios Especiales. Mexico City, Mexico.

Biblioteca Elvira Cape. Santiago de Cuba, Cuba.

Biblioteca Géner y del Monte. Matanzas, Cuba.

Biblioteca Nacional José Martí. Colección de Música. Havana, Cuba.

Casa del Caribe. Santiago de Cuba, Cuba.

Centro de Apoyo a Investigaciones Históricas. Mérida, Yucatán, Mexico.

Centro de Investigación y Desarrollo de la Música Cubana. Havana, Cuba.

Centro Nacional de Investigación, Difusión e Información Musical "Carlos Chávez." Archivo Fotográfico. Mexico City, Mexico.

Centro Regional de Investigación, Documentación y Difusión Musical Gerónimo Baqueiro Foster. Colección de los Hermanos Concha y Colección J. J. Cuevas. Mérida, Yucatán, Mexico.

Fototeca Nacional del Instituto Nacional de Antropología e Historia-Módulo Cd. de México. Fondo Casasola. Mexico City, Mexico.

Green Library, Cristóbal Díaz Ayala Collection of Latin American Music, Florida International University. Miami, Florida, USA.

Hemeroteca Nacional. Mexico City, Mexico.

Hogan Jazz Archive. Tulane University. New Orleans, Louisiana, USA.

Instituto de Lingüística. Havana, Cuba.

Museo Nacional de la Música. Havana, Cuba.

Unión de Escritores y Artistas Cubanos. Santiago de Cuba, Cuba.

Williams Research Center. Historical New Orleans Collection. New Orleans, Louisiana, USA.

NEWSPAPERS AND PERIODICALS

Album Literario. 1892. Mérida, Yucatán, Mexico.
Bohemia. 1964, 1976, 1979–1980, 2011. Havana, Cuba.
Carteles. 1958. Havana, Cuba.
Daily City Item. 1891. New Orleans, Louisiana, USA.
Daily Picayune. 1885–1898. New Orleans, Louisiana, USA.
Diario de Matanzas. 1878–1883. Matanzas, Cuba.
El Espectador. 1911–1914. Mérida, Yucatán, Mexico.
El Club de Matanzas. Periódico de Literatura, Ciencias y Bellas Artes. 1881–1882. Matanzas, Cuba.
El Fígaro. 1886–1906. Havana, Cuba.
El Universal. 1917. Mexico City, Mexico.
El Universal Ilustrado. 1919. Mexico City, Mexico.
El Mundo Ilustrado. 1907–1908. Mexico City, Mexico.
El Recreo Artístico. 1892. Mérida, Yucatán, Mexico.
El Sonido 13. 1925. Mexico City, Mexico.
Girón. 1986–1989, 1991, 1998, 2001, 2003, 2006. Havana. Cuba.
Granma. 1971, 1989. Havana, Cuba.
Islas. Revista de la Universidad Central de Las Villas. 1959. Las Villas, Cuba.
J. Jacinto Cuevas. 1888–1894. Mérida, Yucatán, Mexico.
Juventud Rebelde. 1986, 1999. Havana. Cuba.
La Aurora del Yumurí. 1878–1882. Matanzas, Cuba.
La Fraternidad. 1886–1896. Sancti Spíritus, Las Villas, Cuba.
La Gaceta Musical. 1895. Mérida, Yucatán, Mexico.
La Igualdad. 1893–1895. Sancti Spíritus, Las Villas, Cuba.
La Política Cómica. 1895–1906, 1916. Havana, Cuba.
La Prensa. 2007. Mexico City, Mexico.
Lírico. 1910. Mérida, Yucatán, Mexico.
Metro. 2007. Mexico City, Mexico.
Música Cubana. Havana, Cuba. 2005.
Pimienta y Mostaza. 1892–1894, 1903. Mérida, Yucatán, Mexico.
Proceso. 2010. Mexico City, Mexico.
Revista de Mérida. 1876, 1898. Mérida, Yucatán, Mexico.
Revista de Revistas. Suplemento Musical. 1917, 1922–1923. Mexico City, Mexico.
Revista Musical de México. 1919–1920. Mexico City, Mexico.
Revolución y Cultura. 1979, 1988. Havana, Cuba.
Trabajadores. 1979. Havana. Cuba.
Tropicana Internacional. 2008. Havana, Cuba.
Tropicana Magazine. 1997. Havana. Cuba.

PERSONAL INTERVIEWS

Aceituno, Rosalinda. Event Coordinator at Plaza del Danzón. Mexico City. 17 September 2011.

Acosta, Ildelfonso. Composer and cultural promoter. Matanzas, Cuba. 2 December 2011.

Aldana Linares, Ángela. Leader of the Havana Círculo Amigos del Danzón. Havana, Cuba. 12 December 2006.

Arcaño, Antonio. Flute player and director of Arcaño y sus Maravillas. Havana, Cuba. 16 July 1992.

Arreguín, Mina and Benjamín Bautista. Danzón promoters from Guadalajara, Mexico. Havana, Cuba. 22 March 2007.

Ayala, Maru and Miguel Velasco. Danzón promoters from Monterrey. Monterrey. Mexico. 22 February 2010.

Bada, Miguel. Founding member of Tres Generaciones del Danzón Veracruzano. Veracruz, Mexico. 16 December 2008.

Banks, Brian. Composer. Cholula, Puebla, Mexico. 18 July 2009.

Castaños, Alejandro. Composer. Electronic communication. 2 May 2012.

Corrales. Alberto. Flute player and director of Orquesta Panorama. Havana, Cuba. 3 December 2011.

Cruz Sánchez, Javier. Manager of Salón Sociales Romo. Mexico City. 18 November 2009.

Díaz Díaz, Edgardo. Musicologist. Electronic communication. 22 November 2011.

Fernández Failde, Ethiel. Flautist and band leader. Matanzas, Cuba. 1 December 2011.

Gallardo, José. Vice-president of Amigos del Danzón. Havana, Cuba. 4 December 2011.

González, Dayramir. Jazz pianist and composer. Havana, Cuba. 16 December 2009.

González Peña, Hipólito. Timbal player of Danzonera Acerina. Mexico City, Mexico. 22 February 2009.

Guzmán Loyzaga, Daniel. Conductor, arranger, artistic director of Rotterdam Conservatory Orquesta Cuba and Danzonera SierraMadre. Monterrey, Mexico. 19 February 2010.

Igualada, Heidi. Singer and songwriter. Electronic communication. 21 May 2012.

Jara Gámez, Simón. Former owner of Salón Colonia and danzón promoter in Mexico City. Havana, Cuba. 29 March 2007.

Juárez, Nelly "Nelly de Veracruz." Dancer. Mexico City. 15 February 2009.

Juárez Flores, Jesús "El Cebos." Dancer. Mexico City. 22 February 2009.

Lapique Becali, Zoila. Musicologist, historian. Havana, Cuba. 1 October 1993.

León, Tania. Composer. Telephone interview. 9 May 2012.

Loyola, José. Flute player and director of Charanga de Oro; former president of the music division of the Union of Cuban Writers and Artists. Havana, Cuba. 30 November 2011.

Madrigal, Eutiquio. Former danzón promoter. Veracruz, Mexico. 31 January 2009.

Márquez, Arturo. Composer. Tepoztlán, Morelos, Mexico. 21 September 2011.

Martínez Alayo, Ageo. Leader of the Círculo Amigos del Danzón Electo Rosell from Santiago de Cuba. Havana, Cuba. 22 March 2007 and Santiago, Cuba. 7 December 2011.

Martínez Furé, Rogelio. Musicologist, choreographer, co-founder of the Conjunto Folklórico Nacional de Cuba. Havana. 20 January 1994.

Martínez González, Raúl. Güiro player of Orquesta Siglo XX. Havana, Cuba. 29 September 2011.

Matus Meléndez, Eliseo "Manzanita." Leader of Manzanita y su Son 4. Veracruz, Mexico. 1 February 2009.

Miller, Sue. Flute player and musicologist. Electronic communication. 8 March 2012.

Moliner Castañeda, Israel. Historian and Matanzas Chronicleer. Matanzas, Cuba. 2 December 2011.

Morales, Mario. Dancer. Mexico City. 24 January 2009.

Navia, José B. Founder of the Asociación Provincial Amigos de Danzón Miguel Faílde Pérez. Matanzas, Cuba. 10 December 2006.

Nieto, Miguel. Owner of Salón Los Angeles. Mexico City. 14 September 2011.

Núñez, Jr., Arturo. Manager of Orquesta de Arturo Núñez. Mexico City. 21 February 2009.

Olivares. José Guadalupe "Pepe el Elegante." Dancer. Mexico City. 24 January 2009.
Ortiz Chibás, Fidel. Percussionist of the Orquesta Guillermo Rubalcaba. Havana, Cuba. 5 December 2011.
Ortiz Pichardo, Guillermo. Director of *Danzón No. 2*. Mexico City. 22 September 2011.
Pereira, Juan and Carlos Manuel Ruiz Verrier. Timbal and güiro players of the Piquete Típico Cubano. Havana, Cuba. 3 April 2009.
Pérez Abreu, Marcela. Güiro player for Gonzalo Romeu's ensemble. Telephone interview. 5 October 2011.
Pineda Burgos, Natalia. Founder of Tres Generaciones del Danzón Veracruzano. Veracruz, Mexico. 11 February 2009.
Portillo, Bertila. Dancer. Matanzas, Cuba. 2 December 2011.
Portillo Álvarez, Hayron. Dancer. Matanzas, Cuba. 10 December 2006.
Riande Uscanga, Tomás. Dancer. Veracruz, Mexico. 4 February 2009.
Rodríguez Cervantes, Caridad. President of Amigos del Danzón. 1 April 2009.
Romeu, Gonzalo. Pianist and arranger. Mexico City, Mexico. 26 September 2011.
Rubalcaba, Guillermo. Band leader. Havana, Cuba. 5 December 2011.
Ruiz Torres, Edmundo. Founding figure of the danzón movement in Monterrey. Monterrey, Mexico. 8 February 2009.
Salazar Hernández, Roberto. Dancer. Mexico City. 22 February 2009.
Sánchez, Armando "El Suavecito." Dancer and dance teacher. Mexico City. 24 January 2009.
Sigal, Rodrigo. Composer and electronic music performer. Electronic communication. 27 April 2012.
Terrón, Jesús "Comandante Terrón." Dancer. Mexico City. 26 February 2009.
Terry, Yosvany. Musician. Telephone interview. 1 June 2012.
Ulloa, Francisco. Director of Piquete Sanitaguero. Santiago de Cuba. 6 December 2011.
Urbán, Felipe. Director of Felipe Urbán y su Danzonera. Mexico City. 17 February 2009.
Valdés Abreu, Armando. Leader of the Amigos del Danzón movement in La Víbora, Havana. Havana, Cuba. 28 November 2011.
Varela, Gonzalo. Director of Danzonera La Playa. Veracruz, Mexico. 31 January 2009.
Vargas, José Jesús. Dancer. Mexico City. 15 February 2009.
Vistel Colombié, Jorge. Cornet player and director of Piquete Típico Cubano. Havana, Cuba. 28 November, 2011.
Vitier, José María. Composer. Havana, Cuba. 5 December 2011.
Witmer, Ruth "Sunni." Ethnomusicologist. Electronic communication. 21 December 2009.
Zamudio Abdalá, Miguel Angel. Danzón promoter from Veracruz and founder of Centro Nacional para la Investigación y Difusión del Danzón, A.C. Veracruz, Mexico. 16 December 2008.

SELECTED DISCOGRAPHY

Alberto Corrales y su Orquesta Panorama. *Danzoneando*. Cinquillo CD 123. 2006.
Amadito Valdés, Jr. *Bajando Gervasio*. Pimienta Records 245-360-551-2. 2002.
Amaury Pérez. *De vuelta*. EMI LP 58027. 1987.
Arcaño y sus Maravillas. *De nuevo el monarca*. Artex CD 069. 1993.
———. *El mulato en el morro*. Orfeón CDL 16479. 2004.
———. *Grandes orquestas cubanas*. Areíto CD 0034. 1992.
Arturo Márquez. *El danzón según Márquez*. Concaulta, without catalog number. 2006.
Arturo Sandoval. *Danzón (Dance On)*. GRP Digital Master CD GRD-9761, 1994.
Barbarito Diez. *Don Barbarito Diez y la Orquesta de Antonio María Romeu*. EGREM CD 0021. 1992.
Belisario López. *Orquesta de Belisario López 1942–48. Prueba mi sazón*. Tumbao Cuban Classics CD TCD-069, 1995.
Beto Villa. *Beto Villa. Father of Texas Orquesta, Vol. 1*. Arhoolie Records CD 9059. 2007.
Carlos Campos. *Danzones melódicos*. Musart 1930. 1998.
———. *Joyas Musicales. Para bailar danzón con Carlos Campos*. Musart 3MCD-3243. 2004.
Chucho Valdés. *Chucho's Steps*. Four Quarters Records CD 1823. 2010.

————. *Live at the Village Vanguard*. Blue Note CD 7243 5 20730 2 3. 2000.

Columna B. *Enclave*. Mas CD009. 2010.

Control Machete. *Artillería pesada, presenta . . . Control Machete*. Universal 314 538 944-2. 1999.

Danzonera SierraMadre. *Siéntate*. Consejo Mexicano para la Divulgación del Danzón, without catalog number. 2012.

Dayramir González. *Dayramir & Habana EnTRANCe*. Cinquillo Colibrí CD097. 2007.

Emiliano Salvador. *Puerto Padre*. Yemayá Records YY9428. 2003.

Eugenia León and Danzonera Dimas. *Que devuelvan*. El Hábito CDFL-1312. 1996.

Flaco Jiménez. *The Best of Flaco Jiménez*. Arhoolie Records CD 478. 1999.

Francisco Ulloa y su Piquete Santiaguero. *El camaján*. Indigo LC-03428. 2001.

Frank Emilio. *Cuban Danzas & Danzones*. Yemayá Records YY9437. 2007.

Gonzalo Romeu, *Danzones de Cuba y México, Vol. 1*. Caibarién CP07. 2007.

Gonzalo Rubalcaba. *Mi gran pasión*. Messidor CD 15999-2. 1988.

Grupo Manguaré. *Regálame tus manos*. Areito LD-42841985. 1984.

Heidi Igualada. *En la línea de mi mano*. Cinquillo Colibrí CD 120. 2008.

————. *Serenata*. Unicornio UN-CD7014. 2002.

Inaudis Paisán. *Al estilo de Paisán*. EGREM CD S0040, 2004.

Irakere. *Irakere Vol. 1. Selección de éxitos 1973-78*. Areito cassette C-4003. 1980.

Israel López "Cachao." *Superdanzones*. EGREM CD 0225. 2000.

Joseíto Fernández. *Música popular cubana*. Areíto LP LD-3575. Without date.

Juan Trigos. *DeCachetitoRaspado*. Quindecim QP089. 2002.

Julio Valdés y su Orquesta. *Danzones Chá*. Vedisco 5144-2. 1996.

La Charanga Nacional de Concierto. Areíto LD-3486. 1975.

La Maldita Vecindad y Los Hijos del Quinto Patio. *El Circo*. SONY B000005LEN. 1991.

Liuba María Hevia. *Del verso a la mar*. Eurotropical EUCD-19. 1999.

Orlando Valle "Maraca." *Tremenda rumba*. Ahi Namá Music CD AHI-1034. 2002.

Orquesta Aragón. *Danzones de ayer y hoy*. Discuba CDD 515. 1990

————. *Danzones de ayer y hoy, Vol. II*. Discuba CDD 532. 1989.

Orquesta Félix González. "Que volumen." Victor 78 #72381-2. 1919.

Pablo Milanés. *Aniversario*. Areíto/EGREM LD-3805. 1979.

Paulina Álvarez. *La emperatriz del danzón*. EGREM CD 0048. 1993.

Piquete Típico Cubano. *Danzones*. Self-produced. Without date.

Quinteto Diapasón. *Quinteto Diapasón. Son . . . de Almendra*. EGREM CD 0213, 1997.

Roberto Juan Rodríguez. *Baila! Gitano baila!* Tzadik Records TZ7189, 2005.

————. *El danzón de Moisés*. Tzadik Records TZ7158, 2005.

————. *Timba talmud*. Tzadik Records TZ8140, 2009.

Rotterdam Conservatory Orquesta Típica and Charanga Orchestra. *Orquesta Cuba. Contradanzas and Danzones*. Nimbus Records, CD NI 5502. 1996.

Silvio Rodríguez. *Tríptico, Vol. 2*. Ojalá Records CDO-0007. 2004.

Tom McDermott and Evan Christopher. *Danza. Tangos, Choros, Waltzes and a Little Jazz*. STR CD 1009, 2000.

Various artists. *Antología del danzón*. Areito LD-3724. 1962.

Various artists. *Argeliers León. Grupo de Renovación Musical*. Instituto Cubano de la Música CD/DVD/CDROM 151. 2009.

Various artists. *Bajo el laurel 2. Banda de Música del Estado de Oaxaca*. CD P.D.A. 033 C1, 2000.

Various artists. *Centenario del danzón: 30 danzones clásicos*. Discos Orfeón, 099441000625. 1993.

Various artists. *Danzones All Star*. Discos Continental. CD LEGCD-11517. 2005.

Various artists. *Early Cuban Danzón Orchestras 1916–1920*. Harlequin CD HQCD-131. 1999.

Various artists. *Early Music of the North Caribbean 1916–1920*. Harlequin CD HQCD 67. 1995.

Various artists. *Historia del danzón*. Musart M-114. 1954.

Various artists. *Hot Music from Cuba, 1907–1936*. Harlequin HQCD 23. 1993.

Various artists. *Tejano Roots: Orquestas Tejanas*. Arhoolie Records CD 368. 1993.
Various artists. *The Cuban Danzón. Before There Was Jazz*. Arhoolie Folklyric CD 7032. 1999.
Various artists. *The Cuban Danzón: Its Ancestors and Descendants*. Smithsonian Folkways FE 4066. 1982.
Virulo. *Historia de Cuba*. Areito LD-3471. Without date.
Xiomara Laugart. *La Habana entera*. Bis Music B148. 1996.

SELECTED VIDEOGRAPHY

Ávila Morán, Tito. "Noche de danzón," *Al fin es viernes*. Televisión Metropolitana. Mexico. 1999.
Castaño, Rodrigo. *La ruta del danzón*. Dirección de Producción Canal Once. Mexico. 2005.
Dvorák, Cordelia. *Bailar para vivir*. Vanguard Cinema. Mexico. 2003.
Fernández, Emilio. *Salón México*. Clasa Films Mundiales. Mexico. 1949.
Figueroa Hernández, Rafael. *Danzón. Entrenamiento musical para bailadores, Vol. 1*. www.comosuena.com. Mexico. 2008.
Galindo, Alejandro. *Campéon sin corona*. Raúl de Anda. Mexico. 1946.
Gámez, Rubén. *Tequila*. Clasa Films Mundiales. Mexico. 1992.
García Agraz, José Luis. *Salón México*. Televicine. Mexico. 1996.
Gómez Landero, Humberto. *El hijo desobediente*. As Films y Producciones Grovas. Mexico. 1945.
Leduc, Paul. *Frida. Naturaleza viva*. Clasa Films Mundiales. Mexico. 1984.
Moreno, Antonio. *Santa*. Compañía Nacional Productora de Películas. Mexico. 1932.
Novaro, María. *Danzón*. IMCINE / Televisión Española / Tabasco Films. Mexico. 1991.
Ortiz Pichardo, Guillermo. *Danzón No. 2*. Universidad Iberoamericana. Mexico. 2012.
Pineda Barnet, Enrique. *La bella del Alhambra*. ICAIC / Televisión Española. Cuba. 1989.
Rivero, Antonio del. *Cómo bailar danzón, por el maestro Enrique Tapia*. TV UNAM. Mexico. 1994.
Rodríguez, Ismael. *Ustedes los ricos*. Rodríguez Hermanos. Mexico. 1948.
Rodríguez Esponda, Luis Vicente. *Amor, pasión y cadencia. Danzon/era*. Experimental Films. Mexico. 2006.
Valdés, Oscar. *Danzón*. ICAIC. Cuba. 1970.

INDEX

Printed in the USA/Agawam, MA
November 21, 2013

582208.059